Merry Christmas, Baby
♡ 1989

VARIETIES OF VISUAL EXPERIENCE

EDMUND BURKE FELDMAN

PROFESSOR OF ART, UNIVERSITY OF GEORGIA

VARIETIES OF VISUAL EXPERIENCE

THIRD EDITION

HARRY N. ABRAMS, INC., PUBLISHERS, NEW YORK

TO MERRILL

1928–1972

Project Director: Margaret L. Kaplan

Editor: Teresa Egan

Photo Researcher for the Third Edition: Susan Sherman

Art Direction: Dirk Luykx

Designer: Gilda Hannah, with Gayle Jaeger

Library of Congress Cataloging-in-Publication Data
Feldman, Edmund Burke.
  Varieties of visual experience.
  Bibliography: p. 509
  Includes index.
  1. Art—Psychology.   2. Composition (Art).   3. Visual
perception.   I. Title.
N71.F4   1986   701   86-9333
ISBN 0–8109–1735–1 (hc)

Third Edition 1987

Illustrations copyright © 1987 Harry N. Abrams, Inc.
Published in 1987 by Harry N. Abrams, Incorporated, New York
All rights reserved. No part of the contents of this book may
be reproduced without the written permission of the publishers

Picture reproduction rights reserved by S.P.A.D.E.M. and
A.D.A.G.P., Paris, where relevant
Times Mirror Books

Printed and bound in Japan

CONTENTS

PART TWO
THE STYLES OF ART

PART THREE
THE STRUCTURE OF ART

PREFACE AND ACKNOWLEDGMENTS

This book is meant to stimulate thought and discussion about art as it affects our private lives and our common existence. At a time when many works of specialized scholarship are available, only this purpose seemed a valid reason for adding to the list of books on the subject. My guiding assumption has been that art illuminates life as nothing else can. Therefore I have tried to talk about the recurring features of human affairs as they are discovered through visual form. I deal with the functional and thematic values of art before taking up stylistic, formal, and technical considerations; this approach seemed best for gaining the interest of readers who want to know how art is useful in daily life, how it speaks, and what it means.

I hope readers will feel free to differ with the interpretations of various artworks in this book. That would mean they have been stimulated (or provoked) into raising questions—or proposing alternative evaluations of the objects being examined. Art is too important, and we should care too much about it, to be satisfied with bland acceptance of or plain indifference to any serious discussion of its uses and merits. As a teacher, I would be disappointed if students did not respond vigorously to any presentation I had made. I especially hope my captions and visual comparisons will stimulate further inquiry about many issues—social and cultural as well as artistic and aesthetic. Indeed, many works have been selected because their presentation at a particular place in the text makes a critical point, or tests the reader's understanding of a theoretical position while leading to an appreciation of the meaning and quality of the work itself.

Any book that tries to initiate a dialogue with the reader grows out of many dialogues carried on over the years with teachers, colleagues, and students. I was fortunate in being able to study with artists who liked to talk about art while trying to teach me the rudiments of drawing and painting. Questions were raised for me in conversation long before I realized their significance in the world of scholarship. Later, I learned the labels for those questions and answers, and now I submit them in book form. But they have passed through the crucible of so many conversations that I cannot honestly say who is responsible for the ideas that I, following a common delusion of authors, believe to be my own. So here let me thank them—teachers, students, colleagues, and friends—for what they have given me in countless ways.

PREFACE TO THE THIRD EDITION

The acceptance of this book by so many kinds of readers—artists and teachers, historians and critics, specialists and generalists—has been tremendously satisfying. The criticism chapters, especially, have been well received. I like to think that the rest of the book is a demonstration of critical intelligence applied to the major issues generated by the visual arts in our time.

In the present edition, a number of new illustrations by contemporary artists have been added, and, wherever possible, they are in color. The main text has been thoroughly edited and revised, and the captions for many of the illustrations have been extended. My principal effort has been devoted to clarifying the language of the text, making it accessible to a broader readership without, I trust, weakening its ideas or point of view.

The production of this new edition owes a great deal to the able people at two fine publishing houses. At Prentice-Hall, I am indebted to Norwell (Bud) Therien, and at Abrams to Margaret Kaplan and Teresa Egan for editorial guidance, as well as to Gilda Hannah who, with Gayle Jaeger, has completely redesigned the book under the art direction of Dirk Luykx. Susan Sherman has been especially resourceful in securing the hundreds of illustrations—old and new—without which an art book would have only a pale existence. To all of them, and to Virginia Seaquist, who has prepared the manuscript, I am most grateful.

EDMUND BURKE FELDMAN

PART ONE

THE FUNCTIONS OF ART

The idea that art functions, that it is useful in human affairs, may seem far-fetched; we tend to believe it is the product of surplus energy and wealth. As a result, art is often considered *uniquely* useless—unnecessary for meeting the basic requirements of living. Still, the arts have existed throughout human history and they seem to be thriving today. How can we explain this? Is art tolerated because of some blunder? Can we do without it? No. We need art because it satisfies vital personal and social needs. In this book I hope to show why the visual arts—painting, sculpture, architecture, industrial design, the crafts, photography, films, and television—are essential for human survival.

Furthermore, contemporary art performs the same functions as the art of the past. It continues to satisfy (1) our personal needs for expression, (2) our social needs for communication, celebration, and display, and (3) our physical needs for useful objects and structures. But even if art gives us flashy advertising designs, soaring airport terminals, and good-looking refrigerators, we still wonder how fantastic images and constructions in paint, metal, stone, or plastics affect the quality of our lives. Merchants and manufacturers may need designers to attract buyers, but what function is performed, what need is satisfied, when paint is splashed on a canvas that is then exhibited for the amazement of honest men and women?

Why should we spend time trying to understand the work of artists who have not taken the trouble to make their meaning clear? Can't we live full lives without these visual "experiments"? Is there any connection between today's art and the masterworks of the past? Answers to these questions—or attempts to answer them—are what the following pages are about.

CHAPTER ONE

PERSONAL FUNCTIONS OF ART

Although we are social beings who must live in groups to survive, we have a private and separate existence, too. We can never escape the consciousness of other persons, but we also feel that thoughts occur to us uniquely. Inside each of us many events take place, and often we want others to know about them. To share these feelings and ideas we use different languages; art is one of those languages.

As a type of personal expression, art is not confined to self-revelation; it can also convey the artist's attitudes about *public* objects and events. Basic human situations, such as love, death, celebration, and illness, constantly recur, and we can see them in a fresh light because of the personal comment made by an artist. For example, the sadness of adolescence is shown in the sculpture of Wilhelm Lehmbruck; a peculiar aroma of death hovers over every picture by Edvard Munch; and in the paintings of Frans Hals we sense an irrepressible love of living. For these artists, people, places, and events are *opportunities* to present a personal outlook, even a personal philosophy.

Perhaps all artworks function as individual expressions for the artist. Although many works are created to promote official ideas, they cannot help being vehicles of the artist's private vision. In the modern world, this subjective element is treasured above all others; the personal function of art seems to constitute its very essence.

ART AND PSYCHOLOGICAL EXPRESSION

Visual images preceded written language as a means of communication. However, art goes beyond the communication of information; it also expresses a whole dimension of human personality—our inner, or psychological, states of being.

Why distinguish between communication and expression? Because art is more than a language of standardized signs and symbols; it does not communicate in the same way that a newspaper headline or a traffic light does. Art may employ standardized symbols, but fundamentally it involves the forming of lines, colors, and shapes so they embody an artist's values or convictions or life experience. In this process the materials and techniques of art become the vehicle of expression; they give existence to an artist's intention and meaning. Without art, then, without using certain materials in certain ways, there would

be no way of expressing certain states of feeling. A poem or a song does not mean the same thing as a painting or a sculpture about the same subject; different meanings are created by different materials and techniques.

Man Pointing by Alberto Giacometti (1901–1966) illustrates the point. Here we see a uniquely visual expression of loneliness in the image of a person who is physically and spiritually remote. The same is true of Germaine Richier's (1904–1959) *Leaf*. The proportions of the figures, the indistinctness of the bodily parts, and the elongation of the forms create an impression of human distance. It would be difficult to communicate with either of these individuals; they seem surrounded by silence. Discovering such qualities in art shows that visual forms can convey exceedingly intimate emotions. They show how artists comment on a universal problem: men can multiply the media of communication, but they are not able to *reach* each other. In a sense, all of us are isolated.

Although the feelings expressed in the works by Giacometti and Richier are widely shared, the portrait of a specific person has fewer universal implications; it concentrates on individual personality. In *The Poet Max Hermann-Neisse*, George Grosz (1893–1959) offers us the "map" of a singular man. The artist's linear style, highly developed during his career as a German newspaper satirist, gives us a painfully truthful account of the bones of the man's skull, the veins of his temple, and the worried wrinkles in his face and forehead. The carefully drawn hands, although folded, convey a strong sense of agitation. The brooding quality of the poet is accentuated by his rumpled clothing: those folds seem to be in seething, turbulent motion. Grosz was a

Suzanne Valadon. *Reclining Nude*. 1928. The Metropolitan Museum of Art, New York. Robert Lehman Collection, 1975

The nude and psychological expression. Notice the defensive arm, the hand nervously clutching a piece of drapery, the tightly crossed legs, and the feet that cannot relax. The model's body looks strong and healthy, but her face betrays fear, vulnerability. Compare this woman with Manet's proud, almost arrogant Olympia (page 225).

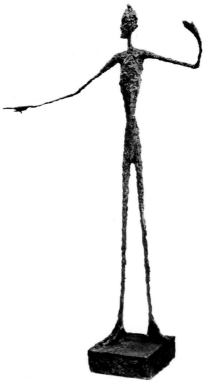

George Grosz. *The Poet Max Hermann-Neisse.* 1927. Collection, The Museum of Modern Art, New York. Purchase

Alberto Giacometti. *Man Pointing.* 1947. Collection, The Museum of Modern Art, New York. Gift of Mrs. John D. Rockefeller 3rd

The tragedy of Giacometti's man is that he wants to communicate but "they" won't listen. So he can't break out of his spiritual isolation. Richier's man is trapped in a loser's self-image: he has defined himself as a victim, a person predestined to fail.

Germaine Richier. *Leaf.* 1948. The Hirshhorn Museum and Sculpture Garden, Smithsonian Institution, Washington, D.C.

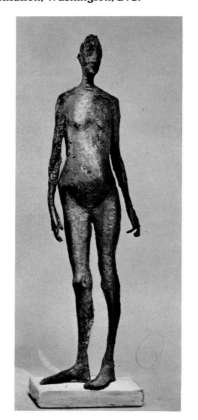

Juan Gris. *Portrait of Max Jacob.* 1919. Collection, The Museum of Modern Art, New York. Gift of James Thrall Soby

brutally honest reporter who tended to stress the fact that man is, after all, a peculiar-looking creature. Obsessed with social and moral depravity, Grosz used art to express the far-from-ideal character of everything he saw. Even in a person he liked, he could not help seeing the countenance of sickness, ugliness, and, perhaps, cruelty.

The *Portrait of Max Jacob* by Juan Gris (1887–1927) deals with a man of about the same age as Hermann-Neisse, and in a similar pose. But the effect is much more placid. Grosz expresses the restless Gothic or Germanic temperament, but Gris portrays the more relaxed and classic qualities of the Mediterranean world. The drawing is excellent, too, but Gris does not distort the forms he sees; the sitter's gentleness is emphasized. Again, we have a kind of facial map; the artist seems to be making a chart of the convolutions of his subject's face, hands, and body, as if in preparation for a painting. Yet the

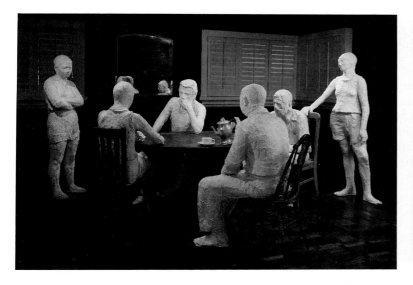

drawing itself has a quality of gentle humanity; it communicates the artist's delicacy of feeling and psychological insight.

Portraits are obviously suited to the expression of personality, but landscapes present a different problem. Still, *An April Mood* by Charles Burchfield (1893–1967) reveals the psychological possibilities of Nature when man projects his moods upon her. The trees, stripped of leaves, give Burchfield the opportunity to characterize them as witches or druids. Then, by exaggerating the heavy character of the dark clouds, which frame the light forms in the center, the artist creates a dramatic, emotionally charged stage. Nature provides theatrical occasions, of course, but only because we see them as the working out of our private dramas of menace and threat, deliverance and jubilation. Here, the upraised arms of the trees seem to join in a weird incantation, a strange imitation of primitive sun worship.

Another example of art as psychological expression is seen in George Segal's *The Dinner Table*. Segal (born 1924) creates sculpture by placing plaster-soaked rags on the bodies of his models. After the plaster sets, the rags are removed and assembled into cast-plaster figures. The final forms, therefore, are replicas of living forms, but without the exaggeration or simplification of carved or modeled figures. The artist then installs props to create a "real" environment. Segal finds his creative role in the identification of commonplace people in commonplace situations, and his technique gives them a lumpy, sluggish quality. He is not in the business of displaying sculptural virtuosity. The unnatural whiteness of the plaster figures contrasts with the realism of the objects used as props and suggests the purity and idealization of classical Greek sculpture. Yet here we have grubby, ungraceful human beings—neither handsome nor ugly, not sick but not well, either. The artist's theme is *the ordinariness, the artlessness,* of our everyday lives. He expresses the indistinctness and colorlessness of the human environment, and his people seem to have the characteristics of vegetables.

LOVE, SEX, MARRIAGE

In addition to describing the varieties of personality, art deals with major interpersonal themes such as love, sex, marriage, and procreation. The treatment of love can range from the physical embrace of Auguste Rodin's (1840–1917) *The Kiss,* to the maternal affection in Mary Cassatt's (1845–1926) *La Toilette,* to the motherly pride of Jacob Epstein's (1880–1959) *Madonna and Child.*

Usually, it is the female figure that is used to express our feelings about love and sexuality. And in the work of a single sculptor, Gaston Lachaise (1882–1935), we see two interesting variations on a sexual theme. His *Standing Woman* of 1912–27 combines elegant hands and feet with idealization and exaggeration of the fleshy forms associated with procreation. There is sexual feeling too, but the figure's eroticism is tempered by lightness and agil-

left: **George Segal.** *The Dinner Table.* **1962. Private collection, Kings Point, New York**

There is a frozen quality about both groups of diners. But the immobility of Le Nain's peasants is intended to suggest their fundamental dignity and self-respect. Segal's people are immobile because they seem to have nothing important to do.

right: **Louis Le Nain.** *Peasants at Supper.* **1641. The Louvre, Paris**

Venus of Willendorf. **c. 30,000–25,000** B.C. **Museum of Natural History, Vienna**

An early "love" object—really a fertility symbol. Here the personality of woman is wholly submerged in her biological role.

ity in the feet and a rather buoyant grace in the hands. By contrast, the forms of the *Standing Woman* of 1932 are much more exaggerated and stylized, with an almost athletic emphasis on childbearing. The feet are solidly planted in the earth, while the muscles of the shoulders and abdomen aggressively assert the female biological role. Because there is less gentleness in the transitions between forms than in the earlier bronze, this figure expresses a kind of procreative arrogance; we get few of the tender meanings of love.

left: **Charles Burchfield.** *An April Mood.* **1946–55. Whitney Museum of American Art, New York. Gift of Mr. and Mrs. Lawrence A. Fleischman and purchase**

The animation of nature. Burchfield converts the landscape into drama: the trees impersonate people against a theatrical backdrop. But Van Gogh's landscape is no stage play: he sees nature going through a real convulsion.

below: **Vincent van Gogh.** *Landscape with Olive Trees.* **1889. Collection Mr. and Mrs. John Hay Whitney, New York**

Auguste Rodin. *The Kiss.* 1886–98. Rodin Museum, Paris
Love as tender eroticism.

Jacob Epstein. *Madonna and Child.* **1927.**
The Riverside Church, New York

Love as maternal pride.

Mary Cassatt. *La Toilette.* **c. 1891. The Art Institute of Chi-**
cago. Robert A. Waller Fund

Love as protective concern.

In contrast to the fleshiness of Lachaise, Amedeo Modigliani's (1884–1920) *Reclining Nude* is a more elongated version of the female. Woman is now a sinuous object of pleasure. Her sleep seems to express complete sexual fulfillment and the subordination of all feelings and functions to the erotica—fusion of the ideas of love and contentment. Finally, we encounter a generalized idea of the female form in *Torso Gerbe* by Jean Arp (1887–1966). Here the specific character of the woman is suppressed in favor of a kind of impersonal, organic meaning. Arp has carried the abstraction of living form as far as one can go without abandoning what is biologically human. But even if the work is impersonal and semiabstract, it still looks sexy.

In our culture we are exposed to a great deal of sarcastic humor about love in marriage. Much of it deals with the loss of the mystery and illusion that feed romance. Still, many of us believe in romance, and that is what Marc Chagall (1887–1985) celebrates in *Birthday*. Here is a work dedicated to the notion of love as perpetual courtship: exchanging symbolic gifts, pretending shyness, continuing the games of pursuit and resistance. Chagall's *Birthday* charms us because of the hope that we can sustain love forever if we continue our romantic rituals.

Oskar Kokoschka (1886–1980) offers a more cynical view of love in *The*

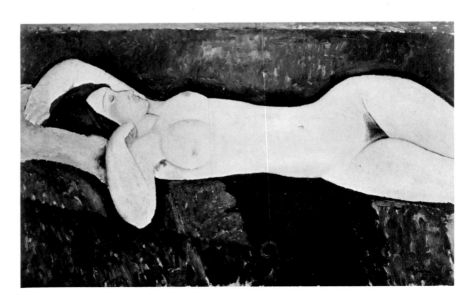

Marc Chagall. *Birthday*. 1915–23. The Solomon R. Guggenheim Museum, New York

Love as levitation. She skips; he flies . . . without arms or wings.

Tempest, or *The Wind's Bride*. Here a couple is shown swirling in space under a moonlit mountainscape. Love for them, as for Chagall's couple, has performed the miracle of levitation. Chagall's people are magically lifted up, but Kokoschka's are violently *swirled*. Words in both titles for the Kokoschka— "tempest" and "wind"—suggest the *sturm und drang*, the storm and stress, of a Germanic conception of human relations. While the bride sleeps, wrapped in tender and trusting emotions, the groom stares into space—starkly and stiffly awake. He may be levitated by the power of love, but he seems unable to suppress strong feelings of gloom.

Oskar Kokoschka. *The Tempest (The Wind's Bride)*. 1914. Kunstmuseum, Basel

Love as levitation. She dreams; he can't sleep.

above: **David Hockney.** *The First Marriage.* **1962. The Tate Gallery, London. © David Hockney 1962**

Hockney's view of a May and December marriage, outdoors, next to a palm tree, under the California sun. He has one foot in the grave; she looks confidently toward the future, like an ancient Egyptian princess.

below left: **Carl Hofer.** *Early Hour.* **1935. Portland Art Museum, Portland, Oregon**

Love and domestic life: comfortable but still a puzzlement.

below right: **Barbara Adrian.** *Bed of Stones.* **1964. Collection Mrs. Alexander Rittmaster, Woodmere, New York**

Love on the rocks; comfort doesn't matter.

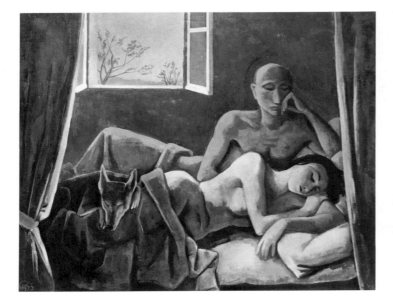

In *Early Hour* Carl Hofer (1878–1955) carries the theme of *The Wind's Bride* one step further to disillusioned domesticity. The crisp morning light reveals the husband, already awake, coldly studying his wife's sleeping form. A dog sleeping at the foot of the bed completes the picture of familial routine. The man's head—lean and bald—creates an impression of asceticism, of an intellectual resigned to marriage but not happy about it. It is interesting that in both works the woman is shown in contented slumber while the husband is wide awake, in the moonlight or skeptically contemplating his situation in the clear light of morning. The marital outlook does not look very good in either picture.

We see another version of the same theme in *Conjugal Life* by Roger de La Fresnaye (1885–1925). Here the Cubist process of breaking up figures and converting them into geometric shapes has begun. But there is enough resemblance to visual reality to allow resistance to the depersonalizing effects of a fully developed Cubism. We recognize a casual, comradely quality about this couple, accentuated by the matter-of-factness of the woman's being nude while her clothed husband reads the newspaper and enjoys his pipe. They exhibit a kind of mutual indifference based on the comfortable intimacy of a long-established relationship. This idea is strengthened by the way the figures lean toward each other: the principal lines and masses seek the center and lock the figures into a tight, formal structure. Compare this composition—and the idea behind it—with the sardonic comment of George Grosz in *Couple*.

Clearly, artistic attitudes toward women, sex, and marriage serve as an interesting index of values in our culture. In Lachaise, the sexual-reproductive attributes of woman were glorified, but at the expense of her femininity and completeness of personality. Modigliani frankly admires the sexual-hedonic qualities of woman. For Chagall she is a little girl; for Kokoschka and Hofer, an enigma, a source of puzzlement; for La Fresnaye a warm, comfortable creature to have around the house. These attitudes are not new; they confirm what we have always known—that matrimony is comfortable but also presents problems. Contemporary art has been candid enough to say so.

left: **Roger de La Fresnaye.** *Conjugal Life.* **1912. The Minneapolis Institute of Arts**

Why isn't he undressed, too?

right: **George Grosz.** *Couple.* **1934. Whitney Museum of American Art, New York**

Why do old couples seem to look like each other?

DEATH AND MORBIDITY

Death fascinates and frightens us; we cannot solve its mystery: Why does vitality and personality inhabit matter in one instant and leave it in another? From the Stone Age cave images of dead animals to African sculptures of departed chiefs, art embodies our desire to understand, if not to master, the fear of death. Science may learn to control many of death's causes, but only art can express our feelings about what happens afterward. This was always the case. Sculpture originated in efforts to provide habitations for the souls of the dead. The monuments of Egyptian art were, in their principal motivation, enormous state-supported enterprises aimed at overcoming the fears caused by the death of a king who was revered as a god. Perhaps today's artistic treatment of mortality is an extension of the anxiety that everyone feels, but which in ancient times was expressed mainly for the benefit of kings.

Artistic Expressions of Mortality In a lithograph by Käthe Kollwitz (1867–1945), *Death and the Mother*, we see the almost insane terror that grips a mother whose child is about to die. The imagery gains some of its symbolic force from medieval personifications of the devil as the messenger of death. Despite our relative freedom from such superstitions, we are disturbed by this work because it exploits fears we can barely suppress. An impersonal phrase like "infant mortality" has powerful emotional content; the viewer experiences real dread and wants to strike out against the death symbol.

A peculiar portrayal of mortality and fate occurs in *Death on a Pale Horse (The Race Track)* by the American painter Albert Pinkham Ryder (1847–1917). Here death carries his conventional attribute, a scythe, as he rides a white horse around a racetrack. No one—except a serpent (at bottom)—is there to witness the sinister scene, and, curiously, there are no competitors. Like other paintings by Ryder, this one looks as if it had been dreamed. Actually, the painting was a response to a real experience: Ryder knew a man—a waiter—who had gambled his savings on a horse race, lost his money, and then committed suicide. But the real-life origin of the painting should not interfere with our interpretation of it. (See Chapter Sixteen for a discussion of interpretation.) Although the figure on the horse unmistakably personifies death, the question remains: How does he do his grim work? Well, he cuts people down with a scythe. But why is he riding around an empty track, watched only by a snake? Here, the artist's mythic imagination is at work: Ryder suggests that life is a mysterious game played by Death and Evil; the track is a magic circle that lures men with the promise of riches. But it is really a death trap; there is no possible outcome except man's destruction; the tree inside the track bears no fruit. Competing against Death and Evil (the system), no one can win. Ryder's dream scene gives us a *magical* explanation of Everyman's life and its inevitable end.

The Dead Mother by Edvard Munch (1863–1944) is more pathetic, not so much in the image of the mother, who is beyond suffering, as in the portrayal of the child, who holds her hands to her ears as if to stop the *sound of death*. Here the psychological realism is more thoroughgoing than that of Kollwitz

above: Edvard Munch. *The Dead Mother.* 1899–1900. Kunsthalle, Bremen

right: Ben Shahn. *The Passion of Sacco and Vanzetti.* 1931–32. Whitney Museum of American Art, New York. Gift of Edith and Milton Lowenthal in memory of Juliana Force

Pablo Picasso. *Girl Before a Mirror*. 1932. Collection, The Museum of Modern Art, New York. Gift of Mrs. Simon Guggenheim

The image in the mirror reflects her fear of becoming a woman.

and Ryder, who employ conventional death symbols. Munch presents the actual death scene and studies its psychological impact on the child. She cannot understand death; she has no adult mechanisms for protecting herself, for softening the blow. So she acts out the meaning of death: it turns out to be a very bad sound. The date of this painting is 1899–1900, a time when art tended to sentimentalize harsh truths. But in Munch we have an artist who, like Ibsen, had the courage to examine the pain of life realistically.

The Passion of Sacco and Vanzetti by Ben Shahn (1898–1969) deals with the death of two men who were convicted of the murder of a paymaster and a guard during a robbery near Boston. The mourners are shown as "respectable" members of society—politicians or lawyers, and an academic—who have played a role in a miscarriage of justice: they have contributed to the execution of innocent men. The background shows a courthouse and a portrait of a jurist taking his oath of office. The scene is heavy with irony: lilies, symbols of resurrection, are held over the open coffins of two immigrant men who were tried by a prejudiced judge. The men are shown in death as defenseless and foreign-looking; their mourners look guilty and crooked. Thus Shahn created a work of bitterness and sympathy: contempt for a society that wants vengeance and compassion for the little men (we see only parts of their faces) caught up in large events that have destroyed them. Death is understood as the matter-of-fact, logical outcome of social and political hypocrisy.

In *Girl Before a Mirror*, Pablo Picasso (1881–1973) pictures the morbid anticipations of a young girl as she becomes aware of her biological woman-

Théodore Géricault. *Madwoman.* c. 1821. The Louvre, Paris

Chaim Soutine. *The Madwoman.* 1920. The National Museum of Western Art, Tokyo. Presented by Mr. Tai Hayashi, 1960

hood. We see a kind of X-ray image of her actual figure on the left and its reflection in the mirror on the right. The left image also shows what may be a spinal cord; both images deal with the shapes of female organs of reproduction and nurture. The girl's innocent face (at left) is reflected in the mirror as a dark, hollow-eyed face surrounded by black and blue moon-shaped crescents. The head on the left has a bright halo, with a yellow passage on the side where a shadow would be expected. This clear-eyed "sun-face" symbolizes her unclouded youth; the "moon-face" in the mirror symbolizes reflected light, an "old" moon, a dying woman. Yet the girl's arm reaches across to the image of her fears. Is she straightening the mirror? Well, the painting is divided vertically into two halves; perhaps the arm moving across the canvas is meant to unite the picture compositionally. But the gesture may also represent the end of her innocence, an expression of sympathy for her other self—the self that ages and dies after bringing life into the world.

Picasso's painting might be compared to the treatment of the same theme by Munch in *Puberty*, and to a highly naturalistic lithograph, *Adolescence*, by the English artist Gerald Leslie Brockhurst (1890–1978). All three works show art reaching across the barriers of age, style, and gender to deal with the apprehensions, the fears, the uneasiness of the human soul.

Artistic Expressions of Illness   The expression of love in modern art may be sentimental or cynical (usually the latter), but when it comes to illness and disease, we see a frank, almost clinical, kind of imagery. Of course, artists are not interested in pathology from a medical standpoint; but they often use sickness as a symbol of the human condition in general. Artists may not be fascinated with morbidity for its own sake, but they refuse to ignore a dimension of experience that helps to define our humanity.

An early portrayal of mental illness can be seen in *Madwoman* by Théodore Géricault (1791–1824). Here the artist examines a woman carefully while she seems to be confronting some real or imagined threat. Perhaps she is truly crazy. But without the title we could interpret this work as a character study, as the portrait of a somewhat suspicious, possibly eccentric, peasant woman. Is Géricault saying that the difference between crazy and eccentric is hard to see? His picture should be compared with *The Madwoman* by Chaim Soutine (1894–1944), painted in 1920, about one hundred years later. Here the artist has attempted to convey *the experience* of the sick person: every part of her trembles with fear; there is no question in our minds that she is mentally ill. Géricault maintains his objectivity, whereas Soutine enters into the life of his subject. We call Géricault a Romantic painter because he chose strange or emotionally demanding subjects. Romantics describe abnormal behavior, human reactions in emergencies, or the loss of rational controls when under stress. Soutine is called an Expressionist because of his subject matter *and* his agitated technique. The Expressionists took the Romantic fascination with violence and incorporated it into the act of painting itself. Artistic imagery then becomes a record of convulsive form and emotion. But even though the frightened eyes and tortured hands of Soutine's woman announce her illness, the picture rises above illness: we recognize a fellow human being who is suffering.

In *The Frugal Repast*, an etching made when he was young and poor, Picasso portrays a gaunt, emaciated couple at a meal. The man is blind; both are almost starving. Their condition offers the artist an opportunity to stretch out their bodies, especially their hands, giving them a weak, feverish quality. But even if the man is handicapped and both are undernourished, the couple seem resigned to their situation; they have a little food (in France, wine is a food) and each other. This etching is a highly civilized tribute to romantic love; what appears to be a morbid interest in the effects of malnutrition on lovers becomes a human triumph over deprivation. Weakness is converted

Pablo Picasso. *The Frugal Repast.* 1904. Collection, The Museum of
Modern Art, New York. Gift of Abby Aldrich Rockefeller

into tenderness, and the artist discovers a peculiar kind of beauty in the withered bodies of people who care for and love each other.

Works like *The Frugal Repast* are not meant to gloss over the reality of poverty. However, one of the great strengths of art is its capacity to reveal the values people hold despite the situations they must live with. Puccini's romantic opera *La Bohème* deals with a theme much like Picasso's: the composer found aesthetic value in the love of a consumptive, dying girl for an impoverished poet. Picasso's etching was made in 1904, when he was twenty-two and an ardent devotee of tragic love; this was only eight years after the first performance of *La Bohème*. Both works express the romantic idea that love can be carried to intensity *because* of affliction and *in spite of* the world's indifference.

There is an aesthetic—that is, a whole system of ideas about art—based on the experience of illness. In Géricault and in Soutine, this interest is part of a concern with the total human condition. In Munch, death is a permanent fact of life. In Shahn's *Passion*, death is part of a satiric-ironic statement about justice. In Picasso's etching the signs of deprivation have a sympathetic, even erotic, significance. In Ivan Albright's *Self-Portrait* and Karl Zerbe's *Aging Harlequin*, a certain ugliness associated with aging (compare Domenico Ghirlandaio's [1449–1494] *An Old Man and His Grandson*) is recorded in fascinating detail. Zerbe (1903–1972) enlists compassion for the harlequin, despite his ravaged countenance. Albright (1897–1983) shows himself drinking champagne and sadly contemplating the fate that is written in his face.

Perhaps the ultimate image of deterioration is seen in the work of Hyman Bloom (born 1913) and of Alberto Burri (born 1915). In *Corpse of an Elderly Female* we witness an artist's fascination with death; he employs no artistic device to soften clinical accuracy. Bloom's interest in cadavers is probably a reaction to the slaughter of civilians during World War II. Here we are forced to confront death without knowing who has died or why. The Italian artist Alberto Burri works much more abstractly. His *Sacco B.* is made of burlap sacking stretched and sewn around what appear to be open wounds and incisions. Burri was a military doctor, and many of his compositions reflect his surgical experience; the dramatic focus is an opening in the flesh. One can view these works as simple arrangements of gauze, burnt wood, and burlap, but they also have an expressive purpose: the rips in the sacking are the result of some mysterious, nonmedical surgery. Although Burri's surfaces suggest disease, surgery is portrayed as a kind of primitive handicraft. A rather disorderly death hovers over the entire composition. It is a far cry from the Thomas Eakins painting of modern surgery in 1889, *The Agnew Clinic*, with its confident presentation of the doctor's technique as a triumph of science.

Examples could be multiplied. We have seen how one of the personal functions of art—now as in the past—is the confrontation of death and all the feelings associated with it. Obviously, art cannot postpone death, but it can help us to face the experience and understand it as part of the process of living. Art seems to be saying that our fears, curiosities, and aversions can be expressed in a form that enables us to see life clearly and whole.

SPIRITUAL CONCERN

We should distinguish between religious art and an art of spiritual concern. Religious art usually expresses collective ideas about human life in relation to the divine. It may have spiritual qualities, but it can also function as education or as history or as a kind of visual preaching. Nonreligious, or secular, art can also exhibit spiritual qualities, as in Van Gogh's *The Starry Night*. Ironically, religious art may exhibit very little spirituality, as in *Christ Preaching at Cookham Regatta* by Stanley Spencer (1891–1959). By contrast, Georges Rouault's (1871–1958) works seem to have spiritual content even when the subject matter is secular, as in his *Three Clowns*.

above: Ivan Albright. *Self-Portrait.* 1935. Collection Earle Ludgin, Chicago

left: Domenico Ghirlandaio. *An Old Man and His Grandson.* c. 1480. The Louvre, Paris

Aging brings many indignities and few joys. Grandchildren are one of the joys, but we need a fifteenth-century master to tell us about it.

right: Karl Zerbe. *Aging Harlequin.* 1946. Collection Dr. Michael Watter, Washington, D.C.

far right: Photograph of Melvyn Douglas as he appeared in the CBS Television Network presentation "Do Not Go Gentle into That Good Night." 1967

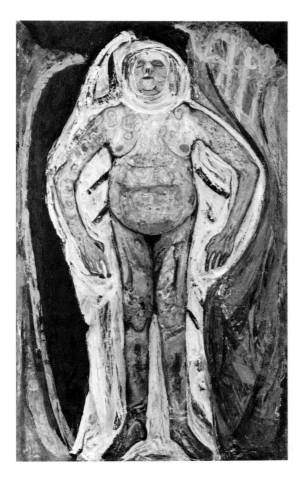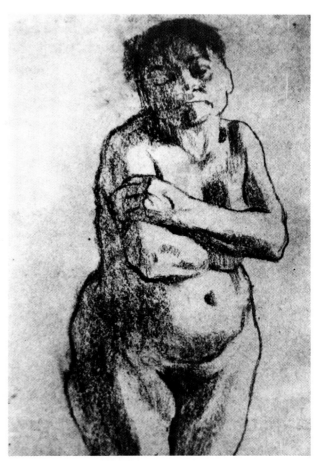

What accounts for this paradox? Well, religious art usually tells a sacred story, encourages morality, or tries to sustain faith in the context of worship. Spiritual art tries to reveal what is sacred or holy in everyday life and in human nature; often it discovers God in unexpected places. A spiritual art does not necessarily come with theological labels. Furthermore, it tends to express the *questions* an artist may have about man's place in the universe, whereas religious art tends to deal with *answers* that have been institutionally established. For our purposes, then, an art of spiritual concern is *any search for ultimate values through the use of visual form.*

Today especially, the artistic enterprise is identified with search and inquiry. In the past, people were more certain about life's origin and man's destiny, and artists could deal with commonly accepted ideas about human existence. But the modern era has witnessed profound changes in the expression of fundamental values. The scientific, industrial, and political revolutions of our time have caused almost universal questioning of inherited dogmas and philosophies. Yet our era has not been especially successful in providing alternatives that hold true even for a lifetime. For that reason, perhaps, today's intellectual, spiritual, and artistic activities have emphasized searching and questioning. Artworks that deal with personal values have been characterized more by uncertainty than by conviction.

Still, we cannot tolerate uncertainty forever. A deep layer of conviction often lies beneath our questions about the meaning and value of existence. Art makes that "layer of conviction" visible. On the surface, *The Starry Night* of Vincent van Gogh (1853–1890) is a picture of a village at night, with prominent cypresses in the foreground and large circles and spirals of light emanating from the stars and the moon. It is a scene animated by flamelike shapes in the trees and active brushwork in the hills and the sky. Everything appears to

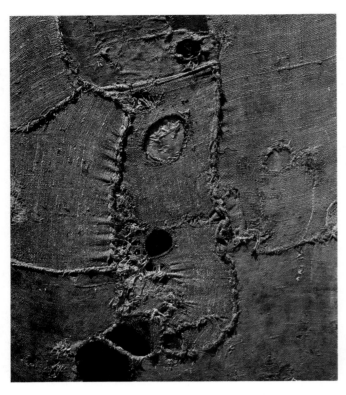

Alberto Burri. *Sacco B*. **1953. Collection the artist**

The clinical ritual of surgery converted into aesthetic drama: open and closed, woven and sewn, wet and dry, alive and dead.

below: **Thomas Eakins.** *The Agnew Clinic.* **1889. The University of Pennsylvania, Philadelphia**

The ritual of surgery portrayed as a triumph of mind over flesh.

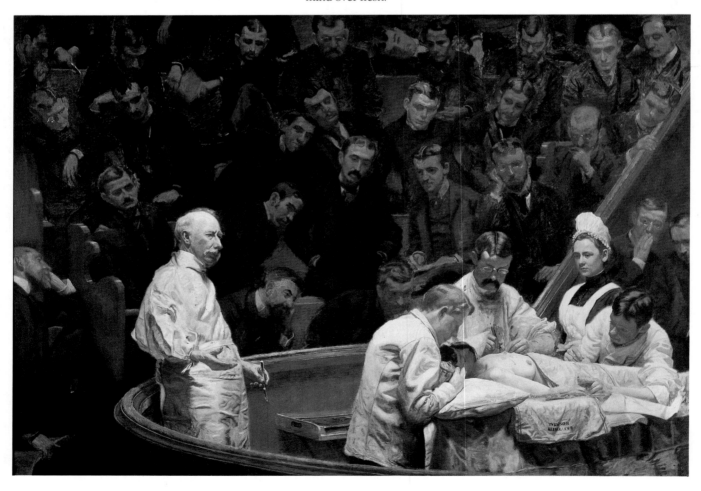

Stanley Spencer. *Christ Preaching at Cookham Regatta: Series No. VI: Four Girls Listening.* 1958. Arthur Tooth & Sons, Ltd., London

Georges Rouault. *Three Clowns.* 1917. Collection Joseph Pulitzer, Jr., St. Louis

Vincent van Gogh. *The Starry Night*. 1889. Collection, The Museum of Modern Art, New York. Acquired through the Lillie P. Bliss Bequest

The useful and the secular often converge in the spiritual: Van Gogh's painting begins with an everyday theme and culminates in a mystical statement.

be alive and in motion; only the houses and the church are at rest. This landscape has a kind of life we do not normally see; the differences between solid and void, organic and inorganic, hardly exist. Van Gogh has shown us the sacred where we did not expect to find it. For those who do not possess his spiritual gifts, the experience of this painting offers a glimpse into a hallowed world: we share in the vision of a "God-intoxicated" man.

The art of Rouault illustrates the same point—in a different way. What accounts for the spiritual character of his *Three Clowns*? First, we see the similarity, with minor variations, of the three men. We view them as a group rather than as distinct personalities; collectively, they can symbolize all men—humanity. Second is the coarseness of their features: the artist has deliberately avoided physical beauty. Because of their rough faces and the harsh transitions from light to dark, we realize we are not dealing with the beautiful, the harmonious, or the elegant. Third is the passive, accepting expressions of the men's faces; the body of humanity is described as suffering and unresisting. Finally, there is the huddled arrangement of the figures; they seem to symbolize the oppressed, fearful, and victimized condition of all those who are weak.

All of these factors, working together, tend to express the wretchedness of the human condition. Certain themes at the heart of Christianity—the virtue of humility and the significance of suffering—are presented in a form that gives them universal application. It appears that the artist wants to reveal our authentic nature—what humanity is really like as opposed to what man thinks he is.

Whereas the spirituality of Rouault grows out of one essential insight—the pain and anguish of being human—the sculptor Henry Moore (born 1898) stresses spiritual affirmation and renewal; his figures cast humanity in a monumental role. Now, monumental sculpture usually celebrates victories of one sort or another. But if Moore celebrates any victory, it is the triumph of *durability* in men and women, of their refusal to be beaten down. The massiveness of his UNESCO sculpture creates a powerful sense of stability: its large forms, abstracted from the thighs and torso, look like the shapes of old hills and eroded mountains. They are also punctuated with deep hollows and full openings and crowned by a head that seems to symbolize the dominance of intelligence over matter. Those openings and hollows are not merely "negative" shapes; they function positively by allowing the environment to become a part of the sculpture.

Without obvious dramatic devices Moore's figure suggests the resurgence of a human being after having been struck down. The forms become symbols of human determination operating against every kind of adversity. The image is Promethean: man suffers but is still defiant. His reclining position may suggest defeat, as in the *Dying Gaul*, yet he is capable of physical and spiritual renewal. Compared with Rouault, Moore is less obsessed with the weakness and corruptibility of man. Instead, his sculpture expresses human tenacity, the courage of an earth creature that slowly rebuilds itself, even if it knows that the powers of the universe will strike it down again.

Henry Moore. Sculpture for UNESCO Head-quarters, Paris. 1958

RECUMBENT AND FALLEN FIGURES AS SYMBOLS OF DEATH AND RESURRECTION

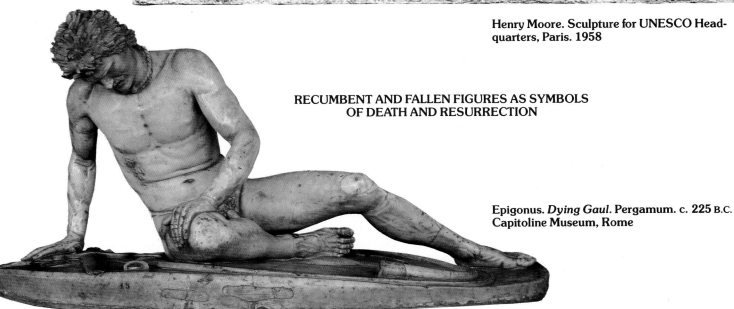

Epigonus. *Dying Gaul*. Pergamum. c. 225 B.C. Capitoline Museum, Rome

Jackson Pollock. *Number I, 1948*. 1948. Collection, The Museum of Modern Art, New York. Purchase

A different expression of modern spirituality is found in the work of Jackson Pollock (1912–1956). *Number I, 1948* shows his typical paint surface: we see tangled threads of pigment dripped and spattered on the canvas, creating an endless maze of pattern and movement. Viewing the work as a whole, we are aware of an overall texture as well as the repeated black calligraphic marks overlaid with paint splashes and spatters, knots and spots of color. And because this is a huge canvas—nine by seventeen feet—we can feel drawn into the center of a jungle. Without representational elements, the painting directs the viewer back to the artist's act of execution. The imagery is at once dance-like and trancelike; no single movement is fathomable in terms of a deliberate departure, journey, and return. We seem to be looking at multiple voyages, all sorts of terrain, and multiple arenas of conflict. Yet the viewer cannot fail to be excited by the energy of the work, mainly because of its explosive release of painterly forces, its kinetic power. But we feel entrapped, too. The experience, which intrigues us at first, can leave us frustrated.

The disturbing quality of Pollock's work would not have attracted such wide interest if it did not constitute a faithful reproduction of the spiritual landscape of our time. If we could see the lives of others from the inside, they might look very much like Pollock's "voyages." But we might also see signs of satisfaction and hints of fulfillment. This would not invalidate Pollock's relevance to the spiritual condition of modern men and women: he remains the painter of our energetic and industrious failures.

AESTHETIC EXPRESSION

Aesthetic needs and impulses are not the specialized interest of some elite; everyone is concerned with what is beautiful or pleasing. Most of us are interested in harmonious forms wherever they can be found—in people, in nature, and in objects of daily use. However, some artists specialize in creating images and objects that are *intrinsically* satisfying, apart from any other use they may have. Such artworks turn out to be useful in a psychological sense: they help to satisfy aesthetic needs—needs that exist at the deepest levels of personality.

In earliest times, humans were concerned with forms, colors, shapes, and textures mainly because they were signs of danger or opportunity. Vision was a matter of supreme importance, since life depended on how accurate it was and how intelligently it was used. We still have remarkable capacity for interpreting optical experience. However, the conditions of modern life may not demand as much of our perceptual ability as we are equipped to supply. In complex cultures, therefore, some forms of visual art have evolved as a means of engaging unused perceptual capacity. Perhaps that is what aesthetic pleasure is—the satisfaction we feel in employing our innate capacities for perception to the fullest.

An elementary aesthetic pleasure might be called "the thrill of recognition." Obviously, recognition has always played an important role in human survival, and that may explain the popularity of art that is easily identified. When we *recognize* something in a work of art, we are, in a sense, rehearsing our survival technique, sharpening our capacity to distinguish between friend and foe. It is only a short step from the ability to make subtle visual discriminations to the ability to enjoy perception itself. Thus, we suspend the impulse to fight or flee, and we learn to linger over visual events. That maximizes our pleasure.

For Georges Braque (1882–1963) painting was mainly a source of visual delight. He was an early associate of Picasso in the creation of the intellectual austerities of Cubism, but he also employed Cubist principles to paint pictures of considerable sensuous appeal and decorative ingenuity. In *The Round Table* we see his mastery of shape and texture and his wit in exploiting visual habits and pictorial conventions for pleasure and humor. The table can be recognized easily enough, with its top tilted up to show a number of ordinary objects: a mandolin, a knife, fruit, a magazine, a pipe, and so on. The objects in themselves are unimportant; but they have shapes, colors, and textures that Braque can rearrange. He can show the top and side view of an object at the

Marsden Hartley. *Indian Composition.* 1914. Vassar College Art Gallery, Poughkeepsie, New York. Gift of Paul Rosenfeld

Indian symbols, patterns, and motifs organized into a painting that functions mainly as an aesthetic object. But aesthetic potency is often rooted in magical-religious function. The forms created by the Hopi and the Crow still have the power to stir emotion.

Georges Braque. *The Round Table.* 1929. The Phillips Collection, Washington, D.C.

opposite: Helen Frankenthaler. *Rapunzel.* 1974. Collection the artist

Whether dealing with the landscape, natural processes, or a fairy tale, Frankenthaler speaks directly in the language of sensation. Her areas of stained or brushed color communicate by their size, intensity, and placement more than by their shape. In other words, despite its lyricism, its highly personal expression of feeling, this painting is *designed*. Hanging those forms from the top edge of the canvas—and making them function simultaneously as narrative and music—is a pure feat of the aesthetic imagination. Compare the imagery to Jim Dine's *Five Feet of Colorful Tools* (page 482).

same time; he can paint opaque objects as if they were transparent; he can reverse the expected convergence of lines in perspective; he can exaggerate ornamental shapes with white lines and exchange light and shadow areas arbitrarily; or he can paint shadows that are lighter and brighter than the objects that cast them. The purpose of these "violations" and surprises is not to create a picture *of* something; the picture must *be* something, a kind of organism that lives according to its own cockeyed law. That "law" seems to state that any twisting, slicing, distortion, or reversal of shapes, colors, or textures is permitted if it adds to our pleasure in looking.

But how does a painter please the eye? Well, once the logic of reproducing appearances is abandoned, the possibilities are endless. The artist becomes a kind of intuitive investigator of forms that are somehow appealing, or unexpected, or both. Usually, his artistic conscience will not permit the use of literary associations; our pleasure has to come from pictorial organization and painterly technique. Accordingly, Braque surrounds the table shapes with thick and thin white outlines in order to flatten out the form and destroy the illusion of deep space. He creates three-dimensional effects, which are then pressed into two dimensions. The viewer is forced to read the painting as if the walls and the floor were in the same plane as the table base. There is a subtle visual humor or, at least, visual trickery in Braque's painting; it doesn't make us laugh out loud, but we know there is something funny going on.

The development of an art of aesthetic purpose was closely followed in our time by the emergence of abstract and nonobjective art. As painters and sculptors have largely abandoned the storytelling function, they have increas-

above: José de Rivera. *Construction "Blue and Black."* 1951. Whitney Museum of American Art, New York

below left: David Hare. *Juggler.* 1950–51. Whitney Museum of American Art, New York

Machine-man metaphors. Hare's Juggler is having a good time; Lanceley's Personage is having a nervous breakdown.

below right: Colin Lanceley. *Inverted Personage.* 1965. Albion College, Albion, Michigan

ingly concentrated on the internal problems of form creation in the hope of generating purely aesthetic emotions. The sculpture of José de Rivera (1904–1985), *Construction "Blue and Black"*, is an example. Here we have a work of almost absolute precision and geometric beauty, but it refers to nothing beyond itself. The sculpture "works" only in an aesthetic frame of reference. Perhaps the design of some useful object will be inspired by it. But we do not ask what this work represents: its theme or subject matter is the formal organization of the thing itself.

Alexander Calder (1898–1976) invented a new sculptural type—the mobile—which pleases us mainly through the movement of abstract shapes. His *International Mobile* is a whimsical work; the slightest movement of air in the space around it imparts a wavy, rollicking motion to the carefully balanced parts. They shift into an infinite number of constellations, arriving at temporary periods of equipoise by trembling, wriggling routes. Although mobiles do not obviously resemble trees or people, their motion can suggest anything from the sway of branches to the maneuvers of a belly dancer. But these are only one viewer's responses, stimulated by a very original—and often comic—artist. Calder's work is highly intellectual and controlled, even in its seemingly random motion. Moreover, his sculpture "uses" the atmosphere and light of its environment. The climate of the room collaborates with the artist; he may be our greatest "ecological" artist.

The *Juggler* by David Hare (born 1917) is another work in which a playful abstraction of motion is the principal theme; the juggler's muscular exer-

The linear forms in Stuart Davis's 1940 street scene fill his canvas with jazzy, comic energy. But in the 1960s sculptures of Voulkos and Paolozzi we see only sinister signs: amputated arms coming out of a truncated head, and slithery, squirmy legs attached to a terrible machine-body-face.

above: **Stuart Davis.** *Report from Rockport.* **1940. Collection Mr. and Mrs. Milton Lowenthal, New York**

below left: **Peter Voulkos.** *Firestone.* **1965. Los Angeles County Museum of Art. Museum Purchase with Contemporary Art Council Funds**

below right: **Eduardo Paolozzi.** *Medea.* **1964. Kröller-Müller Museum, Otterlo, The Netherlands**

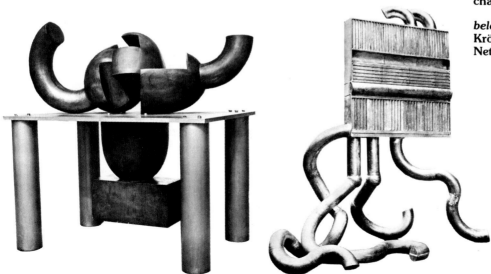

Käthe Kollwitz. *Self-Portrait.* **1934. Los Angeles County Museum of Art. Los Angeles County Funds**

The frontal pose, the masterly control of tones, the clear articulation of form, even the regularity of the paper grain showing through the grays: all these factors produce a sense of aesthetic order, an order that simultaneously expresses age, wisdom, and personal integrity.

tion and striving for balance become an excuse for making a strange steel "thing." It looks as if the artist was searching for a living creature that would fit into his agenda—the creation of form by using modern technologies to manipulate modern materials. The juggler must have represented an opportunity to make a construction out of wire and welded steel. Our aesthetic pleasure is based on the tension between the normal idea of a juggler and what happens to that idea as it is translated into cut, bent, hammered, and welded metal; the process has to show. Viewer expectations are crucial, too. The artist plays with the interactions between *your* idea of a juggler and *his* idea of art. So we have a game or a contest—whichever you like.

Calder's mobile and Hare's sculpture do not perform any of the world's work. But they do something for us as viewers: they yield pleasure based on our ability and willingness to follow the artist as he makes comparisons or metaphors that relate images, ideas, objects, sensations, and memories. Since these works have no practical value, we have to approach them with a fresh mental set, a logic that is different from the one we use in the everyday world. We are not trying to prove we know a juggler when we see one; we want to see if there is any fun or knowledge or insight to be found in recognizing the *difference between* a juggler and a welded steel construction.

A personal and very enjoyable development of Cubism was created by the American painter Stuart Davis (1894–1964). In *Report from Rockport*, he used flat, geometric, somewhat spastic shapes to describe the things he liked: street signs, billboards, gas pumps, automobile horns, city noise, and the architecture of Main Street. The problems that worry traffic engineers gave pleasure to Davis; he liked the confusion of the signs and lights that bedevil motorists; he rejoiced in the gasoline gulches that seem to spring up along every new highway. Davis was an early and devoted follower of the jazz played in the saloons of Hoboken and Newark, New Jersey, and this interest is echoed in the dynamism and staccato rhythms of his painting. Building on the pictorial devices of Picasso and Braque, he developed a personal style that conveys the impact of our distinctively American chaos. Davis was not a social critic: his paintings accept the disorganization and commercial hype in our environment. But he adds to our fund of aesthetic values by teaching us to see highways and shopping districts as gloriously funny—confused, disordered, cacophonous, but peculiarly healthy.

The range of personal expression in today's art is enormous. We have seen works that cry out of loneliness and isolation; works that cross over the boundaries of sanity; works that compare people to machines or machines to people. We have looked at strange visual puns and outrageous visual metaphors. There are works that celebrate the excitement and energy of places we normally regard as ecological disasters. Beauty, defined as ideal form, is not a common trait of today's aesthetic expression. As for the human figure, when it appears, it is often ugly or mutilated: In the work of Bacon, Dubuffet, Paolozzi, and de Kooning, it tends to be angry, awkward, or hateful.

Why? The reasons are complex and beyond the scope of this chapter. It might be fair to say that, using their various methods, artists are trying to tell us something about our civilization. It is certainly true that artistic expression has never been so varied, individualized, and surprising. Perhaps that is a cause for rejoicing: look at the array of aesthetic choices we get.

CHAPTER TWO

THE SOCIAL FUNCTIONS OF ART

In a sense, all works of art perform a social function, since they are created for an audience. Artists may claim to work only for themselves, but this really means that they set their own standards. The artist always hopes, secretly perhaps, that there is a discriminating public that will admire his work. Artworks may be created because of some private or personal need, but they still call for a social response.

There are, however, narrower and more specific meanings for the social function of art. These meanings relate to the *character of the social response* that an artwork evokes: How do groups of people act because of their art experience? Here we hope to show that art performs a social function when (1) it influences the collective behavior of human beings; (2) it is made to be seen or used in public situations; (3) it describes collective aspects of life as opposed to personal kinds of experience. In all these cases, viewers respond with the awareness that they are members of a group.

Many works are deliberately designed to influence group thinking. Artists may try to make us laugh at the same things; to accept certain religious, economic, or social ideologies; to identify with a particular class or ethnic interest; or to see our social situation in new ways. The visual arts can function as languages of praise and celebration, anger and protest, satire and ridicule. In other words, art tries to influence collective attitudes and emotions and, ultimately, the way we act. Advertising art is a common illustration: its purpose is to influence purchasing behavior. Wartime art is another example: governments use it to stimulate patriotism, to encourage self-sacrifice, to spur enlistments, to increase production levels, or to arouse hatred of the enemy. Whether the social goal is war or peace, production or consumption—art plays a role.

Some people think that art designed to influence social behavior is corrupt, impure, "mere" propaganda, and so on. And, given certain assumptions about the "appropriate" functions of art, they may be right. But we could not present a complete or accurate picture of art if we ignored its role as propaganda, for example; the history of art offers many examples. It also shows that the excellence of an artwork is often unrelated to its purpose. In other words, some propagandistic art is bad—badly conceived and badly done. But it can also be very good.

Samuel Laroye. Bicycle mask of the Gelede Secret Society, Yoruba tribe. 1958

Art and social change. For the Yoruba sculptor there is nothing wrong in combining a modern man-on-a-bicycle with a traditional head mask. The mask is used in ritual, and ritual unites the past with the present. Art is the visible expression of that idea: it absorbs and assimilates everything into the *now*.

Eugène Delacroix. *Liberty Leading the People*. 1830. The Louvre, Paris

Much blood, gore, and commotion: all classes are involved in a highly "participatory" uprising, with an allegorical figure, *la belle France*, to inspire and guide them.

Auguste Rodin. *The Burghers of Calais*. 1886. The Hirshhorn Museum and Sculpture Garden, Smithsonian Institution, Washington, D.C.

The public monument is a social art form. It enables an abstraction—society—to become humanly real; it builds our collective memory and, we hope, our civic conscience.

ATOMKRIEG NEIN

"VERY WELL, ALONE"

POLITICAL AND IDEOLOGICAL EXPRESSION

Some artists are interested in the freedom to solve special problems of style or technique. Others use style and technique to express their social and political views. They may speak of their artistic responsibility: art does not exist merely to entertain, it must guide and instruct; it must improve our collective existence. As long as there are wrongs to be righted, art should enlist on the side of right: it should help shape the attitudes that can improve human existence. This view is opposed by those artists who feel they serve society best when they concentrate on the honest expression of their personal experience, the creation of new form, and the refinement of the forms they have inherited.

Cézanne, for example, could generate aesthetic emotions merely by painting apples or vegetables; other artists require themes with obvious social relevance. Eugène Delacroix (1798–1863) seemed to need great human spectacles to make an artistic statement; his *Liberty Leading the People* is one of the early monuments of revolutionary art. Thus social and artistic liberty seem to be interdependent: for some artists, society is free only if they can express their private feelings without fear or censorship; for others, freedom means the right to deal with important ideological themes—in any way they choose.

Revolutionary Art: Latin America   In this century, Mexico has produced three major artists whose work has been frankly revolutionary: José Clemente Orozco (1883–1949), Diego Rivera (1886–1957), and David Alfaro Siqueiros (1896–1974). Their paintings, often in mural form, deal with themes like the poverty of the Mexican masses, the conquest of the Aztecs by Spanish invaders, and the exploitation of peasants by oppressive landowners. The range of these works is from obvious political propaganda to an intense concern with human anguish. In *Echo of a Scream* (compare this socially oriented work with a psychologically oriented work, Edvard Munch's *The Scream,* page 177) Siqueiros employed a fantastic, almost hallucinatory pictorial device to convey the idea of poverty. The word "echo" in the title, the repetition of the screaming child's image, and the deserted wasteland setting extend the theme of the work to the entire body of humanity; the suffering of *all* abandoned children is symbolized here. This painting has an emotional *and a political* strategy; it forces us to confront a painful social reality and to ask Why?

A particularly bitter comment on society is made in Orozco's *Gods of the Modern World,* a part of the fresco mural in the Baker Library at Dartmouth

left: **Hans Erni.** *Atomkrieg Nein (Atom War No).* **1954. Collection, The Museum of Modern Art, New York. Gift of the designer**

right: **David Low.** *Very Well, Alone.* **c. 1940. Cartoon by permission of the David Low Trustees and the *London Evening Standard***

Maoist poster. Library, University of Georgia, Athens

The cult of personality built around Mao Zedong did not hide powerful impulses toward Westernization, as in this patriotic poster, which borrowed heavily from the war cartoons of a Briton, David Low.

David Alfaro Siqueiros. *Echo of a Scream.* 1937. Collection, The Museum of Modern Art, New York. Gift of Edward M. M. Warburg

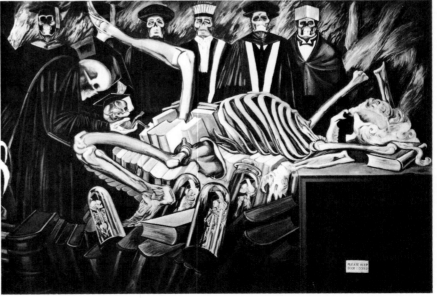

José Clemente Orozco. *Gods of the Modern World.* 1932–34. Trustees of Dartmouth College, Hanover, New Hampshire

With his denunciation of universities in 1932, Orozco anticipated many of today's attacks on the "relevance" of academic study.

College. It shows a dissected corpse stretched on a pile of books and attended by a deathly figure in academic costume. Presumably, the corpse has given birth to an infant skeleton, also in academic cap, with the death figure acting as midwife. In the background stands a collection of professors wearing their regalia. The humor is really gruesome, especially since the mural is in the library of a distinguished American university. The academic function of preserving and transmitting ancient knowledge is presented as a necrophilic ritual. What we see is a type of revolutionary disgust with established social institutions, a typical trait of the satirist who genuinely detests what he ridicules.

Diego Rivera's art has the same revolutionary commitment as Orozco's, but its formal organization is less violent. As a designer, he is perhaps the best of the Mexican threesome. But slick designer or not, he drives his *political* message home with unsubtle force. *The Billionaires* and *Night of the Poor* convey the message of a morality play: the greed of the rich, engrossed in the pursuit of profit, is contrasted with the innocent sleep of the poor, some of whom study at night to escape illiteracy. While this goes on, middle-class types in the background show their disapproval.

These artworks illustrate the stereotyped portrayal of social classes and racial groups according to Marxist dogma. Political ideas are presented in greatly simplified form because they are intended for the uneducated. The principal objective is to persuade the masses that they belong to an oppressed class. Just as early Christian art tried to explain basic concepts of sin, expiation, and redemption in simple terms, so also does revolutionary art try to explain oppressors and victims, wealth and poverty. It is not surprising that Latin American artists, growing out of a tradition in which the religious influence on culture is very potent, employ art in a manner that is similar to that of the medieval Church. But, ironically, the art of Rivera and his associates is violently hostile to organized religion.

Luis Cruz Azaceta. *Apocalypse: Now or Later.* 1981. Courtesy Allan Frumkin Gallery, New York

An ironic statement about war and the end of the world, using the biblical symbol of a horseman galloping over dead and maimed figures. In Dürer's woodcut *The Four Horsemen of the Apocalypse,* War was represented by a skeletal old man carrying a pitchfork; Azaceta's rider is a ridiculous-looking warrior blowing a bugle.

Diego Rivera. *The Billionaires* **and** *Night of the Poor.* **1923–28. Ministry of Education, Mexico City**

Mural art as an instrument for developing class consciousness.

below: **George Tooker.** *Government Bureau.* **1956. The Metropolitan Museum of Art, New York. George A. Hearn Fund, 1956**

In these mechanically repeated spaces, the same sinister eyes watch the same people. According to Tooker's surreal image, we have become interchangeable units because that is what bureaucrats want us to be.

Artistic Expressions of Humanitarian Concern A modern industrial state faces social problems radically different from those of a feudal, agrarian society. Our problems with the regulation of a complex economy, the conduct of international relations, and the administration of justice must seem unreal to people who suffer the anxiety of living in a state of peonage. But we have our own anxieties—for example, those caused by a remote and impersonal government. This theme is well expressed by George Tooker (born 1920) in *Government Bureau*. Using repetition of figure and space, like receding images in parallel mirrors, Tooker creates a quality of Surrealist terror in a government building: it has the atmosphere of an orderly, methodical, and thoroughly dismal nightmare. Is this the image of government by bureaucracy that stands behind our fears of political overcentralization? Tooker has dramatized the vulnerability and alienation felt by ordinary people when they become involved with government, represented by this cheerless, administrative labyrinth.

In *Employment Agency,* Isaac Soyer (1907–1981) portrays the operation of our economy in pathetically human terms. When economists speak of different kinds of unemployment—structural unemployment, transitional unemployment, the displacement of workers with obsolete skills, and so on—we understand only vaguely what they mean. But how are real people affected? How do they cope with an economy that seems to work against them? Soyer depicts the waiting room of an employment agency as a kind of theater where several dramas are being played out at once. Here unemployment translates itself into the feeling of being unwanted by the world, one of the most profound spiritual experiences of our time. As an artist, Soyer can offer no economic solution, but, whether we have a job or not, he makes us experience what the unemployed feel.

Can a sculpture deal with industrial phenomena in social terms? Yes. In *Mine Disaster,* Berta Margoulies (born 1907) has created a kind of memorial to the wives of the men who are periodically trapped and killed by mine accidents. Margoulies stresses the psychological dimensions of the event: women clinging to hope in spite of what they know. This has been the experience of mining people for generations. As in other works of social protest, the device of huddling the figures is employed, along with the portrayal of mixed emotions in the faces—hope, suspense, and despair.

left: Isaac Soyer. *Employment Agency.* 1937. Whitney Museum of American Art, New York

right: Berta Margoulies. *Mine Disaster.* 1942. Whitney Museum of American Art, New York

Alfred Stieglitz. *The Steerage.* 1907. Philadelphia Museum of Art. Stieglitz Collection

The photograph by Alfred Stieglitz (1864–1946), *The Steerage,* is a work that shows human degradation and hope. It is also a great historical document. The picture was taken in 1907 at the height of a great migration of people from all parts of Europe to America. The steerage was the lowest, most squalid part of a ship—and the cheapest way to cross the Atlantic for the desperately poor who came to the United States seeking a new life. Stieglitz has given the scene a timeless quality: his photograph reminds us of a medieval religious work in which condemned people, confined in some hellish place, come out to greet the light.

Perhaps the most monumental work of social protest in our time is Picasso's *Guernica.* This mural-size painting was executed in 1937 to memorialize the bombing of the Basque town of Guernica by Nazi aircraft (flying for Generalissimo Franco) during the Spanish Civil War. Here Picasso invented the imagery that has influenced succeeding generations of artists in their treatment of war, violence, chaos, and suffering. Using only black, white, and gray, Picasso created a work that expresses multiple perceptions of a single catastrophic event: newspaper accounts of the bombing, the screaming of victims, the laceration of human flesh, and the meaning of a type of war in which civilians are the first victims. Images such as the fallen statue, the burning building, the mother and dead child, the shrieking horse, and the spectator bull describe the bombing in terms of modern *schrecklichkeit*—new, skyborne methods of terror.

While Picasso's painting is relevant for our time, it exists within the same frame of reference as Goya's series The Disasters of War, created early in the nineteenth century. But is it equal to the challenge implied by the millions of casualties that might be sustained in a war of nuclear destruction? Probably not. Picasso could still think of war as a catastrophe that has *individual* consequences. Today, the scale of war has been so enlarged that some artists feel compelled to use a more abstract and dehumanized form-language to cope with it. For an idea of the really big bang, we can look at Adolph Gottlieb's *Blast II* (page 214).

SOCIAL DESCRIPTION

Art can perform its social function by describing life without implying that there is a problem to be solved. By concentrating on everyday "slices of life"

Pablo Picasso. *Guernica.* 1937. The Prado, Madrid

Francisco Goya. *"Nothing more to do."* From the series The Disasters of War. Issued 1810–63. The Hispanic Society of America, New York

Despite the mechanization and depersonalization of war, the cruelty of individual executions has not greatly changed—from Goya's nineteenth-century etching to Segal's twentieth-century *tableau vivant*.

George Segal. *The Execution.* 1967. The Vancouver Art Gallery, British Columbia

Marisol. *The Family.* 1962. Collection, The Museum of Modern Art, New York. Advisory Committee Fund

This imagery could have come from a snapshot taken on the front porch about 1910. Everyone squints; the kids look as if they are clones; the mother looks stout and stolid; and the father is absent—or maybe she is a widow. In any case, she raises them alone. The line between social description and satire is very thin.

the artist can focus attention on the quality of our lives together—especially as it is affected by our environment. When an artistic "frame" is constructed around places and events it seems easier to discover their distinctive flavor.

What about the environment of a pool hall? (Remember what Professor Harold Hill said in *The Music Man:* "You got trouble.") In the *Pool Parlor* by Jacob Lawrence (born 1917) we see a "heavy" drama that exploits our stereotyped attitudes about life in the ghetto. The artist created mock-sinister silhouettes of black men engaged in a deadly game of skill under glaring lights. They look like "pool sharks" who are playing for keeps. Lawrence used flat patterning and angularity of shape to make us believe this is a real war—a war fought on green felt tabletops. Actually, the picture is a parody of pool-parlor folklore and the "cool" style of the black ghetto: probably, no one will get hurt, but it has to look as if someone will.

The cultural patterns of ethnic groups—particularly of the first and second generations in America—have been the subject of much study by sociologists. One of their findings is that the first American-born generation is anxious to forget its ethnicity. The next generation, feeling more secure, is often proud of its heritage and wants to revive the customs of its immigrant forebears. Louis Bosa (1905–1981) deals mainly with old-country Italian family customs, perhaps because he knows how hard it is to maintain traditions, to transplant them, somehow, into a new soil. *My Family Reunion* shows an olden "tribal" feast, set in Italy but seen through American eyes. Bosa emphasizes the strangeness of Mediterranean customs, especially if they are seen through Anglo-Saxon lenses. These people look awkward and suspicious and slightly conspiratorial. Their festival is more than an eating occasion: important information is being collected; major decisions are being made.

Images of the landscape or the cityscape have social connotations whether we see people in them or not. There are always signs of human use: care or

Louis Bosa. *My Family Reunion.* 1950. Whitney Museum of American Art, New York. Gift of Mr. and Mrs. Alfred Jaretski, Jr.

Louis Guglielmi. *Terror in Brooklyn.* **1941. Whitney Museum of American Art, New York**
A Surrealist version of the sense of loneliness and menace that the city's streets can evoke. Compare the terror of these Italian women with the mysteriousness of Louis Bosa's family scene in "the old country."

Jesse Tarbox Beals. Photograph of Italian children. 1900

George Tooker. *The Subway.* 1950. Whitney Museum of American Art, New York. Juliana Force Purchase

The subway (without graffiti) felt by urban woman and man as a descent into hell.

neglect, pride or abandonment. The environments people build influence their builders; at the same time they reflect human choices, human ingenuity, and human limitations of imagination. In *Landscape near Chicago,* Aaron Bohrod (born 1907) makes an ironic comment on that halfway region we can see on the outskirts of any American city, with its homemade, cinder-block architecture, piles of rusting machinery, and signs of projects started but never finished. Bohrod's detailed naturalism is ideal for painting the portrait of a house, and, by implication, of its inhabitants—people who occupy the lonely, undefined space between city and country. Much as they try, these people cannot mold their environment into a convincing imitation of a human community.

Edward Hopper (1882–1967) painted a similar building portrait in *House by the Railroad,* although here we see the faded glory of a Victorian mansion. (Bohrod's house never knew glory.) But Hopper's house is only a relic now; perhaps it has become a rooming house. Once it stood for "class"; it represented elegance and, of course, money. The railroad changed all that. Still, the house has its own wilted dignity, conferred by the artist's presentation of its forms as a unified, coherent, sculptural mass, isolated but wearing its dated architectural adornments with a certain forlorn pride.

In 1936 Mark Tobey (1890–1976) tried to capture the flashy illumination and glaring sound of a great American thoroughfare in *Broadway.* He was fascinated by the light from a thousand signs—its capacity to express the search for fun by millions drawn like moths to an electric fire in mid-Manhattan. Later, in 1942, the Dutch abstractionist Piet Mondrian (1872–1944) surrendered to Broadway's glitter with a sparkling canvas, *Broadway Boogie Woogie.* Tobey's tempera painting is "written" in light, a sort of neon script blurring into a white haze at the center of the picture. Mondrian saw the Great White Way as a musical composition, but the restrictions imposed by a rectangular mode of composition would not permit Tobey's freedom of description. Still, by using dozens of little squares and abrupt changes of primary color, Mondrian could give us the flickering, dancelike quality of light and energy, the scurry and halt, of Broadway's "mell-o-dee."

The Los Angeles Fine Arts Squad. *Isle of California.* **1971–72. Butler Avenue, West Los Angeles**

An immense mural that records the effects of a real earthquake while prophesying the end of California's freeway civilization. No people, no cars, no cityscape: the sight is strangely peaceful.

Two houses facing two kinds of adversity. One house has fallen on hard times; the other never knew any good times.

Edward Hopper. *House by the Railroad.* **1925. Collection, The Museum of Modern Art, New York. Given anonymously**

Aaron Bohrod. *Landscape near Chicago.* **1934. Whitney Museum of American Art, New York**

The neon spectacle of Broadway can be expressed as white writing, or as little squares of alternating color, or by shaping the neon tubes themselves into an abstract simulation of the glittering scene.

right: Piet Mondrian. *Broadway Boogie Woogie.* 1942–43. Collection, The Museum of Modern Art, New York. Given anonymously

below left: Mark Tobey. *Broadway.* 1936. The Metropolitan Museum of Art, New York. Arthur Hoppock Hearn Fund, 1942

below right: Chryssa. *Fragments for the Gates to Times Square.* 1966. Whitney Museum of American Art, New York. Gift of the Howard and Jean Lipman Foundation, Inc.

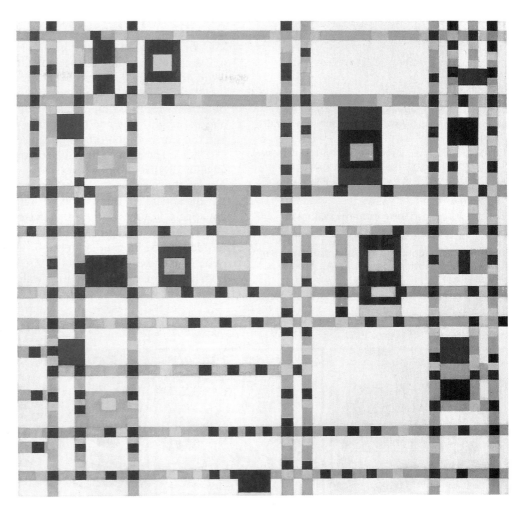

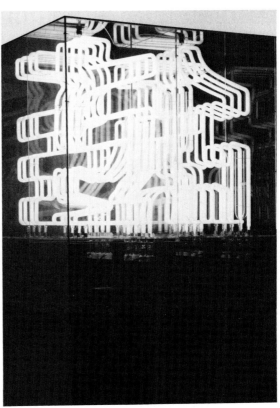

SATIRE

The social function of satire is to ridicule people and institutions so that they will change. Or, at least, stop what they are doing. Also, as a type of humor, satire gives us the feelings of relief and superiority we usually get from laughter. But remember: satire is aggressive in intent. It makes fun of its subject—bitter, derisive fun. Humor may be involved, but satire is a *serious* art form. It cuts the mighty down to size; it loves to show up hypocrisy; it likes to dramatize the gap between official promises and actual performance.

Societies often go through solemn phases when satire is considered negative or divisive, if not subversive. A government's humorless image of itself may be due to the personalities of its high officials and variations in their capacity to "take it." But we can be sure of one thing: satire hurts. Does it have any special features or traits that make it more painful than ordinary criticism?

First, it probably makes us more uncomfortable to be ridiculed than to be scolded. To be laughed at in public is very humiliating. We feel as if we have been ostracized—thrown out of the human community. Second, laughter is both physiological and psychological; it involves the total organism and it fully

below: **Al Capp. Panels from *Li'l Abner* Ugly Woman Contest. 1946. Copyright News Syndicate, Inc.**

Capp's professional interest in comic repulsiveness was fully echoed by his readers, who generously contributed drawings of their candidates in a contest for the supreme ugliness accolade.

bottom left: **Caricature from the ceiling of Horyu-ji, Nara, Japan. 8th century** A.D.

bottom right: **Leonardo da Vinci. *Caricature of an Ugly Old Woman*. Biblioteca Ambrosiana, Milan**

When satire dwells on the ugly, it has a timeless and universal character; very little separates Al Capp's twentieth-century version of ugliness from the repulsive countenance drawn by a Japanese artist twelve hundred years ago.

58

implicates the viewer in an act of ridicule. We tend to remember the satirical image of a public figure long after we have forgotten what he or she did. Finally, artistic satire uses caricature, which exaggerates the physical shortcomings of its victims. Needless to say, we know about our imperfections; to see them magnified is very painful, especially if our psychic defenses are not very strong.

Satire has roots in our fascination with the grotesque, and making grotesque images of real or imagined people is a universal practice. Children are especially intrigued by fantastic or incredibly ugly faces. So are great artists. Leonardo da Vinci (1452–1519) made many caricatures—in his investigations of deviations from the beautiful. From a psychological standpoint, these images are similar to those made by children; they amount to explorations of the frontiers of the human. Caricatures are comparable to the rich body of spoken and written insult most of us know about. Adolescents are especially good at insults, and comedians can convulse audiences for hours with detailed descriptions of their ugly relatives. So the fascination with ugliness is widespread; it may be as pervasive as our interest in the beautiful. This obsession with ugliness seems to be malicious, but it probably has roots that are only partially related to malice: we may just want to exercise our powers of aesthetic discrimination.

Perhaps the greatest political satirist of World War II was the Briton David Low (1891–1963). His cartoons were in many respects visual counterparts to the speeches of Winston Churchill: he could ridicule the Fascist dictators, summon up the courage of the British people when they were taking a terrible beating, express defiance when Britain faced invasion, appeal for help from America, and grieve over the valorous dead. Low was very good at personality formulations, especially in his characterizations of Der Führer and Il Duce. At a time when their racial and military insanity had succeeded in terrifying the civilized world, David Low made Hitler and Mussolini look like asses—dangerous, to be sure, but asses nevertheless. These cartoons were not entirely complete (the quality of evil is usually missing), but they encouraged a hard-pressed people to carry on. The dictators were reduced in size; that meant they could be beaten.

Low's political satire is seen at its best in the cartoon *Rendezvous,* which deals with one of the strange consequences of political expediency—the Russo-German nonaggression pact of 1939. By this treaty the Russians hoped to avert an invasion by Germany. And Germany hoped to secure the neutrality of Russia during its planned attack on Poland. So, the mortal enemies, soon to be locked in a bitter struggle, greet each other with exaggerated gestures of courtesy while employing their customary rhetoric of insult. They meet over the body of a dead soldier. This is how Low dealt with evil: with a few brushstrokes he revealed the tragic underside of political hypocrisy.

left: **David Low.** *Rendezvous.* **1939.**
"The scum of the earth, I believe?"
"The bloody assassin of the workers, I presume?"
Cartoon by permission of the David Low Trustees and the *London Evening Standard*

right: **Jack Levine.** *The Feast of Pure Reason.* **1937. Extended loan from the United States WPA Art Program to The Museum of Modern Art, New York**

Willem de Kooning. *Woman, I.* 1950–52. Collection, The Museum of Modern Art, New York. Purchase

Peggy Bacon. *The Patroness.* 1927. Collection, The Museum of Modern Art, New York. Gift of Abby Aldrich Rockefeller

H. C. Westermann. *Nouveau Rat Trap.* **1965. Collection Mr. and Mrs. Robert Delford Brown, New York**

Art satirizing art: a semiabstract sculpture that pokes fun at the Art Nouveau style.

We expect satire in the graphic arts, especially in news media, but it also occurs in "serious" painting. Most of the work of Jack Levine (born 1915) is satiric, with stress on the ugly rather than on the humorous. *The Feast of Pure Reason* is a typical example. There is a bitter irony in the contrast between the title, which celebrates rationality, and the realities of civic decision-making: a cop, a politician, and a businessman meet in a dark room to "cut a deal." It is interesting that, no matter who his target is, Levine identifies moral corruption with physical grossness. There is nothing funny or redeeming about his people; they are ugly, hence corrupt, hence detestable.

Woman, I by Willem de Kooning (born 1904) can be seen as satirical, too, although the violent execution may prevent our finding much humor in the work. The artist presents an older woman, seated, heavyset, wearing a flimsy shoe, overexposing her body. Apparently, she wants to appear bewitching, but her smile could freeze your blood. Her fiercely staring eyes are probably the result of too much makeup; she seems to be wearing ill-fitting dentures, and her tiny ankle can't support her massive superstructure. Perhaps we are witnessing the furious and pathetic exertions of a "mom" gone berserk. Are there such women? Well, she must have been real enough to de Kooning. Clearly, the artist was enraged enough to portray her as a horrible spectacle. His personal anger asserts itself all over the canvas—within and outside the figure. As soon as the forms were established, de Kooning tore into them with a violent, slashing attack. What wrath! What fury! What can she have done to him?

We see another kind of satiric anger in the etching *The Patroness* by Peggy Bacon (born 1895). Here, too, the subject is a fat woman with a low-cut dress. But her ugliness is different from that of de Kooning's woman. Her face is twisted and pinched in contrast to her heavy hands and spreading bulk—a symbol of small-mindedness combined with too much money. This etching may express the artist's resentment of any patron, regardless of his or her looks. Or it may be a case of revenge—a malicious bite of the hand that feeds her. The dog, lower right, probably understands their relationship.

Satire thrives when there is freedom from political repression, and that freedom we have had. But as art moves toward abstraction, we see more satire in the titles of pictures and less in their imagery. (H. C. Westermann's *Nouveau Rat Trap* is a rare and clever exception.) In general, the analysis and refinement of visual language leads artists away from social and political commentary. Pop art had great satiric potential, although it lacked the killer instinct needed for political satire. Its target was very broad: all of modern culture. But it was often difficult to tell whether Pop derided or celebrated the commercialism of our society. Still, it made us aware of the optical noise around us, and it developed some weapons to cope with visual garbage.

Mel Ramos. *Chiquita Banana.* **1964. Collection Ian W. Beck, New York**

Usually, advertising art borrows from fine art. Here, the relationship is reversed: Pop art borrowed everything it could from commercial art, even including the ®—Trademark Registered—over "Chiquita." Today's art belongs to the culture of reproduction, regardless of where it originates.

GRAPHIC COMMUNICATION

We tend to think of art in terms of precious objects, but art can also be an inexpensive public language. Cheaply reproduced visual images communicate with amazing persuasiveness, and, combined with words, their meaning is clear and unmistakable. In our culture, where mass production and distribution have reached great heights, visual art is extensively used to market goods, services, and ideas. Graphic design—especially of posters, packages, books, and signs—is an indispensable tool of communication. Sometimes it is called advertising design, or commercial art. But labels here are not very important; what matters is that art plays a crucial role in carrying information from government, business, and industry to every social group or subgroup we can imagine.

The Problems of Communication What are the problems of information design that the artist must solve? First is the job of arresting the public's attention: Can people be "stopped in their tracks" by artfully designed images? They certainly can. Getting attention is the main problem of all effective communication. Its challenge varies from the five-second glimpse of an outdoor poster to the eight- or ten-minute examination of a magazine page. Next is the problem of sociological and psychological strategy: Which group is the target and what are its interests and motivations? Third is the problem of characterizing a product, service, or idea: How can it be presented quickly and memorably to a public that is under continuous visual assault from competing products? Fourth is the problem of mixing visual and nonvisual material: What should be seen only? What should be said? What should be heard and seen? Fifth is the design of letter forms—a major graphics problem. Here, the design may be more significant than the choice of words, because today's viewers are very sensitive to the look, *the image,* of a word or a phrase. Finally, graphic designers for films and television face a host of new problems that are different from those of the print media: How can visual imagery be related to unseen words or music—material that occupies aural but not optical "space"? Which is in the "background"—words, music, or images?

The main traits of modern information design seem to be visual logic and simplicity. Simplicity implies a bias in favor of open space and clean, bold forms—forms that are quickly seen, easily identified, and readily understood. A successful graphic design will focus on a desired set of symbolic meanings. Like any artist, the designer tries to control the viewer's responses. By visual logic we mean *a sense of connectedness* among the various elements of a design: the image of the product or idea; the words, or copy; and the layout or composition (which is a kind of image in itself). All of these have to reinforce one another. Not surprisingly, graphic designers often draw upon contemporary art to solve problems of innovation and stimulation of visual interest. The following illustrations show how the allegedly useless fine arts have, in fact, been used ("ripped off") by the communications arts.

Graphic Solutions Picasso himself was a great borrower, and many have borrowed from him. We can see the unmistakable influence of his harlequins and musicians in a carnival poster by the Mexican designer Segundo Freire. However, the poster artist retains only the flat patterning of Picasso's Cubism. He does not slice the figure and recompose its elements; that would produce an image which might confuse the viewer. As mentioned above, simplified imagery is essential for quick recognition in advertising; hence, Cubist and abstract painting have been a fertile source of ideas for graphic designers. Notice how the Italian designer Pino Tovaglia created his railroad poster, using, I believe, the style of Fernand Léger (1881–1955). Léger's *Three Women* may not have any machinery, but it does show how all visual forms can be converted into efficient, mechanical equivalents. So we might think of this

George Aptecker. Photograph of a wall at Coney Island. 1968

Communications design practiced as a folk art.

Bruno Munari. *Campari*. 1965. Collection, The Museum of Modern Art, New York. Gift of the designer

Advertisement for film *The Two of Us*. Designed by Saul Bass and Art Goodman. 1968

A word-image combination in which a maximum of characterization is achieved within very narrow formal constraints.

above: **Barbara Nessim. Art produced on a computer, later used for an article about modems in *Ms.* magazine, 1983**

We still do not know the full potential of computer-generated imagery for the art of graphic communication. In this computer painting the artist builds on the bright color and low resolution of images that we see on the computer screen. Compare Nessim's effects with Lichtenstein's use of Benday screening (page 289).

below left: **Pablo Picasso. *Pierrot and Harlequin*. The Metropolitan Museum of Art, New York. Gift of Paul J. Sachs, 1922**

below right: **Segundo Freire. Carnival poster. 1957**

Fernand Léger. *Three Women.* 1921. Collection,
The Museum of Modern Art, New York. Mrs. Simon Guggenheim Fund

Pino Tovaglia. Railway poster. 1957. Courtesy
the artist and Ferrovie Nord Milano

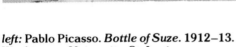

left: Pablo Picasso. *Bottle of Suze.* 1912–13. Washington University, St. Louis

right: Alvin Lustig. Cover design for *Fortune* magazine. 1952. Courtesy Time, Inc.

striking railroad poster as the result of an artistic triple play—from Picasso to Léger to Tovaglia.

The cover design for *Fortune* magazine by Alvin Lustig (1915–1955) reveals the influence of another facet of Cubism—collage. About 1912, Picasso and Braque began to combine pasted material with drawn or painted forms, as in Picasso's *Bottle of Suze.* Here we see a pasted, not a painted, picture, made of construction paper, newsprint, wallpaper, and a label from a liquor bottle. In Lustig's design of 1952 the words and type faces of the collage material have been used to reinforce a communications theme—"the language of advertising." The shapes are taken from television masts and billboards. Thus, the designer reinforces his message two or three times, and with different formal devices. The Picasso collage, on the contrary, has no explicit message: it communicates an *aesthetic effect.* The newsprint is there to be experienced as color and texture; it is not meant to be read—except for the liquor label. Here we have a crucial difference between poetry and advertising.

We see an especially interesting example of cultural diffusion in a Japanese cosmetics poster by Tsuneji Fujiwara. His two faces are remarkably similar to those painted by Amedeo Modigliani, an Italian-born artist who spent most of his working life in France. Modigliani started out as a sculptor and was especially influenced by African wood carving, as in the example illustrated. We can see how Modigliani translated these basically African forms into the small mouth, the ovoid face, and the stylized arches over the eyes of the woman in his painting. As for the Japanese designer Fujiwara, he must have found an ideal of female beauty in Modigliani's work. Somehow, that ideal connects with soap or cologne or face powder.

INFORMATION DESIGN

The forms in the poster by Saul Bass (born 1921) for Pabco Paint Company would not be difficult to trace to Joan Miró (1893–1983). What interests us is the adaptation of Surrealist imagery to advertise house paint. The design strategy makes marketing sense: a manufacturer wants to persuade women that they can do house painting—do it and enjoy it. Now Miró's work is a kind of "research" into childlike imagery; it emphasizes fun and games despite an occasional ghost or goblin. The imagery says, in effect, that we can face our

above left: **Mask, from Ivory Coast. Collection Peter Moeschlin, Basel**

above right: **Amedeo Modigliani. Detail of *Anna de Zborowska*. 1917. Collection, The Museum of Modern Art, New York. Lillie P. Bliss Collection**

left: **Tsuneji Fujiwara. Cosmetics poster. 1957**

Here is the best possible demonstration of the internationalism of today's art and the functional interchangeability of its forms.

67

José Zaragoza. Cover for Brazilian edition of *Vogue* magazine, on the subject of plastic surgery. 1984

An elegant use of the Cubist devices of overlapping, displacement, and repetition of shapes in graphic communication. The subject—plastic surgery—might suggest blood and pain, but here it appears as the epitome of high fashion.

B. Martin Pedersen. Dustjacket for *Typography 5*, the Annual of the Type Directors Club of the United States. 1985

Here the graphic image operates simultaneously at several levels: as a discreet announcement of *Typography* plus the number 5; as a demonstration of the Gestalt principle of figure-ground ambiguity; and as a painting in which bold, abstract shapes bend, squeeze, and float in a golden space.

Giovanni Pintori. Poster for Olivetti 82 Diaspron. Courtesy the artist

Purely visual communication. This work represents a brilliant wedding of the qualities of the machine—accuracy of engineering, measured shape, controlled motion—and the traits of its product: the scrutable mark, the precise word, the significant symbol.

Paul Rand. Poster for Advertising Typographers' Association of America. Courtesy the artist

The picture of an idea that was first expressed by the philosopher Alfred North Whitehead. It succeeds through a clever graphic creation: the arrow penetrates the apple, and that makes its red color flow down into the letter A.

Walter Allner. Cover design for *Fortune* magazine, February, 1965. Courtesy Time, Inc.

Here a graphic designer functions almost like a sculptor. Working for an audience of industrial executives, Allner created a dazzling composition of old and new metallic objects. The design has a powerful, tactile appeal, yet it operates within a graphic format. Why? Because the miracle of photography makes us believe this imagery is real; we can touch it with our eyes.

Joan Miró. *Nursery Decoration.* 1938. Collection
Mr. and Mrs. Richard K. Weil, St. Louis

Saul Bass. Poster for Pabco Paint Company. 1957.
Courtesy Napko Corporation, Houston

fears and laugh at them. The woman with the paintbrush in Bass's design is
having a good time: house painting is a romp, easy enough for a child to do.
This poster also tells us something about the advertiser's perception of wom-
en and their purchasing behavior; it seems they require a childlike approach.
Although the image is exceptionally simple, the designer made sophisticated
use of unconscious suggestion to attain his objective.

With these examples, the dependence of information design on fine art
should be clear. Yet, there is much originality and excellence in graphics. In
our society, relationships among patrons and artists, or clients and designers,
are very complex. Unfortunately, most fine artists live and function in the
time-honored tradition of economic malnutrition, whereas designers do
quite well. All of them—at least the good ones—ought to flourish, especially
since their talents and training are similar. Perhaps, then, we can look forward
to a new Renaissance era, one in which no line can be drawn between artists
and designers because, with few exceptions, they are the same persons.

Victor Vasarely. *Vega.* **1957. Collection the artist**

Since many viewers are disoriented by Op art, it seems logical to exploit Op-art effects in the jacket design for a murder mystery dealing with hallucinatory drugs.

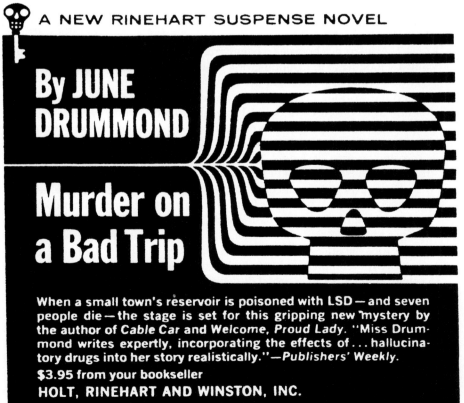

A NEW RINEHART SUSPENSE NOVEL

By JUNE DRUMMOND

Murder on a Bad Trip

When a small town's reservoir is poisoned with LSD — and seven people die — the stage is set for this gripping new mystery by the author of *Cable Car* and *Welcome, Proud Lady*. "Miss Drummond writes expertly, incorporating the effects of . . . hallucinatory drugs into her story realistically."—*Publishers' Weekly*. $3.95 from your bookseller HOLT, RINEHART AND WINSTON, INC.

Advertisement for *Murder on a Bad Trip* by June Drummond. Holt, Rinehart and Winston, Inc., 1968. Courtesy Denhard & Stewart, Inc., New York

CHAPTER THREE

THE PHYSICAL FUNCTIONS OF ART

Paintings and buildings can be symbols, but only buildings serve a physical function. The art of "physical function" refers to objects that are made to be used as tools or containers. By "containers" we mean objects that range from a carton of milk to an office building. Both have to be shaped and built according to the requirements of their contents (if people can be thought of as "contents"). As for a "tool," it can be a tablespoon or a locomotive: small and simple or large and complex. Both have to be designed to operate efficiently, but an important aspect of their operation is appearance: they are seen as well as used. In other words, a tool or a machine looks like something; it has to look like what it does, and it should look good.

The difference between a painting and a building is that we use a painting only by looking at it; a building or a tool is used by doing something *in* it or *with* it. Formerly, we thought the artist's role was to create "skins" that concealed the working parts of useful objects. This notion may survive in a debased conception of industrial design called styling: engineers solve functional problems and artists take care of surface beauty. But now we realize that appearance and function are closely linked. Many useful objects are *totally* created by artist-designers. Their profession, industrial design, constitutes a fruitful synthesis of art and engineering—and marketing too.

During the Renaissance, artists were often architects and engineers simultaneously. The separation of art from the functional aspects of making and building took place during the Industrial Revolution of the eighteenth century. That was when civil, mechanical, and industrial engineering developed as professions separate from art and architecture. As a result, society experienced a proliferation of ugliness in the large- and small-scale environment. Of course, engineers can be good designers, but in the early stages of mass production, technical specialization often resulted in fake or pretentious design—machine-made trash.

Between the eighteenth and the twentieth century, handicrafts survived mainly as obsolescent vestiges of preindustrial modes of production, serving as status symbols for the few who could resist engineer design or as focal points of idealism for craftsmen like William Morris. He hoped to reverse the march of industrialization and capitalism by reviving medieval artisanship. His motives were pure, but his solution was unworkable.

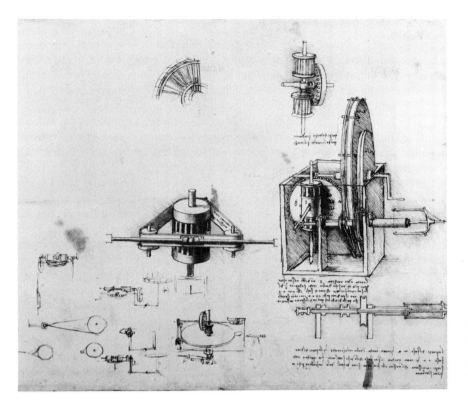

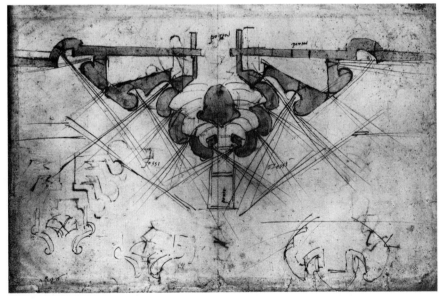

Both Leonardo and Michelangelo were "design-ers"; they could tackle anything—from fortifica-tions to industrial machinery. For the Renaissance artist, drawing was a process of discovery, inven-tion, and visualization—from inside to outside or from surface to depth. The radical separation of art and engineering had not yet taken place.

Today we have industrial designers; they can create anything—from earth movers to cigarette lighters to houses to storefronts. Art shares responsi-bility for the built environment: how it looks and how it works. And here, art means more than embellishing or beautifying surfaces. A successful environ-mental design is the end product of a complex set of relationships between art and law, sociology and engineering. Most important, environmental design has to be done in the light of a total philosophy of human behavior, social interaction, and aesthetic response.

The physical functions of art, therefore, affect us in our private lives and in our public lives as citizens—as people who use and are used by an artificial organism called the community. The most familiar unit of that organism is the house, or dwelling.

ARCHITECTURE: THE DWELLING

Of all building types, the dwelling is the earliest, the closest to our daily lives, and perhaps the best illustration of the combined effects of art, technology, and design. Architecture is a social art, and in the dwelling we see how it influences the basic social institution: the family. Here we might examine some of the interactions between family life and domestic architecture.

The home today is intended almost exclusively for a couple or for a small child-rearing family. Usually, it has no room for aunts, uncles, grandparents, or other relatives. It rarely has a library, parlor, pantry, or front porch. Instead, there may be new rooms or spaces—a game room, patio, family room, recreation room, bar, sauna, sundeck, and carport. Compared with the homes of a generation ago, there is more open planning, less privacy, and fewer single-purpose spaces. Partitions are often eliminated entirely; those that do not go from floor to ceiling do not really separate spaces and insulate sounds. In addition, houses are usually built on one level or on split levels; they seldom have three or four distinct layers. One-level living has its advantages: the ranch-type dwelling promotes mobility within and ease in getting out. It does sacrifice privacy, but perhaps we need less privacy.

Multipurpose rooms allow a reduction in the overall size of a house and intensify the use of space and the wear of equipment. Labor-saving devices and gadgets now absorb a greater proportion of the home's cost, and for many people they are a principal index of its value—economic and aesthetic. That is, we probably love our dishwashers, air conditioners, automatic ovens, tile bathrooms, and built-in stereo sets more than the qualities of light and space that good design can bring to the home.

It often seems that Le Corbusier's dictum—"The house is a machine to be lived in"—is accepted in practice if not in theory. What factors have made it possible for the modern dwelling to operate as an efficient machine while retaining some of the warmth of the old idea of home? Obviously, technology is the key: it cuts down the space and time needed for food preparation and storage, laundering and house cleaning, heating and cooling, decoration and maintenance. Modern building techniques have enlarged the possibilities open to the designer: light; strong structural elements, some of them metal and plastic instead of wood; new insulation materials, adhesives, and fasteners; new surface materials—paints, plastics, and man-made fibers; and prefab-

Bruce Davidson. Photograph of people on East 100th Street, New York. 1967

Architecture is a social art—design for human beings living together. The trouble is that poor people cannot afford to live in spaces designed around their needs. So, like the rest of us, they make do.

Kenneth Isaacs. Ultimate Living Structure. 1968
Here all of an individual's physical needs for domestic living have been packaged in a single double-decker unit. It looks like a triumph of rationality—a real "machine for living." But without social interaction, design is easy.

ricated units, especially for kitchens and bathrooms. Most important of all is the universal availability of low-cost electricity. Remember that until the 1930s many rural homes had no electric power.

Plate glass may be the most influential material affecting home design. Ideal for warm climates, it is widely used in temperate and cold climates. It brings the outdoors in—optically. We have enthusiastically accepted one of the main principles of modern domestic architecture: indoor and outdoor space should interpenetrate. The contemporary house is designed so that its outer shell is a screen more than a barrier. The one-level dwelling keeps us in close touch with the environment. Visually, there is the lamp-and-picture-window combination, facing what we hope is more inspiring than someone else's backyard. That picture window is so essential that even apartment dwellers have them, with a balcony substituting for a patio (although the balcony is rarely used). The main point is that plate glass makes it possible for nature (or city traffic) to be part of our interior decoration.

There are good technical and structural reasons for the widespread use of glass: (1) The walls of modern buildings can be penetrated at almost any point because they do not bear weight. (2) The loss of heat through glass can be reduced by double paning, while the framing around the glass is tight and well-insulated. (3) Plate glass is strong and durable, even over fairly large areas. (4) Intelligent orientation of the house on its site and proper location of windows lets in the sun when it is wanted. Architects can cooperate with nature by designing eaves, overhangs, or sunbreaks so that summer sun is blocked out but winter sun is invited in.

Air conditioning has become a symbol of philosophic disagreement in modern architecture. We have the technology (expensive, of course) to air-condition all interior living space. (Someday, we may be able to air-condition the out-of-doors, too.) Already, shopping centers, department stores, and sports arenas are air-conditioned. Yet our domestic architecture, especially under the influence of Frank Lloyd Wright, seeks *continuity* with nature; we want technology to make structures look as if *they belong to and grew out of* their surroundings.

In the philosophy of the International Style architects, exemplified by Walter Gropius, Ludwig Mies van der Rohe, and Marcel Breuer, the dwelling—or any building—is conceived as *wholly separate* from nature. These architects have designed buildings without windows and without any modification of exterior form in response to climate or view or topography. Masterful engineering enables us to ignore the environment, so the architect can concentrate on designing beautiful interior spaces. And where the focus of activity is almost wholly internal—as in a museum, a laboratory, a department store, a gymnasium, or a factory—such buildings can be successful.

But again, technology affects aesthetics. The high-speed elevator, the steel-frame skeleton, and light curtain-wall construction enable us to build almost as high as we wish. With computerized controls we can create a uniform atmosphere throughout a structure. Sometimes. There may be some disturbing rumbles, too: the costs of climate control are getting too high, and when the technology is not working well, uncomfortable temperature variations develop. When there are no windows, the inhabitants want to look out. When the air conditioning does work, people wish they could smell spring. Or they hanker for the odor of gasoline fumes and damp city streets, the sound of automobile horns, and the sight of pedestrians racing for cover. Office workers may need certain noises and aromas to remind them that they have sense organs. Just like dwellers in the suburbs, for whom the sound of a neighbor's lawn mower and the fragrance of burned barbecue are worth the interest on the mortgage.

Frank Lloyd Wright Perhaps our greatest artist-poet of the dwelling was Frank Lloyd Wright (1869–1959). In a long and controversial career he brought a pioneering and distinctively American genius to the art of creating human shelter. He was independently ahead of European architects in many ways: in understanding how to use (rather than be used by) modern technology; in his revolt against the architectural baggage of the past; and in his aesthetic innovations—that is, in his ability to deal with the dwelling as an art object, as something beautiful to look at and to live in. Wright's adventures in social philosophy and community planning have not been universally praised. But his houses—especially his Prairie Houses—are great monuments. Indeed, when we look at a building as fresh and vital as the Robie House, it is difficult to realize that it was built in 1909.

The most widely reproduced house by Wright is probably Fallingwater, built in 1936 at Bear Run, Pennsylvania. It is at once a triumph of architectural romanticism and an example of the brilliant exploitation of technology. Only steel-and-concrete cantilever construction would allow such graceful but massive overhanging slabs, complementing the rugged natural setting with crisp, rectangular precision. There is an echo of the International Style in these plain cubical masses, but the overall conception is romantic. Heavily textured masonry in the vertical forms connects the house to the materials on the site, an association that is an axiom of Wright's philosophy of building.

Wright's ideas about the internal organization of a house still provoke controversy, although many of them have been accepted. He believed that a huge fireplace and hearth should be the physical and psychological center of the home. And he had strong dislikes: basements and attics; materials like paint, plaster, and varnish; and wood trim. Ornament should not be *applied;* it should result from the natural patterns of materials; it should grow logically out of the processes of forming and fabrication. Cooking and dining facilities should be next to the living room, which should be located in the center of the house, away from exterior walls. He called the kitchen a "work area"—a

Frank Lloyd Wright. Robie House, Chicago. 1909

Frank Lloyd Wright. Fallingwater, Bear Run, Pennsylvania. 1936

Frank Lloyd Wright. Interior, Taliesin East, Spring Green, Wisconsin. 1925

tall space behind the fireplace. Wright believed that cooking odors should flow up and out rather than into the house. (There we may differ.)

Rooms should radiate from the fireplace core; hence Wright's houses usually have a cross-shaped plan. The arms of the cross are thus open to the outdoors on three sides, with horizontal bands of windows around them and wide eaves creating porchlike spaces underneath. Of course, this increases exterior wall area, adding to heating costs, but Wright was a genius, and genius doesn't worry about money.

The interior of Wright's own house, Taliesin East, in Spring Green, Wisconsin, shows the inviting warmth and variety of surface, space, and light that he built into his Prairie Houses. Oriental rugs are used to break up the floor space and to define functional areas, with Chinese and Japanese art objects located on ledges set at different heights so that the eye will be encouraged to linger and refresh itself. Wright's interiors were sometimes criticized for being too dark, but he calculated the modulation of light more than designers who simply flood a room with light. Wright did not force people to install acres of drapery to gain privacy and control over outside illumination. His corners are delightful little zones of peace or sociability. To be sure, his living room suggests a cave more than a tent or a metal cage. Why not? Wright understood our atavistic desires—the deep need for feelings of safety and comfort we inherit from our Stone Age ancestors; he remembered what we remember.

Ludwig Mies van der Rohe The austere style of Mies van der Rohe (1886–1969) can best be understood against the background of Art Nouveau, a somewhat frivolous style of design and decoration that affected all the arts early in the twentieth century. The subway, or Métro, station, designed for the city of Paris by Hector Guimard (1867–1942), shows many of the features of an Art Nouveau structure: ornamental and structural elements of cast iron; the concealment of right angles; heavy reliance on a serpentine, or "whiplash," line; and curves at every joint or change of direction. After World War II this style had a revival that reached its peak in the early 1960s.

Perhaps wealth encourages playful impulses in design and fashion. The somber doctrine of Mies, that "less is more," seems life-denying; people want elegance or playfulness or both. But Art Nouveau was not elegant in the classical manner; instead, it tried to unite art and nature almost literally—nature conceived as a forest grove or a garden filled with plants, vines, and creepers.

The International Style architects loved the austere, severe right angle as much as the Art Nouveau designers loved the S-curve. Accordingly, from the 1920s until about 1942—with the exception of buildings by Wright and his followers—avant-garde houses were plain white cubes, empty of ornament, faced with glass, and covered by no-nonsense flat roofs without eaves. Small wonder that the popular reaction to these buildings was chilly, and that the style was known to some as "gas-station moderne."

In the hands of a master like Mies, the International Style was restrained but rich, as can be seen in his Tugendhat House in Czechoslovakia, designed in 1930. Floor-to-ceiling glass, black marble partitions, polished metal columns, silk curtains, and Oriental rugs: these created an atmosphere of refinement and sensuous appeal within a controlling intellectual framework. Despite his severity, Mies had the instincts of a craftsman; he never abandoned the ideal of beauty achieved through well-made and well-proportioned parts. Unfortunately, his less imaginative followers became addicted to design as the simple multiplication of standardized units.

In the Farnsworth House of 1950, built in Plano, Illinois, Mies employed a vocabulary similar to the one he used again in Crown Hall, his School of Architecture building for the Illinois Institute of Technology in 1952. Both buildings are approached from a raised platform, and in both a series of slablike steps are used to make the transition from ground level to the plane of the floor. In the Farnsworth House, large expanses of glass produce reflected images that help establish continuity with nature. We see an extreme simplification of form and function in the white posts that support the roof, acting as stilts that raise the house off the ground. In the Illinois Tech building, Mies hung the ceiling from imposing steel girders that stretch across the roof and connect to black exterior steel columns; the columns also work as satisfying vertical accents. The building is not lifted off the ground, as is the Farnsworth House, but its platform and gently rising steps create that impression. Finally, the repeated horizontals of the steps help balance the vertical rhythm of the columns, giving the structure a sense of classic dignity and repose.

A Miesian house is essentially *one large cube,* with functional space divisions achieved by nonstructural partitions. For Mies, the real work of architecture was the creation of open interior space, which occupants could subdivide

Hector Guimard. Métropolitain station, Place de L'Etoile, Paris. 1900. (Demolished)

Ludwig Mies van der Rohe. Living Room, Tugendhat House, Brno, Czechoslovakia. 1930

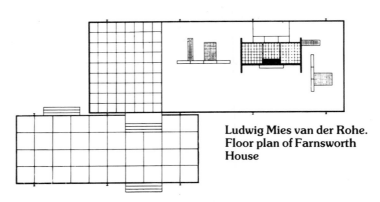

Ludwig Mies van der Rohe.
Floor plan of Farnsworth
House

Ludwig Mies van der Rohe. Crown Hall, Illinois
Institute of Technology, Chicago. 1952

Ludwig Mies van der Rohe. Farnsworth House, Plano, Illinois. 1950

as they wished. Philip Johnson's (born 1906) glass house of 1949 in New Canaan, Connecticut, expresses this point of view, although it probably would not work for a family. But Mies and Johnson are not much concerned about *who* lives in their buildings or *how* interior areas will be used. Instead, they concentrate on designing one of the rarest, most precious commodities in the modern world—pure, undemanding space.

Le Corbusier Le Corbusier (Charles Edouard Jeanneret-Gris, 1887–1965) began with assumptions similar to those of Mies but moved in a more sculptural direction. He preferred poured-concrete forms and left the steel, glass, and brick vocabulary to others. Le Corbusier's Villa Savoye, built in 1929, reveals the strong influence of Cubist painting on his architecture (he was himself an active abstract painter). The house also shows his use of stilts, a brilliant

top and bottom: **Philip Johnson. Glass House, New Canaan, Connecticut. 1949**

81

Frank Lloyd Wright. Interior, Johnson Wax Administration Building, Racine, Wisconsin. 1936–39

structural device that has been widely adopted. These reinforced-concrete columns exploit the fact that steel-and-concrete technology can lift a structure into the air, freeing the space at ground level. This creates a strong shadow pattern at the building's base, which defines the forms above it in almost sculptural terms.

Wright developed "mushroom" pillars (something like stilts) for the interior of his Johnson Wax Building of 1938; they were a structural and decorative device. Since his houses generally rose from a concrete pad, he used cantilevers to open up ground space and to create a strong light-and-dark pattern. But Wright was a horizontal architect—temperamentally attached to the earth. Le Corbusier and the Bauhaus designers would have suspended buildings from a sky hook if that had been possible. Indeed, they designed several classic chairs based on suspension and tension principles.

In the Villa Shodan, built for an Indian businessman in 1952, we see how Le Corbusier's style developed along the directions of the Villa Savoye of 1929. The mastery of poured concrete is now well established, with textures imprinted by rough wooden formwork; this was meant to overcome any mechanical slickness of surface. He also developed the *brise-soleil,* or sunbreak, a device that is especially useful in tropical climates. The occupants can see out, yet the exterior rooms are shaded against the steady sun. From the outside, a delightful articulation of surface and light is produced.

The complicated wooden formwork needed to build these virtually sculptured structures is economically feasible in countries with sources of inexpensive hand labor. Thus Le Corbusier used his poured-concrete vocabulary to build an entire city at Chandigarh, India. But in industrially advanced countries, construction time is precious; variations in shape and space are very expensive and must be held to a minimum. So a building vocabulary of steel frame, glass wall, metal panels, and minor masonry trim is more often used. A notable exception is the Yale Art and Architecture Building, designed by Paul Rudolph (born 1918). Here we see the lavish use of poured concrete combined with a special aggregate to give the building's surface a rich, coarse texture. After the concrete had set, its surface was hand-hammered by workmen, adding to its cost but enhancing its sturdy, grainy qualities. Just right for artists and architects!

Le Corbusier. Interior, Villa Shodan, Ahmedabad, India. 1952
In the interior of the villa, Le Corbusier virtually paints with light through the design of the window perforations, much as in his chapel at Ronchamp (page 400).

Le Corbusier. High Court Building, Chandigarh, India. 1955–56

Paul Rudolph. Art and Architecture Building,
Yale University, New Haven, Connecticut. 1963

Le Corbusier. Unité d'Habitation,
Marseille. 1947–52

The Apartment House   If Wright was poet of the house, Le Corbusier was poet of the apartment and the multiple dwelling. His Unités d'Habitation (apartment houses) have been widely imitated, especially the one at Marseille (1947–52). Le Corbusier conceived of the building as a huge chest of drawers; each apartment is a self-contained, two-level unit that "slides" into a standardized cavity in the building's skeleton. If mass-production methods were fully extended to housing, these "drawers" could be completely fabricated in factories, hoisted into place in the building skeleton, and plugged in. At Marseille, the apartments are sound-insulated by lead sheets between the common walls, something our apartment dwellers would appreciate: acoustical privacy is rare and precious. The kitchens are air-conditioned; living rooms are two stories high and face a balcony with a sunbreak and a view. On every third floor there is a corridor, called an "interior road," which runs the length of the building. Also, two of the interior roads contain indoor shopping centers.

The *Unité* has many of the features of a resort hotel, but it was intended for *permanent* residents. It can accommodate couples, large families, or singles. The seventeenth floor has a kindergarten and nursery; on the roof there is a garden, a swimming pool, gymnasium, running track, solarium, and snack bar. The roof structures for elevators, ventilation, and so on were designed as playful sculptures, and the actual machinery for elevators, generators, and air conditioning was tucked under the first floor, above the stilts.

Le Corbusier wanted urban living to be a supremely satisfying experience, not merely a compromise for people who would rather be elsewhere. His ideas seem relevant to American needs; our population has become increasingly urbanized, and, it seems, increasingly unhappy with the quality of urban living. We have built immense multiple dwellings for persons of all economic levels, but however "modern" these structures look from the outside, they don't seem to promote satisfying patterns of life within. At least, most of those who can escape do so. What is the reason for these costly failures? Do we design and build badly? Is it that Le Corbusier's pattern does not work? Are Americans psychologically incapable of living close to each other? That may be the problem. But the realities of urban life prevent horizontal spread. So those who can, head for the suburbs, where they hope to enjoy low-density life; at least they don't have to live on top of each other. But they pay a price beyond money.

The Modern Dwelling   Wright, Mies, and Le Corbusier were the great innovators of modern architecture. Their contributions to design have been enormously influential, extending even to non-Western societies. The genius of these "form-givers" lay in their ability to create new conceptions of dwelling space based on strong convictions about the nature of living and working together; about the requirements of urban living in an industrial age; and about the new visual options created by modern technology.

What lessons or guiding ideas about the domestic dwelling do we get from these masters of modern architecture?

1. A house does not exist in a physical or social vacuum; it is not primarily a form of self-expression. A house should be oriented to its site so that it seems to belong there. From that orientation it can derive aesthetic as well as practical advantages. Finally, a house must not shut out the environment; it should include parts of the environment within itself.

2. The real substance of a dwelling is the shape of its space, not its fixtures and gadgets. These can be replaced, but the spaces we live in remain fairly constant; space and light are the chief causes of pleasure in a dwelling. A house plan should be shaped around patterns of living rather than the requirements of fashion. This calls for self-knowledge and a realistic assessment of our needs, habits, and resources.

Pierre Paulin. Undulating furniture. 1970. Designed for Artifort Holland. Distributed by Turner Ltd., New York
Furniture is part of architecture—often the expressive part. Here it tries to revive prenatal memories. The repetition of undulating forms in a soft, billowy material reminds us of the security of the womb.

3. The outside of a dwelling is a membrane that reflects the shape of its interior space and selectively transmits light and heat. Traditional features of building—cornices, gables, cupolas—are often costly survivals of obsolete building technologies. On the other hand, the old-fashioned porch probably deserves a revival: it gave much pleasure without being very expensive. As for exterior surfaces, beware of too many types of material—combinations of wood, brick, stone, stucco, glass, marble, metal, and plastic look like overcompensation for failures in design. Simplicity of material is a virtue in building.

4. Interior decoration (Wright called it "inferior desecration") means more than the selection of furniture, the application of ornament, and the display of objects. But since interiors are experienced visually as well as used physically, they have to be considered from an aesthetic as well as a practical standpoint. In apartments, where architectural options are generally limited, the right choices in furniture, color schemes, and lighting can be very satisfying. Ultimately, the problems of unity, focus, and expressiveness have to be solved by reconciling a given space to the needs of a particular set of individuals. This is not easy, but it has to be done, no matter how rich or poor we may be. We can do it ourselves, and we can do it well.

Conclusion Since the time when people lived in caves and tents, domestic dwellings have gone through immense changes; our needs and ambitions have changed enormously. Today, space exploration and scientific fantasy promise residence on distant planets in strange or nonexistent atmospheres. Outer-space technologies may also transform our approach to living on earth. The astronaut's microclimate can be controlled through his or her clothing; so, in time, our only shelter might be our clothing—and that for privacy, not protection. Our dwellings may become no more than storage places for personal possessions, while our lives are lived in special structures designed for special purposes. There may be certain structures for enjoying privacy, just as there are buildings where we go for collective dreams—motion-picture theaters. The difference between home and community may disappear. Perhaps people will live in disposable dwellings like the nests that birds build and discard each year. Designers can accomplish such wonderful (or dreadful) things now, if we wish. But do we wish? Before deciding, we ought to consider what gives communities their social and architectural shape.

LARGE-SCALE DESIGN: THE COMMUNITY
Everyone knows about our problems of crowding, air pollution, traffic snarls, noise, and visual chaos. We know, too, that communities do not have to be in trouble. Cities and towns are built by people, so people are responsible for

the predicament we are in: only people can get us out. What remedies have been proposed to make our cities and towns truly livable? If we think of the community as a work of art—badly or well executed—what are the elements of that art?

We know how to design and construct good buildings and roads, but we seem unable to put them together so that the results are anything short of lethal. If the automobile is a deadly weapon, can we minimize its destructiveness? Can we build cities and towns that are not completely at the mercy of poisonous exhausts and murderous fenders? Is peaceful coexistence possible? Since we are social beings, can we create the physical arrangements that will allow us to enjoy social life?

Philosophers and architects, engineers and planners, have thought about these problems and have made proposals ranging from extreme utopianism to cautious reform. Here we shall examine a few of their ideas.

Ebenezer Howard: The Garden City   In the nineteenth century, as today, people left farms in droves, adding to the congestion of cities. The countryside was depopulated and the cities teemed. In 1898, Ebenezer Howard, an Englishman without architectural training, realized that the problem was not merely to reverse the flow of migration: it was necessary to create communities that would combine the advantages of urban and rural living. His solution: "Town and country *must be married,* and out of this union will spring a new hope, a new life, a new civilization." He wrote a book advancing the concept of the "garden city," a community of concentric belts of land alternately used for commerce or manufacturing and "green" belts or park land. These greenbelts would separate functional areas from each other while providing recreation space and a good balance of rural and urban features—the balance needed for a healthy and satisfying existence. Howard planned to locate administrative and recreational buildings at the core of these communities—something like the squares and village greens that gave emotional and visual focus to early American towns and cities.

Land would not be individually owned but would be held and developed by a common body that would limit growth to about thirty thousand; this would prevent land speculation, high density, and impossible costs. Beyond this population, it would be necessary to start a new garden city. The outermost belt of each community might be used to grow food for local consumption, or it would be left uncultivated so it could be used for recreation.

Howard hoped his plan would lead to the decentralization of London—something that never happened. But it *was* translated into reality in several English and American suburbs. The *word* "greenbelt" has been widely adopted, although all of Howard's principles have rarely been applied in a single community: controlled growth; ownership of land by a common authority; and the separation of residential, industrial, recreational, and administrative functions.

It should be stressed that Howard's garden city was to be a *balanced* community—a place where people would live *and* work. Today's suburbs or satellite towns are mainly one-function communities; they have been called "dormitory suburbs." Without an industrial base, it is difficult for them to pay for good schools and other essential services. And as industries are lured into these communities, as highways to the central city grow crowded, and as industrial facilities sprawl outside their corporate limits, the suburbs lose the advantages of decentralization. But that was the purpose of leaving the city. Aside from the morality of suburban parasitism—using urban services without contributing to their support—there are practical disadvantages in an arrangement that grows increasingly insupportable from an economic standpoint and is architecturally monotonous. We have learned painfully that no community is an island.

Daly City, California

Land on the California coast is precious, and the Daly City developers have eaten up every build-able piece of it. Can everyone have "a place in the country"? Does everyone *want* a place in the country? Is this "country"? Is this sprawl necessary?

Conklin and Wittlesey. Town center, Reston, Virginia. 1961

Ebenezer Howard's Garden City concept is given contemporary expression in the town of Reston.

Frank Lloyd Wright. Broadacre City plan. 1933–40. Reprinted from *The Living City* by Frank Lloyd Wright, copyright 1958. By permission of the publisher, Horizon Press, New York

Frank Lloyd Wright: Broadacre City   Of course, one way to deal with the problems of urbanism is to abandon cities, to start all over again by reorganizing society into small, self-sufficient communities. If the problems of cities are too deep-seated to be solved, we can reform *part* of society by creating ideal communities outside the megalopolitan monsters. This might be called the Noah's Ark approach to urban redesign: save at least some of the people. But decentralization—spreading out the population—might overcome the spatial and social problems of urbanism.

Decentralization would enable people to establish a better relationship to land and to nature. That is what Frank Lloyd Wright proposed with his Broadacre City plan of the 1930s. His solution: an acre of land for each person. Farmers would have ten acres, but all would raise some of their own food, supplementing what full-time farmers could grow. Although this procedure would not be very efficient from the standpoint of yield per acre, Wright believed, as did Thomas Jefferson, that moral benefits accrue to people who till the soil at least part of the time. That is why some people live in agricultural communes today; they are as much concerned with the moral advantages of group living as with escaping the evils of urbanism.

In a land area of four square miles, fourteen hundred families, or six thousand people, could live, produce some food, provide each other with personal services, and engage in some light manufacturing. Wright believed that the automobile and the helicopter liberate us residentially and industrially: we need not live next to where we work. The telephone lets us communicate easily with cities if we need to; radio and television broadcast news and entertainment; we can shop by mail; we can watch movies at home. We do not have to live in cities to use the goods and services they create.

But can communities of six thousand create the necessities of modern civilization? How many people are needed to support a good high school? Or a hospital? Thirty-five thousand? Fifty thousand? How many are needed to support a museum, a theater, a symphony orchestra? These are rarely found in small towns.

Wright did not plan to eliminate cities at once, however; he expected them to wither away. The existence of the city was assumed, since some residents of Broadacre would commute there to work. (Today commuters may wonder whether two or three hours of daily travel are sufficiently rewarded by character-building activities in the suburbs, like raising tomatoes and mowing the lawn.) But contemporary suburban life is a caricature of Wright's idea: he really wanted people to raise their own food, to improve the land, to be independent of bosses and wages. Their houses would be beautiful—designed by architects like Wright, who knew how to relate dwellings to the shape of the land. People would not own land but they could hold it as long as they made productive use of it. Land would not be a commodity that is traded for profit; it would be a source of sustenance and delight.

Wright had strong opinions and strong dislikes. We can tell what they were from his list of principles governing the organization of Broadacre City:

> No private ownership.
> No landlord and tenant.
> No "housing." No subsistence homesteads.
> No traffic problems. No back-and-forth haul.
> No railroads. No streetcars.
> No grade crossings.
> No poles. No wires in sight.
> No ditches alongside the roads.
> No headlights. No light fixtures.
> No glaring cement roads or walks.
> No tall buildings except as isolated in parks.
> No slum. No scum.
> No public ownership of private needs.

Le Corbusier: La Ville Radieuse   The garden city is a suburb and the suburb is a tentacle of the city. According to Le Corbusier, it creates more problems than it solves: commuting, too many vehicles, expensive utilities, costly maintenance. And eventually the garden city is absorbed by the spreading central city. Instead, Le Corbusier proposed his Ville Radieuse, a plan for as many as three million people. Unlike Wright, an American who detested skyscrapers, Le Corbusier found them absolutely essential: in effect, they would be *vertical* garden cities.

The Ville Radieuse would have a higher population density than present cities and yet *more* open space. The explanation lies in its huge but widely separated office buildings and apartment houses. Instead of being lined up next to each other to form canyons, as in Manhattan, they would be far apart, open to light and air, surrounded by parks, and approached by unimpeded highways on multiple levels. Highways and subways would radiate outward from the center of the city, like the streets of Washington, D.C. At the outer rings of the city would be large apartment houses of the type at Marseille, fifteen or twenty stories high, with some individual dwellings scattered among them. Industry would be located even farther out from the city, but not too far from the apartments where workers live.

The space opened up in the city by high-density skyscrapers could be safely used by pedestrians since different kinds of transportation would have their own levels. This is an ideal that we still cannot seem to reach: our urban redevelopment schemes continue to locate parking garages in the city's core, drawing vehicles and pedestrians together and forcing them to compete for the same space.

Le Corbusier was reconciled to the existence of cities and their unique culture; he did not seek to escape the city but to change it. And society seems to have accepted his commitment to high-rise structures. But, until recently, we have been unwilling to carry out the radical surgery necessary to rational-

Le Corbusier. Ville Radieuse: Voisin Plan for Paris. 1925

ize the city's transport systems and to admit light, sun, and air to downtown areas by opening up the space around our skyscrapers.

Le Corbusier admired the skyline of Manhattan—from a distance. He deplored the living and working arrangements that it implied: "Our American friends have erected skyscrapers and made them work. They are constructions of an astonishing technique, tangible proofs of present possibilities. But, from the planning point of view, their skyscrapers are tiresome and their towns wretched to live in (though vibrant and meriting the closest attention)." As for detached single dwellings, he said: "Instead of multiplying innumerable suburban houses let us equip ourselves with impeccable dwelling-units [that is, apartment houses] of an appropriate stature."

Le Corbusier insisted that, since cities are an inescapable fact of life, rational ordering of space can make urban life satisfying, even exciting. Great architecture is possible without a return to the building techniques and living patterns of the past. Reinforced-concrete construction ("reconstituted stone," as he called it) can be spiritually satisfying, functionally adequate, and reasonable in cost. Good urban design results when artistic sensitivity is wedded to modern technology and to a realistic assessment of social, industrial, and human needs.

Following are some of the main principles of town planning advocated by Le Corbusier:

> Town planning means designing for four major functions: Living, Working, Recreation, and Circulation.
> The *materials* of town planning are sunlight, space, greenery, and steel-reinforced concrete.
> Enough dwellings should be concentrated in one building to liberate the space around it.
> Pedestrian routes and mechanized-transportation routes should be separated.
> The distance between home and work should be minimized.
> Living quarters should get the best urban sites.
> Pedestrian paths should not be obstructed by buildings, which should be elevated on stilts.
> Autos, buses, and other vehicles should travel on elevated roadways, beneath which utilities should be housed; the result would be easier installation, maintenance, and repair.
> Industrial and residential areas should be separated by greenery.
> Architectural monuments should be safeguarded.

Elements of Planning: Residential Grouping Almost all community plans call for special areas set aside for residential purposes. Mainly, they are occupied by detached, single-family dwellings. These dwellings vary greatly in

New town in Cumbernauld, Scotland. 1965
A plan that avoids the monotony of the grid. We see honeycomb patterning and tilted siting—both attempts to gain visual variety and sunny exposures in low-cost housing with "add-on" possibilities.

cost, quality of design, and orientation on their sites. Most are built speculatively, in huge developments; others are built on an individual, custom-made basis. But cost and type of construction do not always govern the patterning of roads, open spaces, and home sites. Often the builder of a large development has the best opportunity to provide for good overall design.

What objectives are sought in the grouping of houses, the design of roads, and the shaping of open space? The goal of most people who buy separate dwellings is to capture the charm of village life while enjoying urban conveniences. They hope their houses will blend gracefully into the landscape; afford safe and easy access to neighbors; and provide nearby roads for reaching shops, schools, and churches. Most of all they want visual harmony—residence in a community where individualism has not run amok: aesthetically speaking, they want unity in variety.

To provide visual interest and variety, curving roads are best; they also slow down motorists. A main thoroughfare should never pass through a residential area. Where straight roads are necessary, houses need not be set parallel to the road; they can be given a slight, consistent tilt to create varied space intervals and to allow good orientation to sun and view. But if every house in a group is independently tilted, the result can be chaotic. This can be prevented by zoning ordinances for uniform setbacks and minimum distances between houses. As for intersections, the four-corner intersection should be avoided; the simple T-intersection is better. When connecting to large arteries, a variety of road types can be employed: the cul-de-sac, the dead end, the loop street, and the collector road. Wherever possible, natural contours should be respected; good trees and interesting stone outcroppings ought to be preserved: *the bulldozer should be used sparingly.*

Flat terrain lends itself to any pattern, but designers should try to avoid the obvious, especially the rectangular grid. Design should aim at variety where nature has not been generous with trees or rolling landscape. In highways, it has been found that a good view is improved if it is approached by a curved route. Accordingly, even an ordinary row of houses will look better if we do not see them all at once—lined up like boxes on a shelf. In addition to horizontal curves, the vertical curve—the rise and dip of the road—can add interest to a group of dwellings. Also, we like to see dominant roof lines following the slope of the land; houses tend to harmonize if there is some continuity between their roof lines. In general, we like to see houses flow together; good landscaping can promote that effect.

Whether it is efficient or not, the detached dwelling seems to be something everyone wants, although not everyone can afford it. For most Americans, it constitutes a better solution to the problems of shelter than living in a small box, inside a large box, within a large block, in an anonymous grid. That is a solution increasingly reserved for the very rich or the very poor. But unfortunately, the poetic promise of the dwelling, inherited from Frank Lloyd Wright, has not been realized in housing for the millions. Can it ever be realized? Perhaps this is a case where architecture and planning are ahead of politics and economics. The professionals know how to design better communities than they are allowed to build. The solution? Better clients for our designers.

Elements of Planning: The Highway   Trains and buses are more efficient than automobiles. Nevertheless, if we have a choice, we prefer to drive. Why? Because automobiles give us a greater sense of freedom and personal control. Although modern life is increasingly mechanized and automated, driving provides the opportunity to exercise skill and judgment. The automobile is felt as an extension of our bodies; we want to test it against the rigors of distance, the demands of the road, the cars of other drivers, the challenge of the unexpected. Along with the shopping trip, the auto voyage is one of the great experiences of twentieth-century mankind. Despite transportation alternatives and casualty statistics, we are drawn toward concrete and asphalt like lemmings drawn to the sea.

What appeals to us in addition to going somewhere is the opportunity to feel the land moving under our vehicles, seeing the changing sky and countryside at 55 mph, sensing the car's response to the shifting shape of the road. For these reasons, it is not too much to say that highways, parkways, bridges, and viaducts constitute art objects—sources of aesthetic experience for the millions.

Although safety is the chief goal of highway designers, aesthetic considerations are intimately related to safety. Designers can shape the motorist's visual experience: they know how far drivers can see at given speeds, their degree of peripheral vision, their ability to discriminate objects. They know how comfort and pleasure are affected by the banking and grading of a road and the transition into and out of a curve. The well-designed highway *leads* the driv-

Sven Markelius. Vällingby, Sweden. Begun 1953

Le Corbusier's urban planning ideas applied in Sweden. But those connected units, lower left, look like freight cars. Maybe the S-curve helps.

left: **Alfred Neumann and Zvi Hecker. Apartment house, Ramat Gan, Israel. 1960–63**

The sculptural excitement in the apartment building (left) proves that modern technology can generate the same feeling of community that we sense in the adobe pueblo, America's oldest high-rise dwelling (right).

right: **Indian village, Taos Pueblo, New Mexico. c. 1935. Courtesy Museum of New Mexico, Santa Fe**

er's eye; it prepares us for certain operations while offering enough variation to avoid monotony. Unity and predictability versus variation and surprise: these are aesthetic considerations. It is well known that monotonous highway design can be dangerously hypnotic; in other words, bad design is harmful to your health.

The construction of bridges, viaducts, interchanges, side slopes, retaining walls, safety rails, and embankments presents artistic as well as engineering problems. These problems arise whenever we try to bring a highway through a city. Can it be done harmoniously? Can major arteries be visually integrated with the natural and man-made structures that surround them? How should we treat the areas created by the crossing, paralleling, rising, or descending of freeway ramps as they meet local traffic patterns?

And there are other questions: What should be done with road signs? Can we get the visual information we need more concisely, and sufficiently in advance of need? What about the billboards that invade our privacy, exploiting our attention without our permission? Vision is essential to driving, and billboards cannot be "turned off." So, the best efforts of engineers, planners, and designers are frustrated because the visual relationships they create are not protected. The modern highway illustrates our resemblance to the ancient Romans—solid builders and administrators but not especially sensitive to human or aesthetic relationships.

Since 1946, West Germany and Switzerland have demonstrated greater sensitivity to the highway as a form of architecture. But the world's greatest democracy has not yet accepted the legitimacy of spending public funds for sculpture to enliven dull stretches of road. Edward Hopper's painting *Gas* tells the story well enough. Or, perhaps Stuart Davis was right (see page 41): the gas pump *is* our sculpture! Even so, we have to learn that with our frontiers gone and natural resources limited, the visual pollution of the landscape must stop. Highways may be our best instrument for educating the millions to enjoy the countryside and preserve it unravaged.

Elements of Planning: Plazas, Malls, Civic Centers   Television has made our public life a living-room experience. Today we witness momentous events from the same sofa that was formerly used for conversation and courtship. We experience the deaths of presidents and popes on television with the same immediacy and sense of distress that are felt by members of a family. It has been clear for some time that we cannot gather in a single square to watch

above: **Expressway through Lefrak City in Queens, New York**
An automotive conveyor belt surrounded by an anonymous collection of boxes for middle-income apartment dwellers. The result of this architectural relationship is human indifference.

below: **Complex freeway interchange in Los Angeles**
An engineering marvel that looks good from the air. In a car, it's best to close the windows, turn on the stereo, and stay in the same lane.

Terracing along Highway 70 outside Denver, Colorado

Good highway engineering here creates an impressive geologic display as well as an aesthetic effect appropriate to the grandeur of the Rocky Mountain setting.

our leaders debate the issues; our sense of community comes mainly from the media of news and information. But although the media create a community of ideas, opinion, and entertainment, they do not bring us together physically. In fact, they separate us physically. So we still need places—open spaces—where we can come together out of the darkness of our TV dens. There is no substitute for the exhilaration of *being with* people, as opposed to *looking at* or *reading about* them.

What are the outdoor places that bring large numbers of people together? Amusement parks, shopping malls, civic squares, sports arenas, bus terminals, airports, museum gardens, cemeteries, and parking lots. These are the places where we can stroll, window-shop, sit on benches, or watch the passing parade. Given the chance, we would like to browse in an outdoor book stall, shop in an open market, explore a crooked little street, discover a square with a little church, some statuary, a fountain, and a few children playing. This sounds like a civilized way to spend time. Must we go to Europe to do it?

left: **Jacques Moeschal. Sculpture for Mexico City's Route of Friendship. 1968**

right: **Edward Hopper. *Gas*. 1940. Collection, The Museum of Modern Art, New York. Mrs. Simon Guggenheim Fund**

Red Grooms and Mimi Gross. Detail of vinyl tower featuring Blissberg's Old Folks Home from *Ruckus Manhattan*. 1975. Courtesy Marlborough Gallery, New York

The imageries of Dubuffet and Grooms have common origins in children's drawings, street graffiti, and the art of the insane. Both artists are amazed by the idea of people housed like insects in multicelled containers; both think of cities as crazy, rollicking machine-organisms. Both are fascinated by terror, fun, and lunacy.

Jean Dubuffet. *Recycling Machine*. 1978. Albright-Knox Art Gallery, Buffalo, New York. George B. and Jenny R. Mathews Fund, 1979

Donald Ray Carter. Photograph of Galleria Vittorio Emanuele, Milan

Street life raised to the level of an art form. This is what we are trying to accomplish with our shopping-mall architecture. Too bad we can't do it downtown.

Stamford Town Center Mall, Connecticut

Well, the shopping mall is America's answer to the European square—our version of an exciting public space. Of course, it tempts us to buy things: the visual and spatial amenities have to be paid for. But it is also possible to stroll through for free. A shopping mall is often an enclosed structure, with natural light admitted at the top; usually it has generous and exotic plantings, and air conditioning throughout. (Americans can always improve on nature.) Some malls are created by closing off downtown streets; converting a few downtown canyons to pedestrian use can reclaim the city for people. Also, we are learning that good buildings need not be torn down: auto traffic can be re-routed and people can rediscover their feet. But what about the slums and obsolete structures that usually surround downtown areas? Frequently, they are expensively redesigned and their inhabitants are relocated. A better solution is to invite artists to live there; they tend to inhabit marginal areas, and they will fix most things with their own labor. Furthermore, the results will be better looking, less plastic.

So far as massive redesign is concerned, Rockefeller Center in New York City is our great model. Begun in 1931, it provided the impetus for the construction of public buildings and plazas in the high-density core of a modern metropolis. It consists of sixteen buildings occupying fourteen acres of choice Manhattan real estate. They form a complex that surrounds a pedestrian mall and a sunken plaza that is an ice-skating rink in winter and an outdoor restaurant in summer. These massive, slablike buildings represent the first significant departure from the idea of the skyscraper as a sort of oversized church steeple. They also embody a frank, if unspectacular, solution to the problem of getting the maximum light into the interior of very tall structures. No office is more than twenty-seven feet from an exterior wall; all have light, fresh air, and a magnificent view.

The unbroken curtain-wall surfaces of the Rockefeller Center buildings provide an important psychological dividend—a sense of enclosure and protection for the plaza and mall on the ground. That means *the people* on the ground; here we have tall buildings that do not intimidate. In addition, Rockefeller Center gives the pedestrian a feeling of being at the focal point of an energetic and exciting city. Excitement and a sense of protection: this is the

Lincoln Center for the Performing Arts, New York. 1962–69

Two public squares almost a thousand years apart, and yet they perform essentially the same function. They bring people together in an enclosed space to create one of the great spectacles of civilized life: human beings moving freely against a background of monumental architectural forms.

Piazza San Marco, Venice. Begun 1063

opposite: **Charles Moore and William Hersey. Piazza d'Italia, New Orleans. 1974–78**

Urban fun architecture—part stage set, part sculpture, and part Pop painting. Intended to honor the Italian immigrants of New Orleans, the Piazza is not so much a space as it is a potpourri of classical architectural fragments, modern glitzy materials, and hotel-lobby glitter.

combination we want in public spaces. Great cities can be depressing as well as exciting; individuals privately lost in depersonalized routines need to be reminded of their humaneness, their capacity to experience emotions that enlarge rather than reduce the self. That may be the real reason we feel a sudden urge to go to Paris, Venice, or Rome. The time has come to go to San Francisco, Seattle, and Toronto. And Savannah.

Elements of Planning: Industrial and Commercial Structures   Not long ago, a factory was an ugly place—grimy, surrounded by clutter, garbage, and foul smells. Crossing the New Jersey meadows (swamps, actually) and looking at the industrial sprawl from the train window, one wondered how people could stand the sights and sounds once they had overcome the stench. The same was true of the pulpwood mills in the South, the steel-mill towns along the Ohio River, the slaughterhouses of Chicago or Kansas City, and the scarred mining towns of Pennsylvania and West Virginia. Their active and obsolete remains still mark the places where we live and work.

Today, these sights, sounds, and smells are disappearing, mainly because the operations that produced them have become uneconomic: those mills and factories and slaughterhouses were in the wrong locations; they were too costly to maintain; some could be automated; or their managements became concerned about public image. The Victorian notion that industry is inherently ugly has given way to the idea that order, precision, and harmony are essen-

Frank Lloyd Wright. Johnson Wax Administration Building and Research Tower, Racine, Wisconsin. 1936–39, 1947–50. Views by day and by night

tial features of a successful industrial enterprise. These qualities have to be visible in the places where products are planned, manufactured, and distributed. Consumers have become very choosy—or aesthetically sensitive: they associate merchandise with the places where it is made and sold.

A pioneering industrial statement was made, once again, by Frank Lloyd Wright in his Administration Building (1936–39) and Research Center (1946–49) for the Johnson Wax Company in Racine, Wisconsin. To be sure, the structural vocabulary (with the exception of the tower) seems more related to a domestic dwelling than a corporate headquarters. But is that bad? What should a factory or research center look like? A college campus? Why not? Morale may be improved and management can then attract and hold the people it needs to survive in a modern economy.

The Johnson buildings are located in the center of a city that values architectural excellence. So the structural forms have a bold, sculptural quality. This is especially apparent in the Research Center tower, which rises dramatically from a hovering platform. Its horizontal bands repeat the lines of the administration buildings, and its circular roof turrets provide a good solution to that eternal problem of the high-rise—how to top it off. The floors of the tower are cantilevered from a central core, which passes through the building and emerges as a turret on the roof. This structure is clearly revealed at night; we see the Wrightian concept of a tall building as opposed to the Chicago and New York idea of a skyscraper. Today, high-rise structures resting on platforms are increasingly used and with conspicuous success, as in Lever House (1952). The tower is efficient and symbolically potent, and the platform unites it with the site, creating a useful protected space underneath. Does that idea belong to Wright or to Le Corbusier? Well, good ideas don't care who invented them.

Dramatic industrial and commercial structures can also be seen in E. J. Kahn's (1884–1972) Municipal Asphalt Plant in New York City, the St. Louis Airport Terminal by Minoru Yamasaki (1912–1986), and the North Carolina

Skidmore, Owings and Merrill. Lever House, New York. 1952

Epstein & Sons. Kitchens of Sara Lee Administration Building, Deerfield, Illinois. 1964

Compare this building with Mies van der Rohe's Crown Hall at Illinois Institute of Technology (page 80).

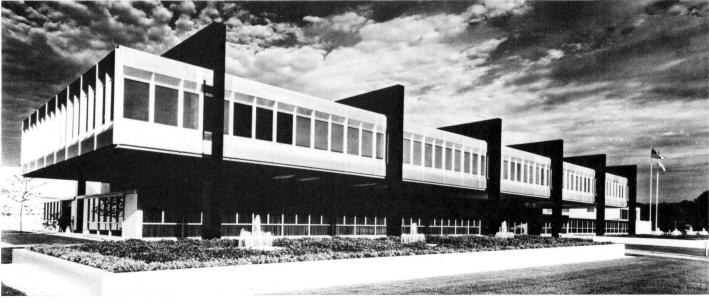

Kahn & Jacobs. Municipal Asphalt Plant (now occupied by the George and Annette Murphy Center), New York. 1944

From industrial plant to temple for arts and sports. A good building is worth keeping, regardless of its original function.

above left: **Minoru Yamasaki. St. Louis Airport Terminal. 1954**

above right: **Matthew Nowicki and William H. Deitrick. J. S. Dorton State Fair Arena, Raleigh, North Carolina. 1953**

Eero Saarinen. TWA Terminal, Kennedy International Airport, New York. 1962

J. S. Dorton State Fair Arena by Matthew Nowicki (1910–1949) and W. H. Deitrick (born 1905). Eero Saarinen (1910–1961) displayed almost theatrical gifts in his TWA Terminal at Kennedy International Airport. All of these examples show that the gap between art and science, or between architecture and engineering, is steadily closing. Great and enduring monuments are created when the artistic imagination is not restricted by a false or forced separation.

Ours is a time of frantic urban and regional transformation. The convergence of several forces has brought this about: (1) We realize that many social problems, now at the stage of crisis, originate in the physical design of the community. (2) We realize that problems of health, transportation, work, and recreation often transcend traditional political units. (3) Modern technology has made it practical to think in terms of large-scale, comprehensive design. (4) Various specialists—architects, engineers, ecologists, lawyers, land-use experts—have developed patterns of unified action in community design. (5) Architectural education now embraces the design of regional environments as well as individual structures.

top: **John Andrews. Scarborough College, University of Toronto. 1966**

The "megastructure" approach to the architecture of great institutions and even of whole cities. Such continuous structures are open to social and technological change because they are designed to receive "add-on" or "clip-on" units, which are mass produced by industrial methods instead of being custom-made on the site.

bottom: **Safdie, David, Barott, and Boulva. Habitat, EXPO 67, Montreal. 1967**

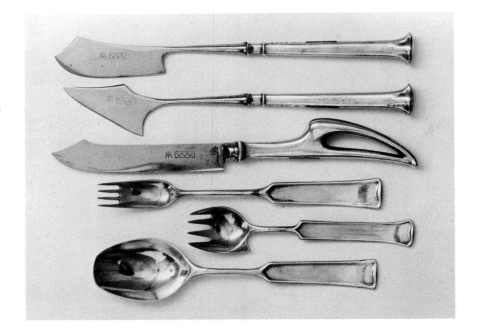

Richard Riemerschmid. Table flatware. 1900. Württembergisches Landesmuseum, Stuttgart

As early as 1900, Richard Riemerschmid combined the rational analysis of function with a sensitive and restrained adaptation of Art Nouveau forms.

Violin made by Antonio Stradivari. 1721. The Metropolitan Museum of Art, New York. Bequest of Annie Bolton Matthews Bryant, 1933

The crafts tend to perpetuate tradition: we do not expect "originality" in the design of a violin.

THE CRAFTS AND INDUSTRIAL DESIGN

We have seen how art performs physical functions through the design of large-scale containers—from single buildings to whole communities. The important point is that art is not only decorative or symbolic, it is also utilitarian. Although there are significant differences between handmade and machine-made objects, we should remember that organizing and shaping them to satisfy human needs is an artistic problem.

At different times the person responsible for making pots and pans has been called an artisan, a craftsman, an engineer, or a designer. In the past, families produced most of their own tools and utensils. The hardworking housewife of colonial days was not called a craftsman or a designer, but she spun and wove her own cloth, cut and sewed garments, made blankets and rugs, painted and embroidered textiles, and performed other tasks we associate with arts or crafts. But here we are not interested in labels; we are mainly concerned with the form and function of useful objects: how they are affected by machine tools and mass production; where the human contribution appears; whether the results have aesthetic quality.

The water jug made by a potter and the aluminum pitcher stamped out by a machine may be similar in shape and function. But the fingers and mind of a potter made the clay jug; making the aluminum pitcher was different. That pitcher grew out of a man-machine *collaboration*. Did it cease to be art when the machine entered the scene? Or do we have something new called "machine art"? If so, do people respond to it differently? Should they? Here we might look at some of the historical, technical, and psychological factors involved in the transition from clay pot to metal pitcher. In effect, we ask these questions: "Have machines been taught to create art? Was it a mistake?"

Qualities of Handcraft   Usually, a craft object has been planned and made by the same person. This is always true if the maker is what we call an artist-craftsman. In the village and cottage crafts of preindustrial economies, there is some division of labor between members of a family, between men and women, between children and adults, between skilled and unskilled workers. Even so, there is a certain unity of control and execution in the handmade object. The "professional" craftsman is different: he or she does all the work, adjusting a design according to the requirements of a customer. A good illustration would be the tailor who makes a garment "to order," that is, according to an individual's personal measurements. Hence, the characteristics of handcraft include (1) unified execution of the object; (2) unified responsibility for the object; (3) adjustment of design to an individual's needs.

The result of the craft process inevitably exhibits variation. That is why we can speak of a craft object as "one of a kind," even if it is similar to other objects of its type. The uniqueness of the object may be based on the craftsman's idiosyncrasies or the special desires of a patron. In either case, that uniqueness is often considered the essence of art. It pleases us to know that we own, or are looking at, an object that is absolutely singular; nobody has one exactly like it.

Another feature of handcraft is, paradoxically, its relative sameness. Variations in detail occur because absolute duplication is impossible in handmade articles. Also, the "true" craftsman does not look kindly on change for its own sake. Like peasants or folk artisans, craftsmen change their modes of thinking and making slowly; they prefer to use patterns and formulas inherited for generations. Now, traditions in the crafts promote a high degree of technical skill; folk craftsmen, especially, concentrate more on mastery of skill than on originality of expression. For them, the problems of meaning and design have been largely solved. The result is a timeless quality in craft objects, a quality that charms tourists—visitors from cultures where tastes change every other month.

Craftsmen of the old traditions care little for novelty, but they do stress the right use of tools and materials and the importance of durability. "Right" means using tools correctly, that is, according to inherited techniques and with respect for the working properties of materials. Since the patron-craftsman relationship is a close one, the craftsman cannot escape responsibility for what he or she has made. Here we have one of the fundamental meanings of craftsmanship: the value of the object is based on a relationship of trust between user and maker. You can go back to the tailor or dressmaker to have your garment adjusted because you have gained weight; try that at your local department store.

Another trait of handcraft may account for the survival of craftsmen today, notwithstanding their struggle with the economic facts of life: it is difficult to produce a great many ugly products by hand. To be sure, there are bad craftsmen, but they are usually weeded out. Furthermore, it is difficult for a human being to make something badly again and again; inevitably, we improve a little bit. But machines can produce trash at a fantastic rate; the results improve only if the designer improves. In the meantime, a vast amount of rubbish is manufactured. Furthermore, excellence in an industrial civilization is often defined in terms of mass acceptance, an acceptance that can be engineered by advertising.

above: **Roy Lichtenstein.** *Ceramic Sculpture I.* **1965. Private collection**

These works rely for their Surrealist impact on the deliberate violation of the craftsman's aesthetic: appropriateness of material, decoration, and mode of making to the form and function of the object.

left: **Meret Oppenheim.** *Object.* **1936. Collection, The Museum of Modern Art, New York. Purchase**

For most of human history, objects of daily use have been made with the aid of small hand tools functioning as extensions of our senses and fingers. We have been thoroughly habituated to the visual and tactile characteristics of handcraft, and it is doubtful that we shall ever escape our emotional attachment to materials worked by hand. But civilization as we know it depends on mechanical and automated forms of making. Since the Industrial Revolution we have been going through a conflict between our emotional attachment to the crafts and the mechanical basis of our economy. Today, that conflict is almost over.

Machine-made products have been accepted by almost all societies. Computer-aided design (CAD) and computer-aided manufacture (CAM) are spreading rapidly. Those newly emerging nations that still depend on handcraft are trying desperately to become industrialized. For them, mechanical-industrial production is a symbol of national prestige, and handcraft is regarded as a survival of colonial dependence. For us, ironically, the practice of the crafts and the ownership of craft objects is often a symbol of taste and cultivation. Or perhaps it is just a hankering for the past. Yet, something in our bones and organs—especially our eyes—craves the touch and sight of hand-made objects. Then, how did we get "hooked" on the mass-production habit?

The Origin and Principles of Mass Production   Clearly, we have to examine the basic processes of mechanization and mass production. Then we can look at industrial design and the implications of machine art for civilization.

The principles of mass production are *duplication, accuracy, interchangeability,* and *specialization*. Casting, the oldest method of duplication, goes back to the Neolithic era—about 8000 B.C. From this *art* (it was art, magic, and technology rolled into one) the metal foundries of the present evolved. Today, there are few manufactured products that do not contain parts cast in metal or plastic. A second Neolithic invention, the potter's wheel, led to the wood lathe and the metal lathe, which is the basic machine tool of metalworking. Die stamping, another method of duplication, was used by the Persian king Darius to manufacture coins in the fifth century B.C. Gutenberg's invention of movable type (c. 1440) was a method of duplication that had effects extending far beyond printing. Movable type involved a kind of *interchangeability,* since the same letters could be used again and again in different combinations. But *accuracy* was not very great and the interchangeable principle was used only on a two-dimensional surface without moving parts. By the eighteenth century, a fair degree of three-dimensional accuracy was developed in steam engines and watches, leading to *interchangeability of parts.* This resulted in the stock of spare parts we now take for granted; manufacturing could be done in one place and assembling in another. These developments depended on uniform standards of measure—agreement about the meaning of dimensions—something handcraftsmen did not have because each craftsman was a law unto himself.

Specialization in mass production refers not only to workers but also to machine tools. The ideal machine is designed to carry out a single operation or set of operations on a particular product. There is talk about versatile robots, that is, multipurpose robots, but this may be a matter of semantic play; efficiency in mass production depends on specialized machines. The ideal factory consists of a series of machines connected to each other, all electronically guided by instructions from a computer. Well, who guides the computer? Here we come closer to the role of the designer.

An assembly line is a manufacturing device that fully employs duplication, accuracy, interchangeability, and specialization in machines and, to some extent, workers. It is mainly associated with Henry Ford, although Eli Whitney set up an assembly-line system to manufacture guns in the eighteenth century. Early in the twentieth century, Ford and other manufacturers realized they

Ford Motor Company assembly line. Early 1900s

could not tolerate hand-fitting because it wasted time. Higher quality and production were achieved by eliminating the possibility of human error. And error could be reduced by taking the human hand out of the process of making!

So the basic idea of mass production might be summarized as follows: The quality of a product can be raised, its price lowered, and greater numbers produced, if component parts are made accurately with specialized tools operated by workers who could not make the whole product alone. The skill resides in the system, not the person who tends the machine or assembles the parts.

Modern manufacturing operations (computerized or not) fall into three distinct phases: plant layout and tooling, duplication of parts, and assembly of duplicated units. These phases follow decisions to manufacture a new product or model—decisions that are guided by research, capitalization, design, engineering, and marketing. Obviously, design interacts with all the other factors, suggesting that an "artistic element" influences every aspect of production. In addition, there is *re*design, which entails costly retooling operations in any industry. Beyond redesign, there is *styling*—a type of designing that changes only the appearance of a product, usually in response to marketing pressures. In the following section we examine some of the ethical and aesthetic questions it raises.

The Emergence of Industrial Design   As we have seen, the Industrial Revolution and mass production caused a steady replacement of the human hand. Until the eighteenth century, no basic changes in manufacturing had taken place since the Bronze Age; tools were more refined but principles of operation remained the same. Then, suddenly, handcraft methods of manufacture became obsolete.

Preindustrial manufacture assumed that the craftsman adds skill and imagination to raw materials that have added value when formed into a finished product. After the Industrial Revolution, craftsmen became *workers* who ceased to contribute skill and imagination: they offered only labor, which became a commodity like wool, leather, metal, or wood. Machines tended by men (or women and children) produced the changes from raw material to finished product with results that were uniform and predictable. The craftsman ceased to be an important variable in production; he became an anonymous, invariable factor.

From a human standpoint, the social consequences of the Industrial Revolution were disastrous. As craft skills lost their unique value, work was turned into labor, often drudgery. Women and children competed to sell their labor with steadily diminishing bargaining power; workers' wages and living conditions were wretched. Ironically, the machines that created wealth and jobs brought poverty and lowered standards of living for those who tended them.

The sordidness of cities, the misery of the working classes, and the monotony of machine jobs led to a romantic escapism in the arts. Sensitive people could not conceive of art in a context that was so ruinous of human resources. And the early products of mechanization gave little contrary evidence: machine tools were used to imitate handmade ornament, with results totally unsuited to the materials and processes used. Craft revivals were attempted, notably by John Ruskin and William Morris, but they could not change the economic facts of life—or art. The artistic problems raised by mass production were not effectively faced until Walter Gropius (1883–1969) established a new kind of educational and industrial institution—the Bauhaus—in the twentieth century.

Gropius realized that the essential difference between craft and machine production lay in *the control* of the process of making: one person in the crafts; a division of labor in industry. He had written a paper, "Industrial Prefabrication of Homes on a Unified Artistic Basis," which urged mass-produc-

above left: **Marianne Brandt. Teapot. 1924. Collection, The Museum of Modern Art, New York. Phyllis B. Lambert Fund**

The Bauhaus-type teapot of 1924, with its perfect geometry and its no-nonsense surfaces, was the product of a love affair with mechanization. An ideological love affair. By 1953, the craftsman felt free to express his organic feelings: machine-form is still honored, but now the shapes are sexier. The idea of biological growth has slipped in.

above right: **John Prip. Silver teapot. 1953. Museum of Contemporary Crafts, New York. Permanent Collection**

German Rose Engine. c. 1750. British Crown Copyright, Science Museum, London

How could the machine tool be humanized? By converting it into "art"—by covering all its surfaces with irrelevant ornament.

tion techniques for building and held out the possibility of high-quality production through industrial methods. The net result of these ideas was the opening of the Bauhaus at Weimar, Germany, in 1919, with Gropius as its director. It was formed by combining a trade school with a school of fine arts.

At first, each Bauhaus student had two teachers, one an artist and the other a master craftsman, because there were no instructors who embodied the qualities of both. It was necessary to give art students experience with machine production so they could provide industry with the *integrated control* it lacked. Beyond machine-forming and craftsmanship, the Bauhaus taught science and economics as well as the fine-arts curriculum of drawing, painting, sculpture, composition, and art history. In this way, industrial designers, as we know them, were first trained.

In 1925 the Bauhaus left Weimar and reestablished itself at Dessau, where a new faculty, now composed of Bauhaus graduates, combined technician and artist in the same instructor. The school became an experimental workshop where models for mass production were continually developed by students and faculty. A mechanical idiom, or "machine style," was created, one that was distinctly different from handcraft styles. Of particular importance, hierarchies and status distinctions between "fine" artists, architects, and craftsmen were largely eliminated.

In 1933, when the Nazis came to power, the Bauhaus was driven out of Germany. Subsequently, one of its younger instructors, Lázló Moholy-Nagy (1895–1946), established an American branch in Chicago, where it was eventually absorbed into the Illinois Institute of Technology. By World War II, it was plain that the Bauhaus had created a new profession, industrial design; at the same time the education of artists throughout the world was fundamentally transformed.

Form and Function Louis Sullivan (1856–1924), Frank Lloyd Wright's teacher, originated the phrase "Form follows function." Applied to architecture or manufactured objects, the phrase became an axiom for all modern design. It means that the outer shape or appearance of an object results from its inner operation; an object should look like what it is and does. There should be no deceptive appearances: metal should not imitate wood, plastic should not imitate marble. The traditional designers of buildings and objects often began with the outer shell or the facade and then proceeded to divide and arrange interior space. As for functional or working objects, ornament was "applied" to cover their nakedness, so to speak. Thus architecture and product design became increasingly decorative. Instead of following function, the form of a product followed prevailing tastes in period styles and ornamentation.

Automobile grilles. Courtesy _Design Quarterly_ magazine

During the 1950s, American automobile designers embarked on a monumental "front-end" binge, which they followed with a tailfin orgy. A true example of American Baroque, the phenomenon had an industrial father and a psychological mother: the manufacturer's need for salable packages mated with the stylist's need to express his sculptural impulses.

Industrial design began as an effort to bring unity and logic to the planning and production of machine-made objects. As it evolved, however, artistically irrelevant factors entered the scene. "Appearance design" emerged when manufacturers and merchants discovered that consumers could not tell the difference between functional design and a new look. Any "redesign" had sales appeal. The new "machine style" could be employed to make a product look as if it had been basically transformed. We got "streamlining"—slick surfaces for everything from automobiles to wristwatches.

Thus we come to a phony version of industrial design—styling. The periodic redesign or styling of products stimulates sales _whether or not_ changes in physical function have taken place. In addition, a newly styled product has the effect of making older designs look inferior. This cycle of design, redesign, and new styling, leading to an apparent loss of value in older models, is called _planned obsolescence;_ it creates a peculiarly modern dilemma.

The quick obsolescence of useful objects has large economic implications: industries need to use most of their productive capacity to keep their workers employed. Obviously, workers cannot buy automobiles and refrigerators if they are not earning wages. So, persuading the public to use and discard goods rapidly is vital to an expanding economy. Without doubt, planned obsolescence has helped to create the American standard of living because it leads to greater use of the productive capacity of industry. But perhaps our standard of living is defined too exclusively in terms of _how many_ things we own and _how often_ we replace them. Today, planned obsolescence

Wilhelm von Debschitz. Inkstand. 1906. Württembergisches Landesmuseum, Stuttgart

An impressive but pretentious solution to the design of a useful object: Von Debschitz tried to transcend utility by disguising the function of the object beneath sculptural gestures.

and disposable design haunt us in the form of pollution, wasted energy, and uglification of the environment.

Clearly, industrial designers belong to the worlds of economics and marketing as well as art. They are trained to analyze a product and find the best combination of materials, processes, and forms to suit its function; their knowledge of production methods equips them to keep manufacturing costs to a minimum consistent with quality; they can design for every phase of production, including packaging, information, and display. But often, they merely fabricate a new "skin" for a product—arriving at a result that is spuriously "different." Can this be changed? Perhaps the competitive forces that made design crucial for successful production will raise the professional and ethical level of the design professions. Generally, we can rely on the integrity of the engineer who designs a bridge or the dentist who extracts a tooth. In time, we should be able to rely on the integrity of the designers who are responsible for what we see—from chairs to locomotives, from saucepans to refrigerators.

Industrial Design: The Chair   Until we sit on it, a chair is a work of abstract sculpture; it is also a complex engineering problem. The habit of sitting in chairs is carried on in many positions, for different purposes, and with a variety of physical apparatus. We expect comfort, support, and stability from our seating equipment, and we would like to get into and out of a chair with a certain amount of dignity. Some chairs have to be portable and light, others must be sturdy to resist abuse; some will be for outdoor use and have to be weather-resistant. Generally, chairs should not be too bulky; today's homes and apartments cannot afford to invest space in a chair that looks like an assembly of mattresses.

As sculpture, chairs possess symbolic value: they can look like thrones, beds, couches, swings, saddles, or wire cages—reminding us of kings, queens, bishops, cowboys, or canaries. Chairs are masculine or feminine, juvenile or adult, shy or assertive. To a crawling child or a kitten, chairs are a forest of legs. To a mother of small children, chairs may represent nonwashable surfaces covered with peanut butter. Thus the practical, the symbolic, and the aesthetic combine in a chair to make it a formidable design problem.

A complete philosophy can be revealed in a chair. The designer uses it to express convictions about structure, truth, strength, comfort, and decoration. For example, the famous Barcelona lounge chair by Mies van der Rohe eloquently demonstrates his architectural philosophy: pay attention to the details; use a minimum of materials; keep it simple; and "less is more." Technological innovation is also prominent: the cantilever principle is used in conjunction with the elasticity of metal; the same continuous metal bar serves as curved leg

left: **Constantin Brancusi.** *Sculpture for the Blind.* **1924. Philadelphia Museum of Art. The Louise and Walter Arensberg Collection**

The biomorphic perfection of the egg can be exploited at several design levels: it can yield practical dividends (the Aarnie chair); or it can be enlisted in the service of tactility (the Brancusi sculpture).

right: **Eero Aarnie. Gyro Chair. c. 1965–66. Distributed by Stendig, Inc., New York**

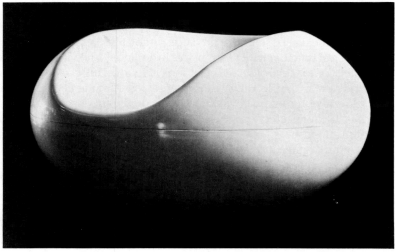

112

Ida Kohlmeyer. *Mythic Chair*. 1984. Courtesy Arthur Roger Gallery, New Orleans

A painter's approach to a chair. The basic bentwood shapes already suggest the armature of a growing thing; Kohlmeyer has merely taken the hints offered by the wooden framework, adding organs and features in hot color. Now the tubular forms really live.

and back support. Aesthetically, the tufted leather cushions provide bulk, warmth, and color in contrast to the thin metal members. A masterpiece of design, the Barcelona chair is likely to endure as a modern classic for years to come—remarkable when we consider its date, 1929.

Where inexpensive, easily stacked and transported seating is required—especially for public purposes—designers often use molded plastic forms with tubular metal legs and supporting elements. Since cost is a factor, molded plastics can replace more expensive and destructible leather or fabric coverings. Because the philosophy of modern design was built on the requirements of a mass market and low unit cost, expensive chair ideas have been regularly "adapted" and sold to a large public at low prices. This was the economic as well as aesthetic achievement of our "pioneers" of design: Charles Eames, George Nelson, Henry Dreyfuss, Russel Wright, and Raymond Loewy, among others; they brought good design to the American masses, creating markets, jobs, and "taste"—a hunger for excellence at low cost.

Today a huge world market for good design has emerged. Production facilities are widely dispersed, international transportation is cheaper, and people in remote places have acquired appetites for quality at reasonable prices. We are entering an era in which the tools of production will be radically transformed—miniaturized, computerized, and electronically linked. There will be many new centers of production and distribution. In this new era, industrial design will be a crucial factor in capturing and holding markets, conserving raw materials, and satisfying human needs yet to be discovered. Or created. Here is where the connections between design and craft become important; we have to answer these questions: Is it useful? Do we need it? Is it worth it? Will it last? Would it be good to have?

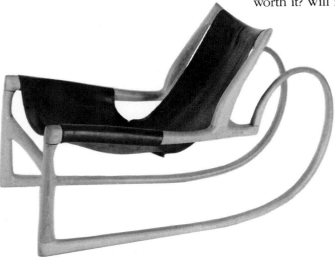

Wendell Castle. Oak-and-leather chair. 1963

Castle is a contemporary craftsman who chooses to develop the sculptural possibilities of the Thonet furniture of the 1860s, the Art Nouveau swirls of the early 1900s, and the tubular-metal construction of the 1920s.

Gebrüder Thonet. Rocking chair. 1860. Collection, The Museum of Modern Art, New York. Gift of Café Nicholson

Ludwig Mies van der Rohe. "Barcelona" Chair. 1929. Collection, The Museum of Modern Art, New York. Gift of Knoll International

Charles Eames. Lounge chair. 1958. Collection, The Museum of Modern Art, New York. Gift of the manufacturer: Herman Miller Inc.

Gunnar Aagaard Andersen. Armchair. 1964. Collection, The Museum of Modern Art, New York. Gift of the designer

Ostensibly, this chair of poured urethane plastic represents the creative marriage of art and technology. But the object makes no real contribution to chair design: it functions chiefly as a fascinating demonstration of liquid tactility.

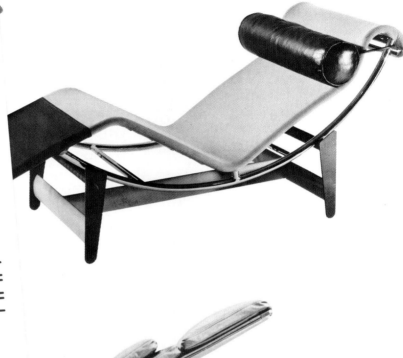

Charles Eames. Chaise longue. 1970. Designed for Herman Miller, Inc., New York

The 1970 chaise by Charles Eames builds on Le Corbusier's architectural solution to the reclining chair (1927). But Eames has new materials to work with: foam-rubber cushions, zippered pillows, and a cast-aluminum frame covered with dark nylon.

Olivier Mourgue. Chairs. 1965
The influence of painters Arp and Miró on contemporary French furniture design.

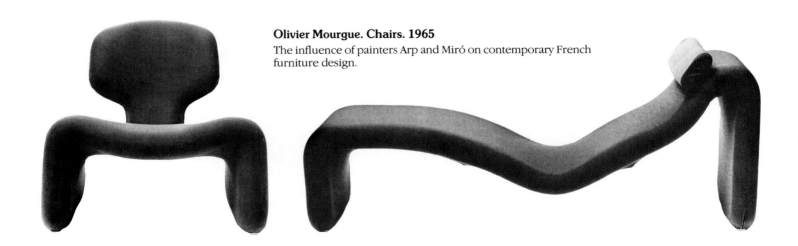

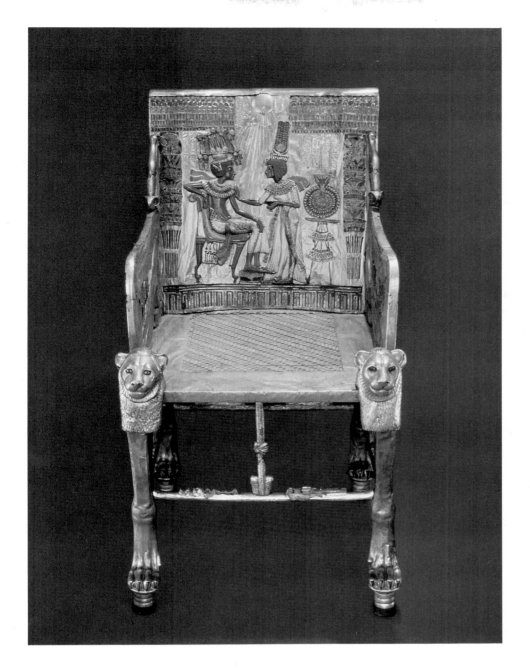

opposite: **Wooden door with carving in relief, from Baule, Ivory Coast. Rietberg Museum, Zurich. Von der Heydt Collection**

There is no difference between the fine and the applied in African art: utilitarian purpose and expressive form coexist harmoniously.

above: **Tutankhamen's throne. c. 1350 B.C. Egyptian Museum, Cairo**

The royal seat is protected by lions, but they don't look very ferocious. The emphasis here is on the symbolism and prerogatives of power: gold-covered carving, inlays of precious gems, the image of an attentive queen, and the sun god shining down on the king, his lineal descendant.

right: **Benvenuto Cellini. *Saltcellar of Francis I.* c. 1540. Kunsthistorisches Museum, Vienna**

Fine art or craft? Obviously, there is more here than a salt-and-pepper container. An extravagant allegory (he represents salt, she represents pepper) was needed to satisfy the taste of a Renaissance monarch. Actually, if he wanted to pour salt, using this object was not a very good way to do it.

Polynesian game board (*konane*) from the Hawaiian Islands. National Park Service, Hawaii Volcanoes National Park. Gift of Mrs. Harry Edmondson, 1956

Only eight inches high, this little table could pass for a monumental sculpture. Why? Because the Polynesian carver concentrated on the essential forms needed to dramatize the supporting function of those fierce little men. Thus the structural elements have tremendous energy. What a powerful game of checkers could be played on that board!

Ice bucket with lid. Magnus Stephensen design executed by G. Pedersen for Georg Jensen Ltd., Copenhagen, Denmark. 1951. Collection, The Museum of Modern Art, New York. Gift of Philip Johnson

This silver container is surely a craft object—handwrought in a precious metal. But notice how its form reflects the influence of machine manufacture. No allegory, no symbolism; all we have is an elegant way to carry ice cubes from the refrigerator to the place where an unfilled glass is waiting.

Micronesian stool for grating coconuts, from the Mariana Islands

Ancient and folk-craft objects, created by anonymous artisans. The jug is one of thousands like it; the stool is a variant of a standard type. Both have almost mechanical qualities of clarity and precision; both exhibit exquisite formal relationships. These objects show that good design is universal and ageless; they would be elegant and graceful even if they were mass-produced in Detroit or Grand Rapids.

Jug, from Kültepe, northern Anatolia. 18th century B.C. Museum of Archaeology, Ankara

These three objects tell the story of craft and industrial design. Vail's bottle is a fetish object; it could be the container for a sorcerer's magic potion. Boccioni's bottle is so intellectual it can't hold anything: it represents a search for the object's inner geometry. Oldenburg's *Lipstick* is a gigantic "put-on"—a burlesque of sex, advertising, mass production, and the Pentagon.

Umberto Boccioni. *Development of a Bottle in Space.* 1912. Collection, The Museum of Modern Art, New York. Aristide Maillol Fund

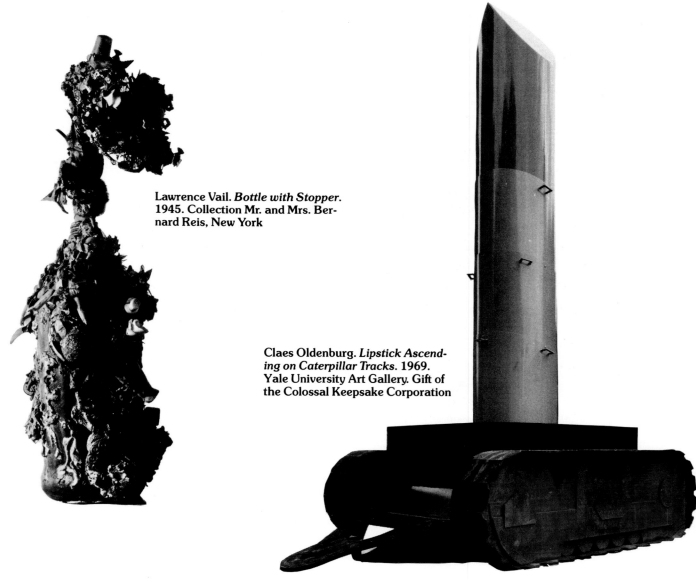

Lawrence Vail. *Bottle with Stopper.* 1945. Collection Mr. and Mrs. Bernard Reis, New York

Claes Oldenburg. *Lipstick Ascending on Caterpillar Tracks.* 1969. Yale University Art Gallery. Gift of the Colossal Keepsake Corporation

PART TWO

THE STYLES OF ART

The concept of style is indispensable for the study of art, and yet it can confuse us because the word has so many meanings. Usually, style refers to the art of a particular historical period, but it may also mean the art of a nation (the Italian Renaissance), or a region (the Barbizon style), or a group of artists (the Pre-Raphaelites). It can also designate an individual artist's quality (Titianesque, Rubensesque, Cézannesque). Style may refer to a technical or artistic approach (Color Divisionism, Pointillism, Photorealism). It can also be used as a term of approval: "He (or she) has *style*." Or, it refers to a new look in cars, clothes, or kitchen appliances; here, "style" is equivalent to the latest fad or fashion. However, all the uses of the concept have one purpose—the classification of a variety of objects into categories that make them easier to recognize, understand, and talk about. At the most general level, therefore, a style is a grouping or classification of artworks (by time, region, appearance, technique, etc.) that makes further study and analysis possible.

As with scientific classification, the sorting of phenomena into categories is based on the observation of common traits or qualities. Styles of art, therefore, can be thought of as families. Just as members of a family have certain features that give them what is called a "family resemblance," works of art may also look like one another. They may have differences, too, but they have *some* common traits that we can see or sense and that make classification possible. The recognizable element may consist of a certain use of line, color, shape, or space; or it may be felt in a qualitative sense. In other words, style may be visible on the surface of an artwork or in its overall feeling. This overall, or *pervasive,* quality of a work is often the basis for its classification; stylistic terms like "classical" and "romantic" seem to rely on the viewer's feelings *in the presence of an artwork* as much as on the artist's technique.

With an understanding of art styles, we can read the so-called hidden language of art. Style helps us find meanings beneath the subject matter and apparent purpose of an artwork. Just as handwriting reveals meanings that are not in words alone, style can tell us much about an artist's environment, values, and heritage. Indeed, archaeologists and anthropologists use style to reconstruct whole cultures: they put pieces of stylistic evidence together like a mosaic, trying to form a complete picture or idea of a culture. Similarly, we can study an art style to build an idea of the inner condition of an artist, a people, or perhaps, the evolution of human consciousness as a whole.

Stylistic Change Although several styles may coexist—especially in modern cultures—there have been periods when a single style was dominant. But every style is succeeded by another, and in recent years, styles have succeeded one another very rapidly. Of all the styles described by art history, only the folk or peasant styles seem to persist regardless of social change—a phenomenon that is probably due to the isolation of folk cultures. Today, however, few groups are completely isolated from world culture; consequently, folk and peasant art is disappearing. This disappearance calls attention to the dynamic and changing character of style in the mainstream cultures.

In the mainstream cultures, then, what accounts for stylistic change? New scientific knowledge? New forms of technology? Fresh artistic responses to the physical and social environment? Can we say that artists invent styles out of whole cloth, so to speak—styles that catch fire, grow into conflagrations, and then burn themselves out?

Scholarly answers to these questions differ according to the discipline of the observer. Art historians may attribute stylistic change to the innovations of artists working out the hints and possibilities of the art forms they have inherited. Critics may see the artist as generating wholly new ways of seeing—ways that become part of our common visual and emotional equipment. Behavioral scientists often attribute stylistic change to shifts in the political, economic, or social climate; thus artists react more than they innovate. I am inclined to believe they do both: they react and they invent; they inherit and they transform.

Why do we try to explain stylistic change? Because we suspect that changes in artistic style may anticipate changes in life as a whole. Perhaps a style that many artists adopt represents a form of adaptation to change in the total culture. In this case, artists serve as social antennae—as scouts, heralds, and prophesiers. Also, there is the possibility that artists *cause* changes in the way people see the world and deal with their experience. In other words, artists may be the ship's rudder rather than its radar.

Regardless of our views about stylistic change, we think we can recognize the emergence of new styles and the decline of old ones. Styles seem to have the traits of living organisms; we speak of their life cycles as if they were flowers that bud, bloom, and wilt; like people, they have a childhood, maturity, and old age. These analogies may be inexact, but they call attention to something we are all aware of: style seems to have a secret connection to overall trends in human affairs.

The reasons for studying the styles of art might be summarized as follows: (1) To acquire useful categories or labels for thinking about the common traits of artworks produced during various periods. (2) To understand the artists, historical periods, countries, or regions in whose art a certain style frequently occurs. (3) To compare or, perhaps, to judge, works of art that are stylistically related. (4) To understand the connections between an artist's technique or creative strategy and our reactions to his or her work. (5) To get special information—"inside dope"—about the future.

CHAPTER FOUR

THE STYLE OF OBJECTIVE ACCURACY

The style of objective accuracy is familiar to most people whether they have studied art or not. They feel confident in judging work in this style since they can compare a painting or a sculpture with its real-life original. (Of course, the real-life original has to be remembered—which is not always easy.) Still, optical accuracy, or convincing resemblance to life, is for many persons the principal way of evaluating artistic excellence.

Most of us have good eyesight, so we believe we are good judges of an artist's skill in creating illusions of reality. To create such illusions, artists often reproduce every visual detail of a model, assuming that a convincingly real work is the sum of carefully observed and rendered parts. Sometimes this kind of artistic approach is called "photographic realism." However, the invention of photography made photographic realism almost obsolete. Yet recently it has made a phenomenal comeback: realism has enormous staying power.

The masters of the past knew how to create realistic illusions without reproducing everything the eye can see: the idea was to seize the essentials. Today, many artists see little reason to compete with the camera; for them the main problem of art is to create credible images through a selective use of the visual facts. Well, what are the right facts? And are they the same for every artist? Objective accuracy seems to require more than good eyesight (or a photographic projector) to be successful.

In this chapter we discuss the varieties of expression possible within a style of objective accuracy. We examine the different ways artists represent reality without reproducing all the details of an object or place. Also, we ask why some artists prefer accuracy of representation to abstraction or distortion. The style of objective accuracy rises and falls in popularity, but it appears to be a permanent way of expressing ideas and feelings. To discover those ideas and feelings we need to distinguish between the thoughtless imitation of optical facts and the use of accuracy to convey meanings beyond what we see.

THE IMITATION OF APPEARANCES

What accounts for our fascination with a painting or sculpture that looks exactly like its real-life model? Why do artists try to imitate precisely what the eye

**Duane Hanson. *Couple with Shopping Bags.*
1976. O. K. Harris Works of Art, New York**
Perhaps this is the ultimate in objective accuracy,
that is, realism without the artist's "personal" inter-
ference. But in his choice of people, their clothes,
and their accessories, Hanson *does* make a
statement.

sees or the camera records? These are fundamental questions, since so many
people believe accurate representation is the basis of art. Also, there is the
evidence of our earliest known art—Paleolithic cave painting: it is highly representational, beautifully accurate. Children, too, want to represent objects realistically, although they do not succeed at first. That is because they don't
understand adult notions of visual logic; but as they grow older, they *do* try to
imitate optical appearances. Accurate imitation, it seems, is part of coming to
terms with the world.

Psychologically, the imitation of reality represents an effort to control reality. At deep levels of awareness, our desire to paint a head so that it seems
alive is part of an effort to develop mastery over life itself. Drawing an object
over and over again creates confidence in our ability to know it or dominate it,
or to make it our own. We think we are less likely to be victims of chance in a
world we cannot understand if we make images that are good enough to replace pieces of reality—pieces of the world we must deal with.

For viewers, realistic works may be fascinating because of admiration for
the artist's skill. At another level, viewers are attracted by convincing imitations because they know they are looking at artistic effects—not *real* flesh,
leaves, cloth, and so on. For that reason many of us enjoy fool-the-eye paintings; we get a peculiar pleasure in being deceived. There are stories going
back to the ancient Greeks about artists who could paint grapes so faithfully
that even the birds picked at them. Perceptually, the appeal of a very lifelike
work relies on a peculiar tension between appearance and reality: we engage
in a continuous comparing or matching operation between what we see and
what we know.

Another kind of accuracy grows out of the interest in narration—telling
the viewer as clearly as possible what happened. From its beginning, art has

Grant Wood. *American Gothic*. 1930. The Art Institute of Chicago. Friends of American Art Collection

Otto Dix. *My Parents*. Kunstmuseum, Basel

played a role in transmitting information. Today, artists have been largely replaced by photojournalists as recorders of events; nevertheless, artists continue to work in a storytelling mode. For example, Andrew Wyeth (born 1917) employs a straightforward descriptive style to tell his stories about the lives of plain people and places. In *Christina's World,* for example, he pictures the lonely struggle of a physically handicapped woman. Through close attention to detail Wyeth establishes a mood of grim reality—plus hope. The tempera medium gives this picture a dry, matter-of-fact quality that heightens our awareness of Christina's hard existence. The selection and location of details are crucially important: notice the high horizon and the low position of Christina's figure: we see more of the earth than of the sky, and this connects her body closely to the ground; distances must seem tremendous in her groping world. Wyeth generates emotion through the skillful use of perspective—in the small, distant building and in the vast expanse of field between Christina and the house. It is not easy to paint a large area of unimportant material—grass—and keep it interesting to the viewer. Yet Wyeth manages to give the field a powerful psychological charge, mainly because of the tension between the woman and the house: we view the grass as space that has to be painfully crossed.

Americans tend to favor accurate, matter-of-fact descriptions of everyday life. This may have grown out of frontier suspicions of Old World culture; traditional civilizations were associated with corruption caused by the pursuit of luxury, whereas we were too young or too poor to be decadent. *American Gothic* by Grant Wood (1892–1942) hints at this idea in its celebration of the plain, simple virtues of rural life. The picture and its title constitute an ironic comment on the soaring complexity of real Gothic architecture. In the background we see a wood-frame dwelling in the so-called Carpenter Gothic style—our version of the illustrious European style ornately carved in stone. But the sardonic force of this work is based mainly on the faces of the farm couple: they are as plain as Gothic is fancy. Their simplicity is severe and slightly pathetic; but authentic, too.

Wood's homely couple might be compared with the double portrait *My Parents* by the German artist Otto Dix (1891–1969). At least, we see similar human types, but Dix is less photographic even though he creates an overwhelming impression of realism. He uses enlarged hands and deep wrinkles—the wrinkles are echoed in the clothing—to convey a feeling of struggle and awkwardness, a feeling that Europeans associate with the peasantry. Wood distorted his heads only slightly, to stress their oval shape (repeated in

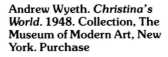

Andrew Wyeth. *Christina's World.* 1948. Collection, The Museum of Modern Art, New York. Purchase

the shape of the pitchfork), whereas Dix employed much more distortion and exaggeration—traits that are usually called Expressionist. Can we say, then, that this is a work of objective accuracy? Yes, because the narrative element, the reportorial details, and those highly believable faces dominate the painting. We are convinced that we are looking at the facts, the real facts.

THE ARTIST AS DETACHED OBSERVER

Another characteristic of objective accuracy is concealment of technique, as though the artist wanted to deny that a picture is made of paint or that a sculpture is made of clay: the final product must not show the marks of the artist's tools. This is because the artist wants to focus attention on the subject, not on the way the picture was put together. There is a certain modesty implied by this approach, artistic self-effacement for the sake of heightening the illusions created by the image. At one extreme, Soutine (page 26) deliberately reveals his brushstrokes; at the other, Charles Sheeler conceals them. Soutine expresses his own and his subject's anxiety; Sheeler uses a smooth, impersonal technique to create a "factual" image of an industrial subject.

Normally, a realistic style does not tell us much about the artist's personality. If we learn anything about the artist as an individual, it is through choice of theme or the overall organization of forms. There is something scientific in this approach: scientists, as we know, try to separate their private feelings from their observations. The hope is that other investigators will come to the same conclusions if they perform the same experiment and examine the same data. The artist-as-realist has a similar goal: his or her work must look true or valid regardless of the observer's personality. The artwork should appear to be almost anonymous, with only the signature revealing the author.

Perhaps the suppression of personality is due to the artist's wish to make vision, the act of seeing, the central fact in experiencing his work. In a sense, the Impressionists fit this description: they used scientific theories of color and optics; they concentrated more on appearances than on their feelings; their images look as if they had been suddenly captured by an impersonal eye.

In the Rouen Cathedral series of Claude Monet (1840–1926) we see a determined effort to represent the same building under different light conditions, according to a theory of color that was considered very "realistic"—that is, based on a foundation in color physics. So we can think of Impressionism as a style of objective accuracy; it was a disciplined endeavor to use scientific discoveries about color to depict objects in their actual atmospheric settings. The Impressionists realized that it is essential for artists to consider the atmosphere and illumination that enable them to see. That realization does not necessarily account for the beauty of their canvases, but it does indicate how scientific seeing—objective accuracy—can have important aesthetic consequences.

In the work of Edgar Degas (1834–1917), we see a style of rich Impressionist color combined with extreme faithfulness to the reality of objects. In *The Glass of Absinthe,* Degas seems to play the role of reporter, of detached observer of humanity: he lets us read the character of the two figures for ourselves. They are caught casually, toward the side of the picture, as if the artist were using a candid camera. As a matter of fact, Degas was influenced by the seemingly accidental compositions of photography; his pictures are designed to look as if their subjects had been suddenly discovered. As a result, Degas's ballet dancers, jockeys, and bathers look exceptionally truthful; we sense they are not theatrically staged. Henri de Toulouse-Lautrec (1864–1901) also employed a photographic sort of composition combined with psychological honesty. He used a similar diagonal device in his portrait *M. Boileau at the Café,* except that the main figure is more centrally located. To be sure, M. Boileau is not portrayed as drunk, depressed, or poor; on the contrary, he is alert, well-fed, and affluent—the solid embodiment of bourgeois self-satisfaction. Whether the subject is prosperous or down-and-out, the style of objective ac-

left: Claude Monet. *Cathedral in Sunshine.* 1894. The Louvre, Paris

right: Claude Monet. *Cathedral in Fog.* 1894. The Louvre, Paris

left: Edgar Degas. *The Glass of Absinthe*. 1876. The Louvre, Paris

right: Henri de Toulouse-Lautrec. *M. Boileau at the Café*. 1893. The Cleveland Museum of Art. Hinman B. Hurlbut Collection

curacy is neutral. Degas and Lautrec used Impressionist color, a compositional method borrowed from the Japanese, and a photographic way of seeing details. Their basic psychological stance was also similar: as detached observers of human behavior, they would not insinuate their own moral judgments. We might call them the radical empiricists of painting: artistic forms should be based on observation of the real world, regardless of how we feel and regardless of what we think we know.

For the detached observer, omission of the observed facts is a vice, a type of visual deceit, a form of artistic immorality. The Philadelphia painter Thomas Eakins (1884–1916) spent much of his career in an almost fanatical pursuit of visual truth—the sort of truth that results from scientific knowledge of what the artist sees. His students were taught human anatomy by dissecting cadavers; and in his own work he was determined to tell "the whole truth and nothing but..." This is clear in his portrayal of the unvarnished facts of surgical technique in *The Agnew Clinic*. Dr. Agnew was not happy with the picture; he was not especially pleased to be shown lecturing with blood on his hands. But Eakins was too stubborn to compromise the facts. He had been just as honest in portraying a blood-spattered surgeon and assistants in *The Gross Clinic*. Eakins insisted on telling everything, whereas those surgeons probably wanted a painting like Rembrandt's *Anatomy Lesson of Dr. Tulp*. There we see a respectful tribute to the pursuit of medical knowledge. To be sure, Rembrandt shows a cadaver, which is not a pretty subject, but he manages to focus our attention more on the searching mind than on the dead man's flesh.

THE ARTIST AS SELECTIVE EYE

An artistic concern with accuracy need not result in photographic realism. Often, illusions of reality can be created by simplification, by eliminating details the eye might see. Or there can be a piling up of more detail than would be visible at one time. This can happen when the artist becomes obsessed with a subject and has trouble leaving it; some artists embellish and enrich a surface

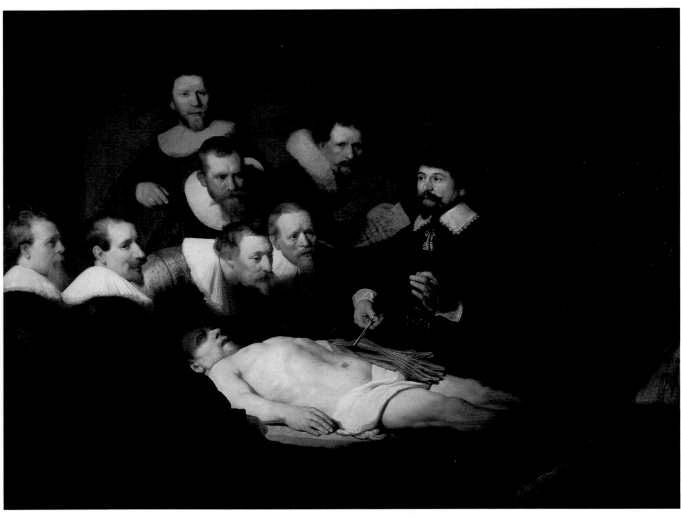

for years, selecting more and more, eliminating less and less: the image becomes a kind of visual storehouse. Ivan Albright's paintings are the result of long, patient accumulation of detail. Appropriately enough, he was chosen to paint the portrait for a film based on Oscar Wilde's *The Picture of Dorian Gray.* As in Wilde's story, Albright's painting grew old and ugly along with its subject. Viewers approach such highly detailed works with great seriousness; the evidence of long and sustained effort induces a special type of empathy. And the artist benefits from that empathy; we respect work, and our respect is converted into belief: Albright *has* to be telling the truth.

Edward Hopper is different; he simplifies while maintaining the strong feeling of a real place. *Nighthawks,* for example, is built out of quiet, uncomplicated areas of color and tone. The brushwork is hardly evident; instead, we sense the physical materials of the place. A mood of silence, of a great city asleep, is created by small inactive figures, crisp shadows thrown by artificial light, and the dominance of vertical and horizontal lines. Hopper is not a "tricky" or dextrous painter; he shows us just enough of a building or a person to permit identification; each area of the canvas is pruned of nonessentials. Like Wyeth, Hopper relies on placement and size relationships for psychological effect. As for his undramatic execution, it builds its own kind of quiet drama. Notice, too, that the mood of this painting depends on an abstract design: the intersection of two horizontal rectangles. But within those rectangles Hopper skillfully manipulates paint thicknesses to get variations of light and dark; it is paint that gives us the solidity of the place and the heaviness of the hour.

In Albright's *Into the World There Came a Soul Called Ida,* accumulated detail is used to describe the wear and tear of the aging process. We can also

Edward Hopper. *Nighthawks.* **1942. The Art Institute of Chicago. Friends of American Art Collection**

see that physical and psychological deterioration fascinate the artist. Almost pitilessly, he focuses on Ida's varicose veins, sagging skin, and the signs of her pathetic desire to reverse the effects of time and a hard life. But we may also sense the artist's compassion; Ida's face is shown in a tragic light, as she realizes that clothes, cosmetics, and hope cannot restore her youth. The buildup of homely detail seems to create a new organism, Ida, who is both painted surface and human document, a woman trapped by time, flesh, and the experience of defeat.

The portrait of Elsa Maxwell by René Bouché (1896–1963) employs a different kind of accuracy to express the drama of aging. Bouché views his subject from below her eye-level, which is not very flattering to a stout, elderly person. Also, the lighting is harsh and the woman's figure overfills the canvas. Finally, there is a nervous, comic quality about her expression. Yet, oddly, a peculiar kind of respect is earned by someone who is presented honestly, without heroics or beautification. The image of Ms. Maxwell reaches a level of human dignity despite—or because of—the fact that the artist presents her in a hard light, at a bad angle, in an uncomfortable position: she rises above her age and her features.

In sculpture, the Italian artist Giacomo Manzù (born 1908) offers us a refined sort of realism. It has roots in Renaissance classicism, and yet it appeals to modern tastes nourished on abstraction. *Girl in Chair* combines careful observation with an elimination of detail so subtle that it is hard to say where the figure has been simplified. Actually, the basic forms have been stripped of all but their most essential qualities of size and shape, yet the figure has extraordinary psychological presence. Even the chair has a curious perfection: its spare, open form provides just the right contrast to the roundness of the girl's figure. In choosing a subject who is neither child nor woman, Manzù faced a difficult challenge: he had to suggest the changing body and personality of a well-proportioned young girl without making her look like a dressmaker's dummy. His solution was to combine strict accuracy in the overall dimensions with slightly softened modeling in the subordinate forms. The result evokes a strong awareness of the figure's geometry and distribution of weight; Manzù approaches abstraction while keeping touch with observed reality.

Ivan Albright. *Into the World There Came a Soul Called Ida.* 1929–30. The Art Institute of Chicago. On permanent loan from the Collection of Mr. and Mrs. Ivan Albright

René Bouché. *Elsa Maxwell.* 1958–59. Collection Mrs. René Bouché, New York

Wilhelm Lehmbruck. *Seated Youth (the Friend).* 1917. National Gallery of Art, Washington, D.C. Andrew W. Mellon Purchase Fund

Giacomo Manzù. *Girl in Chair.* 1955. The Hirshhorn Museum and Sculpture Garden, Smithsonian Institution, Washington, D.C.

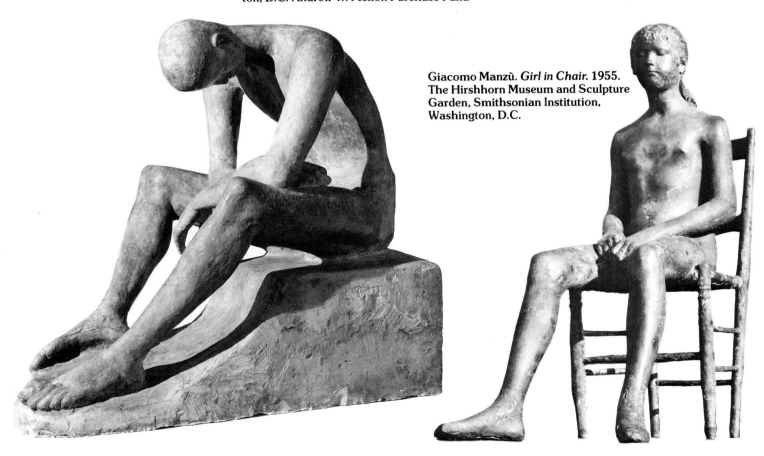

Manzù's pubescent girl might be compared with *Seated Youth* (*the Friend*) by Wilhelm Lehmbruck (1881–1919). Here, too, we see careful observation of the adolescent body together with simplification of surfaces. But Lehmbruck's figure expresses fatigue or despair, in contrast to the girl's more confident attitude. Also, Lehmbruck goes beyond objective accuracy in his elongation of forms. This stretching of the figure's normal dimensions conveys the idea of rapid growth—and the physical unease and psychological tension that adolescents often feel. The possibilities of emotional expression are heightened if the artist, when working in a realistic style, departs—even slightly—from complete physical accuracy.

Suppression of detail does not succeed, however, unless the artist has observed a subject very carefully. He or she must *know* that subject as well as see its surface characteristics. Otherwise, essential traits will be lost: the result will be simple and empty rather than simple and significant. An artwork is the end result of a long process of observation and simplification, whether in Albright's richly elaborated canvases or in the simplified surfaces of Manzù and Lehmbruck. But notice that in departing from the facts, Lehmbruck *created new facts;* his use of distortion represented a decision to sacrifice some visual accuracy in favor of heightened emotional appeal. Apparently, art involves trade-offs; it is a game played according to rules the artist recognizes. One of our tasks is to find out what those rules are; then we can decide how well the game has been played.

VARIATIONS OF THE STYLE

Merely by reporting what they see, artists reveal their individual viewpoints. For example, in his painting *Handball*, Ben Shahn uses a set of strangely separated figures to express his feelings about inner-city life. Those clumsy-look-

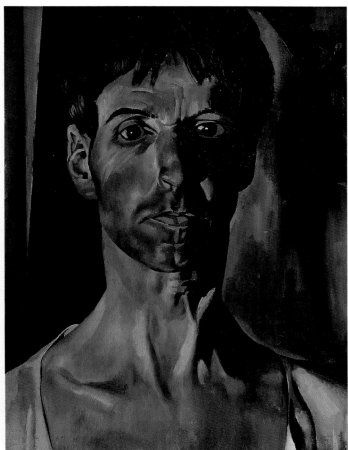

ing boys belong to a world that is totally different from Christina's. Yet both pictures employ isolated figures, and both show large areas of relatively uncluttered space. Shahn paints some urban detail around the edges of the canvas to establish the setting, just as Wyeth shows some farm buildings at the top of his canvas, silhouetted against the horizon. Also, like Wyeth, Shahn freezes the action of his characters. But Shahn's figures look rumpled and lumpy; their bodies lack Christina's peculiar grace. Awkward or not, they are trying to find excitement in exceedingly dreary surroundings. If Shahn's figures look pathetic, it is a general, collective pathos: they are infected by the sadness of their environment. Christina's tragedy is more personal because Wyeth has painted her as the victim of a misfortune that is hers alone. Shahn's realism is mainly devoted to the problems of people in the aggregate, whereas Wyeth concentrates on the drama of the individual.

What about the realistic examination of the self? John Kane's (1860–1934) *Self-Portrait* shows how an untrained artist looks at himself honestly and tries to tell the truth about what he has seen. Stripped to the waist and looking straight ahead, he paints his aging body as accurately as he can. The resulting image reveals a combination of pugnacity, pride in strength, and exceptional candor about the kind of man Kane is. Notice that the edges of the forms are hard and sharp; the modeling of flesh has been achieved with difficulty. Primitive artists tend to use rigid outlines to describe the world. Shadows are difficult, and they can rarely use masses of color and tone skillfully; that normally calls for art-school training. If Kane had wanted to gloss over the facts, he wouldn't have known how; it was a matter of pride to tell the truth, straight and plain. And that explains why we admire primitive imagery; the artist doesn't know any tricks, so he shows us people and places as they really are.

The art of Charles Sheeler (1883–1965) seems closely related to photography; he was, in fact, a distinguished photographer. However, in paintings like *Upper Deck*, the emphasis is on geometric purity of form rather than the real surfaces and edges of things. The machinery in this picture is immaculate-

Charles Sheeler. *Upper Deck.* **1929. Fogg Art Museum, Harvard University, Cambridge, Massachusetts. Purchase, Louise E. Bettens Fund**

The pristine whiteness of these motors and ducts expresses a kind of reverence for machinery.

William M. Harnett. *Old Models.* **1892. Museum of Fine Arts, Boston. Charles Henry Hayden Fund**

ly white, perfectly regular in shape, and without blemish or wear. Sheeler's work may look realistic, but it actually portrays a world in which age, noise, dirt, and confusion have been eliminated. Accurate representation combined with an almost photographic technique creates a very convincing result. However, it is an idealized result because accidents and variation—the effects of time and chance—have been eliminated.

Another type of realism, Magic Realism, falls within the style of objective accuracy. A good nineteenth-century example is *Old Models* by William M. Harnett (1848–1892). Such pictures re-create the retinal image of arranged objects—much like a photograph, but without the texture of paint on canvas. In addition, the arrangement of old or much-loved still-life objects provides a comfortable set of associations: the viewer is invited to enjoy little moments of philosophic contemplation in recognizing the relatedness of things, the beauty of common substances, the failure of art to capture reality completely. And there are the visual thrills of seeing painted nails driven into painted wood, painted letters on painted paper, and so on. The "magic" of this realism lies in the fact that our eyes can be deceived. A painter—a visual artist—forces us to question the reliability of vision itself.

Harnett and the "little masters" of seventeenth-century Holland (who were Magic Realists, too) may have anticipated Surrealism, which also relies on magical illusions. But the Surrealists preferred weird and uncanny juxtapositions of objects, using them to generate psychological shock and a retreat into the unconscious. Harnett, at most, wanted to challenge our faith in sense experience as the only guide to truth. But it is a comfortable sort of challenge; we come away from his paintings feeling fairly good about our optical equipment.

DEVICES OF OBJECTIVE ACCURACY

We have seen several examples of the ways in which artists create convincing representations of reality. Obviously, accuracy of size and shape relationships—"correct" drawing and modeling—are important. Mastery of representation can be learned, but not easily. Reasonably good accuracy can be achieved with the assistance of photographs, tracings, pantographs, and other reproduction devices. Commercial artists and illustrators often use such mechanical aids because they work against deadlines. But even a hand-copied photograph will show departures or omissions from the original; and those departures or omissions can be more interesting than an exact reproduction. It is the drawing "error," the result of the artist's personality, characteristic touch, or attitude, that generates *aesthetic* interest.

In addition to accurate size and shape relationships, the control of illumination helps create realistic images. The source of light, the amount of light an object receives, the shapes and edges of shadows, the transitions from light to dark—the artist learns to observe and control these things by skillful manipulation of his medium. Through the representation of light alone, objects and spaces can be modeled illusionistically. This applies to sculpture as well as to drawing and painting; from Michelangelo to Rodin, sculptors have studied light, attempting to control the way it falls over their forms.

Another device of the artist is focus: sharpness or softness, sameness or contrast, in contour and form. An elementary fact about optics—that objects lose distinctness at the periphery of our field of vision—becomes a tool for governing the spectator's attention. Other things being equal, our eyes are drawn to the center of the most distinctly represented form or object. If the edges of painted forms are softened or blurred, we tend to see them as farther away. In contour drawing, forms in the same plane can be made to advance or recede, depending on the "lose-and-find," "hard-and-soft," "light-and-dark" characteristics of the drawing line. Masters of drawing from Michelangelo (see page 258) to Picasso (see page 208) have used these focal properties of line to make forms seem to move back and forth in the visual field.

Auguste Rodin. Head of Eustache de St. Pierre (detail of *The Burghers of Calais*). 1886. Rodin Museum, Paris

Jacob Epstein. *Head of Joseph Conrad.* 1924–25. The Hirshhorn Museum and Sculpture Garden, Smithsonian Institution, Washington, D.C.

In sculpture, forms may be sharply raised or softly blended, thus controlling visual and psychological attention. The degree to which a form emerges into "full round" becomes a tool of artistic expressiveness. We saw a certain amount of soft focus in Manzù's *Girl in Chair* (page 133) and it appears again in Rodin's head of Eustache de St. Pierre. On the other hand, Jacob Epstein's portraits are sharply focused to heighten the sense of the subject's aliveness. The modeling is exaggerated—that is, the hollows of the eyes, cheeks, and mouth are deeper than in real life. Epstein's rough projections of clay catch the light and bring out the forms very sharply. That sharpness creates a kind of agitation, a sense of emotional activity, even in a head at rest. Compare this with the more melting forms of the Rodin head. Here we are aware of resignation, a slightly unfocused quality that is shared by the eyes. Even so, both heads are convincingly realistic.

Color, of course, is a powerful instrument of representation. Many painters try to create form by color alone; if line or light appears in their work, it is through the edges of color areas or in the sharp contrast between light and dark colors. Traditional painters used color mainly *to describe* objects, whose color varied according to the light they received, its source, and their location in space. Just as we know that focus grows less distinct as objects recede, we also know that color loses intensity as objects recede. Conversely, brightly colored forms seem to advance. So, if brilliance of color is combined with sharpness of focus we have a powerful device for attracting attention—defining forms so that they seem to be vividly and psychologically present.

An interesting variation. Many artists use color arbitrarily or emotively while combining it with precise, representational drawing. Even "realistic" artists exaggerate or invent color, but usually they remain faithful to the observed contours of forms. It seems that where color is concerned the artist has a kind of poetic license—a good deal of exaggeration is permitted. But there can be few if any deviations from optical truth in drawing. Again, we have to know what rules the artist wants to obey.

Perspective is probably the pictorial device most of us know about. It is a science that enables artists to create illusions of deep space on a flat surface through diminishing size relationships. The technical features of linear and

left: **Andrea Mantegna.** *The Lamentation.* **c. 1490–1500. Pinacoteca di Brera, Milan**

Extreme foreshortening in the Christ figure adds to the pathos of the scene. Notice that the crying women are shown in normal perspective, increasing the contrast between life and death.

right: **Édouard Manet.** *The Dead Christ with Angels.* **1864. The Metropolitan Museum of Art, New York. The H. O. Havemeyer Collection. Bequest of Mrs. H. O. Havemeyer, 1929**

Compared with the Mantegna, the foreshortening is less extreme: our eye-level is at the knees, not at the soles of the feet. Manet gets a ghastly, death-white quality from the flat lighting that seems to come from below.

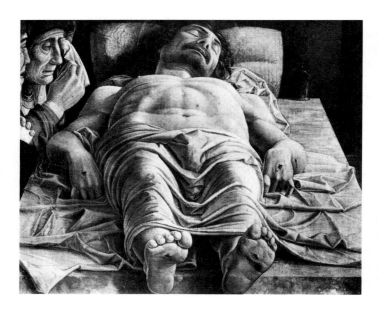

Chuck Close. *Susan*. 1971. Courtesy Pace Gallery, New York

The pursuit of realism by imitating the camera's one-eyed optic. Notice how Susan's ear and neck are ever so slightly out of focus, but we can see each crack in her lips and each pore in her skin. This is not really a picture of Susan: it's a picture of Chuck Close pretending to copy a *photograph* of Susan. There are other ways to reproduce that photograph, yet Close uses an old-fashioned technology: oil paint on canvas. Why?

aerial perspective—the perspective of shadows and reflections, of receding measured forms, of advancing or foreshortened forms, and of single- and multiple-point systems—are quite complex. But even a simple understanding of perspective makes it possible to simulate optical experience credibly. Modern painters, however, have questioned and then largely abandoned the simulation of deep space. The Surrealists used it very dramatically, mainly to create illusions of infinitely receding space, often as a symbol of timelessness. But in the Cubism of Picasso, Braque, and Gris, we see traditional perspective devices combined with anti-perspective, anti-illusionistic, devices. They probably wanted viewers to unlearn what they had learned to do since the Renaissance: read pictures as if they were vistas seen through an open window. Looking at pictures, they seem to say, is a matter of seeing flat surfaces covered with lines, colors, and shapes. And the textures of real materials such as cloth, newsprint, and pressed flowers. And the complex relationships among them. These artists employed a totally different logic, and objective accuracy had nothing to do with it.

Even so, it seems likely that artists will continue to use the devices that create illusions. Certainly, many of our modern masters—from Picasso to Matisse to Klee—possessed the skills for reporting visual experience accurately; and these skills served them well in their most abstract creations. But mastery of realistic techniques is not learned merely in order to discard them later, or to gain confidence, or to suffer. Accurate drawing teaches artists to see, that is, to *understand*, what they are looking at. Only then can they distinguish between surface copying, on the one hand, and knowledgeable representation, on the other. As for viewers, we benefit from the artist's struggle to see and represent. Also, we learn to compare the artist's rendering of reality with the world as we know it. The difference between the two holds many of the secrets of art.

MODERN FIGURATIVE MODES

above: **Morris Broderson.** *Good Morning, Starshine.* **1969. Collection Naomi Hirshhorn, Hollywood**

Using a soft, rubbed-pastel technique, Broderson combines accurate modeling with lush, exaggerated color. Notice the blues and violets in the shadows of the breasts and the glowing reds, oranges, and yellows in the flesh tones. The result is an eerie sort of sensuality—a strange mixture of terror and innocence.

opposite above: **Willem de Kooning.** *Two Women.* **1952. The Art Institute of Chicago**

Pastel again, but the intense color is more aggressively applied. The signs of artistic outrage are everywhere, especially in the treatment of the heads, hands, and feet.

opposite below left: **Philip Pearlstein.** *Two Seated Models.* **1968. Collection Mr. and Mrs. Gilbert Carpenter, Greensboro, North Carolina**

Accurate drawing and modeling combined with understated monochromatic color. Compare these two women with de Kooning's. In both pictures, faces, feet, and features have been arbitrarily cut off. But Pearlstein's almost photographic rendering produces a sense of anonymous, soulless flesh. De Kooning's multicolored torsos look much richer and juicier even though their owners' personalities have been destroyed.

opposite below right: **Chaim Soutine.** *The Madwoman.* **1920. The National Museum of Western Art, Tokyo. Presented by Mr. Tai Hayashi, 1960**

Loaded-brush technique can be used to express agitated or pathological states—in the subject or in the artist. Here twisted contours and convulsive brushwork enlist our sympathy for the subject.

141

Richard Lindner. *Hello*. 1966. The Harry N. Abrams Family Collection, New York

The pose, the clothing, the low angle of vision, the space-age rendering—all combine to create a fearful Amazonian creature.

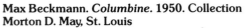

Max Beckmann. *Columbine*. 1950. Collection Morton D. May, St. Louis

Another antifeminine version of a woman, this time in circus costume. Both Beckmann and Lindner revert to a Stone Age fertility image—the so-called displayed or shameless woman motif. But why has this image been revived?

CHAPTER FIVE

THE STYLE OF FORMAL ORDER

The style of formal order is the expression of a preference for stability in art and, by implication, in the world. To the extent that Western civilization carries the imprint of classical Greek thought, formal order has been its constant ideal. The Greeks pursued it through measured form and proportion—through the expression of ideal mathematical relationships. For us, formal order means balance, harmony, and stability in art. It is another term for classicism—a classicism found in the art of many peoples.

The immediate source of proportions for order and hence of beauty was, for the Greeks, the nude human figure. They realized that what we call "beautiful" is the result of a harmonious set of relationships—or proportions—among the parts of any whole. The proportions of the human body are beautiful, they believed, because they reflect the fundamental order in the universe. The problem of the artist was to apply that universal order to the design of buildings, the writing of music, and the making of images. Major works of figurative art were rarely drawn from specific personalities; they were "idealized"—that is, they were based on mathematical averages of the best models the Greeks knew. Artistic creation becomes a search for ideal relationships among three factors: right size and shape, correct proportion, and perfect finish.

We in the West have not always followed the classical ideals of measure, moderation, and order. Periodically, we have been caught up in violent artistic convulsions. But even the Greeks gave way—during the Hellenistic period—to an art of impulsive actions and unstable forms. Our art, too, can be furiously violent as well as smooth and untroubled. Often, in the career of a single artist—Picasso, for instance—we see classical restraint combined with emotional extremes. Apparently, Nietzsche was correct in his division of culture into two principal strains, Apollonian and Dionysiac. The Apollonian strain expresses a dream of order and serenity; the Dionysiac strain expresses frenzy, the discharge of uncontrolled energies. In the past, one strain or the other dominated art; today, both exist side by side.

Because the openness of modern culture permits artists the totally unhampered expression of their Apollonian or Dionysiac impulses, formal order is not our only style of artistic expression. Neither does it represent the

Polyclitus. *Doryphorus (Spear Bearer).* **Roman copy after an original of c. 450–440** B.C. **National Museum, Naples**

Polyclitus designed his sculpture according to an ideal geometric formula, yet this figure looks completely natural. Why? Because of sensitive modeling and the rightness of the proportions underneath the surface.

Leonardo da Vinci. *Studio del Corpo Humano.* **c. 1492**

Leonardo tried to solve an incredibly difficult problem. He wanted to show that a well-proportioned human figure—in action or at rest—fits exactly into two perfect geometric figures: the circle and the square. This would prove that man and geometry, earth and heaven, are harmoniously connected.

taste of an artistic "establishment." Instead, it is the natural expression of artists who are almost instinctively drawn to stable forms and balanced composition; they seem to need a serene vision of the world. So in the West, at least, the style of formal order results from *personality* factors in the artist more than *political* factors in the culture.

Classicism, or formal order, can also be understood as a wish that the world were governed by reason and logic. From the evidence of art, we can see how deliberation and measure, calculation and the weighing of alternatives, overcome the spontaneous and explosive expression of feeling. We see Brancusi instead of Rodin, Mondrian instead of de Kooning. We see the artists planning, measuring, and refining—trying to organize their sensations and govern their emotions. For them, the great danger is loss of control.

THE TRANSIENT AND THE PERMANENT

If there is a single trait that characterizes the style of formal order, it is the search for forms that are permanent. When working with a dynamic subject, the artist emphasizes its steady, unwavering qualities. This means selecting positions where the figure looks stable, avoiding the suggestion that it is about to change. During the late nineteenth century, Rodin's *St. John the Baptist Preaching* was criticized for giving the impression of a figure walking off its pedestal. It was believed that sculpture should look immovable; it should stand still. Then, too, the French identify strongly with the classical tradition; a statue that "wants" to travel outside its assigned space violates that tradition. Psychologically, whatever carries the viewer's eye beyond the art object negates the idea of permanence. Classical artists tried to express the durability of an individual or an idea by stressing the fixed character of its form; viewers

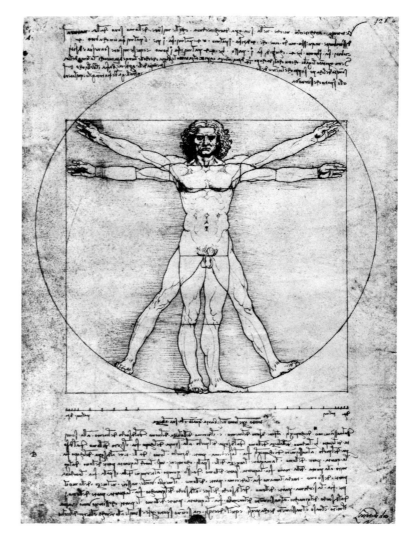

are supposed to feel that a monument has arrested the flow of time. Thus, art represents a victory over transience or change.

Academic art instruction was largely biased in favor of formal order. Students were taught to recognize the positions that give changing shapes a permanent, classical quality. Also, the act of drawing from a rigidly posed model had the effect of freezing movement; to hold a pose, the model had to get into a *balanced* position. The goal of this instruction was the creation of artworks that would look resistant to the forces of change and decay. In effect, the artist was asked to find what it is that can survive amid all the things—including ourselves—that must die.

Students of philosophy will recognize this approach to art as Platonic—the endeavor to know the permanent forms or ideas that lie behind the varied and transient examples of the things we see. The truly beautiful would be the imitation, not of surface appearances, but of ideal and unchanging essences. Such essences must be known intellectually before they can be imitated truthfully. Accordingly, artists must study things of the mind—mathematics (geometry) first and then the ideal dimensions and proportions of things. Only then should they attempt to imitate what the eye sees. This Platonic approach is still alive in art instruction, whether we realize it or not. Artists may also be drawn to it spontaneously: formal order is an emotional bias as well as a philosophic choice.

In *Church of the Minorites (II)* by Lyonel Feininger (1871–1956), we see the style of formal order employed by an artist under the influence of Cubism. In general, Feininger tried to impose the geometric order of crystals upon the visible world. Of course, architecture lends itself easily to this treatment; but Feininger exploited the same form language to represent organic or growing things—even people. Clearly, Cubism had created the breakthrough that Feininger used to express the clean, clear, and restful qualities of the chapel: the building and its world look like facets of a remarkable gem. In Feininger's work there is the implication that our universe has an underlying structure, a structure that is measured, ordered, and perhaps, divinely decreed.

We can see that in the hands of certain artists, formal order has religious implications. This is understandable, since the Greeks had an almost mystical view of mathematics; for them it possessed *divine* beauty, and art was the physical manifestation of the divinity of mathematics. Hence, the implication in Feininger's work that the universe is permanent and perfect is much like

Auguste Rodin. *St. John the Baptist Preaching.* 1878–80. Collection, The Museum of Modern Art, New York. Mrs. Simon Guggenheim Fund

left: Lyonel Feininger. *Church of the Minorites (II).* 1926. Walker Art Center, Minneapolis

right: Philip Johnson. Garden Grove Community Church, Garden Grove, California. 1980

Crystalline structures have been imagined in every time and place, but in our time they have actually been built. Structural steel and plate glass produce this remarkable union of technology and spiritual striving. The Greeks would have loved it.

145

saying that God exists, has created the order reflected in art, and wishes it to continue. That is what a theologian would say; Feininger's painting shows how an artist makes the same statement.

KINDS OF FORMAL ORDER

Although the style of formal order is associated with stability and permanence, there are many variations within the style—different ways of playing out its possibilities. I call these variations *intellectual order, biomorphic order,* and *aesthetic order*. They are not absolutely separate categories, but one or the other tends to dominate a given work or an artist's entire output.

Intellectual Order   Piet Mondrian may be the best known modern master of *intellectual* order. His *Composition with Red, Yellow, and Blue* has been created entirely with vertical and horizontal lines, with areas of unvarying color, and with no representational elements whatever. The elimination of curves, modeling, and subject matter forces us to examine his canvas solely in terms of its restricted formal vocabulary. Yet within this narrow range of pictorial language, Mondrian produces considerable variety—in the shape of the rectangles (their ratios of height to width), in the length of the lines, in the apparent "weight" of the colored areas, and in their spatial relationships. The interactions among the forms are quite complex, yet they are wholly intellectual. By reducing his vocabulary, Mondrian used the activity of the viewer's eye to create mental impressions of motion, opposition, balance, completeness, and rest. We interpret the elements of the design as weight, space, volume, energy, direction, and so on. But the order we experience is based on operations performed by the mind more than the imagination.

An earlier type of intellectual order appeared in Cubism, especially in the stage called Analytic Cubism (1910–12). Braque and Picasso worked together at this time; their work is so similar that it looks as if either one could have painted any given picture. This suggests that the same *intellectual method* of

Piet Mondrian. *Composition with Red, Yellow, and Blue.* **1921. Gemeente Museum, The Hague, The Netherlands**

146

analyzing form was used by both painters; artistic individuality was subordinated to the common requirements of reason or logic. In Braque's *Man with a Guitar* we see straight lines, a narrow range of color, and a figure sliced into geometric shapes. But notice that we learn nothing about the age, appearance, or personality of the subject; instead we see a quiet arrangement of geometric forms that seem to be floating in shallow space. The forms are denser toward the center and more loosely distributed around the edges. Apparently, we are dealing with an approach to the nature of matter—the expression of the idea that, fundamentally, all substances have a common structure. Both Braque and Picasso seem to be saying that the variations in the visible world are superficial; underneath, there is an order like that of physics or mathematics. Here again, the influence of Platonic thought is felt.

Cubism offered an analysis of form that artists could use in many media for various purposes. In sculpture, *The Horse* by Raymond Duchamp-Villon (1876–1918) looks like an attempt to translate an animal into mechanical parts, using the geometric format of Cubism. The painterly language of Cubism was extended by using forms taken from machines or the drawings of mechanical engineers. But, although the artist wants to visualize motion, the stability of classical order predominates. The process of analyzing an animal and reconstructing it along mechanical lines produces an essentially intellectual construct; this horse cannot eat, run, or breed: it exists for the pleasure of the mind.

Raymond Duchamp-Villon. *The Horse.* 1914. Collection, The Museum of Modern Art, New York. Van Gogh Purchase Fund

left: **Charles Demuth.** *My Egypt.* **1927. Whitney Museum of American Art, New York**

Geometry lends itself to a style of order or of emotion. In the Demuth, the forms have been stabilized, balanced, and adjusted to each other. In the Delaunay, they express surging energy—the opposite of balance and rest.

right: **Robert Delaunay.** *Eiffel Tower.* **1914. The Solomon R. Guggenheim Museum, New York**

Engineering and mechanization have been enormously fascinating to artists, whose reactions have ranged from enthusiastic approval to angry rejection. Classical artists, in general, see their ideals of rationality and clarity realized in the machine. Perhaps that is why they borrow mechanical engineering forms so often. But when these forms are employed in art, they also function as symbols. As symbols, they usually express a classical sense of order. That is clearly the meaning of the crisp, Euclidian shapes we see in *My Egypt* by Charles Demuth (1883–1935). But in the *Eiffel Tower* by Robert Delaunay (1885–1941), we see geometric forms in a state of partial disintegra-

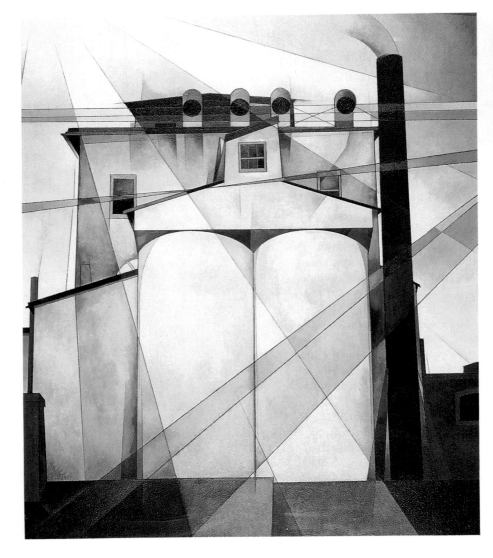

left: Constantin Brancusi. *Torso of a Young Man.* 1924. The Hirshhorn Museum and Sculpture Garden, Smithsonian Institution, Washington, D.C.

below: Jean Arp. *Human Concretion.* 1935. Collection, The Museum of Modern Art, New York. Gift of the Advisory Committee

tion; instead of resting, they seem to be exploding. This shows that the choice of geometric forms offers only a *clue* to the artist's intentions; it is the *organization* of forms that establishes a style.

In architecture, Mies van der Rohe may be our most noted apostle of formal order. As we have seen (page 80), his buildings are classically simple and severely intellectual. This may be due to the crucial importance he attached to absolute purity of surface and space; variations have to be regular and predictable. No matter how they were constructed, his buildings give no visual hint of hand or craft skills. What we see is a product of pure design—that is, of thought governing the organization of standardized parts. Like Mondrian, Mies restricted himself to a narrow vocabulary; he gave up the emotional associations of curving lines to create an intellectual order that, strangely enough, has an almost sensuous appeal.

Mies's style has been widely imitated because it fits so logically into a world of computers and machine technology. It has been equally well used for apartment houses, libraries, and college buildings; it reflects the classicist's search for permanent and unvarying form. Indeed, Mies said he wanted to create space that could be used for any purpose. So his buildings do not reflect differences in function or location. But that is a virtue from the standpoint of intellectual design: it illustrates the victory of architecture over the limitations of climate, handcraft, and tradition. It shows art transcending the personality of the artist. And the client. And the rest of us: we have to *fit into* these structures.

Biomorphic Order The term "biomorphic" designates forms that look as if they had developed in the same way that living organisms develop—through the subdivision of cells. An example can be seen in Jean Arp's *Human Concretion.* While some artists think of nature as chaotic, this artist found perfection

Henry Moore. *Family Group.*
1948–49. Collection, The Museum of Modern Art, New York.
A. Conger Goodyear Fund

left: Marcel Gromaire. *Nu, bras levé, sur fond gris et or.* 1957. Galerie Leandro, Geneva

Classical artists often feel the need to reach an understanding with machines. Here we see them trying to reconcile the forms of the human body with the precise, measured shapes created by engineers.

right: Oskar Schlemmer. *Abstract Figure.* 1962. Bronze copy after plaster original, 1921. Collection Frau Tut Schlemmer, Stuttgart

in the simplest forms of organic life. The material of this work is stone, yet Arp gave it a soft, fleshlike quality. The connection with the human may be remote, but the identification with living form is strong. Again, in *Torso of a Young Man* by Constantin Brancusi (1876–1957), biological and geometric forms meet in the same work. Brancusi was devoted to a kind of mathematical perfection of form, but he was also determined not to break the connection with organic life. His truncated cylinders stimulate memories of ancient art—the armless or headless figures unearthed in classical Greek ruins. At the same time, the trunk and thighs recall the African sculpture that so obviously influenced Cubism. So we have another classical idea: complex evocations achieved through the sensitive adjustment of simple forms.

Henry Moore, also a classical artist, creates sculpture which is less abstract than that of Arp or Brancusi. His family groups and reclining figures are monuments to human heroism and vital response, as in the bronze *Family Group.* Moore may stress the roundedness of human forms, yet we think of

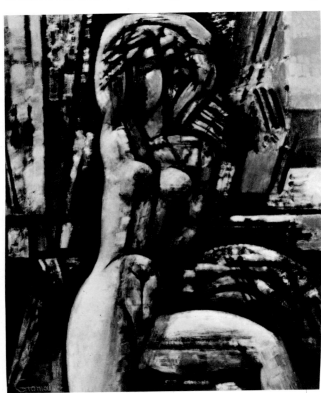

left: **Edward Weston. Photograph of halved artichoke. 1930**

The similarity between the forms here is no accident: both deal with "architecture"—the creation of protected space. The emotions generated by Lundy's church have the same source as those evoked by Weston's halved artichoke.

below left: **Victor Lundy. St. Paul's Lutheran Church, Sarasota, Florida. 1959**

Frank Lloyd Wright. Interior, The Solomon R. Guggenheim Museum, New York. 1959

his people as strong, not soft. This is because there is a virile sense of structure underneath Moore's smooth, curving surfaces; a dynamic system of thrusts and counterthrusts supports his massive bodies. Moore successfully solved the artistic problem of the human and the abstract—of monumental size and surface control, of rounded form and structural power. His work is one of the most powerful statements of the human capacity for regeneration made in the twentieth century.

In architectural construction, biomorphic order has received fresh energy from new materials and devices: collapsible domes with curved metal skins, concrete shells sprayed over inflated balloons, ribbed ceilings of almost botanical delicacy, paraboloid roof structures combined with daring suspension systems. The dome, which has always expressed biomorphic impulses, is a device that goes back to the Stone Age *tumulus*, or burial mound. Its shape is associated with our wish to live inside a womblike enclosure: either the grave mound, uniting us with Mother Earth, or the curved dome of the heavens, symbolizing a benevolent, maternal universe. All of these structures have more than engineering significance: they create an order that symbolizes the ultimate biological and religious meanings of existence.

Frank Lloyd Wright practiced what he called an "organic" philosophy of architecture—one in which buildings assert their kinship with nature through rugged materials, cavelike spaces, and natural forms. His Solomon R. Guggenheim Museum is actually based on the structure of a living creature—an enormous nautilus shell. The spiral form of that shell has both practical and

symbolic significance. It converts the life cycle of a snail into one continuous chamber for the display of art objects. The curved walls and gently descending ramps of the museum also resemble a glorious kind of parking garage that transforms motorists into devotees of a strange aesthetic religion. Because of Wright's museum, a real garage may look like a sort of automotive Guggenheim whose outer skin has been stripped away; it, too, becomes a gigantic concrete seashell, holding gasoline engines by Ford and Chrysler, instead of paintings by Kandinsky and Mondrian.

Aesthetic Order   Aesthetic order is seen in artworks of mainly sensuous appeal. The artist organizes and adjusts the various surface appeals of a work so that they give us pleasure—mainly in their shape, color, size, texture, and arrangement. Aesthetic order relies very little on the optical imitation of reality; it depends on an immediate sense of satisfaction. The simplest analogy is to our pleasure in the taste of food: the pleasure of taste does not mean something beyond itself; it does not look like something; it does not tell a story. It appeals to something within us—a sense of rightness—that responds with the emotion of delight. Perhaps there is an ideal organization of bodily energies—a type of internal balance or homeostasis—that is encouraged by works of aesthetic order. They produce feelings of gratification that seem valid in themselves.

In *The Breakfast Room* by Pierre Bonnard (1867–1947), for example, we see a symphony of color not unlike the symphony of tastes in a gourmet dinner. In addition, Bonnard weaves a tapestry of textures suggested only partly by the objects before him. The table, the window, the fragmented figure, the scene through the window—these are only barely established. They really constitute opportunities for the artist to play variations on yellow, yellow-green, yellow-orange, violet, blue-violet, and so on. Deep space is hardly suggested, and the drawing is incidental. Notice, too, that the color does not move back and forth in the picture space; instead, it shimmers on the surface of the canvas. Painters like Bonnard do not try to remind us of the real appearance of sky, fruit, or tableware: the material we are mainly aware of is paint. Bonnard is like his predecessors, Monet and Seurat; he communicates delight in paint and color, apart from what they represent.

Georges Braque, Picasso's early collaborator, directed their common intellectual style toward a sophisticated type of aesthetic order. His *Woman with a Mandolin* stresses the play of shapes, colors, and texture largely for the sake of painterly pleasure. Compared with Bonnard, Braque was a much stronger designer: his organization of shapes is more varied and inventive. And he had a deeper interest in textural variation, whereas Bonnard suppressed every texture in favor of a single one—paint. Braque also used paint additives like sand and ground eggshells to increase the tactile appeal of his surfaces. By exaggerating the wallpaper pattern and bringing it into the same plane as the figure, Braque implied that the sensuous qualities of the wall are more important than its "correct" location in space. Finally, notice that we learn very little about his subject: it functions largely as "stuff" the artist manipulates and rearranges for visual rather than cognitive purposes: seeing for seeing instead of seeing for knowing.

Perhaps the most elegant modern master of aesthetic order is Henri Matisse (1869–1954). His style was greatly enriched by the study of Persian art, which, like much of Middle Eastern art, emphasized opulence of color and decorative detail. So we see an almost oriental emphasis on splendor in the paintings of Matisse—a subordination of expressive meaning for the sake of a rich aesthetic surface. His *Lady in Blue* shows us a work in which the Persian tradition of flat form and luxuriant color is combined with the European tradition of deep space and figurative imagery. Matisse freely chose and discarded; he found what he needed in what was before him: the curving furniture, the rich gown, the flowing ruffles, the string of beads, the ripe features of the

opposite: Pierre Bonnard. *The Breakfast Room.* c. 1930–31. Collection, The Museum of Modern Art, New York. Given anonymously

Georges Braque. *Woman with a Mandolin.*
1937. Collection, The Museum of Modern Art,
New York. Mrs. Simon Guggenheim Fund

154   Henri Matisse. *Lady in Blue.* 1937. Collection
Mrs. John Wintersteen, Villanova, Pennsylvania

Harry Bertoia. **Screen for Manufacturers Hanover Trust Company, New York. 1954**

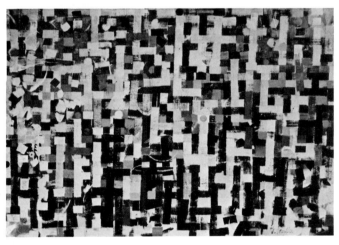

Bradley Walker Tomlin. *No. 10.* 1952–53. Munson-Williams-Proctor Institute, Utica, New York

woman's face, the bouquet of flowers framing her head, and fragments of classical drawings in the background. All of these elements are highly simplified; only shape has been taken from their total reality—shapes that were reassembled to create a new reality. Matisse subordinated everything to one pictorial effect that was meant to be pleasurable as a whole. To enjoy this work, therefore, we must try to see the entire canvas at once; if we let its shapes and colors *fill the eye*, their quantities and intensities will be felt as a kind of mutually reinforcing set of visual thrills.

An American sculptor, Harry Bertoia (1915–1978), designed a wall—a metal screen—that richly exploits the aesthetic relationships of brass, copper, and nickel. It serves as a partition and as a plane against which we see people going about their business in a bank. Because it functions architecturally, Bertoia wisely emphasized the abstract properties of the materials in the screen; symbolic and representational forms do not compete for the viewer's attention. The effect is quiet, orderly, and sensuous at the same time. As a result, there is a mutually enhancing relationship involving the wall, the people, and the space they use.

In the work of Bradley Walker Tomlin (1899–1953), we see a type of aesthetic order that has the qualities of a Bach fugue. Like Bertoia's wall, Tomlin's *No. 10* is totally abstract. We can see that it is a product of measurement, calculation, and simplification; yet there is a sense of freedom—even joy—about it. Works of this type generate feelings much like those we get from ancient

ABSTRACT MODES OF ORDER

Alexej von Jawlensky. *Still Life with Lamp*. 1913. Private collection. Hofheim/Taunus, West Germany

The objects are barely identified; the intense colors try to break loose. However, a strong linear framework holds everything together; color and line are in tension but under control.

Maurice Esteve. *Rebecca*. 1952. Musée National d'Art Moderne, Paris

We see the typical shape and size relationships of an early Cubist still life: smaller forms tightly positioned at the core; larger forms loosely distributed around the center. The colors become lighter and brighter as we move outward. Despite the wavy, emotional quality of the shapes, we sense that they obey an overall logic.

Greek art and architecture. But unlike the Greeks, modern classicists do not build on our associations with the human figure. They rely, instead, on our willingness to recognize the order and rationality of machines, or electronic circuits, or crystals seen through a microscope. Aesthetic order has become a search for the order beneath surface sensation; it seems that we are looking for the key that can make the excitement and confusion of modern life fit into a pattern. In addition to pleasure, we want reassurance.

Richard Diebenkorn. *Ocean Park, No. 22.* **1969. Poindexter Gallery, New York**

This is the sort of controlled abstraction in which the light, color, or shape of a place is lifted out of context, so that its qualities are felt while its identity is obscured.

Jules Olitski. *Magic Number.* **1967. Massachusetts Institute of Technology, Cambridge**

Olitski sets up a vast yellow arena whose dynamics could easily "run away" with the picture. Then he asserts his governance over the scene with some tonal modeling at the bottom of the yellow field, a hint of overlapping in the lower right corner, and a few color streaks along the edges of the canvas. We have formal order achieved with color and space and only a suggestion of shape.

Robert Delaunay. *Homage to Blériot.* **1914. Kunstsammlung, Basel**

Color theory began as a scientific idea and turned into an object—a wheel. Here the wheel becomes a bicycle, a spinning propeller, an airplane, a solar disk. Ultimately it is joined by man as bird, cosmic flyer, and, finally, Superbird.

Stanton Macdonald-Wright. *Abstraction on Spectrum (Organization, 5).* **1914. Des Moines Art Center, Des Moines, Iowa. Nathan Emory Coffin Memorial Collection**

The solar disk again, taken apart and reassembled to make a gorgeous color symphony—or Synchromy, as Wright called it. He was engaged in a daring attempt to put the emotional and symbolic properties of color under painterly control.

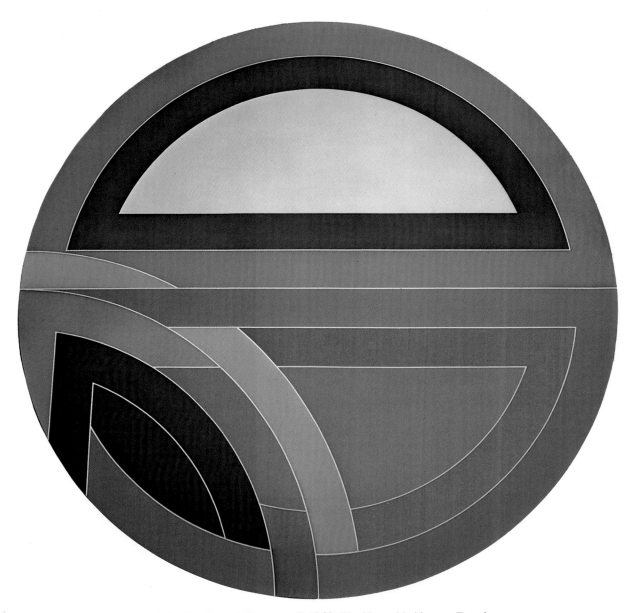

Frank Stella. *Sinjerli Variation I.* **1968. The Harry N. Abrams Family Collection, New York**

The sun disk in a new guise—a set of intersecting protractors. Stella is playing Wright's color-wheel game but according to different rules: painterly emotion is eliminated; color symbolism is gone. We now have precise shapes, perfectly even color, and neat white lines. Design wins over gusto.

André Derain. *London Bridge.* **1906. Collection, The Museum of Modern Art, New York. Gift of Mr. and Mrs. Charles Zadok**

Here color sensations begin to have an independent existence. We recognize the place and its objects, but we experience the sensuous quality of the scene through color alone.

Wassily Kandinsky. *Landscape with Houses.* **1909. Kunstmuseum der Stadt Düsseldorf**

Like Derain, Kandinsky was trying to attend to his sensations rather than to the structures of these buildings and trees.

Pierre Bonnard. *Nude in Bathtub.* **c. 1941–46. Museum of Art, Carnegie Institute, Pittsburgh. Acquired through the generosity of the Sarah Mellon Scaife family**

Bonnard goes further than Derain in separating color from drawing. Now space and shape are subordinated to the orchestration of surfaces with color and a rich mixture of textures.

Wassily Kandinsky. *Study for Composition No. 2.* **1910. The Solomon R. Guggenheim Museum, New York**

Increasingly, Kandinsky looked inward for inspiration. This composition seems to be based on memories of Russian legends and Slavic music. The sensuous force of color and shape is blended into a medley of folklore and mysticism.

161

Sam Francis. *Abstraction.* **1959. Whitney Museum of American Art, New York. Bequest of Udo M. Reinach**

We see color and space, but we feel emotions largely associated with tactility. Francis is a master of the semitransparent mark, the wet stain, the moving spot, the orchestrated splash and trickle.

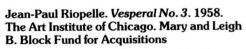

Jean-Paul Riopelle. *Vesperal No. 3.* **1958. The Art Institute of Chicago. Mary and Leigh B. Block Fund for Acquisitions**

Aside from its structural qualities, this paint surface seems edible: the palette-knife technique reminds us of thick slabs of butter and globs of strawberry jam spread on bread.

CONCLUSION

As we have seen, classical styles of art are closely associated with measurement and mathematics—especially geometry. But geometry is not the whole story. The essence of formal order lies in an *attitude* toward motion and rest: rest is good and motion is threatening. When dealing with moving forms, we want them to look measured and predictable. The same assertions could be made about life as well as art. For example, parents often judge their children by their patterns of motion: certain patterns mean trouble, others are reassuring. Apparently, we have learned a visual language of motion and rest, a language that feeds us information about how we should feel and think and act.

Extending this observation to art history, we find that certain social and political settings promote a preference for absolute stability in the visual arts. The art of Egypt and Byzantium, for example, placed a premium on immobility. Does this mean that these civilizations were neurotically obsessed with order? To be sure, they resisted change and managed to endure for at least a thousand years. On the other hand, the sheer durability of a state does not

Morris Louis. *Kaf*. 1959–60. Collection Kimiko and John G. Powers, New York

Through the management of fluid, overlapping stains on unprimed canvas, the characteristic mark of the brush—hence of the hand—is bypassed. We respond to a moist, multichrome mist, seemingly created by nature, not man.

Paul Jenkins. *Phenomena in Heavenly Way*. 1967. Collection Mr. and Mrs. Jack Stupp, Don Mills, Ontario

Wetter than the Louis work, this has more puddle and flow. As the hand and brush become more remote, we enter a world of hydrodynamic engineering made gorgeously visible.

mean that most of its people are living what we would regard as a good life. So, the style of formal order—especially when it is a prescribed style—can be an instrument of social control. Modern dictatorships, for example, almost always promote a trite sort of classicism, possibly because they base their power on society's need for discipline—a discipline imposed from above.

There are times in our lives when stability is what we want more than anything else. At other times, stability—in art or life—strikes us as painfully dull. But from the standpoint of society's health, the opportunity for nonformal styles to flourish alongside classical styles seems essential. For example, the hunger for American cultural products in Eastern European societies is a sign of the boredom and anxiety that a style of forced classicism creates in a population that desperately wants change. And when a stylistic reaction emerges—sooner or later—it takes an extreme form because it has been repressed for so long. The coexistence of opposite styles appears to be one of the best signs of a free society and a healthy culture; it tells us that our social and political institutions are functioning more or less properly.

CHAPTER SIX

THE STYLE OF EMOTION

The expression of feeling occurs so often in the visual arts that we can safely refer to a "style" of emotion. Often, an artist cannot speak in any other language. Van Gogh and Soutine were such artists: their pictures of people, trees, flowers, or even chairs seem to be bursting with passion. For them, what matters is not visual accuracy or the careful construction of an orderly universe; it is the communication of pity, anxiety, or rage; strong feeling takes precedence over everything else.

If we say that emotion is important to certain kinds of artists, do we mean the emotions they feel or their stimulation of emotion in others? It can be both. But as viewers, we are mainly concerned with the way artworks affect our feelings. Sometimes critics give the impression that an artist has in fact experienced the feelings his work arouses. That may or may not be true, but there is no way to find out for sure. Some people assume that aesthetic excellence depends on whether the artist truly felt the emotions we see in his or her work. However, the study of style should focus more on the art object than on the private life of the artist. In judging art it is better to ask: "Does this *work* make me believe in the world it represents?" "Are the emotions I feel based on what I see?" "Am I under the spell of the image or the artist's reputation?"

There is a vast literature about "emotion" and "expression" and "the expression of emotion in art." Here, we take the position that emotions are the *names* we give to neuromuscular reactions that have been triggered by the visual organization of an art object. The *energy* for these feelings comes from the viewer, but the *kinds of feelings* we have are due to the design of the work of art. Accordingly, emotions in art are caused by visual images, shaped and organized so they will *work within us*. Often, that "work" takes place at an unconscious, or precognitive, level.

Naturally, there are variations in the style of emotion. That is, artworks have the capacity to arouse a *range* of feelings and dispositions that are emotional but differ in their content; we can be elated by one work and depressed by another. Our emotional response may be caused by the subject matter of the work, or it may be due to the kind of aesthetic "signal" the work sends out. For example, an abstract work may have no apparent subject matter, yet it can affect our moods and attitudes. Something in its form and design must be responsible for these reactions. Consequently, we have to deal with *two*

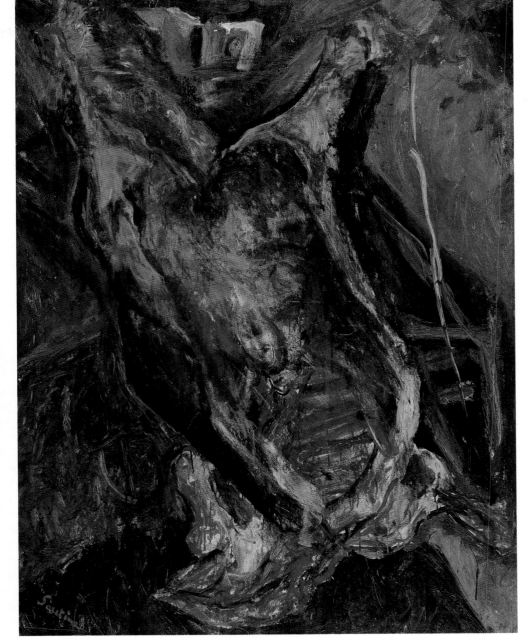

Chaim Soutine. *Side of Beef*. c. 1925. Albright-Knox Art Gallery, Buffalo, New York

Germaine Richier. *The Bat*. 1952. Whereabouts unknown

Henry Moore. *Falling Warrior*. 1955–56. The Hirshhorn Museum and Sculpture Garden, Smithsonian Institution, Washington, D.C.

sources of aesthetic emotion: thematic, or subject-matter, sources and organizational, or design, sources.

The style of emotion uses *any* means of arousing strong feelings, but its most stirring examples usually employ both theme *and* design. We see two examples in the *Side of Beef* by Chaim Soutine and *The Bat* by Germaine Richier. Both subjects are distasteful, and the organization of forms in each case reinforces our normal feelings of revulsion—feelings clustered around the ideas of pain, torn flesh, or the sight of a hideous creature. Henry Moore's *Falling Warrior* deals with killing, too, but its classic simplification of forms seems to purify the theme; we are not aware of any gory qualities. What we know about the subject does not interfere with a peculiar sense of order in the sculpture. The carcass by Soutine, on the other hand, forces us to think about the mutilation of what was once a living creature; it records the slaughter of a beast, not the death of a hero.

Richier's bat, with its webbed limbs radiating from a mammalian trunk, strikes a note of primeval terror because it stirs some instinctive fear in us. This creature bears a resemblance to the human, which arouses mixed emotions—emotions of recognition and dread. We experience disturbing feelings associated with the monstrous and unnatural. Those lumpy, stringy, perforated forms, combined with the symbolic associations of bats, mount a powerful assault on our feelings.

Themes of violence and mutilation, the inhuman and the nonhuman, are frequent features of the style of emotion, especially today. But here we are not concerned with deciding whether we like or dislike this kind of art; we examine it mainly to understand the roots of visual emotion and their connections to our world. If art reflects the times, it is worth attention whether we enjoy it or not. The style of emotion may stimulate us to ask what it is about modern life that leads to images of cruelty and terror. Or it may raise questions about where we find joy—and why.

ROMANTICISM AND EMOTION

As suggested above, the style of emotion often *discloses* an artist's deepest feelings. The attitude of emotional candor, of stressing highly personal reactions, is also called Romanticism. The Romantic tends to believe that the important

Henry E. Mattson. *Wings of the Morning*. 1936. The Metropolitan Museum of Art, New York. Arthur Hoppock Hearn Fund, 1937

Winslow Homer. *Northeaster*. 1895. The Metropolitan Museum of Art, New York. Gift of George A. Hearn, 1910

Paul Gauguin. *The Spirit of the Dead Watching.* 1892. Albright-Knox Art
Gallery, Buffalo, New York. A. Conger Goodyear Collection

Theodore J. Roszak. *Spectre of Kitty Hawk.*
1946–47. Collection, The Museum of Modern Art,
New York. Purchase

aspect of any person, place, or event is his or her feeling about it. The claims of fact seem less urgent since feelings *are* facts. Often, we speak of individuals "losing themselves" in an idea—something that is typical of Romantics. They may even lose their "sense of proportion," the commonsense idea of the rightness of things. For example, *Wings of the Morning* by Henry E. Mattson (1887–1971) makes us feel *drawn into* the sea. Briefly, we forget the difference between subject and object, between the observer and the observed. The ocean is not only a body of water but also a mysterious world in which we could somehow live. By contrast, Winslow Homer (1836–1910), who also painted the ocean—the same vast and powerful universe—portrayed the sea as a *separate* place.

Another trait of Romanticism is an interest in exotic places and dangerous experiences. Romantic artists have often been attracted to distant lands, as Paul Gauguin (1848–1903) was to Tahiti. Faraway places and strange customs can make us forget who we are and where we live; we can get lost imaginatively. Gauguin's *The Spirit of the Dead Watching* has this quality: Tahiti is an exotic place; its people live close to nature (certainly they are not like Parisians); and strange things can happen. Fantastic colors and flowers and a mysterious

Darrel Austin. *The Black Beast.* 1941. Smith College Museum of Art, Northampton, Massachusetts

inscription appear in this picture—"Manaò tupapau" ("The spirit of the dead remembers her"). The girl on the bed looks frightened and paralyzed; an atmosphere of occultism or supernaturalism hovers over the scene. Terror and beauty, innocence and demonism, are mixed in one image: this is the stuff of the Romantic imagination.

In contrast to Gauguin's exoticism, there is the dreamy, strangely threatening world of the American painter Darrel Austin (born 1907). His pictures illustrate the peculiar fascination that violence has for the Romantic imagination. In *The Black Beast* we see a fierce jungle cat with a dead bird under her paws. The animal seems to glow because Austin has illuminated her from below, or within, creating an unreal, phosphorescent effect. That eerie marsh landscape looks unreal, too—like a stage set rather than a jungle scene. Also, the paint surface is exceedingly active compared to the serenity of the cat in the moonlight. The Romantic emotions in this picture are generated by the juxtaposition of the majestic jungle beast with the frail, mangled bird. So the real subject of the work is the duality of nature: struggle and repose, violence and peace, victory and death.

We see another Romantic work in a sculpture by Theodore Roszak (1907–1981), *Spectre of Kitty Hawk*. Here the artist has invented a frightening creature based on the pterodactyl, an extinct flying reptile. Roszak created this monster using steel, bronze, and brass to suggest the mixed results of the invention of flight. But without the title and its reference to the Wright brothers at Kitty Hawk, would we understand this work? I think so. We would experience the same mixed emotions: the feeling of a predatory creature is

Théodore Géricault. *The Raft of the "Medusa."* 1818–19. The Louvre, Paris

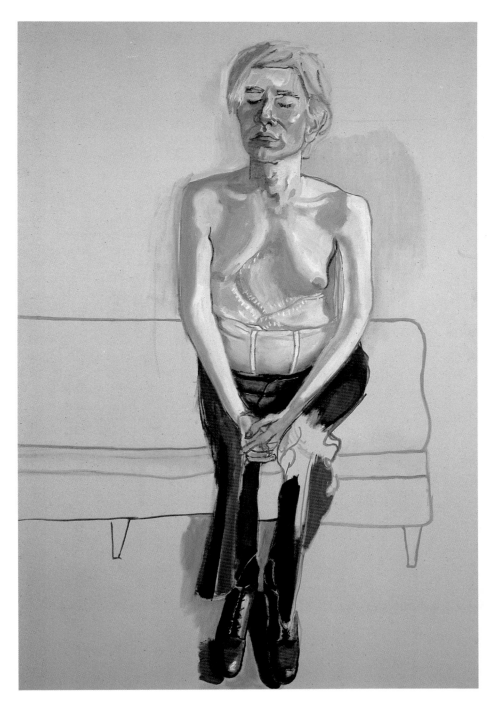

conveyed by the powerful head and claws: the wings, body, and tail suggest an airplane, perhaps after a crash. And there is the hard, hammered material of the sculpture, evoking the metallic glint of a terrible bird-machine.

Because Romantic artists deal with visual forms as well as psychological associations and literary symbols, they take large risks: they have to control a complex type of communication. The dangers of cheap sentimentality and easy emotion are very great. For these reasons, the works of Romantic masters such as Géricault and Delacroix may seem excessively melodramatic. Still, *The Raft of the "Medusa"* survives as a masterpiece. Why? Because of its powerful execution, its visual organization, and its magnificent display of the human figure. We may not know or care about the shipwreck that the work portrays, but the forms carry conviction even though the subject has been forgotten.

EMOTION GENERATED BY SYMBOLS

Jean Dubuffet. *Leader in a Parade Uniform.* **1945. Collection Mr. and Mrs. Morton Neumann, Chicago**

Dubuffet's imagery derives its emotion from a source that was ignored until the twentieth century: the art of children, primitives, and the insane.

Adolph Gottlieb. *Dialogue No. I.* **1960. Albright-Knox Art Gallery, Buffalo, New York. Gift of Seymour H. Knox**

Two immaculate disks float over a terrain filled with dirty splotches and wild writing. The painting symbolizes the world before and after it was civilized.

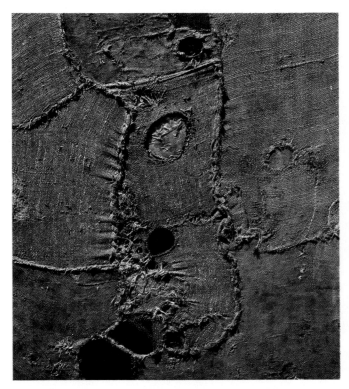

Alberto Burri. *Sacco B*. 1953. Collection the artist

An open wound is visible through a tear in a rotting and patched sackcloth cover; other holes are burned out, dead. Does biological survival—or civilized life—depend on a fabric so worn and makeshift?

Robert Motherwell. *Elegy to the Spanish Republic, No. XXXIV*. 1953–54. Albright-Knox Art Gallery, Buffalo, New York. Gift of Seymour H. Knox

In the background we see the bright, sunny colors of Spain. The melancholy forms in the foreground almost blot them out; they speak of death, of a maddened animal—a bull?—who will kill or be killed.

Arshile Gorky. *The Liver Is the Cock's Comb*. 1944. Albright-Knox Art Gallery, Buffalo, New York. Gift of Seymour H. Knox

These fowl shapes and bright colors seem to come from a cockfight—a maelstrom of claws, beaks, and feathers. We can also recognize hints of human sexual organs. Symbols of pain and pleasure, fighting and sex, living and dying, are mixed to create a beautiful/gory spectacle.

173

Pablo Picasso. *Night Fishing at Antibes.* **1939. Collection, The Museum of Modern Art, New York. Mrs. Simon Guggenheim Fund**

Two women casually watch the spear-killing of fish attracted to a boat by the light of the fishermen's lantern. It is a scene of rich color and dark irony: men are predators at work or play. The women—one executing a pirouette, the other holding her bike and eating a double ice-cream cone—enjoy the spectacle.

Richard Diebenkorn. *Man and Woman in a Large Room.* **1957. Hirshhorn Museum and Sculpture Garden, Smithsonian Institution, Washington, D.C.**

Empty windows, empty walls, empty faces, empty lives. Here shape, color, and perspective barely establish form and space; mainly, they operate as symbols of a physical and human vacuum.

THE ROLE OF DISTORTION

Distortion generates emotion because our feelings are quickly aroused by any departure from the "normal." This is especially true of the human body. But distortion of man-made objects also disturbs us; this is due to a tension between what we know and what we see. Distortion means stretching, twisting, displacing, or otherwise deforming the normal shapes and proportions of things. It also refers to exaggeration of size, color, or illumination; increased contrast between light and dark; or overstated textural and surface qualities. Sometimes distortion is intentional, but usually it is a spontaneous result of the artist's attitude toward a subject.

Because of personality or training, artists may emphasize or suppress certain features of objects; or they may choose to view objects when they look deformed. Even photographs seem to be distorted when their subjects are seen at peculiar times or from unusual angles of vision. But some artists use distortion for expressive purposes. Michelangelo is known for the tormented, writhing quality of his figures, especially for his famous *contrapposto*, an extreme twisting action through the shoulders, trunk, and pelvis. The apocalyptic feeling of *The Last Judgment* in the Sistine Chapel is due, in part, to his representation of faces, muscles, and bodies in tension. Through empathy—through bodily imitation of what we see—we feel those tensions physically and emotionally.

Distortion adds emotional power to an artist's statement: sardonic detachment in Lautrec; feverish anxiety in Munch and Soutine; extreme isolation in Giacometti. Van Gogh's distortion seems to project personal pain and mystical joy into everything he saw. Francis Bacon achieves a macabre, unsettling effect by suggesting that the mentality of savages and madmen lies beneath every civilized surface. But some distortion can be pleasant: the attenuated figures of Lehmbruck give adolescence a special harmony and grace. Modigliani's stretching and simplification of shapes result in a heightening of the figure's sensual qualities. Of course, these artists are basically classicists; when they distort it is mainly to *refine* forms; they make us linger on a contour because it is lovelier than anything we are likely to encounter in real life.

Jack Levine's *Welcome Home* employs distortion to arouse indignation: the longer we look, the angrier we get. The people in this scene are held up to ridicule and contempt; we see their bodies as containers of vice, especially pride, avarice, and gluttony. Levine tends to see social or political prominence joined with moral deformity. Given this mindset, he emphasizes the elegant table service, the obsequiousness of the waiter, the diners' fancy dress, and the sickly glamour of the scrawny woman, upper left, who is supposed to represent the "filthy rich." Noteworthy, too, is Levine's use of a distorting perspective to enlarge the heads; we view these people from above, and that lets us "look down" on them. This kind of satire calls for an artist with a large capacity for outrage. Levine fits the description; he loves the signs of grossness and corruption. For him, distortion is more than an artistic device: it is a physical weapon, a way to express loathing, and a means of enjoying one's disgust.

ANXIETY AND DESPAIR

In this century we have known several terrible wars, and we live with the possibility of extermination in another. So it is not surprising that our art shows symptoms of fear and anxiety. The style of emotion mirrors our periodic lapses into despair, our feelings of doubt that the world can ever settle its problems. Artists, like philosophers and theologians, continually try to explain what is happening to the human species. Some condemn the social or economic conditions that cause wars; others look for the roots of war in human nature itself. Also, many artists are fascinated by images of human pathology: they are peculiarly attracted to the ugliness of human nature, the corruption of our institutions, and the failures of civilization.

Distorted photograph of a man

The high-speed camera reveals distortions the naked eye cannot see. Or, sometimes, it creates distortions, as in this photo. In either case, we try to imitate internally what we see externally. That imitation produces emotion—in this case, queasiness.

Michelangelo. Detail of *The Last Judgment*. 1534–41. Sistine Chapel, The Vatican, Rome

In this self-portrait, Michelangelo wanted to express his personal misery and wretchedness. But notice that he used the same type of distortion we see in the high-speed photo above. Distortion can produce a wide range of feelings—from physical distress to spiritual anguish.

We have an eloquent tradition of artistic protest against war's inhumanity, from Goya's Disasters of War series of etchings to Picasso's *Guernica*. Beyond that, there is a despairing art related mainly to personal suffering—suffering without any apparent social connection. An example of this is *The Scream* by Edvard Munch. It shows a person on a bridge, hands held to the ears, mouth open in what looks like a drawn-out howl. We cannot tell whether the figure is male or female, and we do not know the reason for the scream. But there is something deathly about it, perhaps an anticipation of suicide. In the distance, we see two anonymous figures that symbolize the world's indifference to private tragedy. The drawing lines of the sky and harbor are very generalized; they force all the forms into "echoes" of the scream. Munch has used very simple artistic devices to describe what seemed to him one essential truth: all life is pain and suffering. His painting symbolizes all the invisible anguish of existence.

In the sculpture *Cain* by Lu Duble (1896–1970), the idea of personal torment is more explicit, more violent; we recognize the agony of a man who murdered his brother and fled from society. Cain's suffering is expressed by powerful diagonals that produce a frantic distortion in the head and out-thrust jaw. The held-back head and bared throat tell us that Cain is asking to be killed. This is the way a dancer might use his body to express guilt and absolute surrender; the figure becomes a vehicle for externalizing unbearable psychological pain. Biblical narrative is rarely subtle; it tells us the truth about our spiritual condition in black and white, but with very few grays. And that is what Lu Duble has given us in her sculpture—an image appropriate to the moral scale of the Bible.

Study for a Head by Francis Bacon (born 1909) presents the image of a person who seems to be mad or turning into a beast. Whereas the cry in the painting by Munch suggests human isolation and suffering, this scream declares that we "civilized" men and women are savages. Bacon portrays a well-

Jack Levine. *Welcome Home*. 1946. The Brooklyn Museum. John B. Woodward Memorial Fund
To create satire, indignation is not enough: acute observation and hostile analysis are also required.

Edvard Munch. *The Scream*. 1893. National Gallery, Oslo

Lu Duble. *Cain*. 1953. Whitney Museum
of American Art, New York

Chris Steele-Perkins. Photograph of poster: José Napoleón Duarte, President of Salvador. 1984

Aesthetic emotion originates in real-life situations. In this defaced poster we can see several devices that are deliberately used by Abstract Expressionist painters: the splash, the smear, paint runs, and paint spatters. The paint-drips on Duarte's lapel are especially ominous because they look like bloodstains.

dressed man sitting in a chair, but instead of giving us a character study, he stresses the connection between man and wild animal. Naturally, this is a disturbing image. Does it tell the truth about our species, about the human condition? Well, in this century men have been more cruel than any animal could be. Not surprisingly, Bacon's style has been exceedingly influential. An American painter, Hiram Williams (born 1917), was clearly attracted by Bacon's imagery. The blurred features of his one-eyed *Guilty Men*, combined with their neat business suits, produce the same suggestion of the monstrous that we see in Bacon's work. Both artists employ distortion and human-animal fantasy to upset any comfortable notions we may have about how much we have risen above savagery.

Rico Lebrun (1900–1964) in *Migration to Nowhere* deals with war by making a macabre dance out of the flight of its crippled victims. Through distorted perspective he has enlarged the feet of the figures to dramatize the idea of flight. The vacant horizon symbolizes their hopelessness, the slim chance of escape. Notice, too, that the figures seem to lose their corporeality as they recede into the distance. Yet there is a curious grace in their movement, in their billowing garments, in their use of crutches with the skill of players in a horrible game. Ironically, Lebrun's imagination makes a desperate situation bearable by invoking the agility of the maimed. Bacon, on the other hand, finds nothing redeeming in the image of man: under the well-tailored suit, he is a mad dog.

A subject similar to Lebrun's is treated by Ben Shahn in *Liberation*. Here the figures are deliberately awkward; they look maimed but they aren't; this is an instance of Shahn's ability to find expressive distortion in the freeze-action of photographic imagery. Lebrun's figures, on the other hand, look graceful even though they are crippled. Irony is a major quality in Shahn's work: the children are obviously undernourished; they look for fun in a bombed-out environment; they have to find playthings in rubble. Just as Lebrun found grace in deformity, Shahn found aesthetic interest in the texture of the sky, the tilt of the building, and the coarse rendering of the rubble. The drawing of the children stresses hunger and emaciation, but if we examine their silhouettes, noticing especially the foreshortened, almost spastic, legs, we sense the full horror of broken bodies and broken cities.

Europe's recurrent wars and postwar agonies have produced the type of artistic anxiety that pervades the work of Oskar Kokoschka (1886–1980). In his *Self-Portrait* he employed the typical distortions of Expressionist art: over-sized eyes and hand; a gaunt, bony head illuminated by flickering light and jagged shadows; and a facial expression hovering between profound sadness and deep-seated guilt. The hand seems to accuse the artist, but the mouth cannot speak, cannot say what it is that eats at this man. The restless contours of his face heighten the central idea of the work—that here is a man who can find no forgiveness.

Compared with Bacon, Kokoschka expresses the theme of modern anxiety without surrendering our essential humanity; at least his subject can feel responsibility and guilt. But it would be difficult to attribute such feelings to Bacon's man: an animal is *amoral*; it does not understand guilt. Kokoschka's portrait dates from before World War I, whereas Bacon's picture was painted

left: Francis Bacon. *Study for a Head.* 1952. Private collection

right: Hiram Williams. *Guilty Men.* 1958. Collection Mr. and Mrs. Dalton Trumbo, Los Angeles

Rico Lebrun. *Migration to Nowhere.* 1941. Whereabouts unknown

Ben Shahn. *Liberation.* 1945. Collection, The Museum of Modern Art, New York. James Thrall Soby Bequest

Oskar Kokoschka. *Self-Portrait.* 1913.
Collection, The Museum of Modern Art,
New York. Purchase

in the 1950s. So, on the evidence of these two works, there has been considerable moral deterioration in our time. Of course, this evidence is incomplete; it
may only reflect the opinions of two atypical observers. Does it suggest that
our art must deal with humanity in terms of pain and remorse? Can we find
any aesthetic evidence of gladness or hope?

JOY AND CELEBRATION

Strangely, the same style that expresses anxiety can be used to express joy. As
in drama, there is in art a very fine line between tragedy and comedy. Indeed,
the genius of a comedian like Chaplin lay in the fact that his acting came close
to tragedy, although he appeared to be working for laughs. It seems that celebration in art is related to the tragic *and* the comic spirit; we cry and laugh
during life's exultant moments. Like drama, art can express joy because it

Max Weber. *Hassidic Dance*. 1940. Collection
Mr. and Mrs. Milton Lowenthal, New York

John Marin. *Maine Islands*. 1922. The Phillips
Collection, Washington, D.C.

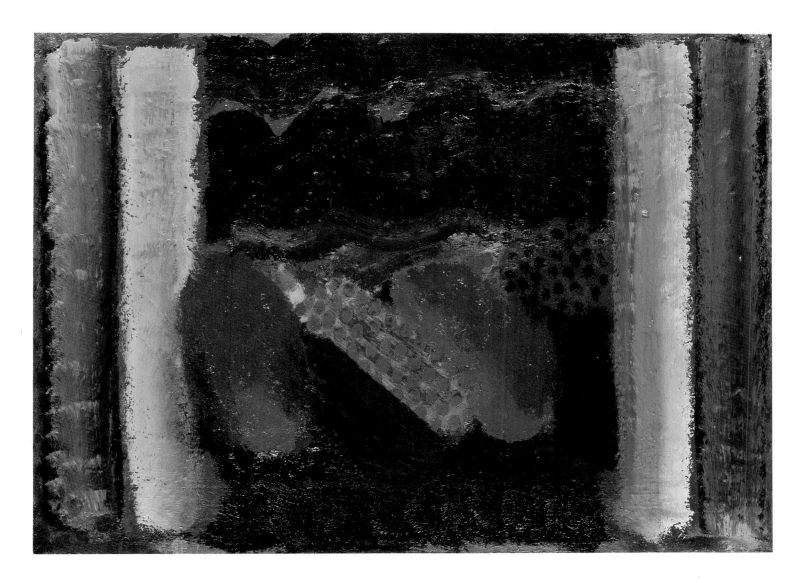

knows about sorrow; it can affirm the goodness of being alive because it has seen how life can be taken away.

We can recognize the connection between comedy and celebration in *Hassidic Dance* by Max Weber (1881–1961). Here the members of a mystical Jewish sect sing and dance to express feelings of exaltation in the created universe; their dance is ecstatic, joyous, and reverent at the same time. The men wear high hats and long, almost funereal garments while dancing in a spirit of what is, for them, complete abandon. The effect is slightly comic, but they don't seem to care: they are worshiping God and that makes them happy. The appeal of this work depends on a set of comic contrasts; awkward men are trying to be graceful; dignified garments are getting tangled up; those high hats may fall off. But the passion of these men makes them indifferent to worldly concerns; what matters is that miracles take place all the time.

From another standpoint and using a different technique, John Marin (1870–1953) expresses joy in the freshness and continuous renewal of nature. Working mainly in watercolor, Marin painted scenes that are alive with energy and movement. With a few slashing watercolor strokes, he can suggest the whole panorama of nature: sky, sun, air, water, and mountains. His style—based on Cubism but not as heavily intellectual—was highly personal; he used an abbreviated, straight-line technique derived ultimately from the carefully hatched planes of Cézanne. But Marin's approach is exceptionally vigorous and slapdash. The generous use of white paper and a fast, wet brush give

Howard Hodgkin. *Day Dreams*. 1977–80. Private collection, London. Courtesy Whitechapel Art Gallery, London

Using rhythmic abstract shapes and large, soft areas of color, Hodgkin manages to convey powerfully erotic feelings. Yet there are no figurative forms—only the chromatic richness and texture of paint, hints of pillows and bedcovers, and a window opening out to the night.

his pictures genuine sparkle and brilliance. This is a happy world: Marin may even paint a few sun rays the way children do. His universe is untroubled, full of radiant energy and growing things: its color and motion and noise are friendly to our species.

To some of us, Marc Chagall's paintings may look naive because of their childlike belief in the power of love—its capacity to remove anyone beyond the "here" and the "now." In *Flying over the Town* a young couple floats above a village as if in a dream; but their eyes are open and the village is real. Chagall pictured the beliefs of childhood: that gravity can be canceled; that love transcends physical facts; that the world is mostly illusion and enchantment. He was a joyous artist completely devoted to the ideals of romantic love: its erotic aspects hardly exist. If he portrayed a female nude, there was no suggestion of physical desire—by her or for her. Just love. Chagall's men and women seem to have been conceived by the minds of children. For that reason, perhaps, love is a weightless sort of joy—a joy so pure that it can liberate us from our rootedness in the earth.

Can architecture express joy? Not easily, since a building must solve the problems of gravity and stability before anything else. Yet the Los Manantiales Restaurant by Ordóñez and Candela has a happy, festive air. Its main engineering device—thin-shell concrete in the form of hyperbolic curves resting on a circular plan—brilliantly solves the problem of structure and expression. The

Marc Chagall. *Flying over the Town.* **1914. Collection Mrs. Mark C. Steinberg, St. Louis**

Joaquín Alvares Ordoñez (architect) and Félix Candela (structural designer). Los Manantiales Restaurant, Xochimilco, Mexico. 1958

Using a circular plan on a masonry base and repeated inverted arches, the General Time Building is emotionally similar to Ordoñez and Candela's building. But the structural devices are entirely different. The common denominator is poured, reinforced concrete, a material that turns architects into sculptors.

Victor Bisharat/James A. Evans and Associates. General Time Building (now occupied by States Marine Line, Inc.), Stamford, Connecticut. 1968

shell structure acts as roof, side wall, and window opening simultaneously; its visual effect suggests the delicacy of curved paper, yet the shell is very strong. To contrast with those wavy shapes, the designers used a rugged masonry foundation and wide, gentle steps; they created a horizontal base for the soaring overhead forms, giving us a feeling of lift and solid support at the same time.

Our pleasure in this building is something like our joy in a great cathedral: we get a thrill from spaces and structures that seem to exceed the limits of human ingenuity. Those curves send signals that can also be found in nature—in leaves and petals or in seashells and ocean waves—but rarely in man-made forms. In architecture, we seldom see mathematical rhythms carried out with the feelings of a frolic. Again, an almost comic idea is connected to the sense of joy: complex calculations have been invested in fun—serious fun. Inert materials have been organized to build a roof that sings but also keeps the rain out. So we get lightness, elegance, and gaiety—something to shout about.

CHAPTER SEVEN

THE STYLE OF FANTASY

As artists manipulate materials, they discover they can invent new forms—forms that have never been seen before. Whereas some will not let their work stray from what looks logical or probable, others enjoy creating strange new worlds. And most artists have the skill to make such worlds seem real. Often, these imaginary creations reflect an artist's determination to change the rules of reality. Such artists create fantastic new forms, or they *let fantastic forms happen*, regarding themselves as instruments that cooperate with universal processes of creation.

Everything in the man-made world almost certainly originated in someone's fantastic imagination. Architects probably imagine new shapes and spaces before they think of any practical purpose for them. Even engineers must have moments when they want to build impossible structures, or possible structures that no one needs. Painters and sculptors, more liberated from practical necessity, are in a better position to pursue their intuitions and visions of form. The important point is that fantasy—the imagination of unreal objects, places, and events—is a universal human trait, and art is its principal outlet.

But if our realities were once fantasies, not all fantasies become realities. Chagall's people flying through the air are fantastic, but they do not anticipate general diffusion of the gift of levitation. (That may happen, but not because of Chagall's paintings.) However, some artistic fantasies have utopian implications: the architect who imagines an ideal city may, someday, cause that dream to become real. As we know, several major architects have proposed utopian structures and communities—fantastic solutions to the problems of social living. City and regional planning might be regarded as the professionalization of our tendency to imagine utopias. Certainly, many of the architectural fantasies of the 1920s and 1930s have become living facts. And today, planning for communities in outer space is beginning to seem quite practical. So private dreams *can* become public realities.

Apart from physical communities, some utopian fantasies deal with personal and social relations. A painting by Edward Hicks (1790–1849), *Peaceable Kingdom*, is based on the Biblical prophecy of a world in which natural enemies live together without conflict, and men (exemplified by William Penn and the Indians in the background) can settle their affairs harmoniously. Why is this painting a fantasy? Because the world it portrays is not the one we

Edward Hicks. *Peaceable Kingdom.* **c. 1848. Philadelphia Museum of Art. Bequest of Lisa Norris Elkins**

Master Gislebertus. Detail of *The Last Judgment.* c. 1130. From the west tympanum, Cathedral of Autun, France

Judgment—who goes to heaven and who goes to hell. The weighing of the souls of the saved and the damned becomes the focus of a struggle between amazingly tall angels and fantastically ugly devils. Notice that the naked souls, waiting to be judged, have fairly naturalistic proportions. It is the angels and demons who are deformed.

live in. The world Hicks painted may be unreal, but the ideal it embodies is real. And, as we have seen, ideals have a way of becoming facts.

Fantastic art originates in both logical and irrational mental processes; accordingly, it has no common set of visual traits. Fantastic artworks may be objectively accurate or subjectively distorted. We can speak of a fantastic *style*, then, only because certain works exhibit a logic based on dreams, utopian hopes, or visual speculation. Of course, the visions of a trained mind may have practical potential. For that reason we can discuss fantastic art in relation to science as well as to myth. So far as art is concerned, science and myth are equally useful sources of imagery. Artists use all kinds of material: the magic of the shaman, the prophecies of wise men, the hopes of religion, and the claims of science.

MYTH

As children we were told stories or fables that we usually accepted without question: they seemed to explain the world in a way that satisfied our curiosity. With greater sophistication, we realized later that these myths were not true. They were entertaining as fiction, but they were not reliable as accounts of history or as accurate explanations of the way the world really works. Still, we could not entirely abandon those early fables: they were converted into folk wisdom and ultimately enshrined in our mental lives in the form of unexamined beliefs and convictions. Officially, we may think of myths and fairy tales as the fantastic entertainments of a stage we have left behind us. But have we?

When an artist like Jean Cocteau presents a fairy tale in a film, our adult sophistication receives a shock: the story is strangely believable; apparently the myth lives on within us. Folktales have the power to stir our deepest selves long after we think we are immune to superstition. In the work of the Swedish film director Ingmar Bergman (born 1918), we usually witness a conflict between the scientific, rational mind and the mythic, poetic, or religious mind. Often, he shows how both tendencies exist in the same person, as in *The Magician*, where a physician succumbs to fantastic fears—fears he thought were overcome by his scientific training.

Why do myths have the power to compel our belief? It is not that they are true in the sense in which science defines truth, but myths establish convincing connections with the way our minds grasp reality. We are not wholly rational, not completely evolved from our primitive psychological selves. In a sense, myths *are* truthful—truthful accounts of the way we have seen ourselves and the world for most of our life on earth. Accordingly, they explain a great deal about the way we think and feel. For the artist this is important: even seeing has a mythic component.

In visual art, as in life, mythmaking goes on continually. The visual arts use plastic fantasy—the creation of strange forms, or strange combinations of known forms. These may be initially suggested by accidental technical effects, as in the "planned accidents" of Max Ernst. Many artists rely on unconscious suggestion—hidden, mysterious sources of form. Some believe that relatively uncontrolled creation will connect their work with the mythic roots of human personality. So, surrendering to fantasy is not an abandonment of truth; it is a way of gaining access to *a special type of truth*—a type that our culture does not value highly but that nevertheless explains much of our behavior.

A well-known fantastic painting that shows the mythic imagination at work is *Hide-and-Seek* by Pavel Tchelitchew (1898–1957). It simultaneously pictures a tree, a hand, a foot, a system of nerves and blood vessels, and then, embryos, babies, and young children. Everywhere we look, passages of wet, flowing color merge with forms of biological life. The blood vessels look like illustrations for a medical text on anatomy; tiny lights beautifully illuminate the rendering of an ear or the place where the veins of a leaf merge with the fine capillaries feeding a human fetus.

Film still from *The Magician*. Directed by Ingmar Bergman. 1958. Courtesy Janus Films, Inc.
A physician, proud of his scientific knowledge, is driven close to madness by a magician using tricks and illusions. But we, as viewers, are not sure those tricks *are* tricks: the magician seems to have supernatural powers.

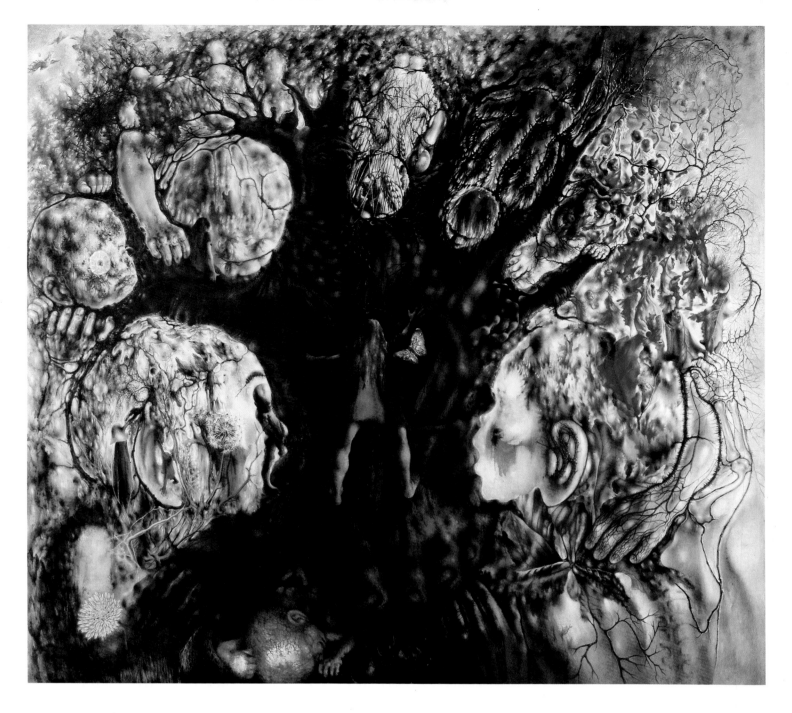

Pavel Tchelitchew. *Hide-and-Seek*. 1940–42. Collection, The Museum of Modern Art, New York. Mrs. Simon Guggenheim Fund

Of course, children do not grow on trees, and the similarity between a hand and a tree is superficial. But for the mythic imagination, things that look alike are aspects of the same reality. Remember, too, that men once worshiped trees, and children are the "fruit" of our bodies; arteries and nervous systems *do* branch out like the limbs of a tree, the fingers of a hand, or the tendons of a foot. However, the painting by Tchelitchew is not a treatise on physiology; it shows how the primitive portion of our human personality confronts themes such as the life of the unborn, the drama of nourishment, the connection between plants and human beings, the tension between consciousness and unconsciousness, the teeming activity beneath the shell of a living thing.

DREAMS AND HALLUCINATIONS

Dreams are further examples of the connection between fantasy and the real world. They seem to lack logical organization after we wake, but while we sleep they look very real, sometimes frighteningly real. Accordingly, artists may employ dream material to get a grip on the viewer's unconscious processes or to shock viewers out of their customary ways of seeing. Often, realistic modes of representation are used, but we see images that remind us of hallucinations, images similar to those caused by a high fever or by drunkenness. Surrealism is the major example of such art. As an organized movement embracing art, music, and poetry, Surrealism may be dead, but as an artistic influence it is very much alive.

We can easily see how an artistic approach that relies on dreams and accidents would encounter resistance from those who think of art as a planned, reasoned approach to creation. However, even the most rational artistic strategy employs some kind of intuition, some reliance on sources of imagery hidden mysteriously in the self. Otherwise, if art were simply a matter of applying known principles to known objectives, artists could be replaced by computers. To be sure, computers are wonderful tools, but so far as I know, they do not dream.

For their interest in dreams, the Surrealists were, of course, indebted to Sigmund Freud. They learned from Freud that dreams are only *seemingly* illogical, that they have important meanings if certain principles of interpretation are known. Not that Surrealist paintings are collections of symbols that require a key—a dictionary of symbols—for interpretation. But they do employ fantastic juxtapositions of images—combinations more like those seen in dreams than in waking life. In Surrealist theory, shock has educative value; it causes viewers to reorganize their habits of perception. Why reorganize our habits of perception? Because—according to the Surrealists—we are hopelessly enmeshed in wrong ways of thinking.

In Salvador Dali's (born 1904) *Soft Construction with Boiled Beans: Premonition of Civil War* we see a highly realistic technique combined with a strangely mutilated and distorted human figure. Employing strong contrasts of light and shadow plus careful modeling, Dali skillfully enhanced the illusion that his fantastic forms are real. The sky and landscape are presented in hues that might be seen in a postcard or a Technicolor travelogue. This somewhat banal naturalism adds to the shock value of the figures and objects. For example, we see an ordinary-looking landscape in which there is a small figure at the lower left; this establishes a monstrous scale for the central subject—huge pieces of female anatomy, skeletal forms, and a grimacing head attached to a breast that is being squeezed by a clawlike hand. We also see a tree trunk merging into a foot that acts as a kind of crutch. Notice the melting of objects—a typical Surrealist trait. We experience that melting in dreams, where persons and objects also exchange identities. From vegetable to animal, from natural to artificial, from mechanical to human: these changes, or metamor-

Meret Oppenheim. *Object.* **1936. Collection, The Museum of Modern Art, New York. Purchase**

The idea of a fur-covered cup, saucer, and spoon is fantastic and absurd. So we laugh. But our laughter is close to panic: this image threatens everyday logic; our world might collapse.

Salvador Dali. *Soft Construction with Boiled Beans: Premonition of Civil War.* 1936. Philadelphia Museum of Art. The Louise and Walter Arensberg Collection

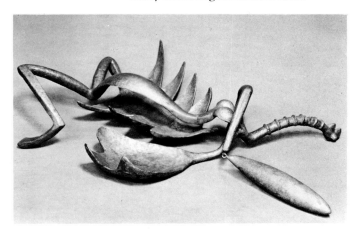

Alberto Giacometti. *Woman with Her Throat Cut.* 1932. Collection, The Museum of Modern Art, New York. Purchase

A gruesome fantasy made all the more lurid because it is rendered with exquisite clarity and loving attention to form.

Art Nouveau chair. c. 1910. Collection Mr. and Mrs. Leo Castelli, New York

A chair that wants to be something else. Wavy plant stems and female heads combine to create an object that seems to be having a terrible dream.

phoses, occur in mythology, too. This type of illogic may or may not hold some sort of truth; it certainly asks us to change the way we think.

We see a strong element of metamorphosis in *Secretary*, a sculpture by Richard Stankiewicz (born 1922). This fantasy has a torso consisting mainly of a cylinder with a typewriter embedded in its abdomen. Pipe-stem arms operate the typewriter, which is part of the secretary's body—an incongruous combination of the human and the mechanical. Many contemporary artworks deal with this theme: persons becoming machines—or machines becoming persons. Here, a somewhat human figure assimilates a machine and then operates on its mechanical innards. Perhaps Stankiewicz is engaged in prophecy—telling us what is happening to machines *and* people: as they rust and age they look increasingly like each other.

We can see a variation of the Stankiewicz fantasy in an advertisement for the Royal Typewriter Company. The idea of a typewriter coming out of a French horn is whimsical and absurd at the same time. At first, it looks like a clever way to get attention. But why a French horn? Because it is a beautiful, carefully crafted instrument that makes a rich sound. When we see a French horn holding a typewriter as though presenting an artwork on a pedestal or giving birth to a perfect "child," we get a complex advertising message, simply and effectively communicated. This is a fantasy in which the two artificial objects are, for a moment, organically united: they have exchanged essential traits; they share each other's excellence.

One of the masterpieces of modern fantastic art is Picasso's etching *Minotauromachy*. This work embodies almost all the elements of fantastic art: dream, myth, hallucination, erotic reverie, incongruous juxtaposition, a man-animal monster, and much more. Picasso deals with the Cretan myth of the Minotaur and with contemporary bullfighting; he also refers to the Greek legend in which Zeus, disguised as a bull, lusts for Europa. Europa, shown as a sleeping or unconscious female matador, is carried off by a badly wounded horse whose entrails pour out of his torn belly. But violent as the scene is, it is calmly viewed by beautiful male and female faces. At the left, an innocent-looking flower girl holds a light up to the Minotaur, who symbolizes chaos

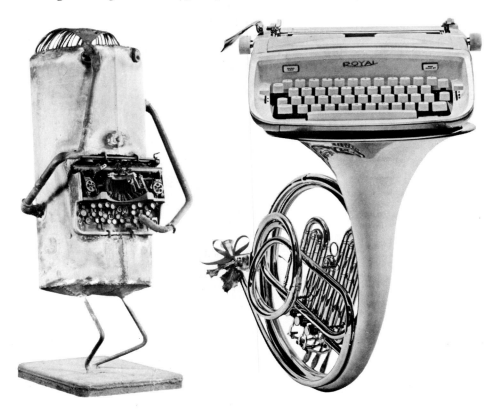

right: **Richard Stankiewicz. *Secretary*. 1953. The Israel Museum, Jerusalem**

far right: **Advertisement. *A Christmas gift with keys so lively, they can go 115 words a minute.* Courtesy Royal Typewriter Company, New York**

and violence. As with dreams, this work is not easily interpreted, but it makes us aware of recurrent themes in ancient and modern European history. For a Spaniard like Picasso, the tauromachy—the ritualistic killing of a bull—reenacts a pre-Christian fertility rite while explaining the universal meanings of love and violence. Picasso explores his Spanish heritage, his erotic fantasies, and his fascination with bullfighting to give us a large piece of history in one concentrated image. Two years later, in 1937, he painted his *Guernica*, commemorating one of the cruelest events of the Spanish Civil War; the *Minotauromachy* anticipated that work. Strangely, Picasso seems to have seen—or prophesied—what would happen to Europe.

In Henri Rousseau's (1844–1910) *The Dream*, we encounter a type of fantastic art that is based on the imagination of a primitive artist. Here "primitive" means untrained or self-taught—and slightly childlike. Rousseau lovingly portrays his dream of a naked woman on a couch, mysteriously located in a jungle where wild birds, animals, exotic natives, and luxuriant vegetation abound. This may be not only the dream of the artist but also the woman's dream. Naive and mildly erotic, it shows us nature's wealth conveniently arranged so that food is easy to find, the natives and animals are friendly, and the environment intoxicates our senses. In this lush setting man and woman can enjoy real love.

Rousseau achieved a magnificent decorative effect through his careful rendering of flowers and foliage. And while his drawing of the nude is a bit stiff, he managed to dramatize her figure with strong illumination and careful modeling. Thus, a "primitive" artist has probably expressed the universal fantasy of male adolescence, making it seem real and attainable by painting each detail with absolute conviction. We have a demonstration of a major principle of fantastic art: for the visionary—whether he uses words or images—conviction is the key; the artist has to believe.

left: Pablo Picasso. *Minotauromachy.* 1935. Collection, The Museum of Modern Art, New York. Purchase Fund

right: Pablo Picasso. *Baboon and Young.* 1951. Collection, The Museum of Modern Art, New York. Mrs. Simon Guggenheim Fund

Picasso's use of a toy automobile for the baboon's head is a good illustration of Surrealistic humor: the logic of the sculpture is stronger than the logic of the "real world."

MYSTICAL TRANSCENDENCE THROUGH PAINT

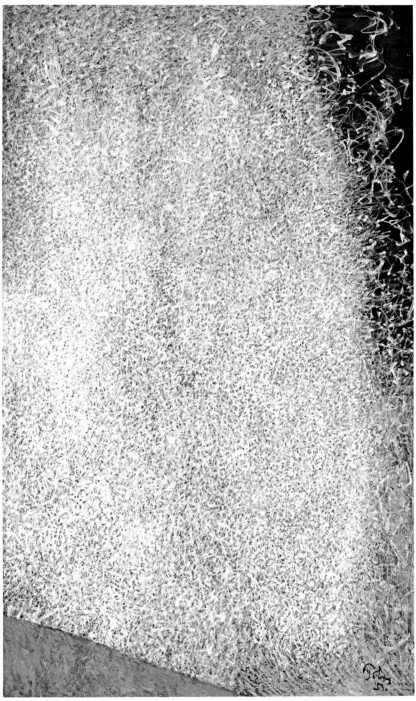

opposite above: Henri Rousseau. *The Dream*. 1910. Collection, The Museum of Modern Art, New York. Gift of Nelson A. Rockefeller

For Rousseau, nature's fertility is generous and benign. For Ernst, nature is an arena of cancerous growth: plants and animals exchange identity; ceaseless reproduction spawns monsters; vegetation threatens to choke out the sky. Rousseau's dream of contentment has been replaced by an Ernstian hallucination. Which vision is right?

opposite below: Max Ernst. *The Joy of Living*. 1936. Private collection, London

Mark Tobey. *Edge of August*. **1953. Collection, The Museum of Modern Art, New York. Purchase**
We cannot tell where this is: Tobey uses a strange sort of writing with light to dissolve the boundaries of places and objects. Line, color, and light combine to produce a mystical sense of oneness.

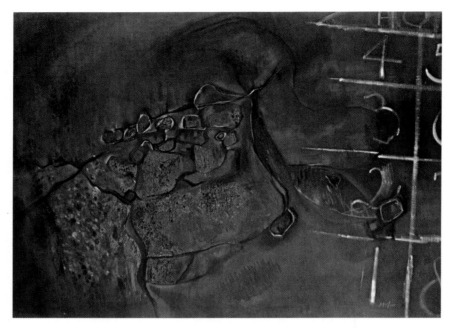

Loren MacIver. *Hopscotch.* **1940. Collection, The Museum of Modern Art, New York. Purchase**

These are the ordinary marks and textures we might see on a city sidewalk—juxtaposed by accident. But MacIver does not overlook them; she changes them into strangely beautiful emblems—signs of truth written in a language we cannot decipher.

Matta. *Disasters of Mysticism.* **1942. Collection James Thrall Soby, New Canaan, Connecticut**

Matta depicts a gorgeous explosion of energy in outer space. We feel a sense of release plus a certain amount of cosmic anxiety. There are great fires in this world; if we approach them we might be incinerated.

Barnett Newman. *Adam*. 1951–52. The Tate Gallery, London

Newman's vertical divisions represent a parting of the pictorial field, which then opens to the viewer a vast primordial space: the world at the beginning.

Arthur G. Dove. *That Red One*. 1944. William H. Lane Foundation, Leominster, Massachusetts

Dove tried to work his way out of nature and then back again, cleansed by abstraction and armed with the radiant force of a powerful symbol: a black sun.

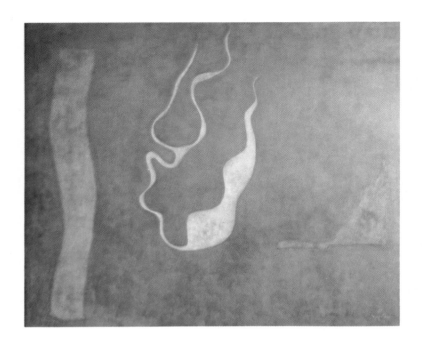

William Baziotes. *The Sea.* **1959. Collection Mr. and Mrs. H. Grossman, New York**

For a certain kind of artist, the miraculous emerges in the discovery that the act of painting can evoke a natural world nature does not know.

Mark Rothko. *Earth and Green.* **1955. Galerie Beyeler, Basel**

Because of its size (almost eight feet high) and the floating, looming qualities of the color, Rothko's painting becomes an environment in which we feel ourselves absorbed. Our sense of self is dissolved in the act of visual contemplation.

SCIENTIFIC FANTASY

Science and technology dominate our lives, so it is not surprising that artists have adapted their symbols. Science raises questions about outer space and submicroscopic matter—questions that fascinate the popular imagination and stimulate endless speculation. *Artistic* speculation about technology is part of a natural process of humanizing concepts, which can radically change our notions of space, time, energy, and matter. These new concepts are often threatening; we tend to cope with them indirectly—in dreams, jokes, and tall stories. Artists do the same thing, employing their own language or imagery. They may want to know whether new scientific ideas can be used expressively in their private worlds of feeling and intuition. Also, they wonder how new discoveries about motion and energy will change the way they see and think. This sort of speculation may not add to the fund of knowledge regarded as scientific truth, but it is important because it tells us how science affects the human psyche, our collective modes of thinking and feeling.

In *The Conquest of the Air* by Roger de La Fresnaye we see a tame work of scientific fantasy—tame when compared to today's space exploration. Cubist forms were used to cope with the intellectual aspects of extraterrestrial travel. The picture includes a balloon in the distance and a sailboat at the right, with a French flag floating above it. Two men are in thoughtful conversation. Presumably, they are symbols of the connections between thinking, sailing, and flying. At the same time, a new technology is related to the historic intellectual achievement of France. If this picture had been painted by an American, he would probably have been called a chauvinist. But since it was painted before World War I, we realize that it reflects an essentially nineteenth-century nationalistic attitude toward science. Today, science is considered an international endeavor. Of course, we wanted to be first on the moon.

In the work of the Chilean painter Matta (Echaurren) (born 1912), we see another artistic effort to deal with the world of outer space. He builds on a Surrealist foundation, which encourages the artist to pay attention to dreams of flying, floating, and wandering in nonresistant environments. The result is a fantastic universe with an astrophysical look. Some of this imagery reminds us of microphotographs of subatomic particles, showing their orbits, velocities, and collisions, and describing their short but interesting life spans. As the particle paths overlap or combine, they also produce forms that have both geometrical and organic qualities. In Matta's fantasies, a biological note, a hint of living form, is always present. Together with the movements of particles guided by the laws of physics, there are water, air, sunlight, moonlight, and stars. Outer space is not all rocks and radiation surrounded by nothingness: there are bodies out there, and some of them are burning.

Matta has not built a model of the real universe. Instead, he paints a world that might be seen by some superior eye, an eye that can understand the imagery of science and art simultaneously. In other words, Matta gives us art, not talented technical illustration. Perhaps the best analogy to his work can be seen in the late medieval paintings of Hieronymus Bosch (c.1450–1516), where the torments of Hell are described in loving detail. Bosch painted what no one had seen but what everyone thought about—the incredible tortures of the damned according to then-current notions of cosmology and theology. Notice that the fifteenth-century Hell depicted by Bosch bears an uncanny resemblance to the fantastic twentieth-century world pictured by Matta.

FANTASY AND ILLUSIONISM

Artists want us to believe in their fantasies, so they use a variety of representational devices. Like shamans and magicians, they work hard on the creation of illusions. As we shall see, the style of fantasy calls for thorough mastery of realistic technique.

Infinite Divisibility by the French-American Surrealist Yves Tanguy

Roger de La Fresnaye. *The Conquest of the Air.* **1913. Collection, The Museum of Modern Art, New York.**
Mrs. Simon Guggenheim Fund

Matta. *Here, Sir Fire, Eat!* 1942. Collection, The Museum of Modern Art, New York. James Thrall Soby Bequest

Hieronymus Bosch. *Hell* (detail of *The Garden of Delights*). c. 1500. The Prado, Madrid

Yves Tanguy. *Infinite Divisibility*. 1942. Albright-Knox Art Gallery, Buffalo, New York

(1900–1955) employs the naturalistic lighting and modeling we would expect in a conventional still-life painting. The objects are certainly inanimate—*nature morte* (dead nature), as the French say. Light comes from a single source, causing the strange objects to cast sharp shadows that obey the laws of perspective as they move toward a horizon we cannot see. In the distance there are glowing light centers coming from the sun—or several suns. Their light passes through an atmosphere much as sunlight sometimes reaches us on earth—through a cloud haze. The objects themselves belong to a skeletal system. But whose? They seem to have organic *and* mechanical origins: some resemble sticks, stones, or geological forms. Yet a machine is suggested by the geometric construction at the left.

In Tanguy's world, everything dissolves into a luminous haze after we have examined the sharp, carefully rendered forms in the foreground. An infinite horizon creates the mood of a dream and an atmosphere of silence. Since the color is mostly a silvery gray, this painting has an almost photographic quality. The effect of the work is not to shock but to induce a calm acceptance of an otherworldly environment. There is no violence in Tanguy's "lunar" landscape; it seems to exist in a time *after* violence and passion have spent their force. So this universe—so bare of the essentials needed to sustain life— is amazingly peaceful. Perhaps that is because these creatures are no longer alive. This may be the world as it would look after we (and everything else) are dead.

A different kind of illusionism is employed in *The Bride* by Marcel Duchamp (1887–1963). Here we have the convincing representation of geometric solids connected by some sort of mechanical-biological circulation system. The title adds a touch of Surrealistic irony by contrasting the romantic-erotic meanings of "bride" with a quasi-Cubist picture of what might be human viscera. We are shown the insides of a mysterious system that hints at human internal organs and arteries. This is the sort of imagery we might see in a catalogue for a plumbing manufacturer. Is it a Surrealist "gag"—a mad, ironic, and well-rendered image of a human being?

Surrealist illusionism depends on visual discoveries made as early as the Renaissance. Today, many artists have abandoned that type of illusionism, preferring to use real objects that are glued, nailed, soldered, or welded together. *Masculine Presence* by Jason Seley (1919–1983) is an example. This figure is made of welded automobile bumpers and a grille (possibly from a 1955 Buick). The result looks like the muscle and skeletal systems of a man, with the convex machine parts producing a remarkably organic effect. Seley's work suggests an interesting relationship between industrial design and sculpture. The original purpose of an automobile bumper was to provide a sturdy defense for the car's easily damaged metal skin. But over the years, designers "improved" the rugged old bumper with a variety of curvilinear shapes. That is, they treated it like sculpture, giving it quasi-figurative, usually female, quali-

above: Jason Seley. *Masculine Presence.* 1961. Collection, The Museum of Modern Art, New York. Gift of Dr. and Mrs. Leonard Kornblee

left: Marcel Duchamp. *The Bride.* 1912. Philadelphia Museum of Art. The Louise and Walter Arensberg Collection

ties. Seley understands this. But in reassembling these automobile parts, he has changed their sex, returning them to the human body from which they came. And perhaps—as sculpture—that is where they belong.

For a more whimsical fantasy we turn to Marisol (Escobar) (born 1930), who made *The Generals* out of painted wood, plaster, and assorted odds and ends. We can recognize a barrel in the body of the horse and an ordinary table or bench in the legs. Marisol's sculpture plays with several levels of representation and meaning at once: it has an overall hobbyhorse quality, particularly in the horse's neck and head. The stiffness and boxlike construction of the generals suggest children's soldiers; but their painted faces and helmets (inverted cereal bowls?) give them the rigidity of dedicated warriors. Their legs and boots are painted on the barrel, like children's book illustrations of wooden soldiers; so it is hard to take their generalship seriously. For a heroic equestrian statue, the horse will not do. And why are two generals riding the same horse?

Marisol hardly tries to create fool-the-eye illusions; only modest craftsmanship is required to mount boxes on a barrel or a barrel on a bench. Yet, with the visual hints Marisol has given us, it is easy to imagine these silly soldiers on horseback. Her art consists in planting ideas in the viewer's consciousness: that generals look like boxes; that military posturing is a child's game. Also, we know that generals don't go into battle on table legs (or on anything else); that knowledge is part of the work of art, too.

Traditional artists had to "persuade" paint, clay, or stone to look like flesh, hair, or cloth; contemporary artists can employ real objects along with illusionistic fragments to create several levels of reality in one work. We have seen how Seley and Marisol "play with" the viewer's frame of reference. The result can lead to fresh insight, a vacation from reality, or a good laugh. We should remember, too, that every artwork is, in a sense, a fantasy. Artists always operate in the realm between illusion and reality, encouraging us to look a little harder at the real world. Sometimes they make us wonder what makes it real.

PART THREE

THE STRUCTURE OF ART

When we were learning to speak, we tried, almost from the beginning, to express desires, feelings, and ideas. Adults helped us to pronounce words, but they did not give us definitions of nouns, verbs, and adjectives and ask us to put them together. Somehow, we learned to say words and to understand them at the same time. Human beings possess innate language capacities, but we learned to use language mainly through trial and error and meaningful reactions to our talk. Much later, teachers dissected the language for us, broke it down into parts of speech and rules of usage. Before that, without consciously knowing the rules, we managed to understand what people were saying.

The same is true of art: we have been using its language; now we are about to study its *structure*—its parts and how they are put together. Now, studying the structure of art may not be absolutely necessary for understanding its overall meaning: our innate visual and intellectual equipment enables us to understand images without formal instruction. However, there are other reasons for examining the structure of artistic forms.

First of all, the parts and organizational devices of a language have meanings that are expressive or enjoyable in themselves. Listening to the way a soprano sings certain notes yields pleasure over and above what we get from her song as a whole. Also, there can be passages in a painting, parts of a sculpture, sections of a building, that are very good even though the complete picture, sculpture, or building does not seem to work. This overall breakdown gives us our second reason for studying the structure of art: to find out what is responsible for an artwork's success or failure. Finally, we need to understand the principles of artistic organization—how a work is designed—because design is itself a source of information and pleasure; it tells us how the artist thinks. So the discussion in the next two chapters concentrates on parts and wholes; we study the building blocks of art and the plans, schemes, and strategies that make them work together.

CHAPTER EIGHT

THE VISUAL ELEMENTS: GRAMMAR

P eople see images, not things. Light sensations falling on the retina are carried as energy impulses to the brain, where they are almost simultaneously translated into a meaningful entity called an image. Not that there is a picture, an optical projection, in the brain. The optical processes are in the eye alone; perception is a function of brain, body, and mind. Because of that "mind connection" we cannot experience sensations without characterizing them. An image, therefore, can be defined as *the result of endowing optical sensations with meaning*.

The images we see are labeled with words such as house, tree, sun, and sky. And just as words can be broken down into letters, images can be broken down into their visual elements: line, shape, color, and texture. Furthermore, we can learn to focus on those visual elements. In fact, when we focus on *part* of an image, that part becomes a complete image: our minds have a tendency to create wholes out of parts.

Here we are concerned with the visual elements as they are employed by artists. But after seeing them in art, we may recognize them in nature, too. We see the visual elements in the natural world because we *project* upon nature the habits of perception that our species has found useful or pleasurable. For that reason, studying the structure of art yields indirect dividends—added satisfaction from the perception of images regardless of their source.

Labels for the visual elements tend to vary according to the user, but what they refer to is fairly consistent. It does not matter greatly if one authority uses "shape," another, "contour," and a third, "form" (shape is flat and form is three-dimensional). Mainly, we want to understand the visual effects that the labels designate.

LINE

There is a difference between *a* line and *line-in-general*. A line is the path made by a pointed instrument: a pen, a pencil, a crayon, a stick. A line implies action because work was required to make it. Line-in-general suggests direction or orientation. An impression of movement can be achieved by a series of shapes; none of them needs to be thin, sharp, or linear, but collectively they can suggest a sequence, a direction, a thrust. In other words, *a* line is a mark made by a sharp, moving instrument, whereas *line-in-general* is a conclusion by the viewer that a set of forms is going somewhere. Here, we shall be talking mainly about *a* line, a distinct series of points.

opposite: **Poncho section from Peru.** A.D. **700–1000. The Metropolitan Museum of Art, New York. The Michael C. Rockefeller Memorial Collection. Bequest of Nelson A. Rockefeller, 1979**

Almost all the basic visual elements—line, shape, color, light, and texture—can be seen in this superb Peruvian fabric. Yet, despite its extreme geometricization, the design is representational: it depicts a feline deity holding a human-headed staff. The imagery looks highly abstract, but for the ancient Peruvians it read like a book. For us, the lesson is that abstract forms are most powerful when rooted in real objects, places, and events.

Norbert Kricke. *Raumplastik Kugel.* **1955. Collection Hertha Kricke, Düsseldorf**
Compare Kricke's white-wire construction to the paintings of Matta (pages 196 and 201). Both artists use linear systems to describe subatomic-particle trajectories, or the motion of bodies in outer space.

Pablo Picasso. *Diaghilev and Selisburg.* **1919. Collection the artist's Estate**

Victor Pasmore. *Linear Development No. 6: Spiral.* **1964. Collection Mrs. John Weeks, London**
A system of drawn lines serves as a visual analogy for processes in nature: growth, flow, resistance, and mutual adaptation.

Because all of us have used lines to write, to make marks in the sand or on walls, we know that drawing a line calls for thought: a choice must be made about where the line will go. In learning to write we discovered that "wrong" lines produced letters that could not be understood. That is, there can be right and wrong lines. In writing, a "wrong" line is one that doesn't follow certain rules. To write legibly we have to agree about what letter forms should look like; then we need the muscular coordination to make them. In drawing, too, we try to control lines so that there will be a resemblance between the shapes we make and visual reality. The idea that there are linear agreements about how lines communicate was established early in our lives.

When we were young, line combinations had magical properties: a circle could be the sun, a face, a flower; lines were alive with possibilities. Professional artists often try to recapture these magical-symbolic properties of line, using them in fresh combinations that may become new artistic conventions. And people seem to understand them immediately. Picasso's linear treatment of the crying woman in *Guernica* (page 51) is a good example: we recognized what it meant the first time we saw it.

Uses of Line in Works of Art   For a demonstration of line employed simply but eloquently, we might examine Picasso's drawing of the ballet impresarios Diaghilev and Selisburg. Here the artist who gave us so many distorted human images shows his mastery of naturalistic contour drawing. Mainly, he uses an accented line to describe the weight and volume of enclosed forms. M. Selisburg's fleshy hands and face are executed with a line of utmost precision. The absence of shading gives an almost classical elegance to these well-fed gentlemen. Notice, too, that Picasso knows how to use the power of geometric forms; we sense the underlying ovals, cylinders, and rectangles in this deceptively simple but strong drawing.

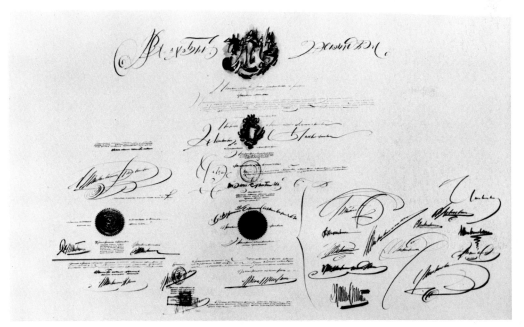

The idea of linear energy appears often in the work of Paul Klee (1879–1940). Line not only describes the shapes of things but also calls attention to itself becoming something else. Klee enjoys a kind of metaphysical wit; he creates illusions of reality and then tells us we have been deceived. Actually, he lets us in on a private joke: the artist is not sure whether the image he draws is "out there," somewhere inside himself, inside us, or just an illusion that everyone shares.

In Klee's *Flight from Oneself*, we see a marvelous, funny-sad pattern of lines that visualizes the ridiculous antics of a split personality. The gestures look like decorative echoes until we realize that they represent twin aspects of the same person. The meandering line, which seems to be a disciplined scribble, is duplicated exactly in two scales, producing two figures that are separate but joined, attached to each other by the same cord that gives them life. With

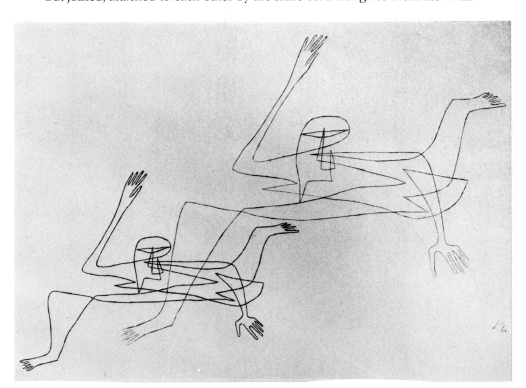

Paul Klee. *Flight from Oneself.* **1931. Paul Klee Foundation, Kunstmuseum, Bern. Permission Cosmopress Geneva, 1966**

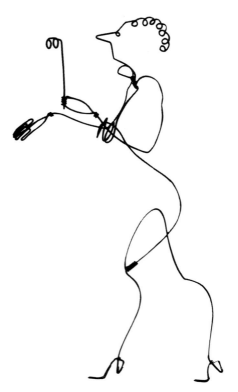

Alexander Calder. *The Hostess*. 1928. Collection, The Museum of Modern Art, New York. Gift of Edward M. M. Warburg

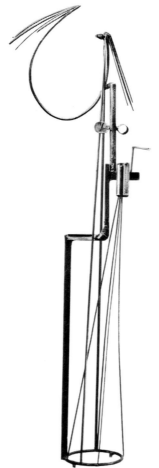

Julio González. *Grande Maternity*. 1930–33. The Tate Gallery, London

one continuous piece of string, Klee has portrayed the shifting reality of mind and body.

Drawing-lines occur in sculpture, too, except that they move in three dimensions. A good illustration is a humorous little wire sculpture by Alexander Calder, *The Hostess*. Here we see how much line can accomplish through suggestion. The penetration of solid sculptural forms has encouraged new directions in welded sculpture, too. Julio González (1872–1942) was one of the first modern sculptors to exploit the linear properties of iron rods. Logically enough, his work grew out of the rich Spanish tradition of decorative ironwork. In *Grande Maternity*, welded iron rods form a stately, monumentally dignified sculpture of a woman. González composed by elimination, arriving at form by implication rather than addition. The sweeping lines of the rods and the cagelike structure of the skirt are remarkably effective in suggesting the movement and grace of the female figure.

In *Royal Bird*, David Smith (1906–1965) plays almost musical variations on a dominant horizontal line. Here, as in Theodore Roszak's *Spectre of Kitty Hawk* (page 168), a bird's skeleton is the basis of sculptural form. The calm horizontal axis is counteracted by a fierce beak-and-jaw construction and the aggressive stance of an angry bird. Notice that the rib-cage pattern, translated into metal, suggests the armor of a medieval knight more than Thanksgiving leftovers. But, if we can suppress our associations with turkey and see the horizontal pattern as a script, we can almost read this sculpture as metal calligraphy.

Klee's psychological use of line appears again in his drawing *And I Shall Say*. Here, too, the figure seems to have been produced with a slightly directed scribble. The hands and feet imitate children's drawing, but the face had to be drawn by a trained artist. Klee united several kinds of line to produce this psychologically convincing characterization. It is an approach that has been used by legions of contemporary artists, designers, and cartoonists. Klee's line can be a nervous impulse, a contour, a notion about to collapse, or a soul rebuilding itself. Notice how the inner-directed eyes express the idea of the child in the adult; we see a person pathetically wrapped in fantasy. Her mouth is closed, her mind is speaking; she listens to herself answering someone in an imaginary dialogue. All this is accomplished with what looks like a scribble.

Line is perhaps the most expressive of the visual elements. Why? (1) Because the *outlines* of things are crucial keys to their identity. (2) Because of our almost universal experience with line in writing and drawing. (3) Because line is precise and unambiguous; it forces artists to "speak" clearly. (4) Because line leads the viewer's eye, implying movement and direction. (5) Because line (for some inscrutable reason) symbolizes thought.

David Smith. *Royal Bird*. **1948. Walker Art Center, Minneapolis**

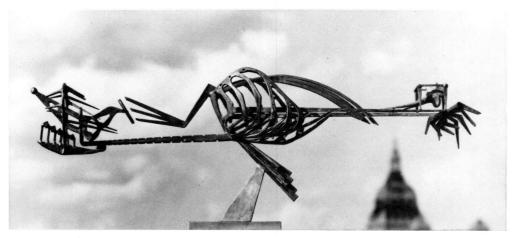

Paul Klee. *And I Shall Say*. 1934. Paul Klee
Foundation, Kunstmuseum, Bern

SHAPE

Our discussion of line touches on shape because closed lines become the
boundaries of shapes. However, shapes can þe created without lines: when a
painter establishes a color area or a sculptor builds a three-dimensional form.
In both cases, drawn lines are unnecessary. Shapes do have *linear* quality
when our attention is drawn to their edges or their orientation, but usually we
think of shapes as areas or as silhouettes—containers of more-or-less homo-
geneous stuff.

The shapes that artists create have many sources: some are taken directly
from nature; others reflect the marks of the tool used to make them. Then
there are shapes that are "invented" by artists. But we cannot help seeing
them—no matter how abstract—in terms of our experience with reality. That
is, we cannot see a triangle without relating its corners to something sharp
and pointed, something that can puncture. So triangular shapes are potentially
dangerous. But not necessarily. A triangle resting on its base also suggests rest
or immovability, like an Egyptian pyramid. The expressive meaning of a shape
depends on which of its properties the artist has emphasized. If an artist uses a
triangular shape to describe something that is normally curved, that may give
us a clue to its aesthetic meaning. Why, for example, does the horse's tongue
in Picasso's *Guernica* (page 51) come to a sharp, dagger-like point? Because
that shape, in that place, symbolizes pain—the pain of the Spanish people.

Seeing lines and shapes involves a certain amount of guessing about
where they came from. When we encounter a perfect geometric shape, we
doubt that it was made by hand: perfect straightness or curvature usually implies a mechanical origin; irregularity of shape usually suggests handmade
forms. Because machine forms are the product of human planning and design, they usually have precise, essentially intellectual, qualities. Of course,

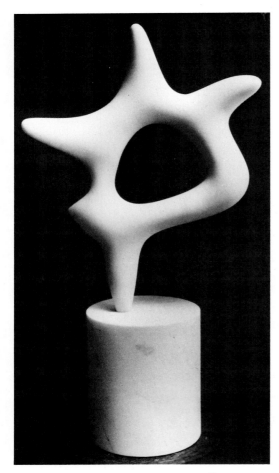

Jean Arp. *Star.* 1939–60. Collection Édouard Loeb, Paris

geometrical shapes can be found in nature—in crystals, in snowflakes, and in certain geological formations. But the natural objects we see with the unaided human eye usually have irregular, uneven shapes.

Our bodies and the bodies of animals are a main source of curvilinear shapes, which are modeled ultimately on the patterns of organic growth—growth through the division and integration of cells. But this principle is violated by crustaceans, living creatures that have sharp, jagged, almost geometrically shaped armor. Their armor—which has been so suggestive to sculptors—is like our fingernails; it lacks nerves and blood vessels, and, thus, the capacity for sensation. So "armor" shapes look as if they feel no pain; they look as if they can *inflict* pain.

In *Star,* a sculpture by Jean Arp, we see a rounded, organic shape given to something usually conceived in geometric terms. A star is, after all, light from a distant body; we do not see its source, just its light waves, usually shown as straight, not wavy, lines. But Arp has chosen a living model for the conventionally pointed star diagram; his star renounces geometry and radiating lines. Instead, it has skin and flesh, bones perhaps, and an opening in its center. This contradiction between the standard idea of a star and Arp's organic version invites us to think of "bodies" in outer space; perhaps the universe is a *biological* system.

Architecture is an unlikely source of organic shapes since its structural devices are usually geometric. However, the development of reinforced concrete has greatly enlarged the architect's vocabulary. Indeed, some contemporary buildings are criticized for being *too* sculptural; they create exciting shapes at the expense of functional efficiency. But in Le Corbusier's chapel at Ronchamp, functional requirements are satisfied while organic shapes enhance the building's symbolic expressiveness. Notice the roof shape, which might be compared to a fish. It does, in fact, resemble a sculpture by Brancusi called the *Fish.* Perhaps it is forcing the comparison to suggest that the roof is a literal image of the fish, an early Christian symbol. Still, the biomorphic shapes in the building increase our awareness of the chapel as a living body—a religious idea that is here given eloquent visual form.

left: Theodore J. Roszak. *Sea Sentinel.* 1956. Whitney Museum of American Art, New York

below: Spiny lobsters
The weapons and armor of crustaceans offer a form language that has a curious fascination for contemporary painters and sculptors.

Le Corbusier. Notre-Dame-du-Haut, Ronchamp, France. 1950–55

The shapes we see in Le Corbusier's roof and in Brancusi's *Fish* are surprisingly similar. Can this be explained? Perhaps the same idea speaks to us through a similar process of abstracting from living form.

Constantin Brancusi. *Fish*. 1930. Collection, The Museum of Modern Art, New York. Acquired through the Lillie P. Bliss Bequest

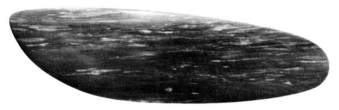

We see another architectural use of organic shapes in the facade of the Casa Batlló in Barcelona, designed by Antoni Gaudí (1852–1926). Plainly, he has avoided geometric shapes wherever he could. In Gaudí's architecture, doors, windows, chimneys, and balconies are converted into fantastic forms, usually resembling human or animal bodily parts. His style appears to be a triumph of the imagination over the character of materials. We see shapes performing architectural, sculptural, and symbolic functions at the same time.

Antoni Gaudí. Detail of Casa Batlló, Barcelona. 1905–7

The fleshy facade Gaudí designed for the Casa Batlló acquires strength and firmness through the thin, bony columns that seem to support enormous Surrealistic eyelids.

right: Jean Arp. *Madame Torso with Wavy Hat.* 1916. Hermann and Margrit Rupf Foundation, Kunstmuseum, Bern

far right: Adolph Gottlieb. *Blast II.* 1957. Joseph E. Seagram and Sons, Inc., New York

left: **Billowing spinnakers**

Shapes also possess volumetric meanings: we perceive them as the containers of dynamic forces. The beauty of a sailboat (as well as its female associations) is based on the container idea, here expressed in the spinnakers.

right: **Paul Klee.** *The Great Dome.* **1927. Paul Klee Foundation, Kunstmuseum, Bern**

In Arp's *Madame Torso with Wavy Hat*, shape has a comic purpose. We can easily identify madame's hourglass figure, but her head and hat have changed into something else. An Ionic capital? Ocean waves? An upside-down handlebar mustache? Notice, too, how the convex forms of the hips are balanced by *concave* shapes located where the thighs would fit into the torso. These shape relationships are dramatized by shadows cast by the raised relief of the figure. But why do these shapes look funny? Because organic forms without structural firmness seem to wriggle like jelly. And jelly is funny because it has no bones.

Blast II by Adolph Gottlieb (1903–1974) gives us a laboratory demonstration of the properties of shape. The canvas is occupied by two forms of the same area and mass, but the upper one is smoothly rounded whereas the lower one is ragged, chaotic, and smeared at the edges. The title suggests that we

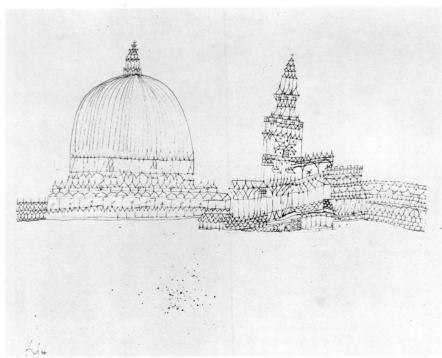

are looking at an abstract version of a nuclear explosion. The circular form above must represent the mushroom cloud, while the agitated shape below symbolizes destruction. The cloud has a serene, floating quality that contrasts with the angry shape underneath. Notice the blotched quality of the brush-strokes around its edge: the artist emphasizes its violent, "dirty" character. Obviously, the artist is exploiting the ironic contrast between a sooty, black shape and the clean, brushed-out form floating over it.

Paul Klee gives us a striking illustration of the two major types of shape—the biomorphic and the geometric. *The Great Dome* might be considered a statement about sexual symbolism in the guise of architectural description. The structure on the left represents a monument of our architectural tradition—the heavenly dome. At the same time, it describes the female breast, the symbol of maternal nurture. At the right Klee portrays a tower, a symbol of maleness that stands erect because of a geometrical system of triangles. These basic shapes seem to be opposed, but they are connected along the base of the composition. To engage in some amateur psychologizing, it might be said that Klee is using these shapes to say that man and woman are fundamentally different, but that they are fundamentally (at base, at rock bottom) united. In other words, the sexes have to be joined to create a complete picture.

We see an extreme example of geometrical shapes representing human beings in *Composition: The Cardplayers* by Theo van Doesburg (1883–1931). (Perhaps Cézanne's earlier *Card Players* anticipated the analysis of form in

Theo van Doesburg. *Composition: The Card-players.* **1917. Gemeente Museum, The Hague, The Netherlands**

Paul Cézanne. *The Card Players.* **1890–92. The Louvre, Paris**

final Proof Hundertwasser 屋根の上の川

彫 川嶋達夫
摺 清水昭男

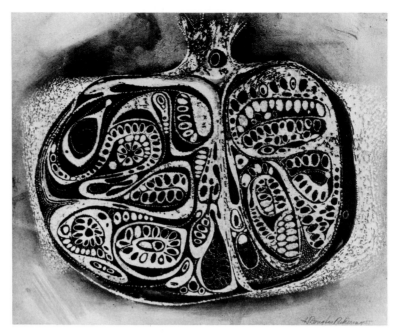

left: **Printed circuit (used in television sets). 1958. Collection, The Museum of Modern Art, New York. Gift of Warwick Manufacturing Company, U.S.A.**

Printed circuitry and a section of fruit; their similarity shows how advanced technology approaches art and how both approach the organic.

above: **H. Douglas Pickering. *Pomegranate*. 1955. Collection the artist**

Van Doesburg's work.) This painting consists of a system of rectangles, loosely packed on the outside and densely packed in the center. A few large L-shapes suggest shoulders, knees, and chairs. But the organization of these geometrical shapes takes precedence over visual representation. Life's irregularity has been converted into strictly measured, precisely placed units of form. It should not be surprising to learn that devices now exist which can create patterns for electronic circuitry—patterns that bear a remarkable resemblance to Van Doesburg's painting. These patterns are made by a technician using an instrument called a "coordinatograph." Perhaps Van Doesburg unwittingly anticipated today's computer circuits. Can we expect better coordinatographs to replace painters and sculptors? Will electronic engineers create art? They can try.

LIGHT AND DARK

It is reported that on his deathbed Goethe uttered the phrase "More light." In the eighteenth century, philosophers of the En*light*enment spoke often about "the light of reason." For them, light dispelled darkness; it symbolized mind or reason illuminating what is hidden and mysterious. Perhaps it is unfair, but light is also a masculine symbol; all the ancient sun gods were male: Apollo, Mithras, Mazda, and Horus. The earth and the moon, which *receive* or *reflect* light, are female symbols. Without these female bodies, however, light would be invisible. Reality, or form, requires light *and* dark—yin *and* yang.

Regardless of the bad reputation of darkness, artists use it as a positive tool: they work with shadows to imply light. Symbolically speaking, they use both male *and* female elements. The light in Klee's *Self-Portrait* is the absence of shadow; the exposed paper is perceived as light because of its *contrast* with the black-painted areas. Without contrast, we would have the sensation of light but would be unable to see line or shape. The *Suprematist Composition: White on White* painted by Kasimir Malevich (1878–1935) shows how the reduction

Technician using coordinatograph to prepare pattern for microelectric circuit

opposite: **Friedrich Hundertwasser. *End of Waters on the Roof*. 1985**

Symbolic shapes. Hundertwasser's cityscapes are cryptic images of himself—the tightly wound spiral, or snake person, in the center of the composition. He looks out through mysterious window-eyes at a fence, or barricade, made of houses. They seem to be spear points or teeth. Will they devour Hundertwasser? Or is their main function to protect him from strangers?

217

left: **Paul Klee.** *Self-Portrait. Drawing for a Woodcut.* **1909. Collection Felix Klee, Bern**

right: **Kasimir Malevich.** *Suprematist Composition: White on White.* **c. 1918. Collection, The Museum of Modern Art, New York**

The eye requires contrast to see form: contrast in light and dark, contrast in color, or contrast in "temperature." Malevich gives us contrast in temperature, which is almost invisible in black and white.

of light-dark contrast almost eliminates form. Actually, Malevich played a trick: he used two kinds of white—one warm and one cool—so that perception is possible because of a "thermal" difference rather than light-dark contrast.

Since colors differ in degree of lightness or darkness, they can be used to establish light-dark differences and thus produce form. Pure yellow is lighter than red; pure blue is darker than yellow; side by side they create contrast. Sometimes, however, colors are mixed to the same degree of lightness or

Henri de Toulouse-Lautrec. *Maxime Dethomas.* **1896. National Gallery of Art, Washington, D.C. Chester Dale Collection**

Here the silhouette shape directs our attention outward: it creates pictorial space and alerts us to an interesting exchange of glances between the masked woman and M. Dethomas.

darkness, and then the eye has to discriminate between them on the basis of their chromatic quality alone.

The simplest type of light-dark contrast is visible in the silhouette. Usually a solid black against a white ground, the silhouette provides a maximum of contrast and visibility. The viewer's eye is normally drawn to its shape as a source of information. Silhouettes occur in nature, as when we see an object against the light, but usually, objects get some light, or they are illuminated by several light sources. This results in a play of light that can be imitated in art. The manipulation of light and dark to create illusions of form on a two-dimensional surface is called "modeling"—a term borrowed from sculpture. Objects can be "modeled" using only the stark contrast provided by two "values"—black and white. But more convincing and subtle representations can be created by imitating a wider range of light intensities. This type of mod-

eling, which was perfected during the Renaissance by Leonardo da Vinci, is called *chiaroscuro*.

With much painstaking effort, a painter can imitate photography, as in the style called Photorealism (see page 422). However, the human eye (and the camera) can discriminate more degrees of light intensity than the artist's skill and pigments can reproduce. Consequently, most artists do not try to compete with nature *or* the camera. Usually, they look for *patterns* of light and dark which they can use to create believable and expressive effects.

Much of the symbolism of light is mythic in character. Yet in art, the transitions from light to dark have their own distinctively aesthetic meanings. The gentleness or abruptness of halftones can create emotional responses. The source of illumination—from above or below—affects our feelings. The distinctness or indistinctness of shapes can be controlled by the manipulation of light and dark. Some shadows seem empty or opaque; others look luminous and full of life. They invite closer inspection or they direct us back to the light. We have seen how architects use light: some bathe their interiors in strong light, but others design forms that break up light or cast mysterious shadows. The great architects *compose* with light as much as with space.

As with line and shape, our perceptions of light and dark are guided by our life experience. And in life we avoid too much of either: we can be as blinded by light as by its absence. In art, strong light-dark contrasts are usually equated with sharpness of focus, which usually implies closeness to the viewer. Because the eye prefers to avoid extremes of light or dark, the late afternoon seems to provide the most optically pleasing halftones and shadows. From four to seven is a good time for social life: people past the bloom of youth seem to know this. Only teenagers have the courage to have a date in the glare of fluorescent lighting or at the sun's peak. The rest of us get together when the shadows are falling.

One result of the use of intense color in modern painting is the tendency to think of light mainly in terms of color. Nevertheless, the creation of form by manipulating light and dark has been with us for a long time; it is not likely to disappear. In the following pages, therefore, we examine some dramatic examples of lighting in both traditional and modern works of art.

Baroque Experiments with Illumination After the masters of the Renaissance perfected chiaroscuro, the later Mannerist and Baroque painters went on to employ unusual illumination to dramatize their subjects. For example, in Caravaggio's (1571–1610) *The Calling of St. Matthew* the source of light from the extreme right is used in a highly theatrical manner: about eighty percent of the figures are in shadow. Viewers can read the forms only with the evidence given by the light that creeps around their edges. This concentration of light, or "information," in small areas increases our visual alertness. "Seeing" such a work of art involves a new kind of viewer participation. Georges de La Tour (1593–1652) went a step further, using *artificial* light to construct solid, classically simple forms of great emotional power. His *Saint Mary Magdalen with a Candle* shows the Baroque painter creating a dramatic stillness with a light-dark patterning that is almost abstract. Yet the result is realistically convincing. Although most of the picture is in darkness, it is a quiet, comfortable darkness because of the calm, reasoned shaping of the lights.

El Greco (1548?–?1614) carried the rich tradition of Venetian color to Spain, but he is best known as a master of flickering light—a light more animated than that of La Tour. Both are Baroque painters, but La Tour's smoothly brushed figures seem less troubled—on the surface, at least—than those of El Greco. Notice the artificial illumination in *The Agony in the Garden of Gethsemane*, especially in the Christ figure, where the light-dark contrast conveys a powerful impression of emotional climax. El Greco seems almost modern in the inconsistency of his light sources. The angel and the swirling figures in the space beneath her receive illumination different from that of Christ, and the

Caravaggio. *The Calling of St. Matthew.* **c. 1597–98. Contarelli Chapel, S. Luigi dei Francesi, Rome**

In Baroque painting, light is an aggressive, liberating force. A small amount of it is enough to reveal the spiritual opportunities that lie hidden in the shadows.

Georges de La Tour. *Saint Mary Magdalen with a Candle.* **1625–33. The Louvre, Paris**

La Tour's light represents the cleanliness of a spirit that has been washed and scrubbed by the effects of endless moral reflection.

El Greco. *The Agony in the Garden of Gethsemane.* **c. 1580. The National Gallery, London**

In El Greco's painting, forms are flames beckoning to each other. The spiritual life is almost always compared to fire—glowing, blazing, consuming, or smoldering.

Rembrandt van Rijn. *Man with a Magnifying Glass.* 1665–69. The Metropolitan Museum of Art, New York. Bequest of Benjamin Altman, 1913

For Rembrandt, light is the device that creates shadows, and shadows are the painter's way of listening to the soul. We see this best in his sitter's eyes—looking out but thinking in.

soldiers and trees in the distance are bathed in moonlight. The result is a scene that looks real and dreamlike at the same time: the natural and the supernatural converge in the same space.

In Rembrandt (1606–1669) we encounter perhaps the most psychologically penetrating of Baroque experiments with illumination. The richness of forms in the light, the cultivation of mystery in the darks, the gradual or sudden buildup of pigment with brush or palette knife: these technical and aesthetic devices have never been surpassed. Rembrandt's transitional tones bear the closest study because that is where he departs from the abstract patterning of light and dark to reveal his distinctive insight into the human condition. Those halftones raise his art above merely skillful modeling. In *Man with a Magnifying Glass* the loss of light in the shadows seems to symbolize all that is human and vulnerable in his subject. The light areas consist of a vigorous, manly impasto swimming in liquid glazes that make the transition to the luminous shadows. The light areas meet our eyes first, struggling to expand and assert their dominance. The halftones represent modifications of light, the feminine element that seeks compromise by resisting in some places and yielding in others. In the deep shadows we see light whose fire has almost burned out; shadows are burial places for fires that have died. But in Rembrandt, light never really dies; it sleeps restlessly underneath his glazes; it can always flare up again.

Rembrandt van Rijn. Detail of *Man with a Magnifying Glass*

Light and Dark in Modern Art   A spectacular break with the traditional use of light and dark appears in the work of Édouard Manet (1832–1883), especially in his "scandalous" painting *Olympia*. His merciless lighting may have aroused the indignation of French critics as much as his subject offended the French public. There were "moral" objections to his candid presentation of a prostitute, but his flattening of form and unsentimental application of paint seriously upset visual expectations. Manet tended to eliminate subtle modeling effects: he painted directly, without glazes, and with a preference for bluish black in the shadows and transitions. So the *Olympia* reminds us of a candid-camera photograph in which the flashbulb has bleached out the half-tones. And, since Manet avoided linear perspective, we do not approach the subject by gradual stages; we confront his woman suddenly and directly. Or she confronts *us*, and that, too, is disturbing. Nakedness, flatness, glaring light, and indecent subject matter: this was enough to launch a pictorial revolution.

below: **François Boucher.** *Miss O'Murphy.* **1752. Alte Pinakothek, Munich**

opposite above: **Édouard Manet.** *Olympia.* **1863. The Louvre, Paris**

opposite below: **Paul Gauguin.** *The Spirit of the Dead Watching.* **1892. Albright-Knox Art Gallery, Buffalo, New York. A. Conger Goodyear Collection**

From Boucher to Manet to Gauguin one travels through distinct modes of viewing woman. At first she is a delightful toy; then she becomes a more complete person—still used for pleasure, but humanized to the point where her stare is embarrassing; finally, she reverts to fearful adolescence as the child-woman imprisoned by the superstitions of a witch.

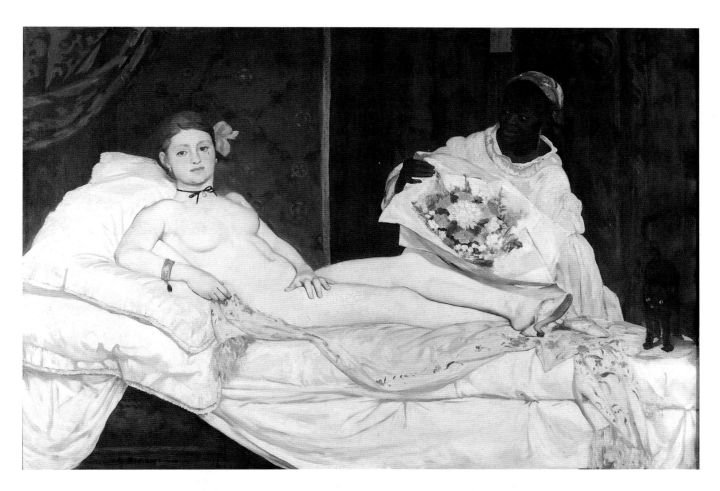

In the woodcut *The Prophet* by Emil Nolde (1867–1956) we see again how the elimination of halftones, plus strong contrasts of black and white, can produce a powerfully expressive effect. Of course, the woodcut medium is highly suited to this treatment of light. But it would be difficult to accept if Manet had not blazed the path. The nose in Nolde's *Prophet* is entirely black, even though that conflicts with the logic of the head's lighting. By 1912, however, an artist could mix descriptive and abstract elements arbitrarily, in this case producing a stern effect through a pattern of darks connecting the nose, brows, and mustache. The tools used to cut a wood block do not change direction easily because of resistance from the wood's grain. The result is a harshness in the shapes, which can be read as traits of the prophetic temperament: righteousness, anger, disappointment, sorrow.

Rouault's *Miserere: Dura Lex sed Lex* (Have mercy: The Law is hard but it is the Law) is very much in the spirit of Nolde's woodcut. Here, too, the pictorial structure is based on an extreme light-dark contrast, with the addition of a few halftones to modulate the glaring light. Using very unconventional techniques, Rouault achieves a rich texture on the printing plate; with aquatint, etching, and helio-gravure, he produces a surface that is more like a painting than a print. The grainy, scratchy whites and the thick, pitted blacks create a painfully hard image, an image in which bitterness and resignation are mixed with acid.

COLOR

There is a vast literature on color theory—much more than most of us have the time or inclination to study. Often it provides answers to questions that artists do not necessarily ask; their knowledge about color is usually based on trial and error, the advice of teachers, borrowings from other artists, or lucky guesses. Some color systems are more concerned with the physics of light and the physiology of perception than with aesthetics. Others have evolved from industrial needs for the classification of dyes, inks, and pigments. At any rate, artists work with color on an intuitive more than a scientific basis. The great colorists tend to make instinctive adjustments to the requirements of their vision rather than apply the findings of color physics. The French Impressionists, however, were very interested in scientific color theory; even so, the paintings of other artists were the principal influence in the evolution of their style. Their opportunity to see the work of Turner and Constable in England in 1870 was a major factor in their artistic and aesthetic development. Still, it does not hurt to know about color wheels, complementary color, analogous color, tonal color, and so on. But keep in mind that our purpose is to understand *how color works in art*—how it affects the ideas, feelings, and information we get from images created by artists.

Color Terminology   Responses to color may be emotional and intuitive, but we need to talk about it. Hence terminology: it permits orderly reference to the properties of color that, we believe, generate aesthetic emotion. Following are brief definitions of the terms most commonly used, chiefly to describe what is done with artists' pigments.

Hue refers to the names of primary colors such as red, yellow, and blue. Note that these are different from the colors of the light spectrum as taught in physics. (The "physical" spectrum, made by breaking down light into its component colors, consists of red, orange, yellow, green, blue, indigo, and violet. Plus all the colors in between, for which we may or may not have labels.) The primary hues are theoretically the basis for mixtures resulting in orange, green, and violet; presumably, they are *not* the result of a mixture; that's what makes them primary. But in practice, the most intense hues are achieved by mixture. The names manufacturers use are a type of labeling meant to distinguish hues and tints from their almost identical cousins made by other manufacturers. Thus we have "Mediterranean Gold," "Colonial Yellow," "Roman Bronze," "Canary Yellow." Artists' pigments have a label history, too: burnt sienna, Rubens red, gamboge yellow, zinc white, and so on. But they mean nothing unless you have used them.

Value refers to the lightness or darkness of a color. As white is added, a color becomes "higher" in value until pure white is reached. Conversely, as black is added—or some other color that has a darkening effect—the value becomes "lower" until pure black is reached. As you approach pure white or pure black, you become less aware of chromatic or color quality and more aware of lightness or darkness, which is to say, *value*. Yellow is already high in value, so it can be used to raise the value of colors darker than itself. Blue is already low in value, so it can lower the value of lighter colors.

Intensity refers to the purity of a color, the absence of any visible admixture. As mentioned above, pigments seldom present a hue at its fullest intensity. For example, the pigment called alizarin crimson is quite dark; it can be made into an intense, bright red by the addition of a small amount of yellow or cadmium orange. Ultramarine blue is very dark as a pigment and becomes an intense blue hue only with the addition of white. But too much white will kill its intensity, producing a "pastel" or a tint, a faded look.

Local color is the color we "know" an object to be as opposed to the colors we actually see. We know a fire engine is red, but depending on light conditions, its distance from the viewer, its reflective quality, and so on, it may look red, violet, orange, or even green in some places. Its highlights might be almost white. At least, a painter would use these colors to represent the "redness" of a fire engine. Similarly, distant mountains appear to be blue and violet, although we "know" that their local color is green and brown.

Complementary colors are opposites. Also, they are across from each other on the color wheel. More fundamentally, the presence of one denotes the absence of the other: there is no yellow in blue; there is no red in green. This means that no other color is as different from red as green. To the human eye, the *afterimage* of red is green; the afterimage of green is red. If red and green are side by side, the red looks redder and the green looks greener; the after-

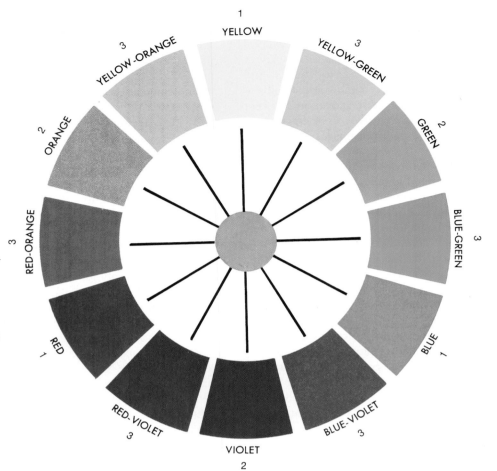

The Color Wheel

The result of arranging the color spectrum in a circle. The number ones are called primaries; the number twos are called secondaries; the number threes are called tertiaries or intermediates.

Color complementaries are pairs that face each other on the color wheel: red-green, violet-yellow, blue-orange, etc. With a larger wheel and more mixtures, we would have more complementary pairs.

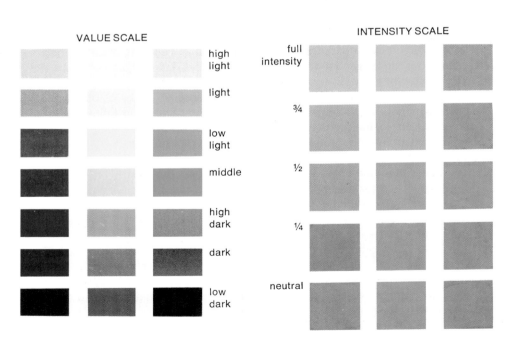

VALUE SCALE

			high light
			light
			low light
			middle
			high dark
			dark
			low dark

INTENSITY SCALE

full intensity			
¾			
½			
¼			
neutral			

The Value Scale:

From light to dark. High values approach white; low values approach black.

The Intensity Scale:

This shows the range of a color, from full saturation to low saturation or neutrality.

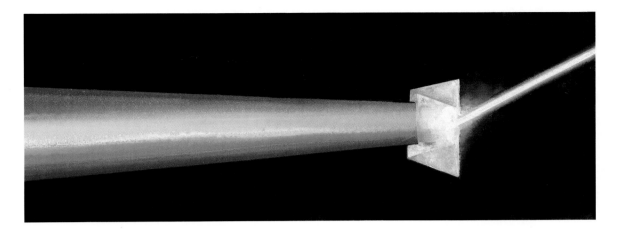

The Color Spectrum. Illustration by John Ad-kins Richardson
The result of passing light through a prism.

image of each enhances the actual image of the other. If complementaries are mixed, they cancel each other out—that is, they produce a gray or, more likely, what painters call mud; they *neutralize* each other. A small amount of red added to a large amount of green will gray the green; white added to the mixture will raise the value; and thus a variety of interesting grays can be mixed without using black.

Analogous colors are relatives, or kinfolk, as opposed to strangers like complementaries. They are related because they share the same "blood lines' —red and orange, orange and yellow, green and blue, blue and violet, violet and red. Analogous colors are next to each other on the color wheel. Families of color do not end distinctly at any point on the color wheel; they seem to "intermarry" with their close neighbors. And being relatives, they "get along," if that is true of relatives. They are harmonious next to each other; they can mix with each other without becoming gray.

Colors are called *warm* or *cool* because of our associations with blood, fire, sky, or ice. Reds, yellows, and oranges are warm; blues, greens, and some violets are cool. But these "thermal" properties are relative (all the properties of color are relative). Yellow-green would be cool next to orange but warm next to blue. Painters can create form by contrasts of warm and cool rather than contrasts of light and dark. When it comes to spatial quality, the warm colors advance, and the cool colors recede. This illusion is due to the fact that the wavelengths at the warm end of the light spectrum are stronger—that is, more visible—than those at the blue-violet end. Ultraviolet, for example, is so weak that we cannot see it at all.

Tone refers to variations—lighter or darker—of a single hue; its meaning is similar to *color value*. *Tonality* refers to the overall color effect of a work in which one color and its variations seem to dominate the whole. Rousseau's *The Dream* (page 194) has an essentially green tonality, for instance. We also speak of a warm or cool tonality, which is a way of referring to the "temperature" variations of the dominant color in an artwork. A painting with a blue tonality may have some reds and yellows, but bluish tones would be dominant because of their *quantity* and *distribution*. In general, tonal painting tends to produce easy color unities because it reduces the number of color variables the artist must work with.

Color as Language   It should be plain that little can be said about colors in isolation; they always occur in a context or relationship—in art and in life. The *quantity* of a color can change our ideas about advancing/receding, expanding/contracting, warm/cool relationships. And, of course, the *shape* of a color area affects its meaning, as does its surface quality or texture. In addition to the optical properties of color, there are symbolic properties to consider. Needless to say, we are affected by the folklore and the psychology of color; so artists must simultaneously consider how we see colors and how we feel about them.

One of the main goals of modern painting has been the use of color as an independent language of feelings and ideas. This is especially true of abstract and nonobjective art. The intention of certain early modern painters was to imitate music, which presumably communicates through "nonobjective" sounds. Wassily Kandinsky (see page 161), who thought of colors in musical terms, is credited with the first nonobjective paintings—works that tried to use color as a pure language of emotion. Before him, the Fauves, or "Wild Beasts," had carried the coloristic advances of Impressionist painting into the realm of arbitrary color. Several other movements—Post-Impressionism, Symbolism, and Expressionism—greatly enlarged the role of color as an independent language. But instead of discussing styles and movements we ought to look at the way color speaks in specific artworks by some of the masters of modern art.

London Bridge by André Derain (1880–1954) (page 160) exhibits the crisp, bright touches of color we associate with Impressionist paint application, but the blurring of edges and the pursuit of atmospheric effects is absent. Notice that the strong yellow marks on the bridge do not hold still; they jump out of their assigned places and try to act independently. Local color is exaggerated, too: we see a bright orange sky without any optical "explanation." The yellow reflections in the water look improbable. As for the drawing, it is clearly subordinate to the pattern of the brushwork and the activity of the pigment. As we would expect, when the innovations of Impressionism were still controversial, Derain's Fauvist color and drawing aroused violent reactions from critics and the public.

Still Life with Lamp by Alexej von Jawlensky (1864–1941) (page 156) dates from the same period as Derain's *London Bridge*. But it moves further in the direction of independent color, retaining only a nominal connection with visual reality. Although the structural organization is strong, it is really a scaffold on which to hang the intense, vigorously applied color. Jawlensky is well on the way to a type of abstraction in which pictorial structure is based on contrasting color intensities. At least four kinds of red compete for our optical attention; two or three yellows also make themselves felt; some greens try to cool things down, and a coarse black framework struggles to hold the work together. Drawing is minimal and modeling is nonexistent. It is color alone that produces this angry lamp and those frantic apples.

The *Landscape with Houses* by Wassily Kandinsky (1866–1944) (page 160) is, like the Derain, fairly close to Impressionism in its gradations and traces of color-vibration technique. Here Kandinsky's edges are not as harsh as Derain's, but his color spots do jump out. We also see an unbelievable blue house, a pair of fiery trees, and some incredible orange rooftops. Kandinsky is not interested in the type of spatial control that Cézanne achieved in the 1890s. Color has become increasingly musical; we can almost hear a flute and a mandolin. Or is it a balalaika?

Mark Rothko (1903–1970) (page 198) is famous for using color to create a mystical light that seems to surround the viewer. His pigment impregnates the canvas like a stain, so we are not aware of it as a brushed-on substance: it seems to radiate color. Rothko's paintings become separate, light-filled worlds. Apparently, he was trying to find a way to change the viewer's consciousness through color. Employing shape very sparingly, his paintings manage to transcend our everyday ideas and associations. We know that color is exceedingly potent in its capacity to affect the human nervous system, but to experience it there must be form—shape, size, location—or design. This is what Rothko produces with his colored rectangles floating in a colored field. Serene, deceptively simple, and pleasing to the eye, these forms find a pathway to our consciousness through our eyes alone.

As we know, Surrealism also tried to alter consciousness. Mainly, it employed outrageous juxtapositions of form and subject matter; the approach was essentially literary. As the public grew familiar with this strategy, however, its capacity for surprise diminished. Rothko, by contrast, found a way to change our physical environment—at least temporarily. He used color to induce agreeable, contemplative states of being. His art suggests that we may be entering an era when painting, largely through color, will be able to communicate directly with the neurological source of our feelings.

TEXTURE

We speak of getting "the feel of things" as if touching were the best way to know something. In fact, feeling things is our *earliest* way of dealing with objects. But as we develop, tactile sensation gives way to visual sensation as the main mode of knowing. Still, we regard touch as more reliable than vision. If you have a bad fall, you are likely to *feel* your body—"looking" for breaks or bruises; something that "looks" all right may conceal damage that has to be *felt* to be discovered. Babies, we know, examine objects by putting them in their mouths—*feeling* them with the lips and tongue. But the time comes when learning about the world through touch or taste is dangerous; seeing is safer.

Adults have learned to look before they touch, but it is possible that their looking is a kind of tactile inquiry. That is, we use vision to find out how something would feel if we touched it. This connection between visual and tactile sensation is so well developed that we can fall in love just by seeing someone: "love at first sight." However, looking contemplates tactility: we hope to hold and embrace. In other words, we move back to our earliest sensory modes when seeking the complete knowledge that love implies.

A texture can be seen as well as felt. But "seeing" a texture really means having a good idea about its surface quality. Much visual representation consists of providing viewers with reliable cues about surfaces. Surfaces, in turn, are sources of very basic information. Think of modern advertising—especially photographic illustration—and its capacity to inform, to arouse desire, and to sell—through texture.

far left: **Nail fetish, from the Lower Congo. 1909. Museum für Völkerkunde, Basel**

The heavily textured surfaces of these sculptures have different functions. The nails driven into the African fetish act almost medically: they are supposed to drive out demons or activate healing energies in the body of a real person. Paolozzi's figure bears the holes left by arrows shot into the body of the martyred saint. It also looks like the body of a man lacerated by every kind of modern illness. In both figures we see a similar symbolic drama. The nails and arrows represent powerful invasive forces that, when released, leave holes for the body's pain or energy to escape. Visually, those coarse textures are signs of a struggle to control the life force inside every person.

left: **Eduardo Paolozzi. *Saint Sebastian No. 2.* 1957. The Solomon R. Guggenheim Museum, New York**

What are the tactile properties of surfaces that can be rendered visually? Essentially, they are phenomena related to the light-absorbing and light-reflecting qualities of materials. These are usually represented graphically in terms of light-and-dark patterning. With pattern, an artist can represent the texture of anything from burlap sacking to the surface of the moon. In the three-dimensional arts, of course, textures are created, not simulated. But painters and printmakers are not far behind: collage has taught them to attach anything to a surface—if glue can keep it there.

The early dependence on touch in human sensory development is reflected in the strength of tactile qualities in the art of tribal peoples. Their art exhibits a textural vividness that is especially popular today—particularly for artists who want their work to make a direct sensory appeal. For the tribal artist, rough textural effects result mainly from using traditional materials, tools, and techniques—usually in ritual. For today's artist, coarse textures fulfill an aesthetic agenda: going back to the source, abandoning representation in favor of composing with real objects, and creating a "primitive" look to shake up the tired sensibilities of the jaded gallery-goer.

Jean Dubuffet. *The Sea of Skin.* 1959. Collection Daniel Cordier, Paris

This "Sea of Skin" comes from the century plant, an organism that flowers once and then dies. Dubuffet has used its textures to make a statement about all the things, including ourselves, that age and die.

The modern desire to return to strong tactility in art may be due to a distrust of remote visual stimulation, as in reading, driving, and scanning—watching the world from a distance. The coarse textures of contemporary art probably express a desperate effort to reach back and down into the deepest strata of human personality. We have grown sick of smoothness and polish—in life as well as in art. Also, we live in a culture where our senses are regularly assaulted by loud noises and violent images; a powerful jolt of texture may be the artist's only way of being heard.

Seymour Avigdor (designer). Interior with patterns. 1969. Material found at Vice Versa Fabrics, New York

The appeal of overall repetitive patterns is fundamentally tactile. The patterns become textures because we cannot deal visually with so many little images—they have to be perceived in the same way that we see grains of sand, beans in a pot, or bees in a hive.

233

CHAPTER NINE

ORGANIZING THE ELEMENTS: DESIGN

No matter what the purpose of an artwork, its elements are organized to be seen. The purpose of a chair is to support someone and *to be seen*. The purpose of a poster is to persuade people and *to be seen*. Stated more accurately, a poster *must be seen* before it can persuade anyone. Consequently, artworks have one common goal over and above their personal, social, or physical goals. That common goal might be called *organization for visual effectiveness*.

The term *design* is often used as a substitute for the phrase *organization for visual effectiveness*. Design is a process that is common to the creation of all works of art. For that reason, we make no distinction in this book between the design of paintings and the design of useful objects, such as chairs or posters or book jackets. Sometimes, the word *design* is restricted to the creation of utilitarian objects, while the creation of "nonuseful" objects like paintings and statuary is called *composition*—a more "artistic" process. But for our purposes, design applies to any art object, regardless of its maker, its material, or its use. Why?

1. Because the useful objects of the past often become the "use*less*" or "fine-art" objects of the present. The status of the object may change, but its visual organization remains the same.

2. Because so-called useless objects (pictures, statues, decorative objects) *do* have a purpose, although it is not necessarily physical: they function by being seen.

3. Because design is the artist's chief tool for controlling what and how viewers see.

By insisting that design is a process common to all works of art, and by refusing to set up a ranking among art objects—calling some *high* art and others *applied* or *minor* art—we gain certain advantages. We avoid being embarrassed by history, as when a fertility figure becomes a "fine-art" object in a culture that uses modern medicine instead of magic to deal with infertility. We avoid classification problems, such as how to distinguish between the physical usefulness, the psychological expressiveness, and the aesthetic value of stained glass in a Gothic cathedral. We recognize the power of images: the

Alexander Calder. *Acoustical Ceiling.* **1952. Aula Magna, University City, Caracas**
Calder's floating forms constitute an immense sculpture designed to improve the acoustical and visual qualities of an architectural space. Aesthetic and practical values are combined in the same construction. Is this art or engineering? Or both?

Brooklyn Bridge is symbolically potent even though it was designed to carry travelers across a river. There must be a visual reason, a *design* reason, for that symbolic power.

As soon as materials are formed and assembled, they become a visual organization that succeeds or not because of the way its elements work together. Now, all works of art exhibit certain patterns of "working together"— patterns sometimes called "principles" of design. These principles are based mainly on the way people see effectively. In a sense, the so-called principles of design are the result of long-term trial and error. Accordingly, the history of art might be considered a history of the types of formal organization that have been found effective in various times and places.

DESIGN IN USEFUL AND "FINE" ART

left: **Ingo Maurer. Giant bulb. 1967**

right: **Murray Tovi. Tovibulb. 1969. Designed for Tovi & Perkins, Inc., New York**
Tovi's light fixture could be a sculpture by Brancusi, but it also has a practical function, like Calder's ceiling. Maurer's lamps are Pop art objects and light bulbs at the same time. In both cases, the designer worked with ideas as well as with sculptural form.

235

We cannot claim that any single design principle—for instance, "unity in variety"—constitutes a rule for artistic and aesthetic effectiveness. Distinguished works can be found that defy the principles of design cited here or elsewhere. Also, unity is experienced differently in different cultures: the unity of a Hindu temple is more apparent to Indian than to Western eyes; in the twelfth century, the Gothic architecture of the North seemed ugly and *dis*unified to the peoples used to the classical forms of the Mediterranean world. Nevertheless, the principles of design are based on fairly common habits of visual perception; they are certainly influenced by the common physiological equipment of the human race.

The habit of reading from left to right, or top to bottom, or right to left produces differences in the way we look at images. But everyone has to measure size relationships, the distance between objects, and the speed of moving objects. Binocular vision and perceptions of size, color, shape, brightness, texture, and depth confer uniformity more than diversity on our ways of seeing. Because of that perceptual uniformity we can speak of design elements and principles as if they applied to everyone. In fact, as languages go, the language of vision may be the best we have for communicating the unity of the human species.

UNITY

Perhaps unity is the *only* principle of visual organization; perhaps the others are merely different ways of achieving it. Ultimately, unity reflects the fact that we are separate individuals who see and feel and think with the equipment provided by our separate bodies and minds. We are also finite individuals; we need to close our visual experience at some point in order to move on to other things. That is the chief reason why we require visual unity. Artists try to help us by organizing the parts of an artwork so that they will be *seen as a whole*. A failure in this effort—ineffective design—results in the premature termination of the viewer's experience; the viewer stops looking. The act of "not looking" might be considered a kind of completion, but not a good one; it represents the breakdown of communication. Therefore, the artist's design objective is to create a *good* unity, an *intentional* unity, among the parts of a work of art *before* they are seen by a viewer. What are the principal ways of doing this?

One is *dominance and subordination*. The artist attempts to control the *sequence* in which visual events are observed and the *amount of attention* they are paid. The dominant element of a work is the one the others depend on for their meaning and their visual value. Dominance is achieved most easily by *size,* the largest form being seen first. It is also achieved by *color intensity.* Other things being equal, an intense color area will dominate a dull, pale, or grayed area of the same size. Similarly, a warm area will dominate a cool area because warm colors seem to advance toward us.

Another way of achieving dominance is through *location:* our eyes are usually drawn toward the center of any visual field: centrally located objects are more likely to receive attention. That is why the head in most portraits is centered between left and right and slightly above the midpoint of a canvas; it corresponds to the location of the viewer's own head. The *convergence* of lines and forms on a point, or their *radiation* from a point, gives dominance to that point. *Light* becomes a dominance factor: the eye—like a moth—finds it difficult to resist a place that seems to radiate light. For instance, we are tempted to look at the bright sun even though we know it will hurt our eyes. Hence, a very light area will dominate its darker surroundings, much as the sun dominates the sky.

Finally, dominance can be achieved by *difference* or *exception*. We know that nonconformity stands out: if an oval shape appears among a number of squares, it will be seen as the exception; it will stick out like the proverbial sore thumb. What is the image you associate with the novel entitled *A Tree*

Paula Modersohn-Becker. *Self-Portrait*. 1906. Kunstmuseum, Basel

Notice that the face is modeled in more depth than the body; its colors are more intense, too. The psychological unity of the portrait is built mainly on the greater dimensionality of the head. Our eyes are drawn to the place where the plastic and chromatic values are concentrated.

Grows in Brooklyn? A slender, green, plant-shaped object surrounded by massive walls of brown brick and gray stone. The tree captures our attention because it is unexpected. In our mind's eye, we see the tree before the bricks.

Coherence refers to the *belonging together* of the parts of a work of art. In life these parts may be entirely unrelated, but in art their colors, shapes, sizes, or textures can be adjusted so that they seem almost indivisible. The sense of coherence casts a kind of spell: once it is achieved, any further change will be felt, and it will seem to ruin the whole work. We respond as if we are in the presence of a living thing; its unity is its life. The viewer comes to believe that the organization or design of an artwork is inevitable: it could not be different and still exist.

Visual coherence is often pursued through analogous color and color tonality—the use of a single color or admixtures of it throughout a work. *Similarity* of any kind—of shape, color, size, illumination, or texture—promotes the impression of coherence. But similarity has its perils, since sameness can lead to boredom. Our tolerance for sameness is limited; we need *variety* to satisfy our appetite for change, but not so much variety that the sense of wholeness is sacrificed. Clearly, the artist has to walk a fine line.

Piero della Francesca. *The Resurrection of Christ.* c. 1460. Palazzo Comunale, Sansepolcro, Italy

Two kinds of unity. In Piero's fresco, the placement of Christ's head at the apex of a triangle creates a powerful symbol of dominance and upward movement. In Rembrandt's etching, Christ is centrally placed but only slightly higher than the others. His figure unifies and dominates the scene through gesture, frontality, and painterly modeling of form.

Rembrandt van Rijn. *Christ Healing the Sick (The Hundred Guilder Print).* c. 1648–50

Unlike forms can be unified by the device of clustering: *closeness* suggests coherence. When surrounded by open space, unlike forms that are near each other tend to be seen as a unit: the eye *prefers* likeness to unlikeness. This principle of unity is illustrated in Braque's *The Round Table* (page 38). There we see a variety of objects, shapes, and textures, almost none of which are alike. But they are held together by the encircling form of the tabletop and the open space around them. To be sure, there is a sense of "spilling up," but that is part of the *fun* of this work.

Unity based on converging or radiating lines is fairly common and easy to use. The designer's problem is to avoid the obvious. An almost pure example of radiating unity can be seen in a wire construction by Richard Lippold (born 1915): *Variation Number 7: Full Moon.* But notice that Lippold creates subsidiary centers of interest; also, the color and shimmer of his fine metal lines have considerable intrinsic appeal, so they divert attention away from the radiant center. In a related type of design, *"and the bush was not consumed,"* Herbert Ferber (born 1906) builds a composition on repeated V-forms—in the sculpture and in the wall behind it. But although the lines seem to converge at the point of the V, Ferber introduces variations in shape and direction to escape monotony. In addition, he uses plant forms to avoid a tedious repetition of the V-shaped device.

An example of unity through central location can be seen in *Nachi Waterfall,* a silk-scroll painting from the Kamakura period of Japanese art. Such paintings had a mystical-religious function in ancient Japan, but we can see them in terms of their masterful pictorial design. The dead-center placement of the waterfall would have been obvious and dull, except for the sensitive adjustment of dark weights and textures left and right, top and bottom. The dramatic climax of the painting occurs at the base, where the falling water strikes an irregular, rocky profile. There the artist introduces several rounded forms and diagonal lines to counteract the dominant verticals. He also reserves the strongest light-dark contrasts for the spot where the water crashes against the rocks; after that, it trickles away to a different tune.

left: Richard Lippold. *Variation Number 7: Full Moon.* 1949–50. Collection, The Museum of Modern Art, New York. Mrs. Simon Guggenheim Fund

right: Herbert Ferber. *"and the bush was not consumed."* 1951–52. B'nai Israel Synagogue, Millburn, New Jersey

Nachi Waterfall. c. 1300. Nezu Museum, Tokyo

Henri Matisse. *Carmelina.* **1903. Museum of Fine Arts, Boston. Tompkins Collection**

Unity through frontality. Everything faces straight ahead—the table, the mirror, the picture, the objects on the shelf—and Carmelina. But her hand positions are not identical, one bottle is slightly turned, and there is some nonfrontal imagery in the mirror. Matisse has used psychological interest and visual variation to produce a very lively composition.

It seems at first that the artist has used an almost mechanical device for achieving unity. Then we recognize his ingenious use of subordinate devices for creating variety. A masterpiece can result from creating an impossible problem and then solving it.

BALANCE

The Leaning Tower of Pisa is famous because it is out of balance but still manages to stand. What keeps it from falling? Are invisible forces holding it up? From what we can see, the building ought to collapse. The fact that it doesn't is both funny and disturbing. All of us have a deep need for balance or equilibrium; that balance can be seen in nature, in the human figure, and in man-made structures. We expect it in art as well as in life.

In architecture, balance is largely a matter of adjusting weights and stresses; in physics, we find it in the laws of energy conservation; in the biological world, it exists in a correlation between the animal population and the food supply. In art, balance is an optical condition; weight, stress, tension, and stability—words that are borrowed from physics or engineering—take on perceptual meanings. It would not be surprising if certain scientific problems were intuitively solved by artists and viewers as they calculate whether the forms they see are pleasing. One thing is certain: in learning to walk we went through a period of instability; remembering that period has made us very sensitive to all signs of imbalance.

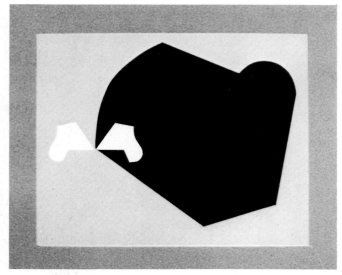

Symmetry is the simplest and least challenging type of balance. It has a spontaneous appeal, which is probably due to the bilateral symmetry of the human body. Also, it requires a minimum of perceptual effort to understand. The elements in each half of an image may be very complex, but as soon as they are recognized as echoes or mirror images of each other, they acquire an interest that is curiously satisfying. Perhaps this pleasure is related to the way electrical charges are distributed over the hemispheres of the brain during perception. Perhaps it is just a visual reinforcement of our physical stability. *Asymmetrical balance,* which is more difficult, provides pleasure, too. But it works indirectly—through a complex system of substitutions and compensations: it "costs more" in terms of perceptual energy.

Balance by weight reminds us of a lever and fulcrum, or a seesaw. We unconsciously assume that the center of a picture (or of our visual field in the case of sculpture and architecture) corresponds to the fulcrum where the lever or seesaw is poised. A heavy weight on one side can be balanced by a lighter weight on the other *if the lighter weight is located at a greater distance from the center.* Here physics and visual perception follow the same laws. Although gravity does not actually operate on the objects in paintings, we perceive them *as if* it does.

The role of gravity in art criticism is probably underestimated. We have already seen that the visual elements have optical weight. Size, shape, color, "temperature," and texture are experienced as if they are heavy or light, solid or transparent, floating or sinking. Also, there is no doubt that colors and textures can tip the optical scales we carry inside our heads. An artist who doesn't know about those scales is trying to walk with one leg; a critic who cannot weigh forms with those scales is trying to see with one eye.

SYMMETRICAL AND ASYMMETRICAL BALANCE

left: **Piero Dorazio.** *Janus.* **1949. Marlborough Galleria d'Arte, Rome**

Janus was a two-headed Roman deity, here treated as a pair of symmetrical forms. Notice how Dorazio produces variation of shape and direction within a basically symmetrical design. Arp balances his *Olympia* (remember Manet's woman of the same name?) by exploiting our interest in the pair of small forms at the left; they counteract the massive torso that occupies most of the picture space.

right: **Jean Arp.** *Olympia.* **1955. Private collection, Switzerland**

ASYMMETRICAL BALANCE USING MECHANICALLY PRECISE FORMS

left: **Ben Nicholson.** *Painted Relief.* **1939. Collection, The Museum of Modern Art, New York. Gift of H. S. Ede and the artist (by exchange)**

right: **Jean Gorin.** *Composition No. 9.* **1934. Private collection**

241

Edvard Munch. *The Dance of Life.* **1899–1900. National Gallery, Oslo**

This almost completely symmetrical composition employs balancing figures at both extremes to symbolize the opposed notions of joy and sorrow, vitality and death.

Alexander Colville. *The River Thames.* **1974. Collection J. H. Clarke, North Bay, Canada**

The thrust of the bridge and the weight of the woman's figure are balanced psychologically by the expanse of water. The river becomes a symbol (of her ambition, her career, her life) whose "weight" counteracts the complex forms and forces on the left side of the composition.

PSYCHOLOGICAL BALANCE

Balance by interest is another asymmetrical device. It is based on stimulation of the viewer's *curiosity*, usually to counteract impressions of weight. Here we deal with the fact that visual attention—its duration and intensity—adds weight. This is something artists may have known before psychologists did: small forms that excite our interest can balance massive forms that leave us cold. How is psychological interest generated? By formal or symbolic complexity. Psychological interest can upset the physical forces at work in a visual image. We know that certain signs—a face, a cross, a flag—can arouse complex feelings and associations; they can influence perception in ways that have little to do with formal structure. For example, it is difficult to perceive Surrealist works apart from their symbolic meanings. Here we might consider a painting by Chagall, *Birthday* (page 19). The small bouquet of flowers—the special gift—carries a great deal of emotional "weight"; it balances the figures psychologically. Without it, the rest of the canvas makes little sense; it doesn't have to.

Balance of weight by interest is humorously illustrated in Miró's *Maternity*, another case where an artwork is virtually a laboratory experiment. Two straight lines cross in the center of the picture, forming an X—or a pair of scissors. The point where they cross becomes the fulcrum for a seesaw. At the end of one line, we see a large form shaped like a wedge of pie; this large form is balanced by a small, insect-like form at the other end of the line. A wormy shape near the insect seems aimed at a circular form on the other arm. Apparently, the wedge-shaped form stands for the male, with the hole in the wedge acting as a kind of eye; the wormy shape is probably a sperm seeking an ovum. The other arm of the X seems to be female, and it is divided by the fulcrum point into two equal segments. One is internal, where the ovum is located; the other is external, where we see a hemispherical shape that looks like a breast. The little feathered creatures at both ends must represent the female biological symbol, ♀: both seem to be engaged in a seesaw game: the ovum swings close to the sperm, and then it swings away. From the title of the picture and what we know about scissors and levers, it looks as if there is going to be a meeting; someone is going to get pregnant. So Miró has created a little play out of the biology of human conception: fertilization seems to be a comic event in which delicate timing, physical engineering, and funny little bugs cooperate with chance.

RHYTHM

The term "rhythm" applies basically to music, dance, and poetry; it relates to measures of time. Time plays a role in visual art, too, but there it is a function of space. In other words, the artist creates visual rhythms by controlling sequences and repetitions of shaped space. We might define rhythm in art as *the ordered or regular recurrence in space of one or more of the visual elements.* We call the main types of rhythm *repetitive, alternative, progressive,* and *flowing.* Usually, it is repetition of the same shape that sets up a rhythm; it makes seeing easier and more enjoyable. For some mysterious reason, our eyes will follow a repeated sequence almost against our will. Visually speaking, rhythm makes it hard to say no.

We know that people march, lift, or pull together with more effectiveness if their effort is regulated by a rhythmic stress, or beat. They tire less easily,

REPETITIVE RHYTHM

Mu Ch'i. *Six Persimmons*. c. 1270. Daitoku-ji, Kyoto, Japan

The rhythm of Mu Ch'i is mainly achieved through repetition of shape, with subtle variations in spacing and tonal values. Each piece of fruit is an individual.

Wayne Thiebaud. *Seven Jellied Apples*. 1963. Allan Stone Gallery, New York

The rhythm here is deliberately monotonous; even the tilt of the sticks is boring. Thiebaud seems to be saying that all those jellied apples have the same sickly sweet taste.

PROGRESSIVE RHYTHM

right: Joern Utzon. Sydney Opera House. Bennelong Point, Sydney Harbor, Australia. Completed in 1973

below left: Andy Warhol. *Brillo Boxes.* 1964. Leo Castelli Gallery, New York

below right: Kasimir Malevich. *Eight Red Rectangles.* 1915. Stedelijk Museum, Amsterdam

too. In performing repetitive tasks, we always try to find a comfortable pace and rhythm. Up to a certain point, *repetitive* rhythm helps to reduce weariness and maximize efficiency. But industrial psychologists have shown that operators who perform repetitive tasks on dangerous machinery—stamping, cutting, and sawing machines, for example—tend to get hurt. Injuries can be reduced, however, by rotating operators after a certain length of time. When the human organism is bored by repetitive action, it resists by breaking the rhythm of that action.

Artists and designers try to exploit the comfortable qualities of repetitive rhythm without creating boredom or monotony. So they employ *repetition with variation,* which is like *theme and variation* in music. Also, simple alternations between black and white, solid and void, warm and cool, can be varied by introducing an unexpected element, a slight change in emphasis; the goal is to "wake up" the viewer without destroying the rhythmic pattern of his or her experience. A rhythm is like a habit: it creates unity, but it can frustrate variety. So artists seek variety *within* unity by temporarily frustrating the viewer's expectations—in other words, with an occasional surprise. But ultimately, the artist has to satisfy the rhythmic expectations that were originally aroused.

A rhythmic sequence rarely occurs as the result of accident: it has to be calculated by the artist. Such calculations can easily become mechanical patterns requiring only the capacity to follow directions. Viewers can sense this and they lose interest rapidly. Some of the Pop artists—Andy Warhol in particular—have made the repetitiveness—the boring aspects of our commercial environment—the main theme of their work. We can think of other examples from architecture and product design that exhibit a deadly sort of sameness. Then, what separates the artist from a patternmaker or a manufacturer of stereotypes? The ability to think of saving variations—variations that can enliven a work without destroying its basic rhythm.

Progressive rhythm involves repetition plus a consistently repeated change. Thus the viewer's expectation is aroused in terms of a goal, a culmination. In architecture we may see it in the order of the setbacks of tall buildings. Or, when moving through a building's interior, we experience a sequence of progressively enlarged or diminished volumes. This builds suspense: we wonder what we'll see at the finish. The architect usually gives us some hints: he may then satisfy our expectations—or pull a surprise out of his hat. But a surprise totally unrelated to what preceded it would sacrifice the unity of the whole. So we have a rhythmic rule: some qualities of the introductory sequence must be found in the dramatic climax. In other words, there are good surprises and bad surprises.

Rhythm as continuous flow is suggested by wave motion: the repetition of curved shapes, the buildup of emphasis at the crests, a sense of pause in the troughs, and a smooth changeover from one form to the next. The crucial feature of this type of rhythm is the transition between forms: How does the artist carry the eye from one nodal point, or crest, to the next? If the transition takes place along a curvilinear path, with no sudden changes of direction, it describes rhythmic or continuous flow. But there can be jagged, or staccato, rhythms, too. We see them in the paintings of Stuart Davis and John Marin. In general, flowing rhythm is more common: in sculpture we see it in the work of Jean Arp and Henry Moore. In architecture, we see it in the work of Candela and Saarinen. Alvar Aalto's bentwood experiment shows how flowing rhythm might be used in chair design. Notice, too, that this comfortable rhythm is based on the contours of the human figure: our pointy knees and elbows have been nicely rounded off.

Marcel Duchamp, in his *Nude Descending a Staircase, No. 2,* and Gino Severini (1883–1966) in his *Dynamic Hieroglyphic of the Bal Tabarin,* dem-

FLOWING RHYTHM

left: Alvar Aalto. Experiment with bentwood. 1929. Courtesy Artek, Helsinki
Aalto has created a rhythm out of the inherent character of a material and the process used to shape it.

right: Hans Hokanson. *Helixikos No. I.* 1968. Borgenicht Gallery, New York
Here the flowing rhythm is enhanced by a vigorous wood-carving texture that runs across the direction of the flow. We get a sense of muscular relaxation.

Marcel Duchamp. *Nude Descending a Staircase, No. 2*. 1912. Philadelphia Museum of Art. The Louise and Walter Arensberg Collection

Gino Severini. *Dynamic Hieroglyphic of the Bal Tabarin*. 1912. Collection, The Museum of Modern Art, New York. Acquired through the Lillie P. Bliss Bequest

onstrate the main rhythmic varieties in single works of art. We see repetitive, alternating, progressive, and flowing rhythms in combinations that can keep our eyes almost endlessly occupied. Duchamp's graceful sequence of forms was much influenced by early multiple-exposure photography; Severini, an Italian Futurist, was fascinated by the precision and energy of mechanical processes. His painting has the quality of a carefully orchestrated and rather agreeable explosion. Both Duchamp and Severini were engaged in humanizing mechanical modes of seeing and making, and it is interesting that they relied largely on rhythm to do the job.

PROPORTION

Proportion refers to the *size relationships* of parts to each other and to the whole. Size or scale in itself has no proportional meaning: a form must be seen in relation to other forms before we can be aware of its proportion. Why do we study proportion? Is it because there are *rules* for correct or harmonious proportions? Or is this a case like color, where artists tend to follow their intuitions about what is right?

We study proportion because viewers respond to it emotionally. For more than two thousand years, there have been attempts to set up rules of perfect proportion—rules that would guarantee pleasing intervals in works of art. The most enduring is the so-called Golden Section, or Golden Mean. It divides a line or rectangle into two parts so that the smaller has the same ratio to the larger as the larger has to the whole. The formula for the Golden Section is expressed algebraically as: $a/b = b/(a+b)$. But, although the Golden Section has been used for a long time, there is nothing magic about it beyond the recognition that a line divided in half makes a dull pair of intervals. Segments of thirds are only slightly better. If we could measure the proportions of all the world's masterpieces, I think we would find that they come close to the Golden Section, but that they vary from it, too. The variations would probably follow cultural norms that differ according to time and place. For exam-

bc is to ab
as
ab is to ac

a   b   c

Golden section

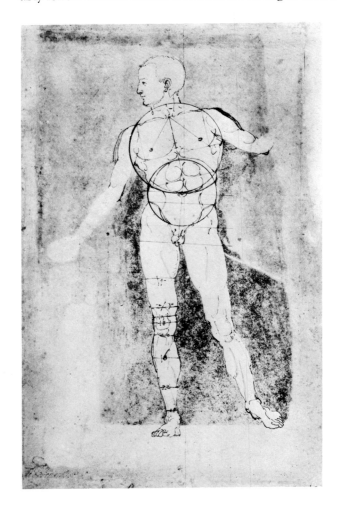

Albrecht Dürer. *Study for Adam*. c. 1507. The Albertina, Vienna
Dürer kept searching for the geometrical secret of classical figurative proportions. Compare this drawing with Leonardo's *Studio del Corpo Humano* (page 144).

ple, we would find little or no similarity in the proportions of Eskimo and Polynesian figurative sculptures. Why? Different economies, different climate, different social organization.

But even if universal rules of proportion do not exist, all of us make judgments about proportion. Certainly we have strong ideas about what constitutes *bad* proportion in art, in useful objects, and in other people. Consider this: we are larger and taller today than the knights who wore medieval armor, so when we see a suit of armor in a museum we conclude that medieval knights generally had stubby figures. Compared with us, they had "bad" proportions! There has been a change in standards of proportion since the Middle Ages, but it is not due to a new geometrical formula: nutrition made the big difference.

The figures in today's fashion illustrations are sometimes ten or twelve heads high. (Mostly, only basketball players can meet that standard.) Yet art students used to be taught that eight heads was right for men, and six and a half for women. If a model did not conform, the head could be drawn larger or smaller as needed. I suspect that the average proportions of the human figure constitute our model for thinking about proportions in all things. That is, we see a doorway or a ceiling in terms of the amount of space it provides above the height of the average person. Most likely, the seat of a chair is judged according to our notions about proportions of the average person's bottom. That average changes as we grow older and more sedentary; designers have to think about these things.

People are continuously engaged in making visual calculations and comparisons. If you say about a friend: "She's my height, but a little stouter," you are making a proportional judgment. You may go into a new apartment and feel uncomfortable without knowing why. Did the builder skimp on the ceiling height, so that you feel squeezed down? You walk along a city's streets and feel depressed for no apparent reason. Are the buildings so high that you cannot see them as multiples of the human figure? Unconsciously, we make proportional judgments in deciding how an image, an object, or a space relates to our physical and, ultimately, our aesthetic, needs.

For centuries, viewers of architecture were accustomed to the proportions of classical Greek and Roman buildings. So early modern buildings—even skyscrapers—were adorned with miniature Greek temples at ground level or on their roofs. This was a recognition of the fact that the classical civilizations solved the problem of proportion and symbolism in major buildings, but we were confused about what to do. In the 1930s, when the severe flat roof of International Style architecture was introduced, it looked stark, naked, and arbitrarily cut off. Viewers still wanted psychological interest at the top of a building as well as at its entrance. That is why our earliest tall buildings had to have something that looked like a "head." Good proportion meant having a *complete body.* The idea that a building needs a capital, or head, is quite literally expressed in the buttresses of the Nebraska State Capitol in Lincoln. Well, those Nebraskans could have been right in 1922, even if they used a somewhat old-fashioned idea to create "capitol" interest. Today, we have returned to the notion that a building needs a head. And we employ abstract forms to do the job; often we borrow traditional forms and give them a modern twist, or break, as in the broken pediment on top of Philip Johnson's American Telephone & Telegraph Company Building in New York City. Underlying the "Chippendale" look is the idea that satisfying proportions in any structure have to be modeled on something we care about. But a cabinet? A chiffonier?

CONCLUSION

Our discussion of unity, balance, rhythm, and proportion has shown that designers have to consider viewers' habits and needs. In other words, perception does not obey abstract, impersonal laws; it depends on perceivers—

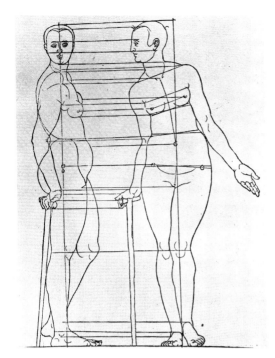

Albrecht Dürer. Study from *The Proportions of the Human Body.* 1528

left: **Fashion drawing**

right: **Female figure. Photograph of Debbie Drake from the jacket of her *Easy Way to a Perfect Figure and Glowing Health,* Prentice-Hall, Inc., 1961**

Proportions through the ages. From Dürer's search for classical perfection, to an elongated fashion image, to an actual woman. But the proportions of "actual" women change, too. Can art be the reason?

Buttress of the State Capitol, Lincoln, Nebraska

John Burgee Architects with Philip Johnson. Model of AT&T Corporate Headquarters, New York. 1978–84

flesh-and-blood human beings. So, in addition to knowing the tools and devices of the designer, we need to know why viewers are interested in them. To a considerable extent, an artist's effectiveness depends on understanding the way people respond to different kinds of visual organization. In addition, we should realize that artists are guided by their personal responses to form; in the act of creation the artist becomes a surrogate for the viewers he hopes he will have.

For us, there may be a temptation to use the "design principles" as standards for judging works of art. But that would be a mistake. Their use should be limited to *explaining* the organization of the visual elements in specific cases. That may give us some insight into the way an image works, why it is exciting or boring, whether it has too much or not enough of something. Here we come close to the problems of art criticism, discussed more fully in Chapters Fifteen and Sixteen of this book. There we shall see that criticism involves philosophic as well as design considerations. But the principles of design are useful: they give us some of the tools we need to do the work of art criticism.

PART FOUR

THE INTERACTION OF MEDIUM AND MEANING

How do the terms "material," "medium," and "technique" differ? We ought to understand them before studying the interactions between artistic expression and the various media. *Material* causes no difficulty: it designates the physical stuff of art, such as paint, clay, metal, or stone. These materials are available in a variety of natural or manufactured forms; artists work with them directly or supervise others who shape and assemble them according to instructions.

Medium is a more difficult term. In the dictionary it is defined as "the substance through which a force acts or an effect is transmitted." In other words, a medium is a vehicle for changing materials into artistic form. In painting, the word *medium* has a technical meaning: it is the *liquid* in which pigment is suspended—wet plaster, linseed oil, egg yolk, varnish, synthetic resin, and so on. But that definition would not work for architecture or sculpture. For a definition that applies to all the arts, let us say that a medium is a special use of materials for an artistic purpose. Thus architecture is not a medium, it is an art. Cast concrete, however, is a medium used in architecture. Sculpture is an art, but welded metal is a sculptural medium.

Technique and *medium* tend to overlap in ordinary usage, but we can define *technique* with more precision here: *a technique is a special or personal way of using a medium.* For example, many artists employ the medium of oil paint, but Jackson Pollock developed a *personal technique* of dripping paint. The sculptors John Chamberlain (see page 340) and Richard Stankiewicz (see page 338) use different personal techniques in the medium of welded metal. The architects Le Corbusier, Nervi, and Candela use the medium of cast concrete, but each in a different way.

In the following chapters, we attempt to show how the nature of a medium influences what is done *with* it and what is expressed *through* it. Obviously, every medium has inherent possibilities and limitations. Some artists submit to

left: Edgar Degas. *Developpé en avant.* 1920. Bronze copy after wax original, 1880. The Metropolitan Museum of Art, New York. The H. O. Havemeyer Collection. Bequest of Mrs. H. O. Havemeyer, 1929

Two representations of woman in motion. Notice how material and technique influence the resultant form and meaning.

right: Robert Cremean. *Swinging Woman.* 1960. University of Nebraska Art Galleries, Lincoln. Gift of Mrs. A. B. Sheldon

the limitations; they seem to know what cannot be accomplished within a medium. Others work on the possibilities: they try to stretch the medium's range. *Craftsmanship* might be understood as the knowledge of what can be done in a medium and the ability to do it. Still, all the possibilities cannot be known in advance: every artistic medium holds out a challenge to the judgment of the person who uses it.

Technique is important but it is not the whole story of art. Although an artist needs technical skill, it is only a means to an end. That is why, as critics, we find ourselves judging the connections between artistic means and ends; we are interested in the *quality of interaction between medium and meaning.* When examining a work of art, we want to find out how the medium has influenced its overall expression. At the same time, we want to know how an expressive purpose has affected the medium's use. Needless to say, critics must know as much as possible about the technical and expressive possibilities of the various media.

Is personal artistic experience necessary to understand media/meaning relationships? It helps, but it may not be absolutely essential. Certainly, none of us has worked in every artistic medium. So the following chapters try to provide some basic information about media/meaning relationships in the major art forms. This is not easy because we are attempting to communicate through words and reproductions the sort of knowledge that is normally gained by direct observation or practical experience. Also, new technologies might make our generalizations about media obsolete. Wherever possible, then, we shall talk about specific works of art; they, at least, will stay put.

CHAPTER TEN

PAINTING

O f all the visual arts, painting is the most widely practiced. Children and grandparents, amateurs and professionals, physicians and prizefighters—all paint, with pleasure to themselves if not always to others. Is there any reason why this art should have attracted so many devotees? There are, of course, several reasons, but one of them concerns us especially: the flexibility and versatility of painting, particularly in oil, tempera, and acrylics.

The discovery of oil painting in the fifteenth century opened up immense pictorial possibilities. It was the type of technological innovation that illustrates our theme: the interaction of medium and meaning. Oil paint has blending and modeling qualities unobtainable with tempera paint. The slow-drying oil vehicle permits the artist to modify a still-wet paint film by adding paint, wiping it out, introducing darker or lighter tones, scratching in lines, and even manipulating paint with the fingers. Yet the paint will dry as a single "skin" in which all of these applications and afterthoughts are physically united.

Because oil paint dries to a fairly elastic film, it does not crack if the canvas buckles slightly. Accordingly, the artist can work on a large canvas as opposed to the small wooden panels required for tempera. Before the perfection of oil painting, mural-size works had to be executed in fresco—that is, dry colors plus fresh plaster—and on the site of the wall itself. With oil on canvas, artists could execute huge works in their studios, afterward transferring them to a permanent site in a building. Using fresco, Michelangelo had to stand on a scaffold or lie on his back to paint the Sistine Chapel ceiling. Like a modern painter of outdoor signs, he could not stand back from his work to admire it or gauge his progress.

Painting appeals to persons who vary greatly in skill and sophistication, whereas sculpture appears to be an art for the hardy few. Sculptors need solid technical preparation, which often requires physical strength. Also, their subject matter is limited. To be sure, Bernini could carve stone to look like lace—a truly virtuoso effect. But painting has a generally larger capacity for creating illusions. Sculptors seeking naturalistic effects had to *paint* their work to close the gap between reality and its representation. In painting, key inventions—like linear perspective, foreshortening, chiaroscuro, glazing, and color complementarity—opened up illusionistic opportunities that nothing could

253

Michelangelo. *Isaiah* (detail from the ceiling of the Sistine Chapel). 1508–12. The Vatican, Rome

The good physical condition of Michelangelo's Sistine ceiling paintings makes us wish that Leonardo had used the same fresco technique in his *Last Supper*. The color in a fresco does not *rest* on the surface; it sinks into, and becomes part of, the wall. Thus a fresco can withstand a great deal of punishment.

match. Finally, sad to say, badly executed paintings endure physically in spite of their poor craftsmanship. Painting has no "built-in" features that might discourage ineptness in technique. Everything survives.

Because the painting media are flexible and tough, because painting is attractive to many temperaments, because painting can treat almost any subject, and because works of indifferent technique can last as long as masterpieces, painting is exceedingly popular. For that reason alone, the criticism of painting is very difficult. The invention of oil painting and of painting with plastic media has had amazing social as well as artistic consequences. But no matter how revolutionary the technical changes have been, we must remember that the human need to create images has been the driving force.

THE FUGITIVE AND THE PERMANENT

In a well-designed building we can see that a truss, an arch, or a dome is *doing the work* of supporting weight and enclosing space. The forms are felt as a physical system that will probably hold together as we use it. But such factors rarely affect our perception of painted forms. Still, the art of painting has a physical basis that, as in architecture, is concerned with durability.

The stone vaults of Gothic churches were developed because fires were so common that wood-roofed churches burned down repeatedly. So the physical survival of man-made structures was very important in medieval communities. This interest in durability was reflected in all the arts. For painting, durability meant resistance to fading, peeling, cracking, warping, and splitting. Since a picture was a valuable commodity, painters had to master "correct" technique—that is, a technique that ensured permanence. So-called fugitive colors could fade, especially blues and violets. Others might turn black or "bleed through." Colors applied to an absorbent ground would "sink in." The knots in a badly sealed wood panel might show through the paint film. A thousand perils hovered over every artist's brush.

During the Renaissance, painters were members of the goldsmith's guild, and although masters like Leonardo, Titian, and Michelangelo had risen above the artisan class, they were deeply immersed in problems of craftsmanship; their training was rooted in artisanship and the guild system. Leonardo and Cennino Cennini wrote treatises on the art of painting that contain lengthy discussions of technical methods. Cennino's, however, is more like a cookbook; Leonardo goes beyond cookery into questions of anatomy, physiology, optics, perspective, and art criticism.

If painting technique begins as an interest in physical durability, it ends as an aesthetic requirement. During the Middle Ages, artists' contracts specified the use of costly materials, much as today's architectural specifications require materials with certain performance ratings. But when the social and professional status of the painter became firmly established, the intangible qualities of his art were stressed; although sound technique was assumed, people realized that genius consisted of more than costly materials.

Many modern painters observe ancient traditions of craft, but mainly for aesthetic reasons. The painter's technique has become a new source of meaning and pleasure; in the past it was mainly a guarantee of durability. For example, notice how Soutine's painted forms remind us of El Greco. However, in *The Madwoman* Soutine employed more direct brushwork in the darks than El Greco would have because Soutine's brilliant cadmiums and alizarins were not available to El Greco. That is, they were not available in chemically stable, lightproof pigments. The old masters would have employed a thin reddish glaze over a neutral tempera underpainting that rested on a luminous white ground. Soutine, on the other hand, was able to apply opaque reds and crimsons directly to the white-primed canvas; he could paint his twisting shadows with loaded brush quite spontaneously. The turbulence of Soutine's imagery

left: **Chaim Soutine. *The Madwoman*. 1920. The National Museum of Western Art, Tokyo. Presented by Mr. Tai Hayashi, 1960**

right: **El Greco. Detail of *Pentecost*. 1603–7. The Prado, Madrid. Copyright © Museo del Prado**

Leonardo da Vinci. Detail of *The Last Supper*. c. 1495–98. Sta. Maria delle Grazie, Milan

Instead of the time-honored fresco technique, Leonardo used tempera on a masonry wall that was badly sealed with a varnish of resin and pitch. Moisture must have passed through the wall into the paint film, which began to peel soon after the work was completed. Since then, it has suffered from poor care and numerous restorations. We can only guess at its original magnificence.

owes a great deal to this type of direct execution; El Greco's flickering effects had to be planned in advance. Interestingly, that flickering effect expresses spirituality in El Greco; in Soutine it becomes a symptom of madness, a sign of the soul in torment.

Inevitably, the durability of goods has a different meaning today than it had in the scarcity economies of the past. For us, an artistic concern with permanent technique seems old-fashioned, since we are reasonably assured of the physical survival of a painting; our concern shifts to its durability as a significant statement. We want to know whether a painting will live as a vehicle of sustained *aesthetic interest*. And we are especially concerned with its *originality*. As George Moore said, "It does not matter how badly you paint, so long as you don't paint badly like other people."

The *time* required to execute a work by traditional methods worked against a casual approach toward artistic subjects. But as the oil-painting medium was perfected, technical skills could be devoted to themes of less than high seriousness. For example, the courts-of-love paintings by Jean-Honoré Fragonard (1732–1806) seem exceptionally shallow, even by modern standards. However, the fluid execution of *The Swing* is a triumph of painterly virtuosity. Beyond the silly theatrics of the situation, the drawing, brushwork, and composition are managed with extraordinary skill. We, on the other hand, often employ a casual and offhand technique for the treatment of major themes. *La Mort d'Attila* by Georges Mathieu (born 1921) is such a work; it represents the death of the "Scourge of God," as the murderous Hun was lovingly known. But visually, it tells us more about Mathieu's wrist than about Attila.

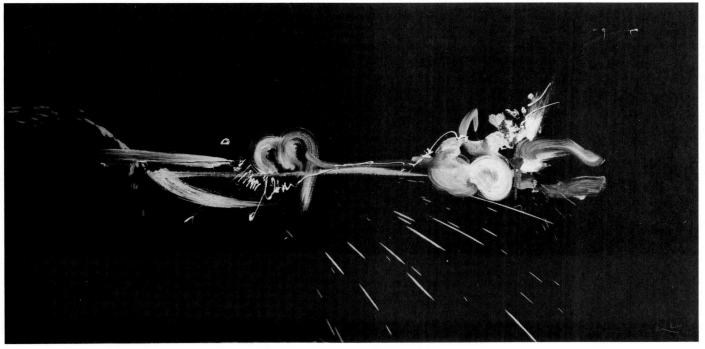

left: Jean-Honoré Fragonard. Detail of *The Swing.* 1766. By permission of the Trustees of the Wallace Collection, London

below: Georges Mathieu. *La Mort d'Attila.* 1961. Collection Jean Larcade, Paris

We do not look at a painting as medieval or Renaissance men did, inquiring into its craftsmanship, its likelihood of surviving as an object that permanently states an important idea. Contemporary collectors are more inclined to think of a painting as a possession they may sell if it ceases to be interesting or if its market value increases. Clearly, we have a different sense of time, a different set of priorities. Under the impact of rapid technical and social change, our confidence in fixed values has broken down. The idea that man-made structures can or should survive seems old-fashioned, just as it would have seemed absurd to medieval men that anything be made *not* to last.

257

But if the decline of the old idea of permanence has cost us certain artistic values, there have also been compensations. Experimentation with new materials and themes has generated dividends in visual variety. Painting is perhaps more entertaining—certainly more shocking—than it was. At the same time, painters have not abandoned serious issues. Although photography, film, and television pose a threat to the survival of picture-making as a handcraft, painters appear to be responding to the challenge vigorously. Certainly, painting is more widely practiced—and the results more widely exhibited—than ever before; the range of social and personal concerns it deals with has been extended; and it competes with every other medium of information and expression. As will be seen, painting has acquired some of the traits of sculpture, architecture, and theater. So painting may be old, but it continues to grow.

DIRECT AND INDIRECT TECHNIQUES

Simply stated, direct painting seeks a final effect immediately; indirect painting calls for a stage-by-stage approach. These two approaches represent fundamental contrasts in technique and in artistic psychology. In general, traditional methods are indirect, systematic, and planned in advance. Modern approaches tend to be direct, spontaneous, and open to happy accidents.

For as long as painting is regarded as an elaboration of drawing, the indirect method will prevail. When painting is a process of applying color to a scheme that has already been worked out, it makes sense to use the indirect method: it amounts to a problem in the division of labor. First comes the conception of the work, its theme, its setting, its specific content, and so on. Next, drawings are made to explore the spatial representation, the arrangement of landscape or architectural features, and the placement of figures. Finally, there may be an oil sketch to indicate the distribution of color and light. Drawing, however, is the main compositional tool, the real decision-making device.

left: **Michelangelo. Studies for *The Libyan Sibyl.* The Metropolitan Museum of Art, New York. Joseph Pulitzer Bequest, 1924**

The drawing is more detailed than the final fresco painting because it truly is a "study"—a device for *knowing* a phenomenon visually and intellectually.

right: **Michelangelo. *The Libyan Sibyl* (detail from the ceiling of the Sistine Chapel). 1511. The Vatican, Rome**

Studies of anatomy, drapery, hands, and facial expressions were undertaken so the artist could be assured of an intellectual and visual grasp of the subject; then he felt ready to transfer his drawings to a prepared surface. Following enlargement to the scale of the final work, the artist could begin painterly execution. The preliminary painting—often in tempera—would usually be monochromatic; this "underpainting" translated preparatory sketches into paint, establishing the compositional scheme, placing the lights and darks, and modeling large forms. Because tempera paint dries quickly and is very opaque, corrections to cover mistakes can be made easily. Oil paint, on the other hand, dries slowly and becomes somewhat transparent as it grows older; thus passages that have been painted out will eventually show through. However, tempera does not blend easily. Egg tempera, especially, is difficult to spread over large areas. So large forms have to be built up by "hatching" (creating small areas of color or tone by a series of lines painted close together); it is an essentially linear technique.

When using the indirect method, the underpainting can be executed in cool tones because warm-tone glazes will probably be applied over them at the end. By manipulating glazes (paint thinned with oil or varnish), the painter can acquire a rich, warm-cool balance. Light areas were usually painted "higher" or "chalkier" than they would finally appear because overpainting and glazing would lower their value. Also, it was assumed that white pigment (usually white lead), together with final varnishing, would tend to yellow the painting. That was another reason for favoring a cool tonality in the underpainting.

Before the wide use of oil painting, most paintings were completely executed in tempera (the other principal media were encaustic, which employs hot wax as a binder, and fresco, which employs water, lime, and plaster as its binder). Tempera is usually understood as any painting medium based on a glue. Older glues came from cooked animal skins—rabbit skin, for instance. As we know from scraping breakfast frying pans, eggs are a powerful adhesive. Casein, a milk derivative, is a modern glue that makes an excellent tempera. Polymer or acrylic tempera comes close to being an ideal medium since it possesses all the assets and none of the liabilities of the traditional tempera and oil media. Until the 1940s, however, tempera paintings were mostly executed with the traditional egg-yolk medium. And some painters, like Andrew Wyeth, continue to employ the classic egg-tempera medium.

Contemporary artists who use the traditional method of tempera painting prepare a gesso ground (thin, white plaster-of-Paris layers applied over a coating of glue) on a wood panel (today it would be Masonite); then they puncture an egg-yolk sac, "cook up" an egg-and-water or egg-and-oil emulsion, and mix the emulsion with powdered dry pigment. The pure egg-tempera medium is quite permanent; it does not darken with age; and it provides clean, bright color. But tempera usually calls for a rigid support and, as mentioned above, it is not well suited for covering large areas. Furthermore, it dictates a slowly built-up, step-by-step mode of execution. And, like fresco, it forces the artist to think in linear terms.

Direct painting began when artists increased the amount of pigment in their oil glazes. The Venetians were probably the first to do this; they employed a technique in which the brush is "loaded" with paint of a pasty, viscous consistency and then applied in short "touches" rather than spread out evenly. This technique permits freer departures from a controlling tempera underpainting. We can see a line of development in the use of direct oil painting from Titian to Rubens to Delacroix. Delacroix may represent the critical departure from reliance on an underpainting; with him, spontaneous execution begins to assert itself forcefully. His contemporary, Jean-Auguste-Dominique Ingres (1780–1867), painted directly but produced a surface on which no brushstroke could be seen. Delacroix, however, exploited the emotive possibilities of brushwork. In his oil sketch for *The Lion Hunt,* we see a tech-

Jean-Auguste-Dominique Ingres.
*Pauline Eléonore de Galard de
Brassac de Béarn, Princesse de
Broglie.* 1853. The Metropolitan
Museum of Art, New York. Rob-
ert Lehman Collection, 1975

nique that relies almost entirely on broad strokes of the brush. Drawing is felt,
but it is subordinate to the painterly development of form. The dynamism of
this composition derives basically from an underlying pattern of whirling
forms that radiate from the center and rotate in a counterclockwise direction.
But Delacroix was not content to rely on linear dynamics: he supported the
movement of the composition with brushstrokes that have a life of their own.

The *Lion Hunt* by Peter Paul Rubens (1577–1640) is obviously the technical and thematic ancestor of the Delacroix oil sketch. Although Rubens employed a preliminary underpainting, he relied on a direct type of overpainting
executed very spontaneously. Today, we can see a similar approach in the
painting of Richard Lytle (born 1935). Direct painting technique has an appeal—for the artist and the viewer—that seems to be unchanged by the passage of time.

top: Peter Paul Rubens. *Lion Hunt.* 1616–21.
Alte Pinakothek, Munich

left: Eugène Delacroix. Sketch for *The Lion
Hunt.* 1860–61. Private collection

right: Richard Lytle. *The Possessed.* 1959. Collection the artist

BRUSHWORK AND EMOTION

The question arises: How does brushwork excite our emotions? Fundamentally, it is through a process of visual imitation: we "act out" the artist's work of wielding the brush and applying paint. All of us have had experience with brushes—either in art classes or in performing personal or household tasks. So, it is easy to simulate inwardly the motions implied by the brushwork we see. This does not mean that viewers perform gymnastic maneuvers in front of a painting that has an active surface. It *does* mean that brush marks stimulate a variety of physiological reactions inside the viewer, and these reactions generate feelings.

In direct technique a great many decisions are combined in the act of applying paint. The brushing gesture takes on crucial importance when color, value, shape, size, and texture are determined as the paint is laid on. Furthermore, the painter is usually trying for a spontaneous look even if he or she works slowly and deliberately. When the desired effect is not achieved immediately, the artist scrapes off the paint and tries again: oil paint is ideal for this sort of trial-and-error execution. But if the artist continues to paint over earlier efforts rather than scrape them off, the result is a labored, rather tortured-looking paint surface. Direct technique, therefore, is not well suited to frequent "overpaints." The color becomes muddy, and the surface looks uncertain; clarity of color and crispness of brushwork are lost.

Because painting is in many respects a *performing* art, viewers are attracted by the evidence of paint mixing and brushwork. Here, Cézanne and Van Gogh are instructive performers to watch. There is a steady buildup of planes in Cézanne, but his "touch," while careful, is rarely hesitant. He did not push the paint around indecisively, and he seems to have known the color and value of each stroke before he committed himself. Frequently, the canvas shows through, as white paper sometimes does in a watercolor painting. Consequently, Cézanne's surfaces have a freshness and sparkle that would not be possible with a more labored, brushed-out technique.

Van Gogh's *The Ravine* demonstrates the emotional power of a different kind of brushstroke: we see a pattern of short, rapid, curved, and angular thrusts. They set up staccato rhythms that reinforce the impact of the vibrating color. The application of the paint contributes to the gushing motion we "feel" in the water: blended colors or luminous glazing would surely ruin this effect. For a completely different approach to brushwork, we must go back to El Greco's *The Agony in the Garden of Gethsemane* (page 221). Here, it is the *shaped areas of light* that create the effect of turbulent emotion. Using indirect painting technique, El Greco came very close to the agitated feeling that modern painters achieve through violent, impulsive brushwork.

If we trace the emergence of brushwork from its beginnings among the fifteenth-century Venetians to its full development in our own time, it seems that its course has paralleled the growth of individualism in society and of autonomy among artists. Direct technique played an important role because of its emphasis on the uniqueness of the painter's style; it appealed to artists who saw the expression of personality as their principal objective. Indirect technique suited more modest or secretive artists—painters who did not wish to display their "handwriting." These contrasting attitudes are visible today. The so-called hard-edge and geometric painters tend to employ a smooth, anonymous technique, relying on design and the optical effects of color to carry the burden of their work. But for "action" painters, the path of the artist's brush traveling across a canvas is often the main theme.

Brushwork has become a declaration of the artist's personal freedom. For a painter, what could be a more forceful assertion of individualism than the bold marks of the brush, left on the canvas exactly as they were applied, unretouched and undisguised? With their brushwork exposed, painters were ready to tell all. In a post-Freudian era, artists declared that there was nothing to hide, nothing to cover up.

Paul Cézanne. *Houses in Provence.* c. 1880. National Gallery of Art, Washington, D.C. Collection Mr. and Mrs. Paul Mellon, 1973

Frans Hals. Detail of *Governors of the Old Men's Almshouse, Haarlem.* 1664. Frans Hals Museum, Haarlem, The Netherlands

Vincent van Gogh. *The Ravine.* 1889. Museum of Fine Arts, Boston. Bequest of Keith McLeod

DIRECT TECHNIQUE

The impression of swiftness and spontaneity calls for considerable assurance on the part of the artist—assurance based on solid knowledge, power of observation, and shrewd grasp of character.

Leonardo da Vinci. Detail of *Portrait of a Musician*. 1490. Biblioteca Ambrosiana, Milan

Michelangelo. Detail of *The Prophet Joel*. 1509. Ceiling of the Sistine Chapel, The Vatican, Rome

What generous expressions! How intelligent the eyes! The noses and chins are constructed as nobly as Greek temples. Even if they are idealized, such men *should* have existed.

THE HUMAN IMAGE IN TRADITIONAL PAINTING

Rembrandt van Rijn. Detail of *Head of Christ*. c. 1650. The Metropolitan Museum of Art, New York. The Mr. and Mrs. Isaac D. Fletcher Collection. Bequest of Isaac D. Fletcher, 1917

For Rembrandt, the image of Jesus posed a special problem: the Catholic Baroque tradition called for an idealized, somewhat mannered personification, but Rembrandt's painterly style and religious commitment had their roots in Protestant realism. His solution: a Jewish model in whose countenance we see a remarkably credible embodiment of manliness and compassion.

El Greco. Detail of *Fray Felix Hortensio Paravicino*. c. 1605. Museum of Fine Arts, Boston

Behind those penetrating eyes, which seem to take one's full measure, the viewer senses the controlled intensity of a totally dedicated man, a "true believer."

Peter Paul Rubens. Detail of *Self-Portrait*. 1638–40. Kunsthistorisches Museum, Vienna

The self-assurance of an older man who has been very successful. An intellectual as well as a highly physical person, Rubens was never assailed by doubts about the ultimate unity of spirit and flesh.

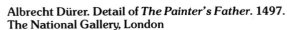

These are stubborn men. So were the artists who painted them—stubborn about telling the whole truth.

Albrecht Dürer. Detail of *The Painter's Father*. 1497. The National Gallery, London

Jan van Eyck. Detail of *The Virgin and the Canon Van der Paele*. 1436. Groeningemuseum, Bruges

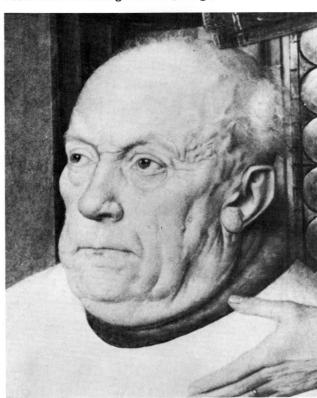

Jacques-Louis David. Detail of *Man with a Hat.* After 1816. Royal Museum of Fine Arts, Antwerp

Even in the work of a classicist like David, the force of a private personality asserts itself—especially in this candid portrait. A new cult of individualism is emerging—casual, studied, self-assured. The manner of aristocrats is now enjoyed by a confident bourgeoisie.

Théodore Géricault. Detail of *The Homicidal Maniac.* 1821–24. Musée des Beaux Arts, Ghent

Pursuing the varieties and extremes of individualism, the Romantic painter examined one of the most tragic forms of human suffering and alienation: madness.

Diego Velázquez. Detail of *Pope Innocent X.* 1650. Doria-Pamphili Gallery, Rome

A work of the seventeenth century, but thoroughly modern in its approach to painting and personality. Its optical realism anticipates Impressionism and photography. The only barrier between the viewer and a complete disclosure of Innocent's character is the aristocratic reserve of the artist.

Édouard Manet. Detail of *The Luncheon in the Studio.* 1869. Neue Pinakothek, Munich

The self-assurance of this young man corresponds to certain arrogant qualities in Manet's style: a frontality based on exceedingly flat lighting, a refusal to tamper with or idealize visual facts, a determination to set the painterly act above pictorial convention.

Eugène Delacroix. Detail of *Portrait of Chopin*. 1838. The Louvre, Paris

Here is an ideal combination: a Romantic composer portrayed by a Romantic painter. Delacroix realized that there could be a correspondence between feeling, form, and technique. We see more than the structure of Chopin's head; we see his turbulent inner life expressed through brushwork.

THE HUMAN IMAGE
IN MODERN PAINTING

From Cézanne to Picasso to Gris, we see the progressive analysis, breakup, and rearrangement of form. Cézanne tried to bypass subjective impressions by destroying objects and reconstructing them along rational, architectonic lines. Picasso went further by attempting to show the interpenetration of solids and voids. Even so, the human qualities of his subject show through. With Gris, we have a different objective: the creation of a geometry of form that could deal with anything—people, objects, places, or spaces. Cézanne would have approved.

Paul Cézanne. Detail of *Victor Chocquet Assis*. c. 1877. Columbus Museum of Art, Ohio. Howald Fund Purchase

Pablo Picasso. Detail of *Portrait of Ambroise Vollard*. 1909–10. Pushkin Museum, Moscow

Juan Gris. Detail of *Portrait of Picasso*. 1912. The Art Institute of Chicago

Georges Rouault. Detail of *The Tragedian*. 1910. Collection
Professor Hahnloser, Bern

Edvard Munch. Detail of *Puberty*. 1894. National
Gallery, Oslo

The common trait of Expressionist art is its capacity to
make us spectators at the moment when a person experiences a very personal dread. The soul, if not the body, is
invariably shown naked and shivering. We see more than
a person's fear of responsibility, guilt, physical deterioration, or a life of emptiness; we witness a sense of awe
when these abstractions become final meanings in personal existence.

Oskar Kokoschka. Detail of *Self-Portrait*. 1913. Collection, The Museum of Modern Art, New York. Purchase

Ivan Albright. Detail of *And God Created Man in His Own Image*. 1930–31. On permanent loan to The Art Institute of Chicago from the Collection of Ivan Albright

Henri Matisse. *Green Stripe (Madame Matisse)*. 1905.
Royal Museum of Fine Arts, Copenhagen. Rump
Collection

Alexej von Jawlensky. *Self-Portrait*. 1912. Collection
Andreas Jawlensky, Locarno, Switzerland

In a sense, Matisse, during his Fauvist period, was responsible for
the development of all these artists—even the Germans and the
Slavs. While pursuing his serene pictorial objectives through a system of arbitrary color, he opened up a new set of emotional options
for figural representation—options that were eagerly seized by artists of restless disposition. Although Matisse was concerned with
the human image only as a motif in a grand scheme of light, movement, and pleasure, these Expressionists followed a different
path—a path of agonizing self-examination and private anguish.

Max Beckmann. Detail of *Self-Portrait in a Tuxedo*. 1927.
Busch-Reisinger Museum, Harvard University, Cambridge,
Massachusetts

Ludwig Kirchner. Detail of *Portrait of Gräf*. 1924.
Kunstmuseum der Stadt Düsseldorf

Karel Appel. Detail of *Crying Nude*. 1956. Collection Mr. and Mrs. Alan Fidler, Willowdale, Ontario

Antonio Saura. *Imaginary Portrait of Goya*. 1963. Museum of Art, Carnegie Institute, Pittsburgh

To the extent that the human image survives in painting, it is either mutilated or ridiculed. Appel and Saura convert Expressionist brushwork into a mode of abuse, trying to summon a kind of mythic power through wild painterly attacks on their subjects. Larry Rivers and Richard Hamilton are cooler: they play Pop-art games with drawn, painted, and pasted image fragments. But the game is violent; the human image is being mugged.

Larry Rivers. Detail of *Celebrating Shakespeare's 400th Birthday (Titus Andronicus)*. 1963. Collection Clarice Rivers, New York

Richard Hamilton. *Fashion-plate study (a) self-portrait*. 1969. Collection Rita Donagh, London

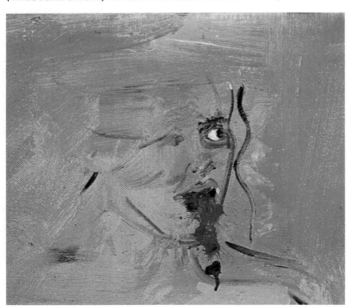

FROTTAGE, GRATTAGE, AND DECALCOMANIA

The spontaneous application of paint with a loaded brush was one type of liberation from the traditional approach to painting. Artists exploited the fact that the marks of tools are expressive in themselves. Once this was discovered, it was a simple step to the realization that new tools produced new possibilities of expression. Artists now devised new techniques for manipulating paint, which, *itself* became the subject of their imagery. Among the most inventive was Max Ernst (1891–1976), a prolific creator of new technical devices.

For most of his career, Ernst was associated with the Dada and Surrealist movements; so, irrational impulse played a major role in his art. *Chance arrangement* was a principle of Dadaist composition; fantasy and the combination of unrelated images guided Surrealism. Clearly, the movements were linked. Ernst's technical discoveries grew out of a search for imagery that could not be known in advance, that could not be consciously calculated. His was an art that originated in "accidents"—seemingly random interactions between paint and process. But, although the process appears to be unplanned, Ernst worked hard to create accidental situations.

Frottage is the best known of Ernst's techniques. Most of us are familiar with it in the popular art of rubbings; pencil or crayon rubbed over paper placed on a textured surface transfers a negative image of the texture underneath. Accordingly, archaeologists use frottage to make copies of stone or metal reliefs. For the artist, abstract patterns, as in wood grains, can be transferred and worked up into recognizable images. Thus, frottage stimulates the creation of fantastic forms. Ernst used it to convert the normal or accidental processes of nature into artistic images. For example, Ernst used frottage in oil painting by placing a freshly painted canvas over a relief texture and then scraping away part of the paint. The unscraped paint left in the valleys and crevices of the canvas created a pattern corresponding to the texture underneath. This process did not involve rubbing, but it resulted in the transfer of a pattern by a frottage-like technique.

As with *decalcomania* (see below), the key to frottage is transfer—*informal printing*. Other informal printing processes involved dipping leaves, kitchen utensils, toy parts—anything that could be held in the hand—into wet paint; the object was then used like a hand stamp to transfer a pattern to canvas. Then the paintbrush was used to heighten or finish the forms suggested by the marks of real objects and processes.

Grattage, another Ernstian technique, is the grating or scratching of wet paint with a variety of tools: a comb, a fork, a pen, a razor, a needle, a piece of

left: **Max Ernst. *The Eye of Silence*. 1944. Washington University, St. Louis**

The painter builds a surface through carving, scratching, and abrading; his picture is something "real" rather than a system of illusions.

right: **Antoni Tàpies. *Campins Painting*. 1962. Collection Mr. and Mrs. Robert B. Mayer, Winnetka, Illinois**

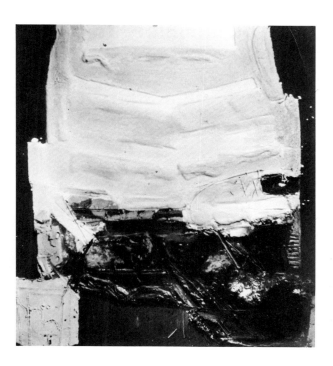

glass. Grattage exploits the plastic character of wet oil paint just as the paint-brush does. But the brush is designed to smooth and blend paint—only secondarily to leave its mark. These tools of grattage treat paint as a kind of colored mud or as a type of building material, like concrete. (Here it should be mentioned that Le Corbusier liked to "scratch" images into the poured-concrete surfaces of his buildings.) The conception of paint as a material that can be scratched, abraded, or otherwise tortured represents a departure from the idea of paint as a descriptive substance. In traditional painting, the pigment was not really "there"; it designated something else. Now paint became a kind of primal substance that miraculously "remembered" everything done to it.

In *decalcomania,* wet blobs of paint are squeezed between two canvas surfaces, which are then separated. Variations in pressure force the paint into random patterns, forming crevices and rivulets that can be exploited for their formal and thematic suggestions: fantastic geological structures, landscapes of unknown planets, monstrous biological specimens, wild projections of the fevered imagination. Still, it is the artist's imagination that acts as the creative instrument. In the end, decalcomania, frottage, and grattage are strategies for making the creative juices flow.

Another Ernstian technique, *éclaboussage,* is widely used today. It involves dropping paint or turpentine from a height to a prepared canvas. Ernst dropped paint from a perforated tin can swung from a string suspended above the canvas. The paint splashes were then manipulated like the squeezed pigment in decalcomania. Turpentine dropped on a freshly painted canvas was also used to create splash patterns, to expose the bare canvas, or dilute the wet paint partially. The turpentine was blotted up or allowed to stand in a puddle or run in random paths. From *éclaboussage,* or *dropping* paint, it was only a short step to *throwing* paint with a brush or dripping it from a stick, à la Jackson Pollock.

For centuries, the brush was an extension of the artist's hand, but when used to splash and spatter paint it became a different tool. One of the most bizarre methods of using paint is the technique of Niki de Saint-Phalle (born 1930), who would fire a rifle at bags of paint suspended before a wall covered with relief sculptures. The firing of the gun and the explosion of the bag of paint created two dramatic events—the performance itself and its visual result on the wall relief. Here, the theme of violence was captured in at least two dimensions: the gunshot becomes, so to speak, an act of execution; the image becomes a collision report.

Once the brush lost its central place in painting, and once pigment became a nonillusionistic substance, the tools and materials of image-making

Photograph of Niki de Saint-Phalle about to paint with a rifle

GOVERNED COMPRESSION

César. *The Yellow Buick*. 1961. Collection, The Museum of Modern Art, New York. Gift of Mr. and Mrs. John Rewald

were almost infinitely extended. For example, a bulldozer might be employed as an artistic tool, as in Morris's *Earthwork* (page 361). Or, images could be created with the powerful hydraulic press used to squeeze junked automobiles into compact cubes of anonymous metal. That is what César Baldaccini (born 1921) did, using a method he calls "governed compression." We cannot escape the impression that these theatrical gestures represented a shift of focus in visual art: from images and objects to the dramatic effects of technology. Increasingly, painters and sculptors want to be performers or film producers or civil and mechanical engineers: they cause objects to be made and environments to be changed. But they don't form objects and images with their hands; they use "foreign" technologies. Are they ashamed of brush, paint, and palette knife? Are they tired of drawing, mixing, and blending? Are they trying to humanize the rifle and the hydraulic press?

The painter's urge to join the performing arts—or engineering—will be discussed below. But here we want to stress artists' attempts to devise new creative strategies. At first, these strategies were tools for making art *objects*. But the next generation of artists was concerned with strategy for its own sake. The *process* of throwing, dripping, or exploding paint opened up possibilities that were felt to have aesthetic value apart from their results. In a subsequent section of this chapter, "Beyond Collage: Assemblage, Environments, Happenings," we shall analyze these developments in painting and/or drama.

Willem de Kooning. *The Time of the Fire.*
1956. Private collection

THE PICTURE AND THE WALL

Abstract Expressionism, or "action painting," which dominated the art scene from 1946 until approximately 1960, reintroduced huge canvases—canvases large enough for a Baroque palace. Dimensions of up to sixteen feet were not unusual. This new scale of painting signaled a fundamental change in the way painting was meant to operate in its setting and for its public.

Action painting depended for its effectiveness on the communication of the artist's brushing gestures—gestures accomplished mainly through the movements of the large muscle groups of the body. This is obvious in a work such as de Kooning's *The Time of the Fire.* To appreciate this painting, the viewer's reaction must be kinesthetic as well as optical. Its reproduction in a book, no matter how faithful, cannot stimulate the appropriate bodily responses: it lacks grand scale.

Large pictures were created in the past, but their size was based on the need to accommodate many figures (often lifesize or larger), plus buildings, interior details, and so on. Scale and format were keyed to the actual dimensions of real objects. With the growing importance of landscape painting, however, large size yielded to mastery of atmospheric perspective: vast spaces could be portrayed on small canvases. Then, with Impressionist painting, the distance of the viewer from the *picture surface* became crucial for understanding the work. At one distance, perception would be of color patches and fragments of form. At a greater distance, color areas and fragments came into *focus*, yielding an image that made sense as a whole, but not in its separate parts, many of which were very small.

The vital, possibly accidental, discovery of the Impressionists was that unfocused color areas could sustain interest as images in themselves. Furthermore, the emotional potential of these color areas could be exploited if they were detached from objects and surfaces. This is exactly what we see in the combination of free color, active brushwork, and abstract design in a huge canvas-mural, *Water Lilies,* painted by Monet about 1920. The work is made up of three panels, each fourteen feet wide, and it is executed in broad, loosely brushed color areas. Because of its size, we cannot see the entire canvas at once. Instead, we see a succession of fragments that are essentially abstract: areas of color take precedence over visual description; the big brushing gestures are as significant as the flowers and water they represent.

opposite: Claude Monet. *Water Lilies.* c. 1920.
Collection, The Museum of Modern Art, New
York. Mrs. Simon Guggenheim Fund

David Teniers. *The Picture Gallery of Archduke Leopold Wilhelm.* c. 1650. The Prado, Madrid

The display of paintings in the seventeenth century emphasized their separate character: each picture represents a self-contained world independent of the architectural setting in which it is encountered.

Office of David Rockefeller, Chase Manhattan Bank, New York. 1961

Here the forms in the painting harmonize with the furniture and floor covering of the room. Painting and architecture are on speaking terms because they use the same abstract language: no figures, no illusions of deep space. Then why does the figurative sculpture from Asia look so right? Because it makes no illusionistic claims; because it occupies real space; because it functions as a real presence.

The large scale of modern painting has important implications. The first is that passages of color and texture are frequently larger than the viewer, making it difficult to maintain an attitude of detachment while we view them. Areas and shapes are not so much objects of perception as *part of the environment;* they *surround* the viewer. Certainly, Mark Rothko made effective use of this factor. We are reminded of the difference between the motion-picture image and the television image. Empathy is easier with the motion-picture screen than with the home tube. Movies communicate emotion visually, whereas the television image feels more like an extension of radio: it carries information through the spoken word. In other words, the small image employs a literary logic; large images employ the logic of the whole body and the emotions.

A second implication of large-scale painting lies in the tendency of the picture to merge with the wall; it becomes part of a building's architecture. It ceases to be a view seen through a window, a device for *dissolving* the wall. Painting thus returns to its mosaic and stained-glass antecedents. This development began with the flattening of space by Cézanne and the Cubists, who realized that illusionistic effects violated the integrity of the wall and of architectural space. Now, the painted image *rests* on the wall surface; it doesn't claim to carve out deep space. Increasingly, modern painting and large-scale graphics function as architectural accents; many of our buildings would be uninteresting without them.

The return of painting to architecture is part of a drive to create environments. In this development, painters have been encouraged by modern architectural practice. Some architects design interior surfaces that function like paintings or like sculptural reliefs. Buildings by Wright and Le Corbusier often look complete without pictures. Indeed, many painters feel that Wright's Guggenheim Museum dominates the pictures in it: the building's design satisfies most of our visual and plastic requirements; pictures become superfluous. Buildings by Mies van der Rohe, however, seem to need painting and sculpture.

In general, there is an abundance of anonymous space and plain wall surfaces in modern American building. Perhaps this creates a vacuum that painters instinctively want to fill. Besides, the large scale of modern painting has effectively removed it from the domestic dwelling; public buildings are its natural, perhaps its only, habitat. Increasingly, painting has become an art for the spacious walls of museums and public buildings or for the corridors and executive suites of banks.

Some small works are still created for private dwellings, but major works by "important" painters rarely fit into homes, even those of the rich. Major collectors have to design special facilities for their collections. Clearly, paintings have escaped the category of Victorian knickknacks. They are too large, too bright, and too disturbing to rest quietly against the wallpaper, sharing the soft light of a table lamp with family photographs, collections of china, and travel souvenirs. Painting has become an art of public statement and public performance.

Today's large-scale paintings are created with the awareness that they are destined ultimately for public ownership and display. What will happen to small pictures, easel paintings? Will they be replaced by Happenings and Environments—visual extravaganzas that can fill virtually any available space? Or will they end up as handmade decorations—wall spots—for motel rooms and doctors' offices? I think pictures as ornaments, traded like furniture and other household items, will continue to be created, but they will not occupy a position close to the heart of painting as a serious art form. Henceforth, large paintings will be created for public architecture. As for the small picture—the serious easel painting—it will be made for reproduction in print and electronic formats that will bring millions of people into contact with the world's best visual thinking.

BEYOND COLLAGE: ASSEMBLAGE, ENVIRONMENTS, HAPPENINGS

In every generation, some painters feel that their elders have carried the art as far as it can go, so they must strike out in radically new directions—in materials, technique, and creative approach. One powerful reason for their dissatisfaction has been the attraction of the film—an attraction that is understandable, since motion pictures are the most important extension of the art of image-making since the Stone Age. Spurred by the need to compete with new media of communication, painters try to cross the line separating their art from sculpture and architecture. They have abandoned representation, creating works that are "real." They have fashioned works that spectators can enter physically, like actors in a play. Such innovations can be understood as the endeavor of "old-fashioned" image makers to compete with new materials and technologies that threaten their existence.

Assemblage is an example. As the word implies, it is art created by putting things together—usually by combining them in new contexts. Because of

The painter as collagist. Bearden used photographic fragments and assorted odds and ends, which he reorganized in a pictorial scheme that combines French Cubism with images drawn from Black American life. The combination makes sense visually and historically: Cubism had African roots.

their training, painters can think of debris and other found objects in terms of line, shape, color, and texture. Instead of imitating surface appearances and textures with brush and paint, the artist employs "real" materials. This reduces the need for conventional skills in the *re*-presentation of reality. For many painters, the old skills have grown progressively less important as photography, film, and graphic-reproduction techniques have advanced.

The technical ground for *assemblage* was prepared by *collage*. These media are similar except that collage calls for *gluing* materials to a surface. Assemblage employs *any* method of joining things together, producing results that look much like sculpture. Many painters have practiced sculpture; but as painters, they usually approached three-dimensionality by creating illusions of depth and by manipulating textures. However, the differences between painting and sculpture began to break down under the assaults of Dada artists such as Schwitters, Arp, Ernst, and Duchamp. As a result, today's painting studio looks very much like a sculpture studio.

Among modernist practitioners of collage and assemblage, Jean Dubuffet (1901–1985) can be compared with Max Ernst in imaginative and technical

Jean Dubuffet. *My Cart, My Garden.* **1955. Collection, The Museum of Modern Art, New York. James Thrall Soby Bequest**

fertility. His mixtures of pigment, asphalt, tar, cement, varnish, glue, sand, and so on convert the artist's canvas into a kind of *wall*. His "wall" becomes a new kind of fresco, this time inspired by *graffiti*, the markings found on sidewalks, fences, toilet stalls, and, alas, subway cars. Like the Dadaists, Dubuffet was powerfully attracted to the artistic possibilities of debris. His works were made with butterfly wings, tobacco leaves, papier-mâché, metal foil, driftwood, banana peels, fruit rinds, coal clinkers, and dirt. Again, the downgrading of paint in favor of discarded and "worthless" materials.

An industrial civilization produces vast and varied kinds of debris—used-up and discarded materials that possess a built-in visual history. Dubuffet took obsessive delight in employing garbage of one sort or another *in place of* paint or in conjunction with it. He also borrowed images from the art of the insane; they, too, are part of society's debris. In much of his work, Dubuffet seemed to be saying that the most interesting things we produce—human, vegetable, or mineral—are the things we ignore or throw away.

Now that pigment is being displaced, industrial debris, garbage, and earth itself—stones, gravel, minerals, and dirt—provide the materials of "painting." Inventing problems with materials becomes one of the burdens of the new painterly freedom: traditional technical constraints are gone. There is no hierarchy of subject matter: one theme is as good as another. As for the public, its hostility toward the new has substantially evaporated. Moving from a position of alienation, painters are often celebrated culture heroes—supported by foundations, employed as "stars" by universities, and encouraged to decorate the walls of important public buildings. For some of them, this combination of social acceptance and technical freedom may seem unnatural; artists have always thrived on resistance: the stubbornness of materials, the restrictions of traditional technique, or the anger of the public. So, without this resistance, artists contrive to reintroduce it. Perhaps that explains the strange substances and the outrageous subject matter: painters keep trying to shock the unshockable middle class.

Pop Art and Combine Paintings　Almost everything in the built environment has been designed to inform, persuade, entertain, or sell. Especially to sell. In our culture an enormous amount of material is reproduced to carry out the functions of visual communication and display. Hamburgers and hot dogs, soft drinks and bathing suits, automobiles and stereo sets: their images greet us on television, jump out of road signs, crowd the pages of magazines, and fill the precious shelf space of drugstores and supermarkets. When we do not see this imagery, we hear it described in other media. To carry on our daily lives, we have to *adjust* to a world of image saturation; we become visually anesthetized, or we learn to see graphic images selectively. The Pop artists have chosen this world as the source of their own imagery; they are determined to make us see what our nervous systems have mercifully managed to suppress.

In the strategy of Pop, large scale is very important. Another major feature is repetition—mechanical repetition, as in *Marilyn Monroe* by Andy Warhol (born 1928). Radio and television commercials rely heavily on repetition—a device that eventually overcomes resistance. So Warhol uses visual repetition in his paintings, prints, and three-dimensional "sculptures"—reproductions of containers for soap, soup, breakfast foods, and so on. Obviously, he is not selling the product; he is making a statement about a large part of our environment. Warhol understands publicity—perhaps even better than Dali.

Anonymity is another feature of Pop. Robert Indiana's (born 1928) paintings based on stenciled signs tell us little about the personality of the artist except his lettering skills, word choice, and determination to capture the viewer's attention. Warhol's Campbell's Soup labels—hundreds of them—might have been painted by some other equally neat designer. Thought and

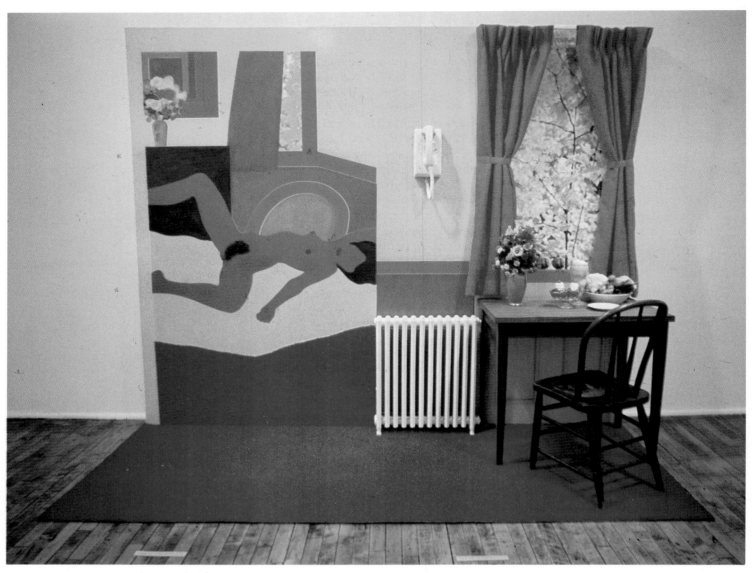

Tom Wesselmann. *The Great American Nude, #54.*
1964. Neue Gallery, Aachen, West Germany

Wesselmann's erotically displayed woman shows that he can "do" a Matisse, a vulgar Matisse, if he wants to. Beyond that, he throws a Pop-art curve: the woman presented as just another cheap object in an environment of cheap objects.

Andy Warhol. *Marilyn Monroe.* **1962. Collection Vernon Nikkel, Clovis, New Mexico**

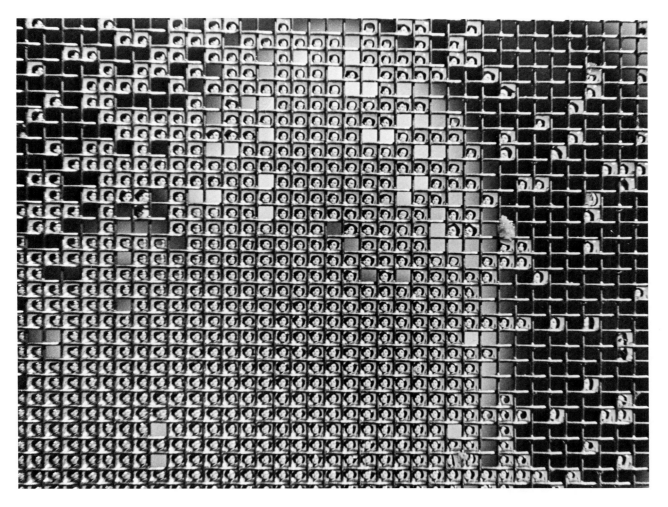

skill are visible, but they do not seem to belong to any particular artist. Thus, Pop echoes the homogenized character of commercial graphics, in contrast to the highly individualized creations of the gallery artist.

Other Pop artists—Robert Rauschenberg, Wayne Thiebaud, and James Rosenquist—approach painting in a more personal manner, but they still draw on the stereotypes of popular culture for their imagery. Rauschenberg

Audrey Flack. *Golden Girl*. 1979. Collection Mr. and Mrs. Walner, Illinois

Flack uses an airbrush technique to produce a Photorealist world of female artifacts and movie-star symbols: lipsticks, makeup, a glossy black-and-white photo, a background of print, and rainbows of paint and light. Marilyn Monroe's tragic career is summed up in a pair of cupcakes with cherries on top, and, in the end, a burning candle.

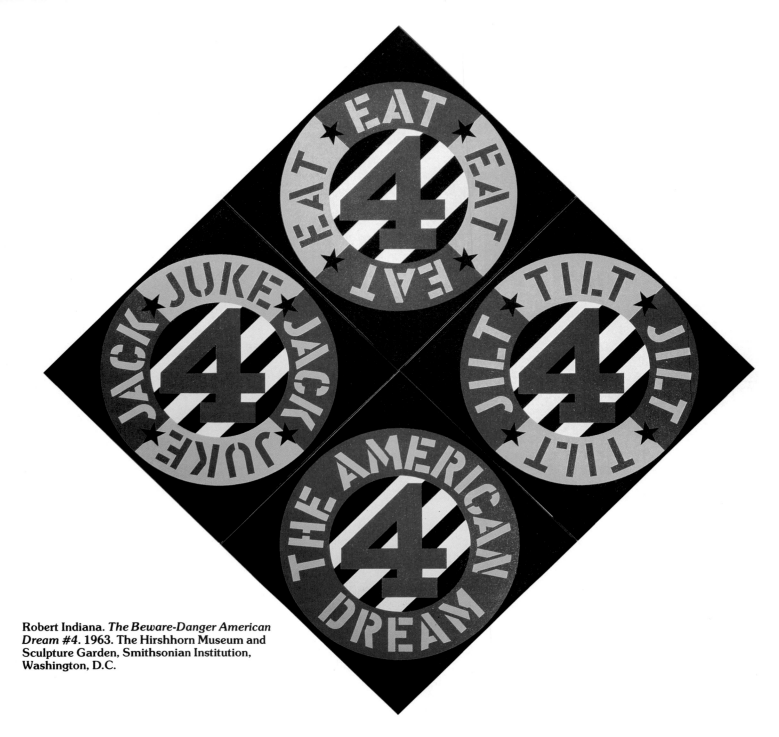

Robert Indiana. *The Beware-Danger American Dream #4*. 1963. The Hirshhorn Museum and Sculpture Garden, Smithsonian Institution, Washington, D.C.

(born 1925) uses this imagery very much like an Abstract Expressionist painter. However, he is more inclined to paste up or silk-screen a photograph than to paint an image. He uses paint mainly to splash or spatter a composition made of reproductions. Paint becomes a kind of visual glue that connects, soils, or insults images manufactured by the world of commerce. Because his vision is essentially that of the collagist, the work of Rauschenberg and the other Pop artists may signify that the "hand-painted" image is dead.

Rauschenberg's "combine" paintings freely associate many of the stylistic and technical developments of twentieth-century painting. In a work such as *Canyon,* the principal ingredient is collage combined with attached objects—a stuffed eagle and a suspended pillow—plus painted areas, paint drippings, and a stick nailed to the wooden picture support. The work is not easy to explain in terms of any single idea that the materials and their organization express. Indeed, as in Dada, the prevailing theme is nonmeaning, the absurdity of art and of everything else.

Robert Rauschenberg. *Canyon*. 1959. Collection Mr. and Mrs. Sonnabend, Paris

The choice of materials tells us something about the world of Pop; it is a world of simultaneous fascination and disgust with the visual environment, particularly as manifested in hard-sell advertising, packaging, labels, and trademarks. The use of printed matter by early collagists such as Picasso, Braque, and Gris was based on the color, texture, and real-life origin of these materials. Pop artists, however, paid more attention to the meaning of the printed words—words like Eat, Love, Pow, Wham, and Gosh. Also, as in action painting, we see the frequent use of paint smears and drippings to simulate mud or other substances thrown at a wall. Splash-and-splatter is now an important tool of painting. For some artists it is a decorative device, but it is also a highly expressive symbol of anger and defiance.

Some Pop artists seem unable to decide what stance to take toward the advertising environment. When viewing the work of Andy Warhol, for example, it is difficult to tell whether he is repelled by our culture's commercialism or whether he wants to merge with it. We look for signs of a point of view, but we receive only an exclamation point. Like Wow! Cool!

Happenings   Architecture is the art of creating a physical environment in which people can live and work. In the past, painting and sculpture were *part* of architecture—focal points of the architectural environment. Now, painters try to create living environments that change as they exist in space and time. Instead of being a statement *about* life, art becomes an activity that is part of life: it is lived as it is created. This art consists of images that are made by ordinary spectators moving through a space organized by an artist. These transient images have been described by their inventor, Allan Kaprow, as "surrounding(s) to be entered into" or "Happenings" and "Environments." They look suspiciously like theater.

Happenings originated in collage and the kind of Environment created by the Dadaist Kurt Schwitters (1887–1948) in his famous Merzbau constructions. Originally built in Schwitters's home in Hanover, a Merzbau might be described as an architectural collage, a modulation of interior space using garbage and found objects as structural and decorative elements. Schwitters worked on one for several years, bringing it to completion about 1924 and giving it the title *Cathedral of Erotic Misery.* Another one, dated about 1933, was more architectonic, less reminiscent of collage techniques. Schwitters built little grottoes into his constructions, dedicated them to friends, and incorporated discarded clothing and other "nonart" items, much as Robert Rauschenberg has included old socks in his "combine" paintings. Significantly, Schwitters was quoted as having said, "Anything the artist spits is art." Spit, splash, and splatter: these have become buzzwords in painting.

Schwitters wanted his constructions to be a synthesis of poetry, architecture, painting, and drama. His was a revolutionary type of creativity that flourished in the generally disillusioned environment of Central Europe after World War I—an environment characterized by a disastrous economic decline and the rise of National Socialism, Communism, and Fascism. These conditions combined to create a watershed in history for many artists and intellectuals who felt trapped by the war and betrayed by their civilization. The forms, values, and institutions that had existed up to and through the war were associated with disaster. Dadaism and its products have to be seen against this background of extreme demoralization.

Happenings and Environments in American art can be regarded as ritualized versions of the Dadaist antiart of the 1920s. Schwitters once made a plaster cast of a friend's discarded socks and put the casting into one of his Merzbau grottoes: that sounds familiar. Such gestures resemble our twentieth-century expressions of revolt: (1) Discarded materials and debris are preferred to traditional media. (2) "Beauty," especially museum-type beauty, is avoided like the plague. (3) The process of creation means more than its result. (4) Defiance of authority is the main source of wit and humor. (5) The

Wayne Thiebaud. *Pie Counter.* 1963. Whitney
Museum of American Art, New York. Gift
of the Larry Aldrich Foundation Fund

Roy Lichtenstein. *Little Big Painting.* 1965.
Whitney Museum of American Art, New York.
Purchase, with funds from the Friends of the
Whitney Museum of American Art

The drips, dribbles, and broad brushing gestures
of the Abstract Expressionist style are meticulously
"reproduced" on Lichtenstein's canvas. What we
have is a hilarious burlesque—the inspired smears
of action painting reduced to commercial art.

above: **Edward Kienholz.** *The Beanery.* **1965. Stedelijk Museum, Amsterdam**

This Environment is the replica of a real place—a bar in Hollywood. Kienholz has carefully reproduced its cozy squalor to make a statement about the mixed assortment of people gathered there—"clock-heads" wasting their "time" and wasting each other.

right: **Kurt Schwitters.** *Merzbau,* **Hanover. 1924–37. (Destroyed)**

gap between art and life is narrowed as much as possible. (6) Caves and grottoes proliferate—both Merzbau constructions and Happenings favor cavernous, womblike spaces.

Even "primitives" are affected. In the 1950s, a relatively little-known American, Clarence Schmidt, created a series of grottoes within his winding, cavelike house on a hill in Woodstock, New York. Schmidt, who had general carpentry and building skills, had no formal artistic training and was almost certainly unaware of Kurt Schwitters. Yet his fantastic house can be compared in important respects with Merzbau constructions. Like Schwitters, he recited poems of his own composition; he may have thought of himself as a reincarnation of Walt Whitman. Schwitters's Merzbau began in the basement of his house; it grew until an attic tenant had to be evicted. Schmidt lived in his "house" and kept adding to it; eventually it resembled a "many chambered nautilus," with new rooms and grottoes appearing as the construction ran down the hill and burrowed into the earth.

The Happenings of Allan Kaprow (born 1927) were more formally staged. They had a script or scenario to control the spectators and the "actors" who moved through the gallery where the event was "staged." Kaprow says these events grew out of his work in collage and assemblage, and he lists the typical materials used: "painted paper, cloth and photos, as well as mirrors, electric lights, plastic film, aluminum foil, ropes, straw; objects that could be attached to, or hung in front of, the canvas along with various sounds and odors. These materials multiplied in number and density, extending away from the flat canvas surface, until that pictorial point of departure was eliminated entirely...." As the two-dimensional canvas was left behind, real environments were simulated: "a subway station, penny-arcade, forest, kitchen, etc." The gallery gave way as a place for staging Happenings to "a craggy canyon, an old abandoned factory, a railroad yard, or the oceanside."

Unlike conventional theater, Happenings had no developed dramatic structure—that is, a beginning, a middle, and an end; plot and character development; conflict, climax, and resolution. They retained connections with assemblage plus elements of other art forms—dance, music, and poetry. Kaprow defined Environments as "slowed-down, quieter, happening[s]"—large-scale dioramas that could last for several weeks; the Happenings compressed time and lasted for only a few hours. Of course, motion pictures are better at compressing or expanding time. And they have the further advantage of being reproducible; a Happening is so spontaneous that it is confined to a single enactment and viewing.

What is the meaning of the Happening for painting? We have mentioned its resemblance to theater and film, although it has less dramatic structure than theater and less pictorial control than film. As painting, the Happening surrenders monumentality and durability: it cannot linger before our vision. But the collage and assemblage origins of Happenings and Environments suggest different objectives. Happenings by Kaprow and Environments-plus-Sculpture, like those of George Segal, may be efforts to discover a hidden order beneath the surface of ordinary events in everyday life. Like Schwitters and Dubuffet, these artists were trying to find meaning in what is apparently chaotic and worthless.

Still, the Happening could not become a vehicle of durable aesthetic value. It worked better as a creative exercise for the artist, as a way of stimulating and focusing energy on fresh sources of imagery. Often, an artist's imagination is stimulated by literature, music, dance, and film; thus Happenings, like collage, represented a fresh way of stimulating shapes and sensations. Furthermore, they satisfied the artist's need for a device that could *interfere with* reality, a device that could take apart events and reveal their unsuspected meanings. In retrospect, they appear to have been significant mainly as a strategy—a strategy foreshadowed in techniques like Merzbau constructions, Surrealist automatic writing, and the nihilistic stunts of the troubled generations that lived between the two world wars.

Op Art   Op, or optical, art followed the premature decline of Pop art in 1964. Painters then attempted to construct artworks that would rely solely on the physiology of vision. In a sense, Impressionist color divisionism (which depended on afterimages to create sensations of colors that were not present) paved the way for the new style. Op painters employed mechanical motion, artificial light filtered through prisms, and images that shift depending on the viewer's angle of vision. Op brought the science of optics into the realm of aesthetics; the sociological comments of Pop yielded to a type of art that bypassed the viewer's mind and imagination. And in its own terms, the effectiveness of Op was undeniable: it produced feelings of physical disorientation or excitement purely by visual means.

The effects of Op seem similar to those of modern biochemistry, but perhaps that is merely coincidental. In any case, Op vividly demonstrated startling new powers in painting. And painting, as a result, found a new claim on hu-

right: **Photograph of Clarence Schmidt in residence, 1964**

below: **Allan Kaprow. From *Orange*. Happening. 1964**

A form of expression that wants to escape framing, geometric positioning, specific location in time or space. Art with limits cannot be exclusive; everyone gets into the act.

man attention: art could compete with tranquilizers and mood-altering drugs as a depressant or a stimulant. Much earlier, Matisse had said he dreamed of an art "which might be for every mental worker...like an appeasing influence, like a mental soother, something like a good armchair in which to rest from physical fatigue." Op, of course, was not especially effective as a pacifier or a soporific; one psychoanalyst compared it to a plunge into a cold shower. But if images could shock the nervous system, perhaps they could also induce the soothing feelings Matisse longed for.

As objects of aesthetic value, Op works are not easy to judge. They create a difficulty that the psychologist Theodor Lipps saw as an obstacle to aesthetic response—awareness of one's bodily sensations instead of ideas and emotions. Also, a purely optical response is often unsatisfying to those who expect emotional, intellectual, or formal nourishment from art. According to a West Coast painter, Jesse Reichek, "The question seems to be whether optical tricks that massage the eyeball, and result, in some cases, in physiological effects, provide a sufficient task for painting. I don't believe such tricks are sufficient."

The desire to transform the physical basis of consciousness has always been latent in painting. We have seen it in Mark Rothko's work (see page 198); in Op art we witness a systematic attempt to seize the human organism and change its psychic condition. But the movement failed to develop a rationale that would guide its further evolution. Its main influence was on psychedelic poster art. In the end, Op was arrested at a stage related more to physics than to aesthetics—a stage where it was unable to join the humanistic mainstream.

Bridget Riley. *Blaze I.* **1962. Collection Louise Riley, London**

Kurt Schwitters. *Cherry Picture.* 1921. Collection, The Museum of Modern Art, New York. Mr. and Mrs. A. Atwater Kent, Jr., Fund

Collage and assemblage might be regarded as an unconscious return to tribal modes of artistry, particularly in their emphasis on textures. But instead of using seeds, shells, and fibers, the modern artist employs commercial garbage—the abundant rubbish of our textile, print, and home-furnishing industries.

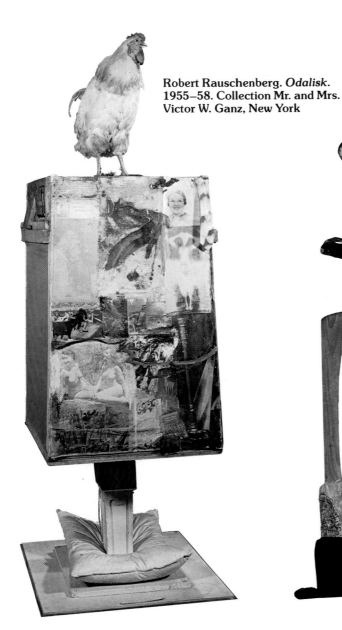

Robert Rauschenberg. *Odalisk*. 1955–58. Collection Mr. and Mrs. Victor W. Ganz, New York

From a certain standpoint, both works can be seen as elaborate displays of the taxidermist's art: stuffed pedestals for stuffed birds. However, the purposes they serve are internal to art: to get away from abstraction, calculation, deliberate design, and cerebral form—to reestablish the status of things as things.

Joan Miró. *Object*. 1936. Collection, The Museum of Modern Art, New York. Gift of Mr. and Mrs. Pierre Matisse

Edward Kienholz. *The State Hospital*. 1964–66. Moderna Museet, Stockholm

As an impresario of mixed media, Kienholz bears a curious resemblance to the Baroque sculptor Bernini: the theatrical requirements of the spectacle take precedence over rules about the separation of painting, sculpture, and architecture. But this spectacle celebrates misery, not mystical transcendence.

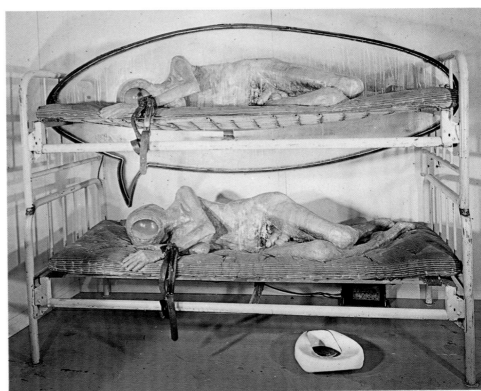

left: **Mirror fetish, from the Lower Congo. c. late 19th–early 20th century. Ethnographical Museum, Antwerp**

The fetish figure has to be a "mixed-media" construction since it functions as a container for magical substances in its abdominal cavity. In the Congolese fetish, a mirror serves to frighten off demons. In the contemporary "fetish" by Arman, tubes of paint embedded in a female torso pour ribbons of color into her polyester belly and womb.

right: **Arman. *La Couleur de mon amour.* 1966. Collection Mr. and Mrs. Philippe Durand-Ruel, Buzenvale, France**

left: **Antoni Gaudí. Detail of spire, Church of the Sagrada Familia, Barcelona. 1883–1926**

Gaudí and Rodia both conceived of architecture as the creation of expressive forms that appear to have grown by natural accretion. This view demanded labyrinthine passages, surfaces like tribal sculptures, and coloristic effects of Byzantine brilliance. A mixed-media approach is almost inevitable when the designer feels that every part of a structure is magically alive.

opposite: **Simon Rodia. Detail of Watts Towers, Los Angeles. 1921–54**

MINIMAL AND COLOR FIELD PAINTING

Reductionism is a persistent tendency in recent art: if painting can cast off its inherited baggage, perhaps it will have a better chance of being itself. Of course, artists disagree about what is essential and what is expendable. But they feel the need to redefine their art periodically, to breathe in an aesthetic environment unconstrained by the aims of their predecessors. For Minimal and Color Field painters, these inherited aims are "illustration," symbol making, social comment, and artistic autobiography. Minimalists react against styles that connect art to history, literature, politics, psychology, or religion.

Josef Albers. *Homage to the Square: Red Series—Untitled III*. 1968. Norton Simon Museum of Art, Pasadena, California

Albers established an important precedent for Minimalist painters by showing that pictorial values can be generated almost solely through the color interactions of simple geometric forms.

What is left? Pure mathematics. Or the ineffable—imagery so pure it can only be seen, not talked about, not understood.

The seeds of this art may have been sown by Malevich, Kandinsky, Mondrian, and, more recently, Josef Albers (1888–1976). It was called "art as art" by the painter Ad Reinhardt (1913–1967), who said: "Art-as-art is a concentration on Art's essential nature. The nature of art has not to do with the nature of perception or with the nature of light or with the nature of space or with the nature of time or with the nature of mankind or with the nature of society." Minimalists satisfy those specifications; they want to create forms complete in

Ad Reinhardt. *Abstract Painting.* **1960–61. Collection, The Museum of Modern Art, New York. Purchase (by exchange)**
Reinhardt forces the viewer to look long and hard, to search, and, perhaps, to meditate. Sometimes, a cruciform image seems to emerge, but its meaning is unclear. All we know is that our eyes desperately search for form in the blue-blackness.

themselves, purely visual, and unsoiled by contact with the world. This is to say that Minimal art aspires to the status of ultimate form, behind which there is nothing more, less, better, worse, or the same as.

In appearance, Minimalist canvases are large, abstract, bright, often hard-edged, and highly simplified or flat in color. They tend to suppress figure-ground relationships created through overlapping, color-value differentials, and perspective devices Especially, they avoid the painter's "handwriting," as in Abstract Expressionism. So there is a certain impersonality about their forms and painted surfaces, which leads viewers to feel they are in the presence of mass-produced objects. The same results are visible in Minimal sculpture, which can be manufactured industrially according to the sculptor's specifications and written or spoken instructions.

Color Field painting is more flexible; it permits considerable formal variation—from floating mists to hard-edge geometry. Its techniques are varied and ingenious: staining unprimed canvas; applying pigment with a squeegee, a spatter device, a paint roller, or an airbrush; pouring diluted paint onto a canvas, which is then turned and tipped to create form through controlled puddles and spills. (We are reminded of Max Ernst, but the color is brighter and wetter.) Although these techniques afford much variety of edge and a wide range of depth, transparency, melting, and interpenetrating illusions, they consistently avoid the brushed look, the drawn line, and the painterly marks of wrist, fingers, and thumb. We have the impression that the medium itself does the job A human being *initiates* the process, but then the process seems to operate according to its own laws or "intelligence." Unwittingly, perhaps, the Minimalists and Color Field painters were preparing us for computer art.

Charles Hinman. *Red/Black*. 1964. Krannert Art Museum, University of Illinois, Champaign

New visual problems are created for the artist who paints on a surface of curved and bent planes. The irregular contours of the canvas no longer "frame" the image; they are part of it. As for color, it sets up a conflict between real and illusionistic space. The painter has to settle a variety of optical and perceptual claims.

THE SHAPED CANVAS

The rectangular canvas is one of many possible shapes. It dominates all the others mainly because of the Renaissance idea of a picture as a window opened on the world. This tradition is so strong that we are hardly aware of it; it even crops up in domestic architecture as the "picture window." In a sense, pictures have always been "windows"—images shaped by architectural design. That was certainly true of mosaics, stained glass, frescoes, mural paintings, and large-scale tapestries. Even cave paintings followed the shape of the rock wall. Historically, painting has obeyed externally determined formats.

But modern paintings move around; they are not meant to hang on any particular wall. In other words, paintings are autonomous images. With the growth of abstraction, the painted image ceased to symbolize something else; the shape of its frame could be determined by internal, that is, design, requirements. Increasingly, the real image has shifted from the wall to the viewer's eye. So the shaped canvas becomes a device for organizing the forces within the viewer's perceptual field.

It would be a mistake, however, to think of the shaped canvas as a type of painted sculpture. The strategy and tactics of this sort of painting are pictorial without being illusionistic. We cannot, as with sculpture, walk around a shaped canvas. So, the painting has been liberated from architecture, yet it falls short of free-standing sculpture; the only space it can effectively occupy is within the eye—retinal space. That is where this new kind of pictorial experience is designed to begin and end.

The older painting traditions endeavored to enlist the total apparatus of vision—eye, brain, and mind. The heart, liver, and spleen, if possible—not the optical organ alone. The patrons of painting—kings, princes and priests—were concerned about the career of the image *after* it passed beyond the retina: How would thought and behavior be affected? Today, the image is in-

"You are now looking out the window . . . please move on."

Clem Scalzitti. Cartoon. Copyright © 1977 by The New York Times Company. Reprinted by permission

This cartoon has sound historical credentials: the idea of a picture as a view seen through a window began with the Renaissance. Today, we are more inclined to substitute the camera's viewfinder. Incidentally, do you like listening to recorded talk while looking at pictures?

Frank Stella. *Pergusa.* 1981. Collection Holly Hunt Thackberry, Winnetka, Illinois. Courtesy M. Knoedler & Co., Inc., New York

Now the shaped canvas has moved into the gray area between pictorial art and sculptural relief. However, Stella's inspiration comes mainly from Abstract Expressionist painting. His old-time geometry and flatness (see page 159) have been replaced by wormy curves and fishlike squiggles. The snaky shape at bottom casts two shadows: one is real and one is painted. We get a rollicking sense of fun and media play—from painting and sculpture to architecture, mosaics, and fabric design.

creasingly controlled by artists themselves, and their expertise lies in the optical arena—a place where complex visual forces interact. Many of them want to create an art that is exclusively retinal, an art that defies interpretation along symbolic or intellectual lines. Frank Stella (born 1936) has put their case well in his comments and his shaped canvases: "I always get into arguments with people who want to retain the old values in painting, the humanistic values that they always find on the canvas. My painting is based on the fact that only what can be seen there is there. It really is an object."

EROTIC AND OBSCENE ART

One of the earliest functions of visual art was the stimulation of sexual feeling, if only to encourage human reproduction. But erotic art continues to be created in societies that have passed beyond the earliest stages of culture. Today, when human overpopulation is an urgent concern, we witness an increase in the creation of artworks devoted to erotic themes. Some of us react with a sense of being liberated from what seems to be the unjustified repression of healthy sexual feeling. Others are offended: they see erotic art as obscene or pornographic and fear that civilized restraints on the expression of sexuality are breaking down.

The public celebration of the human body, especially the female nude, is a well-established tradition in Western art and culture. This public art has usually been accompanied by a more or less underground art in which human figures are shown in explicit sexual practices. But in today's permissive climate, that underground art is created and exhibited openly. The change is not so much in the fact that erotic art exists but that it is abundantly visible.

Joan Miró. *Persons Haunted by a Bird.* 1938. The Art Institute of Chicago. Peter B. Bensinger Charitable Trust

In 1938, Miró's phallic fantasies could be assimilated by the Surrealist format of dream symbolism and sexual horseplay. But before he was a Surrealist, Miró was a humorist.

Jean-Léon Gérôme. *Roman Slave Market*. c. 1884. The Walters Art Gallery, Baltimore

The official art of the nineteenth century was often an exercise in disguised voyeurism. Under the pretext of teaching history, some painters catered to the prurient interest of the public.

Balthus. *The Golden Days*. 1944–46. The Hirshhorn Museum and Sculpture Garden, Smithsonian Institution, Washington, D.C.

The awakening sexuality of the girl adolescent has absorbed much of the career of Balthus. His art thrives on the conflict between bourgeois respectability, as represented by comfortable, well-appointed interiors, and the less-than-innocent reveries of good little girls.

above: Jean-Auguste-Dominique Ingres. *Odalisque with a Slave.* 1840. Fogg Art Museum, Harvard University, Cambridge, Massachusetts. Bequest of Grenville L. Winthrop

The reclining nude has a venerable tradition in Western painting. By the nineteenth century, however, that tradition had been carried to an incredible stage of too-muchness. Still, Ingres was serious about his erotic objectives; Wesselmann satirizes that eroticism, as well as our own commercialization of female bodies.

right: Tom Wesselmann. *Great American Nude No. 51.* 1963. Collection the artist

Francis Bacon. *Two Figures Lying on a Bed with Attendants* (panel of a triptych, *Three Studies for a Crucifixion).* **1968. Marlborough Gallery, New York**

Today artists feel free to deal with the theme of homosexuality. In Bacon's work, this motif is overshadowed by a consistently animalistic view of man—even in his efforts at love, which come to resemble the copulation of beasts.

Larry Rivers. *Celebrating Shakespeare's 400th Birthday (Titus Andronicus).* **1963. Collection Clarice Rivers, New York**

A mutilated female nude, symbol of Venus and maternity; a "cool" diagram of dismembered human parts; the portrait of a solemn black man; and a reference to one of Shakespeare's plays. Here are all the areas of contemporary social concern: art, race, sex, and violence.

Much erotic art is created as a mode of protest. Perhaps that is due to the class antagonisms and intergenerational conflicts that have grown so intense in the industrial nations of the world. In that case, the unlovely or obscene content of erotic art becomes explainable: it is meant to offend the "establishment" by celebrating what is considered to be wrong or ugly. But the "establishment" reacts by co-opting erotic art; it even collects obscene art. It always has.

There are also art-historical reasons for the flourishing of erotic art. For almost a century, the artistic imagination has been dominated by abstract and nonobjective art that tends to divert the impulses we associate with sexual expression. Much of modernist painting, for example, stems from Cézanne, a painter whose genius was inhibited in the presence of the unclothed human figure—male or female. An erotic vision of man or woman appears to have been uncongenial to his tastes as a painter. What he left us was a structural or geometric legacy. And, understandably, Cézanne's artistic descendants built on the foundation he established. His work stands in relation to modern art as the Epistles of Paul do to the development of Christianity.

The emergence of obscene art, then, may be due to the difficulty artists have experienced for close to a century in perceiving the human figure affectionately. They shied away from the voyeurism of a Gérôme or a Bouguereau, on the one hand, and the hothouse eroticism of a Modigliani or a Pascin, on the other. Instead, they explored the problems of color symbolism and space organization opened up by the Post-Impressionists in the late nineteenth century. But space is a medium in which human beings move and encounter each other; ultimately, artists feel that they have to examine all forms of human encounter—even the ugly ones.

Now we are faced with an exaggerated reaction to the expression of anonymity on a vast scale—as in Minimal and serial art, not to mention much of our public architecture. In gallery painting as well as in popular culture generally, we see a great deal of brutal imagery substituting for genuine erotic feeling. Often, it associates sexuality with pathological behavior, as in Larry Rivers's *Titus Andronicus*. These are the excesses that accompany the easing of a long repression, but sooner or later they will play themselves out.

CONCLUSION

The use of trash-can contents in collage by Schwitters; the use of dead leaves, flower petals, fruit rinds, and butterfly wings by Dubuffet; the Cubist and Dadaist incorporation of "real" objects in pictures; the Pop use of package labels and advertising slogans; Happenings that look suspiciously like improvised theater: these and other developments suggest new connections between painting and gardening, spectator sports, refuse collection, psychodrama, and media hype. Everything is fair game: some artworks echo the processes of food preparation, eating, collecting leftovers, emptying the garbage, and then making something new out of garbage.

For many years, Jimmy Durante had a nightclub act in which he tore a piano apart in a kind of comic tantrum. The public loved it. Clearly, the processes of disintegration have their own aesthetic fascination, as might be confirmed by anyone who has watched the dynamiting of a building, a staged auto crash, or a child knocking down a house of blocks. In César's "controlled-compression" sculpture we see the crushing of an automobile converted into an artistic act (see page 277). We might regard these activities as efforts to discover an affirmative meaning in all the acts of needless destruction and senseless consumption that mark our culture.

Artists may not be aware of the ultimate meanings of their work, but civilization operates through them nevertheless. We hope their experimentation with strange new materials, processes, and themes will turn out to have humanizing results. One thing is certain: history will look back and make a surer judgment than we can. In the meantime, we can watch what's Happening . . . with fascination.

CHAPTER ELEVEN

SCULPTURE

L ike painting, sculpture began with the making of figures for primitive magic and, later, for religious ritual. For that reason, sculpture always seems to have a magical quality about it. The Greek myth of Pygmalion and Galatea gives us an idea of the almost supernatural power ancient peoples attributed to sculpture. Pygmalion, a sculptor, fell in love with Aphrodite, and because she would not have him, he made an ivory figure of the goddess and prayed to her. Eventually she took pity on him and entered into his carving, making it live as a real woman, Galatea. Pygmalion married her and she bore him two sons.

The myth expresses the essential ingredients of sculptural creation. The artist's motive for creating arises from an emotional crisis—personal distress plus yearning for the impossible. He tries to control reality by fashioning an object that portrays what he wants. The goddess cannot withhold her pity, so she gives life to the artist's image. Then he falls in love with that image, an image *he* has created. Art thus acquires a life of its own, and the union of creator and creature results in a continuation of life. A man's strange longing for a goddess is converted into living reality by the artist's anguish and compelling skill.

Painting has magical associations, too, but its reality is largely illusionistic, whereas sculpture gives physical substance to the artist's hopes and fantasies. For that reason, sculptures were more commonly used to represent gods and goddesses; to serve as vessels for the souls of the departed; or to function as totems, idols, and cult objects among primitive peoples.

Regardless of material, the capacity of sculpture to occupy real space and to compel belief in its aliveness distinguishes it from painting and graphic art in general. Accordingly, sculpture has remained, throughout its history of changing form and function, the same art that Pygmalion practiced—the art of making three-dimensional materials come alive. It makes fantasies real, it remembers the dead, and it satisfies human longings for perfection.

MODELING, CARVING, CASTING, AND CONSTRUCTING

The sculptural processes are simply the most suitable ways of working available materials. Stone can be chipped, scraped, carved, drilled, and polished,

Tlingit Indian shaman's mask in the form of a bear, from Alaska. c. 1840–60. Peabody Museum, Harvard University, Cambridge, Massachusetts

Sculpture has roots in masks like this one, which enabled a tribal shaman to transform himself psychologically into a bear. The spirit of the bear enters the body of the shaman and makes him potent as a healer. What we regard as art—the superbly carved and painted sculpture—is really magic, the enhancement of the shaman's therapeutic powers. The marvelously active baby otters are his assistants.

so it appeals to artists who are comfortable with highly resistant materials. Wood can be worked by the same processes, but modern technology permits it to be permanently bent and molded, as in the Thonet chair (see page 114). Metals can be cast, cut, drilled, filed, bent, forged, stamped, and extruded. More recently, *powdered* metals have been combined with plastic binders, so they can be modeled, almost like clay. Metals can also be assembled by welding, soldering, and riveting; they can also be joined with adhesives. As for plastics, we are beginning to overcome their associations with cheap imitations of more prestigious materials. Their lightness and transparency hold out far-ranging possibilities: it would be difficult to predict what sculpture will become with our new plastics, metal alloys, and high-fired ceramics.

For traditional sculptors, mastery of the basic processes—modeling, carving, and casting—constituted the principal artistic challenges. These processes remain important, but they are not indispensable because, as in painting, technology permits materials to be formed and assembled by other means. However, modern sculptors confront new problems of aesthetic choice due to the variety of new processes and materials available to them.

Monumental statuary is an example: in the past it was cast in bronze or carved in marble. Today, welded and riveted metal is more common, espe-

Henry Moore. *Two Forms.* **1934. Collection, The Museum of Modern Art, New York. Sir Michael Sadler Fund**
Only eleven inches high, this sculpture has the monumental force of a much larger work. Why? Because Moore knows how to establish a real dialogue between abstract forms: they speak about relationships that matter—between mother and child, between lover and beloved.

cially as figures recede in importance and sculptures virtually become environments. Naturalistic statuary, of course, must be modeled and then cast in bronze; or it has to be carved in stone. It is still seen in public buildings and parks, and it continues to be commissioned by conservative groups. But sculptors who can create such works are a diminishing minority. Contemporary buildings seem to be more friendly to sculpture that is, in general, more open, more geometric, and less monolithic in form.

It would be difficult to conceive of a sculptural group like Rodin's *Burghers of Calais* being created through any process other than bronze casting. The naturalistic treatment of bone and flesh, the psychological characterization of the figures, the sensitive control of light, the variety of volumes and surfaces—these could not be achieved with welding or assemblage processes.

Auguste Rodin. *Burghers of Calais.* **1886. Rodin Museum, Paris**

Yet contemporary sculptors carry out monumental commissions. The subtleties of modeling with clay or marble may be sacrificed, but large scale and a marvelous freedom of extension into space is now possible. Also, the techniques of industrial production and fabrication can be used by sculptors today. The mallet and chisel have been joined by the acetylene torch, the electronic welder, and even the hydraulic press.

The Greeks knew the art of bronze casting, and they also had an abundance of good white marble. But they must have prized marble more for its durability than for its appearance, since their marble statuary was painted. It was not the stone's whiteness or texture they admired so much as its capacity to reveal their love of clear and stable forms. Stone could capture the body in action or repose, and it embodied their conception of ideal human proportions. Through marble sculpture they expressed a typically Greek idea—that reality and perfection can meet in human forms.

For Michelangelo, sculpture was the art of releasing the forms hidden, or imprisoned, in marble. This, too, is a classical Greek idea; it typifies the attitude of the carver—one who begins with the stone block or wood log and cuts away until the form in his mind's eye is revealed. Carving is a *subtractive* process, and it has always been considered the most difficult of sculptural processes because it calls for a conception of the result before the work begins. The carver subtracts nonessential material to liberate an image that *already* exists. Yet the grain of wood or stone significantly influences what forms will emerge. For example, diorite and basalt, hard granitic stones used by the sculptors of ancient Egypt, resist detailed carving; consequently, Egyptian sculpture is characterized by large, simplified forms that closely follow the shape of the stone block as it was quarried.

left: **Michelangelo.** *Crepuscolo (Evening)* **(detail from the Tomb of Lorenzo de' Medici, Florence). 1520–34**

Stone carving: the forms seem to emerge from the marble. But notice that Michelangelo employed an almost Cubist technique to find out where they were.

right: **Luca della Robbia. Detail of** *Madonna and Angels.* **c. 1460. National Museum, Florence**

Polychromed terra-cotta: clay, fired and glazed white in imitation of marble, but capable of being mass produced. For the della Robbias it was an art and a family business.

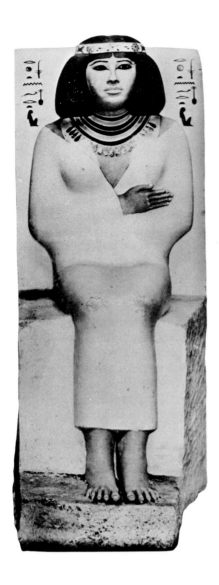

Accurate casting reproduces the forms and tool marks of an original clay or wax model. Its main advantage lies in the translation of clay or wax into a material that is more durable than the original. Also, after casting, a work can be transported without breaking, and it can be duplicated. Today, durability and surface quality rather than duplication are the chief motives for using casting techniques. Bronze, the most common casting material, has beautiful color characteristics. The surface of a bronze casting develops a rich patina with age; it can also be burnished or treated with chemicals to produce a wide range of color from gold to a deep, lustrous brown or greenish black.

It should be remembered that the earliest sculptures were painted, glazed, or inlaid with gems and other materials; their main purpose was to create convincing and vivid effigies. Terra-cotta sculpture was often polychromed to look more realistic. Today, the same effect might be achieved with plastics. Frank Gallo's *Swimmer,* made of polyester reinforced with Fiberglas and wood, gives us an idea of the realism pursued by the ancients, even in its deliberate, Pop art prettification. Gallo (born 1933) often seats his figures in real chairs, creating a kind of shock by juxtaposing a magical effigy with a "real" object made by industry. But the closest modern counterparts to ancient painted sculptures may be found in our store-window mannequins. Made of painted papier-mâché or plastic, adorned with synthetic hair and eyelashes, and wearing real clothes, these figures might be considered contemporary "temple sculptures." No one worships them openly, but they seem to have genuine cultic significance.

far left: The Lady Nofret. c. **2650** B.C. Egyptian Museum, Cairo. Painted stone

left: Jōkei. *Shō-Kannon.* **Kamakura period (1185–1333). The Kurama Temple, Kyoto, Japan. Painted wood**

above: Frank Gallo. *Swimmer.* **1964. Whitney Museum of American Art, New York. Gift of the Friends of the Whitney. Colored polyester, Fiberglas, and wood**

Unlike Michelangelo, Rodin defined sculpture as "the art of the hole and the lump." Although he (or his assistants) produced many carved marble works, Rodin's statement is typical of the sculptor as modeler—one who builds form *additively*. Clay is also more responsive than wood or stone; the marks of the sculptor's hands are visible in the material. Nothing is so personal and direct as clay. But clay has distinct limitations compared to wood or stone: it possesses little strength in tension or compression and hence requires an armature for support; and it is not a permanent material. If a clay work is to be fired, its scale is limited by the size of the kiln and a variety of engineering considerations. Accordingly, clay is mainly used to make preparatory "sketches" for sculpture to be executed in other materials. As ceramic sculpture, however, clay is durable and reproducible; also, it can be given a wide range of color and texture. Most important, clay is cheap: it encourages experimentation with form; it permits the sculptor to take chances.

One of the pleasures of bronze sculpture arises from our knowledge that a soft, plastic material has been "frozen" into a hard, durable material. Bronze castings are actually hollow, but they *look* heavy and solid; they retain the earthy quality of clay or rock. Hence, clay seems to call for bronze casting. For a master like Rodin, the tactile variety of clay—its capacity to modulate light while describing shape—was perhaps its main attraction. Even though bronze casting is difficult and expensive, clay's versatility, its feel, and its look make it one of the most satisfying ways of "thinking" in three dimensions.

Wood is appealing because of its grain, its color, and the sense of its origin in a living tree. Also, it has greater tensile strength than stone, so it can be given projecting forms with less fear of breaking. Unlike metal, which is cold, or stone, which is abrasive, wood is warm and pleasant, even sensuous, to the touch. The disadvantages of wood lie in its dimensional instability—its tendency to warp or crack. Wood can be worked more easily than stone, yet it offers enough resistance to cutting to require carving tools that leave characteristic marks. An important advantage of wood that is often exploited in contemporary work is its adaptability to constructed sculpture. There is also a special expressiveness in wooden joints, whether those of the skilled cabinet-maker or of the sculptor using improvised methods of joinery. Finally, there is a long sculptural tradition of painting wood, covering it with metal or fabric, or embedding foreign materials in it; thus, wood fits easily into modern strategies of collage and assemblage.

A contemporary use of wood can be seen in *Wall Piece* by John Anderson (born 1928). Here, carving and construction techniques are combined in a work that pretends to have some mechanical action. Forms projecting from a slot look like levers, doorknobs, or faucet handles, suggesting that we should pull, lift, or twist them. The fact that these operations cannot be performed does not prevent the sculpture from arousing our expectations: it looks as if it could work *mechanically*. It looks as if it could throw a switch, turn on a light, put an engine into gear. These connections between form and meaning are logical enough, since knobs and levers are meant to be grasped, and wood is inviting to the touch. So we have a curiously magical-mechanical device; through carved forms and limb fragments it makes connections with tribal animistic sculpture; through its knobs and levers it connects with modern mechanization.

The sensuous potential of plywood, a construction material that is usually covered, is beautifully revealed in the laminated wood sculptures of H. C. Westermann (1922–1981). In *The Big Change,* he carves a huge wooden knot, creating a Surrealistic contradiction between shape and material, form and function. In addition to its absurdity and its use of a material without ancient credentials, this work exhibits the unity of form, finished craftsmanship, and monolithic stability of classic sculpture.

Few final sculptures are done in wax because it is not very permanent. Also, it can easily be damaged in handling. But wax was a congenial material

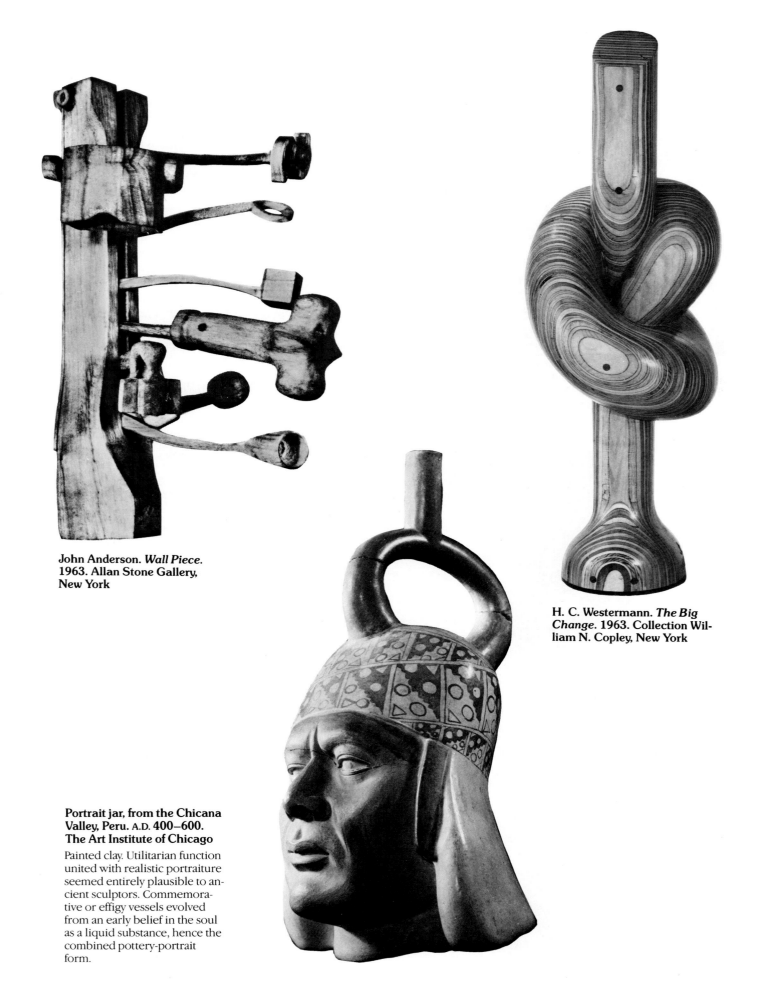

John Anderson. *Wall Piece.*
1963. Allan Stone Gallery,
New York

H. C. Westermann. *The Big*
Change. **1963. Collection William N. Copley, New York**

Portrait jar, from the Chicana
Valley, Peru. A.D. **400–600.**
The Art Institute of Chicago

Painted clay. Utilitarian function
united with realistic portraiture
seemed entirely plausible to ancient sculptors. Commemorative or effigy vessels evolved
from an early belief in the soul
as a liquid substance, hence the
combined pottery-portrait
form.

Medardo Rosso. *The Bookmaker.* **1894. Collection, The Museum of Modern Art, New York. Acquired through the Lillie P. Bliss Bequest**

for the nineteenth-century sculptor Medardo Rosso (1858–1928). In *The Bookmaker*—made of modeled wax over plaster—we see a painterly interest in light similar to that of Rodin and Degas, both of whom executed sculptures in wax. Rosso's figure is unusual for its delicate treatment of a heavy body; it reminds us of Rodin's monumental *Balzac.* The transitions from form to form are so gentle that they seem to be blended with a soft brush. The work may be small, but it suggests large-scale statuary because wax has no grain, no texture visible to the eye. At the same time, wax is capable of almost infinitely detailed modeling.

Enormous changes in sculptural attitude have taken place since Rosso modeled his delicate figures in the 1890s. The critic Clement Greenberg gives an excellent summary of these changes: "Space is there to be shaped, divided, enclosed, but not to be filled. The new sculpture tends to abandon stone, bronze, and clay for industrial materials like iron, steel, alloys, glass, plastics, celluloid, etc., etc., which are worked with the blacksmith's, the welder's and even the carpenter's tools. Unity of material and color is no longer required, and applied color is irrelevant: a work or its parts can be cast, wrought, cut or simply put together; it is not so much sculptured as constructed, built, assembled, arranged."

Auguste Rodin. *Balzac.* **1892–97**

Leonard Baskin. *St. Thomas Aquinas.* **1962. St. John's Abbey Church, Collegeville, Minnesota**

Clearly, we are in the midst of a revolution in sculptural materials and technique, a revolution that reflects the unprecedented social, technical, and spiritual changes of modern life. Naturally, new materials and techniques generate new aesthetic effects, and in the following sections we shall examine the main ones.

THE ANCESTRAL COUPLE

Ancestor figures of the Dogon tribe, Mali. Reitberg Museum, Zurich. Von der Heydt Collection

As long as the original parents are perceived as the source of an awesome generative power—a power still active in tribal life—their effigies must be rigidly frontal, solemn, unmoved. The slightest deviation from verticality is felt as the weakening of a force that must endure through eternity. Notice the variety of forms and spaces that can be achieved within this vertical format.

Heavenly couple from Khajuraho, India. c. 11th century A.D. Archaeological Museum, Khajuraho, India

In India the affection of the ancestral pair assumes an explicitly sexual character. Innocent of Western prudery, medieval Hindu temples were densely populated with "loving couples" in exuberant settings much like their teeming earthly communities.

King Mycerinus and his queen, Kha-Merer-Nebty, from Giza. 2599–2571 B.C. Museum of Fine Arts, Boston

Unswervingly pointed toward eternity, the royal pair also evidences an interest in the pleasures of marital intimacy. This interest is based on the discovery of the body as aesthetically pleasing and erotically exciting—ideas visible in the figures' contrasted forms: his—athletic and virile; hers—soft and rounded.

Detail of sarcophagus, from Cerveteri. c. 520 B.C. **Museo Nazionale di
Villa Giulia, Rome**

To preserve the alive quality of this couple, the Etruscan sculptor shows them
with their hands arrested, as if caught in a moment of animated conversation.
Also, vividly painted eyes, hair, and skin must have compensated for the archaic stiffness of the heads.

Ekkehard and Uta. **Naumburg Cathedral, East Germany. 1250–60**

Conjectural portraits of the founders of the cathedral. One hardly doubts they are a contemporary, that is, a Gothic, couple. Their relationship—more realistic than romantic—seems based on a "sensible" arrangement: the alliance of an influential, somewhat cynical German margrave with a stylish and elegant Polish princess.

Ludwig Münstermann. *Adam and Eve.* **c. 1618. Landesmuseum, Oldenburg, West Germany**

Equally guilty, Adam and Eve cannot face each other. The sculptor—a German Mannerist—has composed their restless forms in parallel to express the idea that they are partners in sin.

FROM MONOLITH TO OPEN FORM

The sculpture of antiquity reflected the tree log, the stone block, or the marble slab from which it was carved. Projecting forms in stone or wood could be broken by the sculptor's hammer and chisel; for that reason, tribal sculptures closely resemble tree trunks, and Egyptian figures follow the form of the granite block. Only by the casting process could long extensions and complex open shapes be produced; but casting was mainly used to fashion weapons, jewelry, and harness decorations. Sculpture in general, and carved sculpture in particular, tended to be monolithic (similar in form to a single stone). A

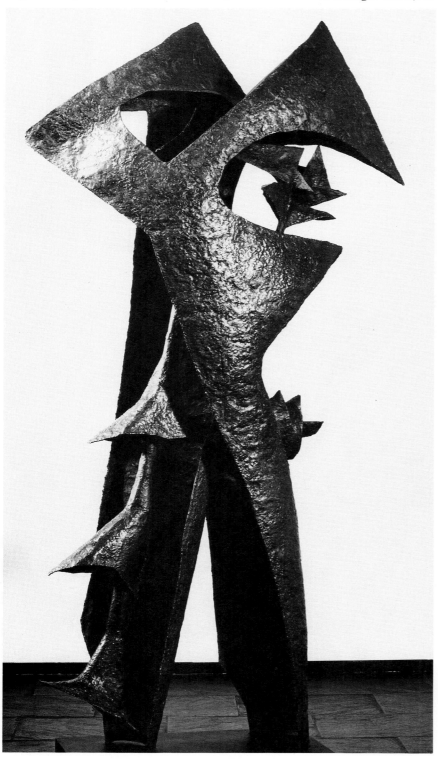

Seymour Lipton. *The Prophet.* **1956. Courtesy Betty Parsons Gallery, New York**

Working directly with modern metallic materials, Lipton creates forms that combine the effects of the acetylene torch's cutting action with the surface qualities of modeled clay.

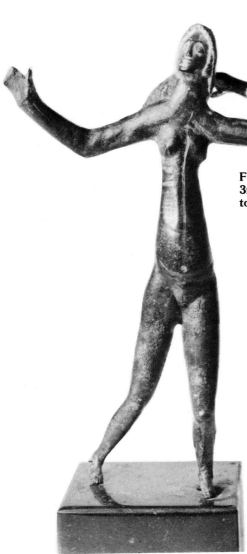

Figure of a dancer. Gallo-Roman, 3rd or 4th century A.D. Musée Historique, Orléans

Henri Matisse. *Serpentine.* 1909. The Hirshhorn Museum and Sculpture Garden, Smithsonian Institution, Washington, D.C.

Extended and penetrated forms in marble and in bronze. The *Laocoön* is anything but monolithic; those holes and projections are more typical of bronze casting. So we get mixed signals: the Gallo-Roman figure and the Matisse look like what they are— bronze castings of clay models. But the *Laocoön* marble also looks like a casting, which is aesthetically disturbing.

Agesander, Athenodorus, and Polydorus of Rhodes. *Laocoön.* Late 2nd century B.C. Vatican Museum, Rome

notable exception, the Hellenistic figure group *Laocoön,* was carved from several blocks of marble, and although it represents a remarkable technical achievement, it is not considered aesthetically successful because its parts seem disunited; the feeling of a single, embracing shape—the *monolithic feeling*—has been lost.

In addition to considerations of material and process, monolithic form dominated traditional sculpture for religious and psychological reasons. We associate permanence and resistance to change with uncomplicated shapes. Open and complex forms suggest motion, the enemy of stability and timelessness. For that reason, in the pyramids of Egypt and the temples of Greece the triangle resting on its base or the triangle supported by repeated verticals was employed. In religious sculpture, too, permanence is expressed through forms that look as if they can resist the ravages of time. The sacred sculpture of all ancient peoples tends to be solid, frontal, and monolithic.

Open-form sculpture comes to us mainly from the barbarian peoples whose invasions of Europe from the steppes of Asia eventually destroyed Greco-Roman civilization. Their nomadic existence and metalworking skill encouraged an art of restless linear dynamism. Heated metal lends itself to curved, serpentine, and spiral shapes—ideal for peoples who are fascinated by ceaseless travel. Accustomed to wandering, hunting, and battle, the barbarian peoples felt free to move in any direction along the seemingly endless Asian plains. Not surprisingly, they were late to discover the concepts of enclosed space and monolithic form. The art of these wanderers, who eventually settled Europe from Russia to Ireland, was one of continuous twists and turns on a flat plane. Their three-dimensional art was created mainly by assembling two-dimensional, linear structures.

left: **Maori prow ornament, from New Zealand. Museum für Völkerkunde, Munich**

Vikings and Polynesians— both warlike, seafaring peoples—created a complex linear art in which spirals, interlaces, and elaborate perforations almost obliterate their much-loved animal motifs.

right: **Animal head, from the Oseberg ship-burial. c. A.D. 825. University Museum of Antiquities, Oslo**

Western art can be seen as a struggle between Mediterranean closed-form, or monolithic, ideas and nomadic open-form ideas. On the one hand, sculptors from Michelangelo to Maillol tended to preserve monolithic form; on the other, Romanesque and Gothic sculptors continued the barbarian obsession with convoluted form. If the Gothic cathedral is the culmination of Christian art, then the nomadic conception of form and space prevailed. During the Renaissance there was an attempt to revive classical notions of form, but the taste for twisting motion generated by barbarian art could not be entirely displaced. With this background, modern sculpture in the West would be expected to reveal anticlassic tendencies: it should resist clear forms and balanced relationships; it should prefer shapes that resemble ropelike knots and coils, and it should favor linear detail instead of simple surfaces.

These expectations are, in fact, borne out in recent sculpture: anticlassic tendencies predominate. The sense of the monolith, based mainly on the carving tradition, has been largely abandoned. Still, the monolith survives conspicuously in the work of a master like Henry Moore, although his holes and serpentine shapes show traces of the old barbarian consciousness.

A good example of monolithic sculpture today is seen in Leonard Baskin's (born 1922) *Seated Man with Owl.* Yet this work seems to be a version of a theme we have seen in Egyptian art, as in the *Pharaoh Khafre.* There, the hawk-god, Horus, is behind the king's head, whereas the bird in the modern work—a rather inflated owl—stands on the man's arm, almost obscuring him from view. Baskin's sculpture shares the frontality and immobile expression of the pharaoh, but otherwise we see a modern personality. Where Khafre is slim, athletic, and youthful, the modern man is middle-aged, overweight, and clumsy looking. The Egyptian sculpture conveys a strong sense of enduring mass because it shows no trace of motion. Baskin's figure, on the other hand, exhibits the ponderous bulk of a flabby man whose sitting down is an act of collapse. The pharaoh looks confidently toward the future while Baskin's man seems bored. Apparently, a monolith can express opposite qualities: power and optimism, or man's resignation in the face of life's everlasting sameness.

Other illustrations—from the work of Maillol, Brancusi, and Arp—would show that monolithic form lives on. However, these sculptors are among the "old masters" of modernism. As we approach the present, artists seem to prefer media that yield twisted, perforated, and abstract forms. Also, their nonfigurative bias suggests that for them the classical, monolithic tradition is dead. But the taste for dynamic, broken forms may be oversatisfied, and a desire for the opposite may emerge. In time, then, the stylistic pendulum may swing back to the monolith.

Henry Moore. *Reclining Mother and Child.* 1937. Walker Art Center, Minneapolis
In Moore's penetrated forms we see the culmination of a long process of accommodation between the nomadic obsession with open, serpentine shapes and the classical Mediterranean concern for balance and stability.

Leonard Baskin. *Seated Man with Owl.*
1959. Smith College Museum of Art,
Northampton, Massachusetts

Pharaoh Khafre. c. 2600 B.C. Cairo
Museum

323

CONSTRUCTIVISM

Constructivism was an early-twentieth-century movement whose adherents tried to abandon the monolith and the central axis as the basis of sculpture. It introduced new materials like plastics, Plexiglas, and metal wire; and it treated the figure like an engineering project. Its leading personalities were two Russian brothers who used different names: Naum Gabo (1890–1977) and Antoine Pevsner (1886–1962). They advocated an approach that would bring sculpture into harmony with physics and mathematics, mainly through the use of engineering principles.

After the Russian revolution of 1917, the Communist government supported the Constructivists, but by 1921 it became unsympathetic to abstract and experimental art. Although Gabo and Pevsner wanted to revolutionize architecture and industrial design as well as painting and sculpture, theirs was a revolution the Party didn't like. So, leaving Russia in 1922, the Constructivists carried their ideas to the Bauhaus in Germany. Gabo settled in the United States in 1946, making his home in Connecticut. By 1960, the Constructivist ideas of Gabo and Pevsner were firmly established in the Western world.

How did the Constructivists influence modern sculpture? Mainly through the qualities of transparency, interpenetration of forms, overlapping of planes, and the use of lines in tension to represent space and energy. In their sculpture we seem to be looking at mechanical drawings executed in three dimensions, as in Gabo's *Linear Construction #1.* Its curves are perfectly regular because they do not record organic shapes. Pevsner's *Torso,* on the other hand, reminds us of the forms in a Cubist figure painting. And, like the sculpture of another Russian, Archipenko, it uses negative, or concave, volumes to represent forms that are actually convex. The materials are translucent brownish plastic sheets and copper; the Constructivists were determined to avoid thick, dense materials. The thinness of wire and the translucency of plastic enabled Pevsner to stress the negation of mass. Thus, two traits of the monolith were undermined: (1) the solidity of forms; and (2) the mass, or weight, of forms.

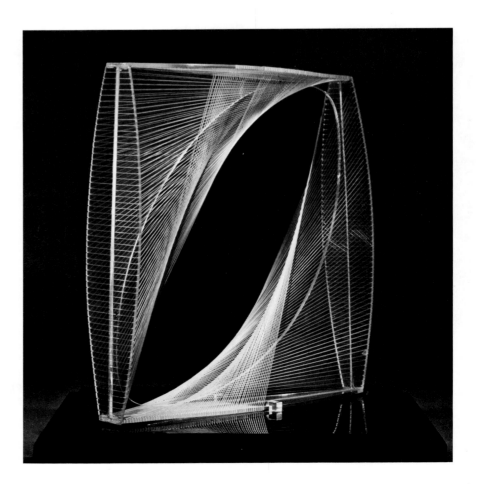

Naum Gabo. *Linear Construction #1.* **1942–43. The Hirshhorn Museum and Sculpture Garden, Smithsonian Institution, Washington, D.C.**

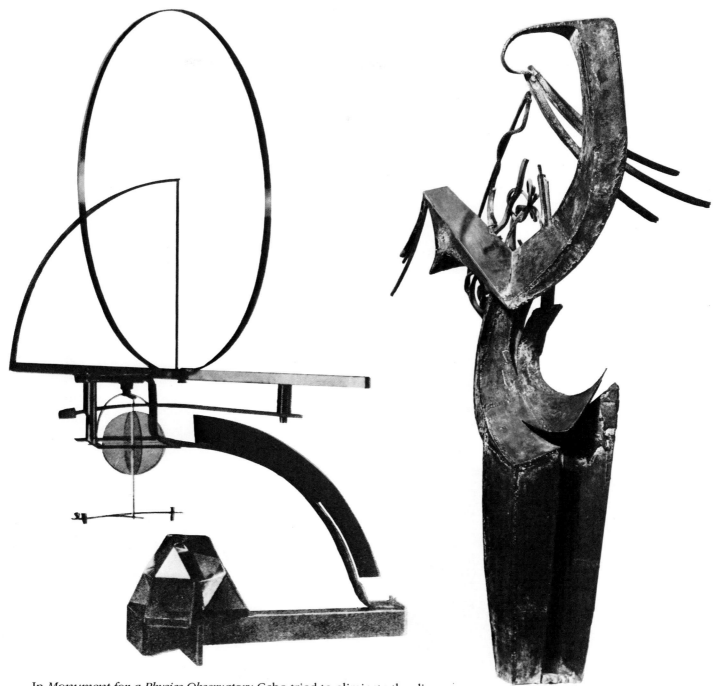

In *Monument for a Physics Observatory* Gabo tried to eliminate the distinctions between sculpture and architecture. The model is made of plastic, metal, and wood, but it bears an interesting resemblance to a wrought-iron sculpture by Julio González, *Woman Combing Her Hair.* Both artists demonstrate the new openness of sculptural space. Liberated from its agelong rootedness in the earth and seemingly independent of the laws of gravity, sculpture now moves confidently into a kind of interstellar space.

Although modern physics has altered our ideas about the concreteness of matter and the uniformity of space, the Constructivists could not entirely abandon opaque, volumetric materials. Even plastics, wire, and glass have shape, weight, color, and substance. Increasingly, Pevsner used solid metals, particularly bronze rods bonded into curved planes, as in *Developable Column.* Apparently, sculptural openness and the nullification of matter have limits. In the end, the sensuous appeal of metal—or even plastic—counteracts the artist's urge to dematerialize form.

left: Naum Gabo. *Monument for a Physics Observatory.* 1922. Collection the artist

right: Julio González. *Woman Combing Her Hair.* 1936. Collection, The Museum of Modern Art, New York. Mrs. Simon Guggenheim Fund

Antoine Pevsner. *Torso*. 1924–26. Collection, The Museum of Modern Art, New York. Katherine S. Dreier Bequest

In the nearly twenty years that separate these two sculptures, Pevsner's forms grew progressively more abstract. At the same time, his surfaces became sensuously richer. There seems to be a law of compensation at work.

Antoine Pevsner. *Developable Column*. 1942. Collection, The Museum of Modern Art, New York. Purchase

COUPLES IN MODERN SCULPTURE

above: Constantin Brancusi. *Adam and Eve.* **1921. The Solomon R. Guggenheim Museum, New York**

In the Brancusi, a scarred Adam supports a smoother and rounder Eve. By presenting the figures in a vertical plane Brancusi creates a type of hierarchy. Giacometti places man and woman on the same horizontal plane; there the man becomes a sexual aggressor.

right: **Alberto Giacometti.** *Man and Woman.* **1928–29. Collection Henriette Gomès, Paris**

Max Ernst. *Le Capricorne*. 1964. Musée National d'Art Moderne, Paris
Ernst compromises the dignity of royalty by presenting this couple as a pair
of hybrid creatures compounded of geometric elements and anatomical portions of man, fish, goat, steer, and giraffe.

Etienne-Martin. *Le Grand Couple.* **1946. Collection Michel Couturier & Cie., Paris**

The united couple is compared to a powerful, earthy generative force by heightening their resemblance to a huge convoluted tree root.

Barbara Hepworth. *Two Figures.* **1954–55. Collection Mr. and Mrs. Solomon Byron Smith, Lake Forest, Illinois**

Which is the man and which is the woman? (I think "he" is on the left.) These figures are so abstract that we can differentiate them sexually only by their height. Perhaps there are some gender clues in the ovals. Or perhaps they are both women.

Henry Moore. *King and Queen*. 1952–53. The Hirshhorn Museum and Sculpture Garden, Smithsonian Institution, Washington, D.C.

In this royal couple, Moore tries to gain access to those mythic feelings that connect the destiny of a land and its people with the strength and harmony of its rulers.

Kenneth Armitage. *Diarchy.* **1957. Private collection, Chicago**
The slablike device makes a literal unit of the couple, forcing us to view the unit frontally and magnifying the impression of obstinate regal power.

Joan Miró. *Man and Woman.* **1962. Pierre Matisse Gallery, New York**
Beyond the cartoony sort of humor, Miró shows how the *range* of sculpture can be extended. This is funny in a *sculptural* way, and it doesn't degenerate into kitsch.

Marisol. *The Bicycle Race.* **1962–63. The Harry N. Abrams Family Collection, New York**

An almost Egyptian solemnity pervades this work. Still, there is something more than a satirical comment about a couple of earnest bicycle riders: he is No. 1, and she is No. 2—and they hate each other.

George Segal. *Lovers on a Bed II.* **1970. Sidney Janis Gallery, New York**
A couple who *succumb* to love; the tawdriness of the setting and their own
plainness make their embrace a compromise between Eros and fatigue.

**Eve Renée Nele. *The Couple*. 1961. Bayerische Staatsgemäldesamm-
lungen, Munich**

This is the fetish pair of a civilization consecrated to engineering: in their abdominal cavities nuts and bolts are renewed, and armatures are magically
rewound.

SCULPTURAL ASSEMBLAGE

Assemblage is revolutionary in the history of sculpture because it abandons carving, modeling, and casting. It begins with materials that already have a rich body of meaning and association. It parallels the flight of painting from the creation of illusions—pretending that stone is flesh or that metal is hair. Seley's automobile bumpers (see page 203) are sculptural because they occupy real space, but they do not cease to be bumpers. In other words, assemblage does not involve the total transmutation of materials; it involves composition with the meaning and substance of materials as they are found.

The sculptor's reluctance to transform materials completely constitutes a profound change in art. During the Middle Ages, alchemists tried to transmute ordinary materials into gold because of their belief in *a hierarchy* of substances. But modern artists will not accept that hierarchy. Science and technology have encouraged this attitude, since so many of the things we value are derived from cheap, abundant substances like coal, petroleum, nitrogen, or soybeans. Furthermore, the process of creating illusions has acquired some of the associations of deceit. The slogan "honesty of materials" has spread from craftsmen and designers to painters and sculptors. They now work in an aesthetic climate in which changing the inherent properties of a material seems unethical or, at least, foolish.

Assemblage is also related to the sense of inadequacy a sculptor may feel when confronting the forming and fabrication achievements of industry. When Cellini made his famous saltcellar, he could rightly feel that it represented the highest degree of technical mastery of his age. But the modern artist is exposed to miracles of miniaturization that make hand carving and casting look like minor accomplishments. Space flight and computerization represent technologies so remarkable that meticulously carved stone and marble seem to be quaint medieval survivals. So it makes practical sense for sculptors to use the products of industry. Their creative strategies shift from an emphasis on forming skills to an emphasis on ideas—composition with meanings already given.

The variety of sculptural effects possible through assemblage with prefabricated materials is enormous; it almost seems as if we are dealing with a new art form. But in the following examples the viewer with a good memory may rediscover some familiar melodies and echoes.

Benvenuto Cellini. *Saltcellar of Francis I.* 1539–43. Kunsthistorisches Museum, Vienna

Ultrasmall electronic circuit, a high-speed binary electronic counter for use in a spacecraft

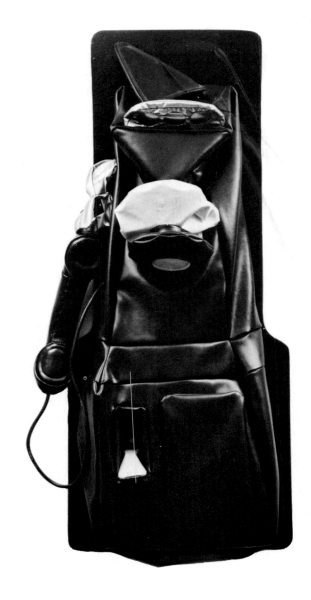

right: Claes Oldenburg. *Soft Pay-Telephone.* 1963. Collection William Zierler, New York
A fire-damaged telephone echoes Oldenburg's soft telephone. Using nonrigid materials like canvas, vinyl, kapok, and foam rubber, Oldenburg has elevated limpness to high status among the expressive qualities of sculpture.

below right: Burned phone, from advertisement for Western Electric Phone Company. 1968. Courtesy Cunningham & Walsh, Inc., New York
Life imitates art. There may have been a tragic fire, but somehow this phone looks ludicrous. Oldenburg bears some responsibility for this.

An Assemblage Anthology   In a relief made of canvas stretched over bent steel wire mounted on a metal frame, Lee Bontecou (born 1931) seems to be using a very old "assemblage" technique. The forms of her sculpture strongly resemble the tribal costume of the Northwest American Indians. At the same time, her technique reminds us of early aircraft manufacture—stretching and gluing fabric over a wire-frame skeleton. But the most prominent elements in her work are ovoid apertures; we cannot help seeing them as eyes or as openings in a strangely hypnotic mask.

The fundamental sculptural metaphors here are the mask and the membrane. The light, sturdy construction of the sculpture suggests the Indian practice of building a canoe by stretching hides over a wooden frame. That membrane arouses primitive, animistic feelings; the air trapped within seems to exert an outward force—an invisible force of the type that holds up airplane wings. Yet all of these ideas depend on a simple and personal mode of assemblage—canvas stretched over a wire frame.

In *Europa on a Cycle,* Richard Stankiewicz draws and constructs with old rods and chains; he uses mechanical parts as they are found, or he cuts metal shapes with a torch. But the various forms of metal—wire, pipe, sheet, rod, spring, tube, bar, and plate—are united by a single method of attachment—welding—and a single color and texture—rust. This simplicity frees the sculptor to deal with problems of volume and contour, movement and balance, illusion and reality. The notion of a beautiful woman carried off by a rusty bike is the kind of Surrealist idea that would have appealed to Picasso; he, too, composed with handlebars.

The Juggler by Robert Mallary (born 1917) is made of especially exotic materials: plastic-impregnated fabric and wood. Using a man's shirt and trousers soaked in plastic and attached to a burnt-wood support, Mallary created a figure out of the clothes meant to cover it. But the hollow arms and legs are almost rigid; they function as real limbs and heavy rags at the same time. The plastic freezes the action of fabric that has been stretched by its own weight and suspended from a wooden frame like a crucifix. Remember too that burnt wood is one of the primal materials of religious sacrifice. Clearly, Mallary has

Painted leather shirt. Tlingit Indians of Alaska. Collected in 1918. University Museum, Philadelphia

The magical motifs of tribal artists are often taken up, either unconsciously or intentionally, by the creators of "museum" art. But little has changed except the labels assigned by critics and historians.

Lee Bontecou. *Untitled.* 1962. Collection Mr. and Mrs. Seymour Schweber, Kings Point, New York

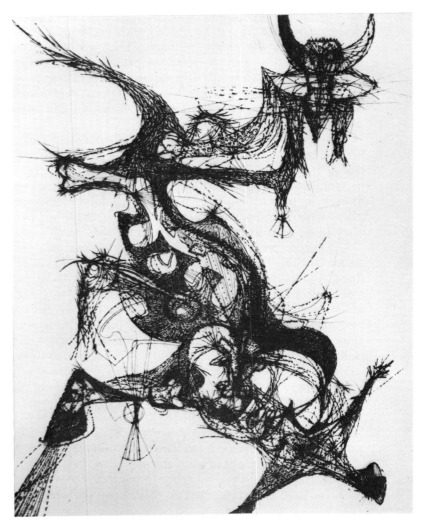

Gabor Peterdi. *The Black Horne.* 1952. Collection the artist

Richard Stankiewicz. *Europa on a Cycle.* **1953. Whereabouts unknown**

Eau de Vroom. **Advertisement for Crêpe de Chine perfume. 1967. Courtesy Berta, Grant & Winkler, Inc., New York**

The sculptural strategy of assemblage is brilliantly illustrated in a perfume advertisement that combines masculine machinery (the Honda), a soft saddlebag (can it symbolize Europa?), and a precious fragrance.

Pablo Picasso. *Bull's Head.* **1943. Musée Picasso, Paris**

assembled some of the basic symbols of suffering and transfiguration. The juggler, while "putting on his act," falls into the position of Christ on the Cross; we get a sense of dying-in-living and failure-in-success—the tragic ideas at the heart of existence.

A Pop version of assemblage sculpture can be seen in *The Stove* by Claes Oldenburg. It consists of painted plaster "food" displayed on a real but antiquated cooking range. The luridly colored food is enough to induce nausea; obviously, sculpture as the pleasing organization of forms is irrelevant here. The design principles of unity, balance, rhythm, and so on have been ignored. Instead, we are asked to look at food and food preparation as disgusting. The artist has directed a program of sabotage against what the housekeeping magazines, with their luscious colorplates, want to sell. We see the nakedness of groceries and cooking, and a familiar event becomes hideously ugly.

Nancy Graves. *Zaga.* 1983. The Nelson-Atkins Museum of Art, Kansas City, Missouri. Gift of the Friends of Art. Courtesy M. Knoedler & Co., Inc., New York

Animal and vegetable parts cast in bronze and assembled to make a creature that might have lived in the imagination of a prehistoric shaman or a medieval wizard. Seeds and roots, ferns and bones, wheels and rods: we seem to be watching an experiment in the laboratory of nature and technology. Graves can produce this strange, floating amalgam of mechanical and growing things because of the openness of modern sculpture.

John Chamberlain. *Essex.* 1960. Collection, The Museum of Modern Art, New York. Gift of Mr. and Mrs. Robert C. Scull and Purchase

César. *Sculpture Picture.* 1956. Collection, The Museum of Modern Art, New York. Gift of G. David Thompson

John Chamberlain's assemblage of crumpled automobile parts looks like an earlier stage in the process of machine destruction visible in the "compression" sculptures of César. Although these parts are found in junkyards, Chamberlain (born 1927) bends, welds, and paints them himself; the total work reflects its automotive origins only partially. In other words, a dead automobile has been used as a source of cheap raw material. The title *Essex* acknowledges a venerable vehicle as its ancestor, but we see the work mainly as a large, colored metal painting. And that is its objective—the creation of an Abstract Expressionist "canvas" in metal. But despite the painterly format and the screaming color, this sculpture cannot "forget" its roots in a machine that regularly commits vehicular homicide. The power of the work depends on aging metal clashing with the shiny new paint film given by the painter-sculptor. Chamberlain forces us to witness a new form of conflict between old and new, tranquility and violence, death and life.

The employment of *wrappings* in assemblage has enlarged the artistic vocabulary of terror. Using methods we associate with mortuaries or shipping rooms, two sculptors, Bruce Conner (born 1933) and Christo (Javacheff) (born 1935) have independently developed a gruesome and mysterious sculptural rhetoric. Both create images in which shrouded objects or figures seem to be struggling to escape their wrappings. The situation has psychopathic as well as sculptural overtones, since it exploits the viewer's fear of confinement; that is the funereal side. The chained or bound figure has a history as old as Prometheus; in Michelangelo's *Rebellious Slave,* for example, we witness a drama of imprisoned form that, in various disguises, appears in almost all his works. Conner's drama of imprisonment—*Child*—shows a mutilated wax figure on a high chair, enmeshed in a gauzelike material made of torn nylon stockings, which also look like cobwebs. The torn nylons function like Francis Bacon's blurred contours, creating an illusion of strangled movement—the quality of a silent, agonized scream.

left: Bruce Conner. *Child*. 1959–60. Collection, The Museum of Modern Art, New York. Gift of Philip Johnson

right: Michelangelo. *The Rebellious Slave*. 1513–16. The Louvre, Paris

above: Christo. *Package on Wheelbarrow.* 1963. Collection, The Museum of Modern Art, New York. Blanchette Rockefeller Fund

right: Rico Lebrun. *Bound Figure.* 1963. Collection Constance Lebrun Crown, Malibu, California

Package on Wheelbarrow by Christo describes the struggle of an unknown thing against a random system of knots and bindings. A sheet wrapping maintains the anonymity of the creature, or object, and the wheelbarrow keeps its secret, adding only the possibility that its writhing form will be carried away. As a result, the viewer experiences strange, more or less abstract, tensions; but an imagination nourished on horror films may discover ghoulishness rather than abstract art at the core of this work.

Little Hands by Arman (born 1928) continues the macabre note struck by Conner and Christo. Consisting of dolls' hands (many of them broken) glued into a wooden drawer, it yields a series of grisly perceptions. We start with a collection of mutilated toys and end with the uncovered mass graves that turn up so tragically in wartime. The drawer functions first as a frame, then as a container, and finally as a tomb (see section below, "Niches, Boxes, and Grottoes"). To equal its horror, we would have to go back to Hieronymus Bosch. But those handmade images lack the clinical detachment of the artist who assembles limbs originally meant to function as parts of a normal body.

In *Chopin's Waterloo* Arman shows his humorous side. Many citizens, it seems, harbor a secret desire to tear a piano apart. Arman has done it for them (as Jimmy Durante used to do) and has given permanent form to the ritual of piano sacrifice. The visual effect is one of splendid destruction—ivories, splinters, and piano wire in gorgeous disarray. Perhaps a piano is more interesting when dismembered than when healthy and whole. By tearing the piano open, the sculptor reveals it as a type of machine. Then, gratifying our desire to annihilate machines, he kills it. For these or other reasons, Jean Tinguely (born 1925), a Swiss sculptor celebrated for self-destroying machines, included a peeled and plucked piano in his kinetic sculpture performance at New York's Museum of Modern Art, *Homage to New York.* Perhaps both pianos represent

Arman. *Little Hands.* 1960. Collection the artist

Arman. *Chopin's Waterloo.* 1962. Collection the artist

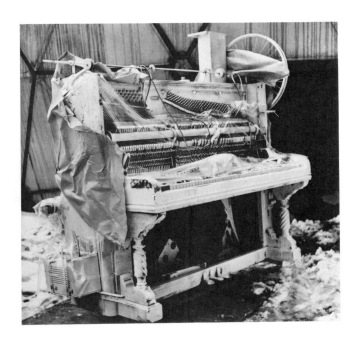

Jean Tinguely. Piano before its incorporation into *Homage to New York*. **Self-destroyed March 17, 1960, in the garden of The Museum of Modern Art, New York**

the aesthetic vindication of small boys who take clocks apart but cannot put them together again.

A fascination with violent or gruesome phenomena is visible in all forms of art and popular culture. For example, there is a vigorous market for the horror films of Vincent Price; all of us like to watch the Marx brothers break up a set; and rock stars have been known to smash their guitars during a performance. Sculptural assemblage can be manipulated to fit the pattern: the sculptor takes a complex object and explores the forces that hold it together. This exploration takes the form of tearing up the object and reassembling it to memorialize the process of destruction. In other words: reverse assemblage.

NICHES, BOXES, AND GROTTOES

The niche is a recessed place in a wall where a sculptured figure or bust can be located. So it is important to think of niche sculptures as *born in* walls, conceived as centers of dramatic interest on a plane surface. The niche encloses the sculpture physically and governs the angle of vision from which we see it. Psychologically, niches defend a sculpture, removing it from full exposure to the elements. This implies that the sculpture needs protection, possibly because it holds a valuable secret.

These psychological meanings of niche sculpture also adhere to the box sculptures and constructions that figure so prominently in twentieth-century art. A box sculpture might be regarded as a detached niche, a secular shrine taken out of an architectural setting that never existed. Looking at the box sculptures produced by our industrial civilization, it is not difficult to project on them all our associations with the cathedral niche or the recess in a temple wall—the mysterious little place we see in private and address in awe and reverence.

MEDIEVAL AND RENAISSANCE NICHE SCULPTURES

left: Apostle. c. 1090. St. Sernin, Toulouse

From the medieval carving, which is part of the wall, to the Renaissance work, which stands free, we can see sculpture moving progressively away from architecture. But not too far: the niche is psychologically necessary; it creates a sense of the sacred, of a person who is divinely protected.

right: **Donatello.** *St. Mark.* **1411–13. Orsanmichele, Florence**

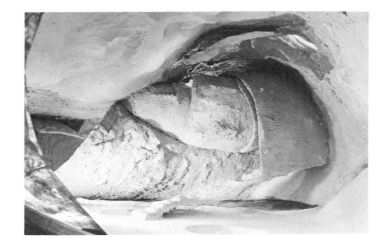

above left: Frederick Kiesler. Interior, Living Room, *Endless House.* 1949–60

above: Lucas Samaras. Detail of *Room.* 1964. Pace Gallery, New York

left: Antoni Gaudí. Original attic (garret), Casa Milá Apartment House, Barcelona. 1905–10

The grotto, like the niche, is a man-made recess or excavation, but it is not associated with the wall; it belongs instead to the convoluted inner spaces of natural caverns. This brings us to the shaped interior spaces of Frederick Kiesler (1896–1965)—a kind of hybrid architecture-and-sculpture. But as a modern art form the man-made grotto has little relation to shelter; it is better understood as interior sculpture. In Schwitters's Merzbau we saw a quasi-Cubist grotto. And in the grotesque—that is, grotto-like—passageways of Antoni Gaudí, we see truly sculptural concavities. All of these interior sculptures remind us that we have never really forgotten our prehistoric existence in caves.

In *Room* by Lucas Samaras (born 1936) we see a twentieth-century grotto, a three-dimensional interior assemblage consisting of possessions randomly(?) attached to the walls of a teenager's cave. Its claim to style lies in a total lack of style, and its realism is reinforced by our knowledge that the room is quite typical. The visual disorganization here makes a comment on American adolescent life-style, but we should remember that it accurately mirrors the large-scale environment created by Americans for generations. Perhaps *Room* is a type of rebellion against the austerities created by Mondrian and Mies; perhaps it exhibits a logic that architects and designers do not yet understand: the logic of the grotto, the niche, and the box.

Boxes differ from niches and grottoes because they can close and become packages—packages that can be carried. The niche is part of a stationary
wall, whereas the box is a portable container for something worth keeping. It
has many of the ancient associations of a reliquary—a container holding the
bones of a saint, a sacred text, or a precious remnant. These religious uses of
boxlike containers suggest the magical ancestry of modern box sculpture; we
see much more than their materials.

The authority of the niche is eloquently demonstrated in the sculptures
of Louise Nevelson (born 1904), sculptures that seem to be collections of
boxes or cells—little rooms. Usually painted black, they convey an impression
of compulsive neatness, of well-arranged, frequently cleaned drawers. Without knowing what the contents are, we sense they have been carefully ordered, put there for a purpose. They consist, in fact, of pieces of wood
molding, bowling pins, newel posts, chair legs, and so on. The secret of *Totality Dark* is not in the origin of its lumberyard odds and ends; it is in the control of their placement. These wooden objects have a power that defies logic.
Why?

Just as the monolith is a sculptural form that expresses order, the box is a
form that commands belief: it convinces on sight. Nevelson's box forms constitute a type of latter-day magical art; she uses this form because she thinks
like a sorcerer or a shaman. The box sculpture is a container for fetish objects
that a shaman typically owns. It is not necessary to know the symbolism of the
wooden shapes so long as we believe they ward off evil—the pains and anxieties we frequently treat with pills. In fact, the namelessness of the box contents enhances our faith in their magical power: the *form of presentation*
dominates the material presented.

In Marcel Duchamp's *Boîte-en-valise (The Box in a Valise)* we see a craft-
ily compartmented little museum within a box that resembles an attaché case.
Its carefully dimensioned spaces make room for small reproductions of each
of the sixty-eight principal works Duchamp created before abandoning art for
chess. Altogether, he built three hundred editions of this little "museum." But
the box is more than a handy container for copies of Duchamp's artistic output; it is an ironic device. By miniaturizing artworks originally meant for a
museum and storing them according to the impartial logic of the valise, Duchamp transformed the objects into a type of business inventory—merchandise in a salesman's sample case. Is that what gallery art is?

Joseph Cornell's (1903–1972) boxes are also surreal containers—collections of objects that seem unrelated until we realize that they are meant to
frustrate commonsense logic. For example, *Soap Bubble Set* has the simplicity

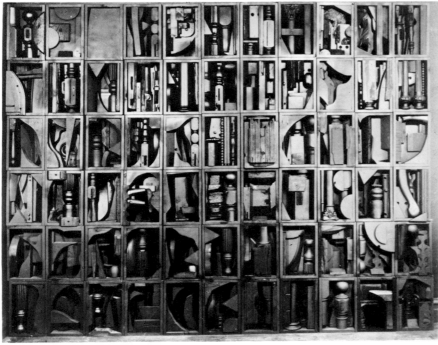

Louise Nevelson. *Totality Dark*. 1962. Pace Gallery, New York

Crafts for Tour advertisement. 1963. Courtesy The 7 Santini Brothers Fine Arts Division, New York

Compare this box to Duchamp's valise—or to Nevelson's sculpture. What principle do they illustrate? Answer: boxes make powerful magic; the container takes over its contents.

Marcel Duchamp. *Boîte-en-valise (The Box in a Valise)*. 1938–42. Dwan Gallery, New York

and serenity of a Chardin still life. But its objects are not anonymous, like Louise Nevelson's wooden fragments; they have identities that induce dreams of old places and possessions, recollections of lost things, like childhood games or tastes or smells. Somehow, Cornell manages to scramble our time sense; he plays with the cues that tell us where our minds have wandered. The experience is slightly disorienting, but it leaves no scars. These collections carry us back to a lost dream time; then the frame takes us home.

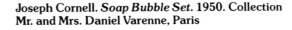
Joseph Cornell. *Soap Bubble Set.* 1950. Collection Mr. and Mrs. Daniel Varenne, Paris

Joseph Cornell. *Blériot.* 1956. Collection Mr. and Mrs. E. A. Bergman, Chicago

H. C. Westermann. *Memorial to the Idea of Man, If He Was an Idea.* 1958. Collection Lewis Manilow, Chicago

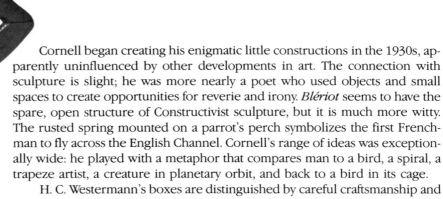

Cornell began creating his enigmatic little constructions in the 1930s, apparently uninfluenced by other developments in art. The connection with sculpture is slight; he was more nearly a poet who used objects and small spaces to create opportunities for reverie and irony. *Blériot* seems to have the spare, open structure of Constructivist sculpture, but it is much more witty. The rusted spring mounted on a parrot's perch symbolizes the first Frenchman to fly across the English Channel. Cornell's range of ideas was exceptionally wide: he played with a metaphor that compares man to a bird, a spiral, a trapeze artist, a creature in planetary orbit, and back to a bird in its cage.

H. C. Westermann's boxes are distinguished by careful craftsmanship and grotesque references to the human body. In *Memorial to the Idea of Man, If He Was an Idea* we see a large, well-made cabinet-and-Cyclops wearing crenellations for a crown, like the battlements on a castle tower. This is a man: the door of his torso, when opened, reveals an interior lined with bottle caps. The insides also contain a headless baseball player and an armless acrobat, plus a black ship sinking in a sea of bottle caps. Incomplete bodies, bottle caps, and baseball—the idea of man! Not much of an idea, according to Westermann.

It is not unusual for the abdominal cavity of a fetish figure to hold magical substances. In *African Art* Werner Schmalenbach wrote: "A [fetish] figure can be used as one only when it is charged with some magic content....Every conceivable thing is used as a magic content: bits of bone, teeth, animal claws.... They are often placed in a cavity hollowed out in the head or belly, or, too, in a little horn on top of the head." Clearly, Westermann follows the African formula: the interior of his box is crucially important even if we don't see it. This approach to sculpture is unlike anything we have seen in museums: the outer form is only part of the statement; the artist fabricates the visceral contents too. The craftsmanship and durability of Westermann's box tell us that he wants to make "real" beings who exist by virtue of their built-in equipment. The fact that their insides are filled with the debris of an afternoon at a baseball stadium is no more remarkable than the fact that our insides contain partly digested hamburger, onions, and Coke.

Kenny Scharf. *Extravaganza Televisione.* **1984. Courtesy Tony Shafrazi Gallery, New York**

The ultimate box—a television set—adorned with Day-Glo stripes and plastic, kitschy add-ons. This could be a way of acknowledging the magic of our principal household shrine. Also, the frame can now compete with its contents.

BEYOND CONSTRUCTIVISM: PRIMARY STRUCTURES

Under the influence of Constructivism, sculptors have tended to discard figurative, gestural, and symbolic meanings. They employ materials and movement as if sculpture were an extension of physics or engineering. At the same time, the penetration of solid forms goes forward, producing a breakdown of classical notions of form. Sculpture seems to be in the process of redefining itself; it is becoming a new type of visual inquiry—the exploration of mechanical and architectural space through primary structures.

Primary structures are not precious objects; they are not designed to be worshiped, admired in private, or employed as architectural adornments. Instead, they are the by-products of spatial investigations undertaken to discover the impact of large-scale forms on human awareness. Often they have an architectural look, except that we live *with,* not *in,* them. They may appear to be abstract and impersonal, but they have a strong physical presence: in seeing these structures we feel the need to arrange ourselves around them.

Images of persons can rarely be found in primary structures, but bodily responses to their openings and enclosures are intended. These kinesthetic responses are what abstract artists invoke when they insist that a humanistic art need not include figurative *representation:* they compose with the perceptual and physiological behavior of human beings in mind.

Primary structuralists vary in the way they employ intuition or calculation in design. Many are willing to surrender the control of form to prepared number systems, equations, and formulas; to them, the computer looks increasingly attractive as a sculptural tool. We should remember that artists have sought a mathematical science of proportion since the ancient Greeks. Presumably, it saves work and is free of human idiosyncrasies. Of course, human idiosyncrasies can be aesthetically interesting. But that kind of aesthetics may be dead. Primary structuralists exhibit our perennial hope of finding laws and creating art that can transcend the chaos of human thought and desire.

Today, labels like "serial sculpture," "systems sculpture," and "ABC art" are used to describe works that rely on simple arrangements of basic volumes and voids, mechanically produced surfaces, and algebraic permutations of form. The impact on the viewer, however, is anything but simple. Architectural emotions are often involved because of the implied invitation to move under, around, and through a sculpture. Also, the forms seem engineered rather than crafted; tactile qualities are conspicuously absent. Of course, textures can be programmed by a computer, but whether that can produce surfaces like those we see in a Rodin bronze or a Henry Moore carving remains to be seen.

Ronald Bladen. *Cathedral Evening.* **1969. South Albany Mall Project, Albany, New York**

An important change in perception occurs when sculpture (or painting) assumes the scale of architecture: we no longer feel ourselves in the presence of represented forms; we tend to regard the object as a primary rather than a derived phenomenon.

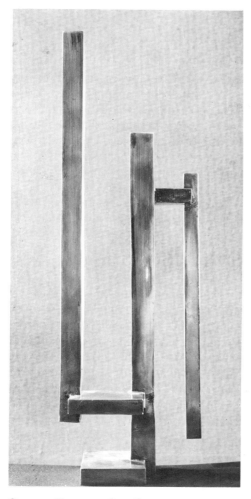

Sol Lewitt. *47 Three-Part Variations on 3 Different Kinds of Cubes.* **1967. Dwan Gallery, New York**

Georges Vantongerloo. *Construction $y = 2x^3 - 13.5x^2 + 21x$.* **1935. Kunstmuseum, Basel**

An early and austere example of sculpture created according to a mathematical equation. But notice the uncontrolled reflections, shimmers, and diffractions in the nickel-silver surfaces. Were they also planned?

Isamu Noguchi. *Floor Frame.* **1962. Collection Mr. and Mrs. Robert A. Bernhard, Portchester, New York**

Sculpture becomes the art of engineering a stately geometric twist, or of subjecting post-and-beam forms to diagonal stresses, seeming to bury and then resurrect them. Despite their monumental scale, these are humorous works.

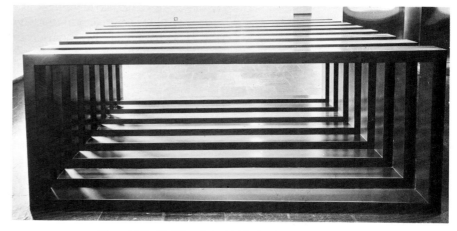

Donald Judd. *Untitled.* **1968. Collection Mr. and Mrs. Frederick B. Mayer, Denver**

Through the absolute predictability of serial imagery, the sculptor tries to empty his forms of emotional and historical "debris." But then a conflict arises: these constructions occupy real space on a real planet whose gravity, atmosphere, and motion (night and day, dark and light) inevitably affect man-made or natural structures and our perceptions of them.

Tony Smith. *Cigarette.* **1967. Albright-Knox Art Gallery, Buffalo, New York. Gift of the Seymour H. Knox Foundation, Inc.**

KINETIC SCULPTURE

Sculpture-in-motion has a history as old as the Trojan horse and as recent as the figures that strike the hour in front of Macy's department store. We see it in the widely owned but aesthetically unmentionable Swiss clock and in millions of spring-driven toys, quartz-driven watches, and transistorized household appliances. The combination of sculpture with mechanical motion occupied some of the best minds of the Renaissance, including Leonardo da Vinci, who received good fees for designing sculptural-mechanical devices for his princely patrons.

Leonardo also designed an early flying machine, repeating the mythic feat of the Greek sculptor Daedalus, who achieved successful flight but with disastrous results for his son Icarus. Icarus flew too close to the sun, which melted his wax wings; so the boy fell into the sea and drowned. This was how the ancients described the fate of men who try to usurp the prerogatives of gods. Daedalus may have been the mythical ancestor of all kinetic sculptors, since he also devised dolls with movable limbs for the daughters of the king of Sicily. (A great sculptor never gives up.) At any rate, the ability to make objects that move by themselves (like automobiles) has seemingly miraculous qualities.

The mystery surrounding motion fascinates artists. Do we see form or do we see movement? Or something else? In kinetic sculpture motion becomes a visual element, like shape or color. The Futurists, as we know, dedicated their art to expressing the effects of movement—especially mechanical movement—which they considered "more beautiful" than Greek sculpture. But the Futurists stayed within the static conventions of painting and sculpture; motion was represented in their art; it did not become part of the art object itself.

In 1920, Naum Gabo created the first modern kinetic sculpture and exhibited it in Berlin. Then his brother, Pevsner, made a statement in *Realist Manifesto* that served as a foundation for kinetic sculpture and Constructivist aesthetics: "We free ourselves from the thousand-year-old error of art, originating in Egypt, that only static rhythms can be its elements. We proclaim that for present-day perceptions the most important elements of art are the kinetic rhythms."

In his sculpture, Gabo concentrated on constructions that penetrate volume and minimize mass, but he created few works that actually employ movement as an element. It was an American sculptor, Alexander Calder, who

Richard Hunt. *Icarus*. 1956. Albright-Knox Art Gallery, Buffalo, New York. Gift of Seymour H. Knox

In Hunt's sculpture, Icarus is supported from below. The original Icarus was not so lucky.

MOTION SIMULATED IN STATIC SCULPTURE

left: Bruno Lucchesi. *Seated Woman #2*. 1963. Whereabouts unknown

right: Luciano Minguzzi. *Woman Jumping Rope*. 1954. Collection Alfons Bach, Palm Beach

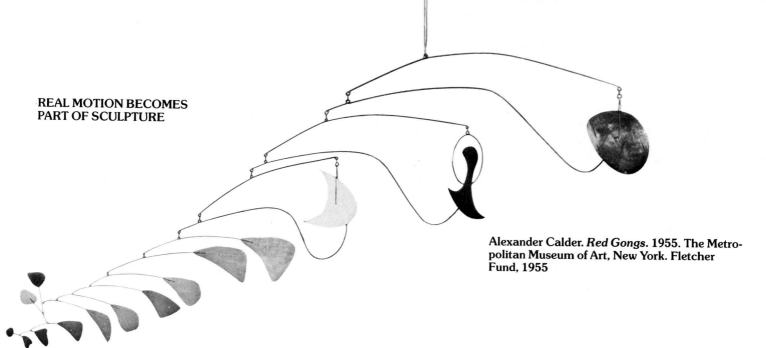

Alexander Calder. *Red Gongs*. 1955. The Metropolitan Museum of Art, New York. Fletcher Fund, 1955

created an art form in the 1930s—mobiles—in which motion is an integral part of the work. Calder's mobiles are sensitively balanced, three-dimensional systems that can move in response to the gentlest of air currents. While receiving their motive force from the invisible environment, the mobile's parts and subsystems travel in orbits especially designed by the sculptor. The energy that actuates them may be random, but the mobile's movement is anticipated, that is, shaped and controlled.

Calder's sculpture can be discussed as if it were static sculpture, but his original contribution was to make it possible for sculpture to control *qualities* of movement. In static terms, Calder's forms look like those of Arp and Miró. Mostly, they are playful and biomorphic—reminiscent of fish, animals, and leaves. But his sculptural *movement* is unique. Some works suggest the stately sway of tree branches; others are as comic as Charlie Chaplin hopping and skipping his way down a street. Mobiles have enormous appeal—they have almost become an American folk art—because their control of motion seems to unlock one of life's great secrets. The mobile and the animated film are quite possibly our greatest twentieth-century artistic achievements.

Examples of Kinetic Sculpture   The machine as an idea and a permanent presence inevitably attracts artists. For kinetic sculptors mechanical motion is especially interesting; the problem is how to use it artistically. Some kinetic sculptures are themselves machines. intended only to exhibit their operation. They are different from real machines in that they perform no "serious" work. The machines of the cartoonist Rube Goldberg (1883–1970) humorously ex-

Rube Goldberg. Cartoon of an absurd machine. Reprinted with special permission of King Features Syndicate, Inc.

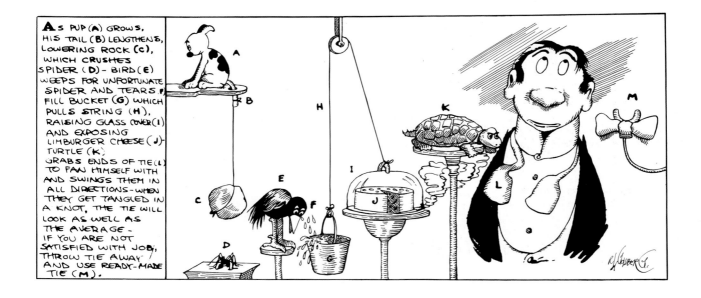

left: Isamu Noguchi. *Big Boy.* 1952. Collection, The Museum of Modern Art, New York. A. Conger Goodyear Fund

Noguchi's little person, though static, aims at the same dynamism as the swinging-girl whistle.

right: **Whistle in the form of a swinging girl, from Remojadas region, Veracruz, Mexico.** A.D. **300–900. The Metropolitan Museum of Art, New York. The Michael C. Rockefeller Memorial Collection. Bequest of Nelson A. Rockefeller, 1979. (1979.206.574)**

ploited this idea: he would "invent" an incredibly complex apparatus to do a minor job like swatting flies or sprinkling salt on French fries. His cartoons had a serious side: they showed how our love affair with machines had reached the stage of disenchantment: mechanization is perfect and absurd at the same time.

A kind of Goldbergian absurdity can be seen in *Music Machine* by Arthur Secunda. This is an operational sculpture consisting of gilded wood, metal, and machine parts built around a music box. Its associations with the mechanics of sound are abetted by radio antennae, a built-in xylophone, a guitar handle, and a variety of electronic odds and ends. Gears, springs, wires, and so on are exposed in an effort to produce visual poetry with mechanized innards.

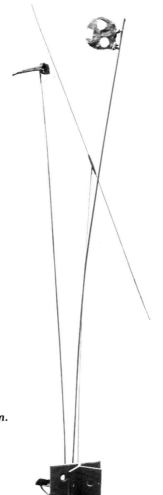

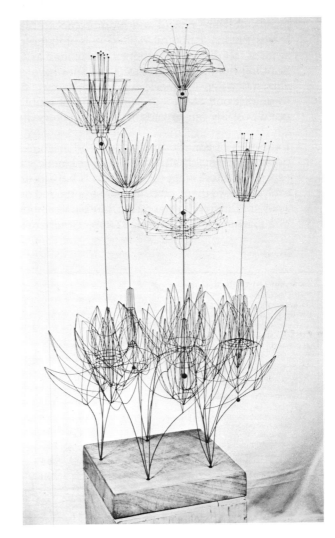

right: **Takis. *Signal Rocket.* 1955. Collection, The Museum of Modern Art, New York. Mrs. Charles V. Hickox Fund**

far right: **Konstantin Milonadis. *Flower Garden.* 1961. Collection Dr. and Mrs. Malcolm A. McCannel, Minneapolis**

Arthur Secunda. *Music Machine*. 1964–65.
Whereabouts unknown

Lin Emery. *Homage to Amercreo*. 1964. American Creosote Works, Inc., New Orleans

Also, there is a hint of human irony in the suggestion that a musician is a machine wired to make noise.

We see a more practical kinetic sculpture in Lin Emery's *Homage to Amercreo,* a mobile fountain whose forms fill with water until they tilt over, empty themselves, and return to be filled again. Although this work functions as a machine, its mechanical action shows the visual delight we can get from abstract forms doing a job clearly and efficiently. The same idea might well be applied to other machines in our civilization. Of course, the purpose of a fountain is to create visual entertainment out of water in motion; that can lead to some strange spectacles. Here we can be grateful that Emery's fountain does not consist of sea nymphs and dolphins acting out an ancient Greek soap opera.

In *Study: Falling Man (Figure on a Bed)* by Ernest Trova, we see an aluminum figure strapped to a circular apparatus that has mechanical-experimental overtones. The work is frightening because the apparatus is so obviously calculated to carry out some sort of dehumanizing job. Trova's figure is a model of urban, middle-aged man—slightly paunchy, swaybacked, faceless, and curiously without arms. He looks a little like a mannequin used in an auto-crash experiment. Trova has created an image of man as ideal subject for clinical experimentation. But we do not know *the purpose* of the experiment. Will he be rocked and rotated like an astronaut undergoing an exercise in weightlessness? Will his manhood survive? Another Trova work, *Study: Falling Man (Landscape #1)* offers three versions of the same man, involved again with mechanical equipment. His nakedness, his high-tech accessories, and his shiny aluminum skin eerily evoke that depersonalized humanity described by George Orwell in his not so fantastic novel *1984.* This harmless creature is about to participate in some remarkable maneuvers. Will he fly? Will the equipment fly him?

Jean Tinguely's kinetic sculptures are mechanical poems about the absurdity of machines and of a civilization governed by machines. His *Homage to New York* was a type of mechanized Happening. In addition to the battered piano mentioned earlier (see page 343), it contained drums, bicycle wheels, Coke bottles, a typewriter, a drawing machine, and a weather balloon. Fifteen rickety motors powered the shabbily constructed affair, which was designed to make music, create drawings, write reports, give birth to machine babies,

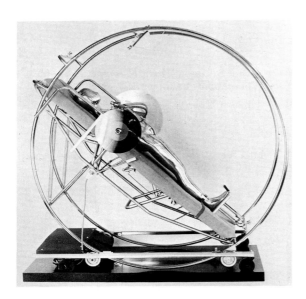

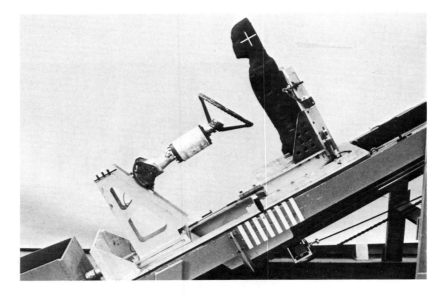

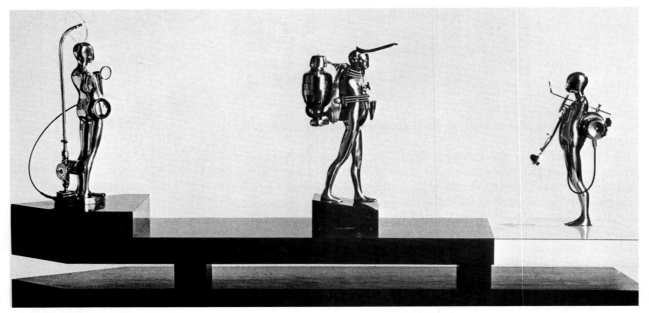

top left: Ernest Trova. *Study: Falling Man (Figure on Bed).* 1964. Pace Gallery, New York

top right: Man-size mannequin, from advertisement for Ford Motor Company. 1966

above: Ernest Trova. *Study: Falling Man (Landscape #1).* 1964. Pace Gallery, New York

Henry R. Martin. Cartoon. Copyright © 1967 by Henry R. Martin. Reprinted by permission

Kinetic sculpture generates its own kind of humor (see Tinguely, pages 243 and 357). When it breaks down, we need a mechanic, not an artist.

"Triangle Electric? Do you repair sculpture?"

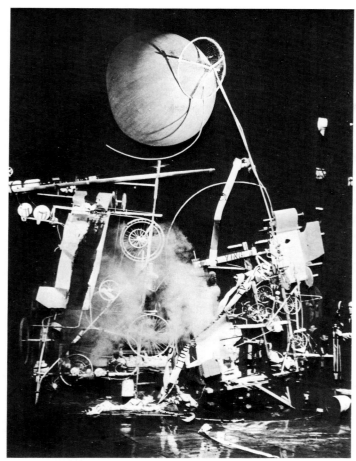

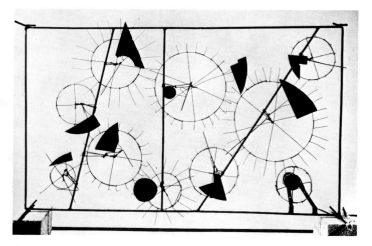

left: Jean Tinguely. *Homage to New York.* 1960. Self-destroyed March 17, 1960, in the garden of The Museum of Modern Art, New York

above: Jean Tinguely. *Méta-Mécanique.* 1954. Museum of Fine Arts, Houston. Purchased with funds donated by Dominique and John de Menil

Louise Bourgeois. *Radar.* 1978. Courtesy Xavier Fourcade, Inc., New York

The table revolves so that the faces of the wooden forms can receive light as the sun moves across the sky. In effect, these maple pieces behave like heliotropic plants. But in the universe of Louise Bourgeois, all living things must obey the laws of geometry.

**Peter Voulkos. *Gallas Rock.*
1959–60. Dr. and Mrs. Digby
Gallas, Los Angeles**

and finally to set itself on fire and "die." The noise, the drawings, the typed reports, and the frenzied activity were aimless, in true Dada fashion. But *Homage* had an aim: suicide. This machine was really a junkyard parody of contemporary civilization.

The short career of *Homage* was witnessed by a distinguished audience in the garden of the Museum of Modern Art on March 17, 1960. Contrary to expectations, the machine did not destroy itself completely, and Tinguely had to intervene to set it on the path to self-immolation. With his aid, the whole whirring, flapping thing began to smoke; at last, it exploded into flame. The "useful" life of *Homage* was ended with a fire extinguisher.

Homage to New York, like Kaprow's Happenings, may belong to theater more than to sculpture because of its brief existence. However, Tinguely has also created works that do not self-destruct. *Méta-Mécanique* exhibits his fascination with bicycle wheels, discarded metal parts, and belt-driven systems for transmitting energy. In general, Tinguely's kinetic sculptures move and sound like a one-man band, with motors substituting for the frantic musician. They thump and pound, vibrate and oscillate, producing to-and-fro alternations or ongoing cycles. In *Homage,* soft-drink bottles were endlessly sent down an inclined plane, but not to be packed, delivered, sold, and consumed; they went down to destruction in a crashing finale. Tinguely was making a statement.

From Greek water clocks to Leonardo's mechanized entertainments for the duke of Milan, to Calder's mobiles, to Rube Goldberg's crazy inventions, to the automated disasters of Jean Tinguely has been a long kinetic voyage. Tinguely's machines never caught up with modern, electronically guided tools; they look more like the equipment that must have filled the bicycle shop of Orville and Wilbur Wright. Today, that comfortable old noise and clutter have been replaced by quieter and more efficient tools of mechanization and automation. Perhaps that is why *Méta-Mécanique* is not frightening but quaint—like antique spinning wheels and sculpture that stands still.

Bruce Kokko. *Paint Can with Brush.* 1965. Whereabouts unknown
This ceramic "craft" object violates all the craft ideals: it can't be used; the paint spills are very uncraftsman-like, and the "truth to materials" principle is ignored.

Roger Lucas. *Three-finger ring.* 1969
Without a visual cue to its scale, this ring might easily be mistaken for a monumental sculpture.

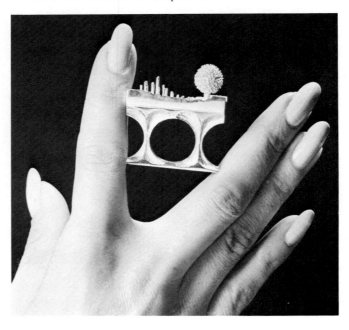

SCULPTURE AND THE CRAFTS

For some time craftsmen have been seeking a divorce from useful manufacture, trying to strengthen their claims to fine-art status. Crafts may have begun as useful art forms, but they are increasingly prized for their *sculptural* values. Handmade ceramic pots, for example, cannot compete economically with mass-produced containers made of metal, glass, or plastics. Yet, they continue to be made by potters, exhibited in museums, sold in department stores, and purchased by collectors. Clearly, they satisfy aesthetic as well as utilitarian needs. Pots are frequently made with no intention that they should function as containers. The potter's wheel has become a tool of sculpture.

Peter Voulkos (born 1924) has been a leader in exploring the expressive possibilities of forms developed by potters. His *Gallas Rock,* which was created by combining hand-built pottery forms, has the quality of a sculptural assemblage. The act of putting these forms together, or crushing them against each other, results in the kind of violence and excitement we associate with action painting. Indeed, Voulkos might be regarded as an "action potter." He has made the crucial move away from the pot as container: now the handles and spouts are gone; the holes and hollows survive as sculptural space.

Similarly, jewelry and metalwork, silversmithing and enameling, look like small-scale sculpture practiced with special materials. Woodworking in combination with metal, fabric, or leather falls into the same sculptural category. The same is true of glassmaking and textile-fiber construction. Clearly, the crafts have emerged from their "previous condition of servitude." This development is welcome, if craftsmen can get better prices for their work. And if sculptors are encouraged to pay more attention to craft, that, too, is welcome. But if utilitarian objects are left to the tender mercies of engineers, we may have cause for regret.

Beyond the Museum: Earth Sculpture   We know that almost everything *in* the environment has been designed by man. Now, many artists want to work on the environment itself. Directly. Their "environment" is more than the local space of human communities; it is the land, air, and water that make up our planet. Like civil engineers they try to shape the earth. Natural land and space become materials for a new kind of sculpture: earthworks, skyworks, and waterworks.

Today, a sculpture can be a cliff wrapped in canvas, a small hole in a park, a trench in the desert, some stones or dirt piled on a gallery floor, shafts of

Otto Piene. Stage of *Manned Helium Sculpture,* one of three days of "Citything Sky Ballet," Pittsburgh. 1970

Michael Heizer. *Isolated Mass/Circumflex.* 1968. Massacre Dry Lake, Nevada

These gestures have little to do with the ecological ethic emerging today. They are meaningful mainly with reference to what they reject: the traditional scale, materials, and purposes of art.

Dennis Oppenheim. *Annual Rings.* Aerial photograph of the frozen St. John River at Fort Kent, Maine, the time-zone and international boundary between the U.S. and Canada. 1968. Courtesy Mr. and Mrs. Kelly Anderson

Walter de Maria. *Mile Long Drawing.* 1968. Mohave Desert, California. Eroded by wind within one month

Alan Saret. *Untitled.* **1969–70. Art Gallery of Ontario, Toronto**

Dirt, assorted trash, and industrial waste have been dumped where they are not supposed to be. We are invited to examine them sympathetically—not as something to get rid of.

Robert Morris. *Earthwork.* **Installed in the Dwan Gallery, 1968. Courtesy Leo Castelli Gallery, New York**

Robert Smithson. *Nonsite.* **1968. Collection Virginia Dwan, New York**

Through the progressive design of the containers for these rocks, Smithson expresses a forming and not merely a collecting intention. Presumably the rocks seemed too anonymous without their shaped enclosures.

light in the sky, or floating, luminescent gas-filled bags of plastic. Like Happenings, these objects, places, and events are often too large, fragile, temporary, or distant to be experienced directly. But we can see pictures of them or read about them. Earthworks can be commissioned, but they are difficult to buy, hard to see, and meaningless to own. Most of them can't be exhibited in museums. And that is the point: earthworks express disdain for galleries and museums; they satirize commodity ownership. The artist issues certificates testifying to the ownership of a piece of an earthwork, just as a broker sells certificates for shares in cotton or grain futures, or pork bellies. We never see the pork bellies we have bought, but we know they exist.

The growth of ecological concern in our time has certainly stimulated artistic thinking in terms of planet-wide ecosystems; we wonder what we can do for, or to, the biosphere, the noosphere, and the atmosphere. Thus, immense creative vistas seem to open up for the artist: perhaps earth sculpture represents the beginning of a marvelous new synthesis between human forming capacities and the earth sciences. Thus far, however, earth sculpture appears to be a type of antiart—a gesture of disillusionment with art institutions and boredom with the artistic traditions of usefulness, object-ness, and meaning on a comprehensible scale. From an airplane, farmland looks better.

Pratt & Whitney RL10 rocket engine, from advertisement for United Aircraft Corporation. 1969. Courtesy Cunningham & Walsh, Inc., New York

The resemblance is accidental, of course. Still, those exhausts look like snakes, and the whole engine has a humanoid look. Why? Because this is the sculpture of the twentieth century. Our technology inspires faith; we want to believe in it.

***Snake Goddess.* c. 1600 B.C. Heraklion Museum, Crete**

**László Moholy-Nagy.
Light-Space Modulator.
1923–30. Busch-Reisinger
Museum, Harvard University, Cambridge,
Massachusetts**

Sixty years ago, Moholy-Nagy anticipated many of today's experiments with light-and-motion sculpture. His machine is not only a working device but also a kinetic sculpture.

CONCLUSION

It can truly be said of sculpture that in the midst of change there is abiding sameness. Magic and sorcery survive even though materials and techniques have undergone radical transformations. Through all the innovations of form and concept, sculpture has retained its identity as an art of physical materials occupying real space, persuading us to believe its forms truly live. In the history of sculpture, the pursuit of vitality remains constant.

Sculpture has lost volume and mass—from the monolith to the metal filament; and it has gained in motion—from the static statuary of ancient Egypt to the kinetic sculpture of the twentieth century. Today, we find sculpture knocking at the door of physics: think of what lasers and holography may do. But it is interesting that artists like Gabo, Pevsner, and Moholy-Nagy—men with strong scientific interests—were increasingly attracted to the sensuous qualities of materials as their careers unfolded. Three-dimensional media make powerful tactile claims—claims that cannot be denied. In other words, sculpture is an art that involves us in physical reality; it forces us to celebrate the world in concrete form. The substance must precede the idea.

opposite above: **Magdalena Abakanowicz. *Women.* 1985. Courtesy Xavier Fourcade, Inc., New York**

Headless, armless figures seen only from the back. They look like mummies, unwrapped after waiting thousands of years to be brought back to life. By using organic materials that have the capacity to age, wrinkle, and decay, and by placing the figures on the same floor we stand on, Abakanowicz draws us into their company—the company of the dead. Seeing sculpture becomes a funereal ritual.

opposite left: **Arnaldo Pomodoro. *Large Sphere.* 1966–67. Mt. Sinai Hospital, New York**

Further evidence of the powerful attraction that contemporary sculpture has, not only for craftsmen but also for industrial designers.

opposite right: **Francesco Bocola. Quasar lamp. 1970**

CHAPTER TWELVE

ARCHITECTURE

Buildings result from the interaction of many factors: site, climate, function, client, building codes, workmanship. For any given structure, one or more of these factors can assume crucial importance. But all of them must be considered in the solution of an architectural problem. We see the physical result but rarely know the priorities that affected the architectural solution. It would be impossible to know all the facts about a building's design and construction, but it *is* possible to know the materials and devices available to architects and to understand how they work.

Architecture relies on structural devices like arches, domes, and trusses, which can be made of materials like wood, stone, or steel. These devices are basic because they govern the space a building encloses. Materials are important because they determine how structural devices operate. For example, a truss can be made of wood or metal; a post can be made of stone or steel. Different materials require different dimensions to do the same job; hence, the visual results depend on the materials and devices the architect chooses.

Now, the art of architecture emerges in these choices. There are usually several ways to enclose space, support weight, admit light, or finish a surface. So architects have to solve their problems in the light of *an idea*—usually an idea about the way shaped spaces affect people. (Churchill once said, "We shape our houses and then they shape us.") If architects did not have to make human choices, their services could be performed by computers, and architecture would not be an art. Alas, some buildings look as if they were designed by computers; the same architectural solution has been used again and again; everyone's convenience (except that of the building's users) has been served. Standardization of materials and construction processes has led to a certain amount of monotony in today's architecture. The *great* modern buildings show that each architectural problem is unique and that design alternatives always exist.

THE CLASSIC MATERIALS

The earliest builders used materials that were close at hand and in good supply. Then as now, building devices and techniques resulted from a combination of ingenuity and the inherent possibilities of available material. Today, the African villager builds with sticks, mud, and grass because these are the

most profuse materials in the environment. For the same reason, Eskimos build an igloo of ice when they settle down for the winter. On the move, they construct with reindeer skins and bone, much as the American Indian built his tepee with wooden poles and animal hides. The igloo is a domical structure resting over an excavation in the ice; in its modest way it solves the same problem as Michelangelo's dome of St. Peter's. The Indian's conical tepee is a type of portable housing; as architectural form it is certainly superior to the modern auto trailer. As for the African grass hut—a cone-shaped roof resting on a cylindrical base—it would be hard to surpass as a useful combination of geometrical forms.

During the great periods of Egyptian and Greek architecture, stone became the favored material when tools for cutting it were developed. The Mesopotamians, having little stone, used brick and glazed tile. In most places, wood preceded stone as a building material; it served as a supporting framework for "curtain-walls" of fiber and mud. Early men used stone for religious and commemorative purposes, as in their mighty *menhir* statues (upright stones that were "homes" for departed souls) and *dolmens* ("table" slabs set on upright stones and used as altars or open tombs). Stone construction grew more complex in the *cromlech*—a circular arrangement of menhirs around a dolmen; it probably served astrological and religious purposes. Oriented toward the sun, the cromlech may be the architectural ancestor of our temples, amphitheaters, and cathedrals.

It is important to recognize ecological influences on the beginnings of architecture. Egypt had an abundance of stone plus a great river, the Nile, which could be used to transport heavy stone to construction sites. The wood of native palm trees was weak and the importation of stronger woods was too

Detail of Stonehenge, Salisbury Plain, Wiltshire, England. c. 2000 B.C.

Moroccan picnic hut. Courtesy Hispanic Society of America, New York. Anderson Spalding Collection

Even basketry has been used in architecture. Notice the progressive rhythm of the geometric forms and the textural interest produced by the woven fibers. The combination is aesthetically pleasing, and it lets in light and air.

Detail of court, Temple of Amon-Mut-Khonsu, Luxor, Egypt. c. 1390 B.C.

expensive, so the Egyptians used stone roof lintels rather than timbered ceilings. But stone cannot span a very wide space, so their interior spaces look like forests of columns.

The Egyptian builders worked with little more than the lever, the pulley, and the inclined plane, but they had, in their slaves, thousands of efficient human engines. For the pharaohs, it was economical to raise grain in the fertile Nile valley, feed it to peasants, and then exploit their labor for a lifetime greater than that of a modern machine. Our civilization would rather convert grain to alcohol and use it as fuel to operate machines. Of course, power machinery had not been invented in 3000 B.C. But remember, too, that slavery discourages invention.

The classic materials—wood, stone, and brick—tell us a great deal about the civilizations that use them. In examining their working properties, we may discover a number of interesting connections between architecture, economics, and politics.

Wood Wood appears in nature as a structural material rather than as an inert mass material like stone. Its distribution in all but the most arid regions and its strength and adaptability to tooling enable it to compete with many specialized materials. It can be a covering surface or a structural member, but its grain, the principal source of wood's beauty, accounts for its structural unreliability. In the natural state, wood varies in strength; consequently, wood construction requires wide safety factors: large dimensions and frequent reinforcement to prevent failure due to hidden defects.

American building has always been lavish in its use of wood, but the disappearance of the frontier, the development of competing materials, and the requirements of new designs will probably reduce the excessive use of wood. Also, wood has distinct disadvantages. (1) It is combustible. What must have been magnificent Scandinavian and Russian churches have been lost to us because of fire. (2) Wood is highly responsive to temperature and moisture changes; its dimensions are not stable. Nails shift and slip as wood dries out and shrinks; joints loosen. (3) As an organic material, wood is subject to attack by rot, fungus, and insects.

Some of these liabilities have been overcome by technology. Because plywood, for example, is made of veneers of wood glued together at right angles, the tendency to warp is eliminated. These veneers, made by a rotary shaving of the log, constitute a very economical use of the raw material. Also, plywood is more consistently uniform in strength than natural wood; it can be used in skeletal structures or in stressed-skin and shell structures. In general, plywood is remarkably light for its strength, which makes it especially useful in the construction of small and medium-size buildings. Laminated wooden beams, a recent invention, create a wide array of architectural possibilities. Indeed, plywood, molded wood, pressed wood, and fiberboard constitute wholly new building materials—a far cry from the tree.

left: **Smith & Williams. Detail of plywood supports, Congregational Church, California City. 1964**

Smooth, slender, and graceful, these curved plywood supports are amazingly strong for their weight. They create an upward-striving effect in contrast to the coarse, earthbound masonry wall on the inside.

right: **Church of Lazarus, Kizhi Island, U.S.S.R. 14th century**

Wood is warm in color, flexible in form, but, alas, combustible.

left: **Stone wall built by the Incas in Cuzco, Peru**

right: **Masayuki Nagare. Wall of the Japan Pavilion, New York World's Fair. 1964**

Stone-masonry wall given a contemporary treatment.

Harbeson, Hough, Livingston & Larson. The Sam Rayburn House Office Building, Washington, D.C. 1965

Stone Our ancestors originally found shelter under stone ledges and in the mouths of caves. They used stone for their tools and weapons and kindled their first fires within stone enclosures. The stone fireplace is still a symbol of warmth and safety in dwellings that otherwise bear no resemblance to a cave. Heavy and virtually indestructible, stone was probably the first material used to commemorate the dead. But piling up stones was not, strictly speaking, building. *Construction* with stone began with the building of so-called Cyclopean walls—made by placing rough stones on top of each other, a type of masonry in which sheer bulk and weight produce a crude form of stability. When satisfactory cutting tools were developed, it became possible to shape and fit stones to create true masonry. It was then feasible to build stone shelters—not only for the dead, but for the living.

The earliest construction employed no mortar. Instead, stone blocks were carefully fitted together. A knife blade could not be inserted into the joints of the masonry used to face the pyramids. The same is true of the stone walls built by the Incas of Peru. The Greeks did not develop mortar until the Hellenistic period, so they used metal dowels and clamps to prevent their marble blocks from shifting. The use of stone masonry with mortar was a great advance: the precision of dry masonry was no longer needed, and greater resistance to shifting became possible. The weight and bulk of stones joined by mortar created a structural fabric of tremendous durability.

But stone is heavy, costly to transport, and expensive to erect. Like brick, it is rarely used in modern building as a structural material. Mostly, stone and marble veneers are laid over steel, concrete, or cinder-block structures. For us, stone masonry is a cosmetic operation—a far cry from the pure stone engineering of the pyramids, the Parthenon, or the Romanesque and Gothic cathedrals. The Romans may have been the first large-scale builders to use stone or marble slabs as a veneer over brick or rubble masonry. The Babylonians used what little stone they had for statuary but followed a practice similar to veneering by facing brick walls with glazed tiles at key locations.

Today, stone has enormous prestige; great cities and important buildings must exhibit large expanses of it. The Sam Rayburn House Office Building for the House of Representatives is an example; it cost between 80 and 100 million dollars, mostly because of the simulated classical masonry that covers it. Almost universally regarded as an architectural disaster, it was described by one critic as "not only the most expensive building of its kind in the world but probably also its ugliest." The lesson here is that poor design cannot be rescued by mountains of marble and limestone.

Brick   Without fuel to fire brick, and living in an arid land where wood was scarce, the Sumerians made sun-dried bricks much like the adobe bricks of the Southwestern American Indians. Even in a dry climate, however, the "mud-brick" wall is subject to erosion and needs to be repaired regularly. Fired brick, however, is durable and maintenance-free. It is really a type of artificial stone that has several advantages over natural stone: cheapness, standardized dimensions, uniform strength and lightness, a wide range of color and texture, and adaptability to mass production.

Since brick is a ceramic material, it resembles mosaic when laid up in a wall. Although it is a structural material, brick is most commonly used as a veneer; so it really *is* a mosaic—a type of wall "painting." Today, brickwork is valued for its color and texture as well as for its association with skilled hand fabrication. Because it is such an ancient material and because of its warm colors and weather-resistant qualities, brick inspires confidence. The viewer knows that a brick wall has been laboriously built by tried and true methods.

left: **The Mission of St. Francis of Assisi, Taos, New Mexico. 1772–1816**

right: **Spiral minaret of Samarra, Iraq. 9th century**

SUN-DRIED BRICK

But brick walls are expensive and their mortar joints are a problem. A large proportion of a brick wall consists of joints that require careful hand labor and are subject to more shrinkage than the brick itself. Brick walls are fabricated slowly, and for large buildings an elaborate scaffolding is required. That is why metal panels are increasingly used for the exterior walls of tall structures. Finally, brick provides good sound insulation but, like stone, it tends to transmit dampness unless combined with additional insulating material.

In the stone and brick architecture of Egypt and Mesopotamia the amount of interior space, compared to the amount of overall volume, was very low. To us, this type of construction is inefficient and appalling in its social implications: it shows that slave labor inhibits architectural imagination. Perhaps the ratio of interior space to overall volume in the architecture of any civilization is an index of its people's freedom. Today's light, thin-walled buildings create interior space almost equal to a building's overall volume. So, aside from aesthetic considerations, architecture tells us something about the valuation placed on human labor, since space is a good reflection of the wages paid to artisans.

To say that wood, stone, and brick are classic materials does not mean they have disappeared from contemporary architecture. They continue to be used, but less frequently for structural reasons. Now their contribution is largely symbolic, since they have lost most of their weight-bearing functions. The classic materials may linger awhile in small-scale domestic dwellings, but even there, glass, steel, aluminum, and plastics are supplanting them. Yesterday's structural material becomes today's aesthetic adornment.

DESIGN IN THE URBAN ENVIRONMENT

Piazza San Marco, Venice. Begun 1063
Underlying the visual pleasure of the piazza is a governing proportion that can be felt only by people on foot—citizens standing, walking, or talking to each other. A marvelously exhilarating arrangement of buildings and space, it depends on a scale that encourages human modes of watching, moving, and meeting.

Rockefeller Center, New York. 1931–37

Compared with the Venetians, who built horizontally, the Americans build vertically. They have to; horizontal space is very, very expensive. So they invented the skyscraper. The only way urban space can be created is by enclosing a shopping area with monumental steel and concrete slabs. The result is a new kind of grandeur—clean and rational but somewhat bland.

John Portman and Associates. Interior, Plaza Hotel, Renaissance Center, Detroit. 1977

An interior space that has many of the qualities of an outdoor park: shrubs, pools, and hanging vegetation, plus cantilevered trees and natural light filtering down between concrete columns and curving ramps. The main excitement comes from the spectacular overhead spaces and the sight of people moving up, down, and around at different levels in an enormous light well.

Bertrand Goldberg Associates. Marina City, Chicago. 1964

Here is Chicago's pragmatic solution to the storage of automobiles (in the first eighteen stories of each Marina City tower), the storage of people (in the rest of the tower), the control of traffic, and even the flow of the Chicago River. These towers generate a feeling of masculine vigor celebrated in Carl Sandburg's poetry about the city with "broad shoulders."

opposite: **John Jerde & Associates. Horton Plaza, San Diego, California. 1985**

How to keep shoppers downtown. Instead of an enclosed shopping mall, the Horton Plaza architects redesigned a substantial portion of the inner city, retaining its crooked streets, sharply angled spaces, and jazzy imagery. The colors are deliberately dirty pastels or ochers; the shapes are large, bold geometrics; the styles, a blend of everything imaginable. Typically American.

left: **Prefabricated stack houses in housing project in Israel. 1965**

Reinforced-concrete rooms, cast on the site, are lifted into place.

right: **Interior, the shrine chapel of Our Lady of Orchard Lake, Oakland, Michigan. 1963**

Laminated wood beams.

MODERN MATERIALS

Steel, concrete, and glass are old materials, but their structural use is comparatively new. The Romans mixed stone rubble with mortar in the construction of walls, a practice that was really an extension of masonry. But the use of *poured* or *cast* concrete, reinforced with steel rods, is entirely different. Similarly, the tempered-steel weapon of a medieval warrior has little in common with the rolled-steel I-beams of modern steel-frame construction. And the lovely opalescent glass bottles of ancient Egypt are only distantly related to the sheets of plate glass used in today's steel or concrete structures.

Architecture has been transformed by these "new" materials because specialized techniques of mass manufacture can produce a superior product at reasonable cost. Today, factory manufacture can reduce costs and improve quality; the handcraft operations that survive in buildings are associated with uneven quality, waste, and frequent delays. Structures of reinforced concrete, or ferroconcrete, are usually formed at the building site, although many concrete beams and slabs can be factory-produced like steel beams. Even so, ferroconcrete fabrication is not a handcraft process in the classical sense; it is better described as manufacturing at the site.

Laminated wooden beams have to be manufactured in a factory and carried to the site. Here again, the techniques of bending and gluing wood were known in antiquity, but the old animal-skin glues cannot compare with today's powerful adhesives. As a result, we have the technology to exploit the lightness, strength, and resilience of wood in continuously curved, load-bearing members that are exceptionally graceful. They permit the spanning of large spaces without interior supports, creating some of the dramatic structural excitement of Gothic stone arches. Laminated beams and arches are monolithic, too, so they can be erected by cranes, thus avoiding the complex scaffolding of stone masonry. The warmth of wood, the pattern of its grain, and the rhythmic effect created by repeated laminations make these beams very attractive. And they are practical for homes as well as for churches and auditoriums.

Cast Iron Cast iron was the first metal substitute for wooden posts and stone columns. It has characteristics similar to stone: great strength and weight; but it is brittle and it develops internal strains as the iron cools in its mold. However, cast iron made it possible to erect tall buildings without prohibitively thick walls. During the second half of the nineteenth century, huge yet delicate structures were built with prefabricated cast-iron columns and beams. Often, they imitated the stone masonry of Italian Renaissance buildings, which accounts for the magnificent factory and warehouse facades built during the 1850s. Now, we are desperately trying to preserve these buildings (they make good artists' lofts) to show the delicacy of a material that is often considered ugly.

George Herbert Wyman. Interior, Bradbury Building, Los Angeles. 1893

Here we see cast iron employed structurally and decoratively at the same time. The effect may seem Victorian, but it is really an elegant demonstration of the delicacy and strength that could be achieved by a sensitive designer using a new building material.

Louis Sullivan. Main Entrance, Carson Pirie Scott Department Store, Chicago. 1899–1904

Sullivan said that form follows function, but he interpreted "function" very liberally. The cast-iron foliage that decorates this building functions psychologically but not structurally.

SUSPENSION-BRIDGE ENGINEERING APPLIED TO ARCHITECTURAL DESIGN

above: Eero Saarinen. Dulles Airport, Chantilly, Virginia. 1962

right: Pier Luigi Nervi. Detail of Burgo Paper Mill, Mantua, Italy. 1964

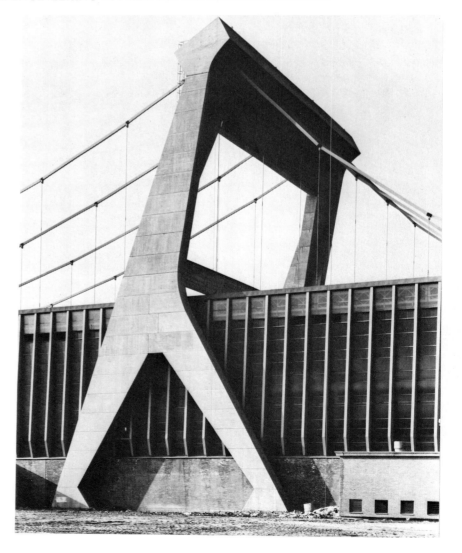

Cast iron set the stage for steel-skeleton construction in the railroad sheds, exhibition halls, and libraries of the nineteenth century. Bridge engineers appreciated iron and steel better than architects, who had used iron structurally (as in the dome of the United States Capitol) but made sure to conceal it. Even today, few architects are willing to expose structural steel. When cast iron was brought out of hiding, it was often given a form based on stone or wood. Since cast iron is a plastic material like concrete, it lends itself to a variety of derivative shapes. So it has been fair game for some questionable sculptural impulses. The ornamental cast-iron columns of the Art Nouveau designers, for example, use the material to imitate terra-cotta panels or High Gothic stone filigree. It was engineers such as Paxton, Roebling, and Eiffel who used metal more authentically. Their aesthetic contribution was to design metal structures that could excite the emotions while performing a practical function.

Suspension bridges made of wood and rope have been used since prehistoric times, but it was nineteenth-century suspension engineering that revealed the structural and aesthetic possibilities of metal under tension. In the twentieth century, designers like Pier Luigi Nervi (1891–1979) and Eero Saarinen employed suspension engineering to create superb interior spaces. An engineer, Joseph Paxton (1801–1865), built the Crystal Palace for the London Exposition of 1851; it was made of prefabricated wrought- and cast-iron units and glass panes. They were manufactured throughout England and bolted together on the site, one story at a time. The result was the largest structure in the world, enclosing seventeen acres under one roof; yet its construction time was only six months. When the Exposition was over, the building was easily dismantled and erected again at another site, where it stood until 1935.

Paxton's use of an iron skeleton anticipated today's riveting and welding of prefabricated steel components into a cagelike structure. He showed that the manufacture of standardized parts for on-site assembly was practical and economical. Masonry vaults and domes, whose strength depended on mass (and iron chains embedded in their mortar), could now be replaced by thin membranes of concrete or glass. Structural strength could be achieved by substituting lightness and precision for heaviness and bulk.

Gustave Eiffel. A joint of the Eiffel Tower, Paris, 1889

Eduardo Torroja. A joint of the Tordera Bridge

Sir Joseph Paxton. The Crystal Palace, London. 1851

Structural Steel The principles of skeleton construction, known in the 1890s as "Chicago construction," were developed with iron. This work, which led to the development of the skyscraper, was carried out with a wrought-iron or rolled-iron framework. Rolled-iron I-beams were a great improvement over cast-iron columns, but iron is not as strong as steel (particularly under tension). Accordingly, high-rise iron structures (above twelve or fifteen stories) were uneconomic; so steel completely replaced iron in modern construction.

The cost of steel per pound is higher than that of any other structural material. Therefore, steel beams are designed in shapes that exploit the material's strength while keeping its weight down. The I-shaped beam is most common because its sections can be quite thin but still resist any force that tries to break it. But large structural members, such as trusses and built-up girders, cannot be manufactured in the form of a single rolled-steel beam; they have to be assembled—usually in the form of latticework—to reduce weight and take advantage of steel's tensile strength. This results visually in complex geometric openings and weblike patterns of metal. From a distance, these openings and patterns seem quite poetic, but when seen close up, they look harsh. Indeed, when we think of engineering as the enemy of art, we are probably remembering some defiantly ugly piece of steel construction.

But the technology of steel manufacture and fabrication has advanced in response to the competition of other structural materials. Today, welded steel connections yield cleaner joints and better continuity within a structural system. And tubular, extruded, and corrugated steel products have opened up new visual possibilities. A few architects have used exposed steel construction with considerable sensitivity, but covering steel with other materials is more common: brick, marble, stone, and glass surfaces remain attractive because of their color, texture, or historical associations.

Oddly enough, the versatility of the steel frame creates problems for designers, especially with the skyscraper: they do not know what to emphasize. Should it be a box, a slab, a honeycomb, or a crystal? Is it a tower or a layer cake? In 1921 Mies van der Rohe proposed a circular steel-and-glass skyscraper; in 1963 Gropius helped design a huge slab with tapered ends—the Pan Am Building in New York City—but not many people like it. The glass skyscraper proposal of Mies was not accepted, but many circular towers have since been built. One of the most successful is Lake Point Tower in Chicago, a modern version of Mies's earlier proposal. Today, steel construction still dominates high-rise architecture; its flexibility has inspired a great deal of experimentation with rooftop forms. But when exciting horizontal space is called for, when we want an arena, a chapel, or an air terminal, the best buildings seem to be made of concrete.

left: **Ludwig Mies van der Rohe. Model for Project: Glass Skyscraper. 1922**

Circular glass towers—alone, clustered, or melting into each other—have fascinated architects for decades. They reveal the amazing lightness of steel-cage construction, and they avoid the boxy look of the typical skyscraper.

right: **Schipporeit-Heinrich, Inc. Lake Point Tower, Chicago. 1968**

Reinforced Concrete The ancient Romans developed a mortar based on volcanic ash, but it was not until 1824 that the first Portland cement was produced by an Englishman, Joseph Aspdin. In 1868, a French gardener, Jacques Monier, hit on the idea of reinforcing concrete flower pots with a wire web, thus creating a small-scale reinforced structure. But reinforced concrete was not widely employed as a building material until the 1890s.

Today's continuously curved and warped ferroconcrete slab is wholly new—a structural member that does not imitate masonry, wood, or metal. Since complex stress patterns are distributed throughout the slab, there is no distinct break between the functions of supporting and being supported. Thus, the curved ferroconcrete slab is the logical and organic fulfillment of the older structural systems. It is also more permanent, more efficient, and potentially as beautiful.

Stone slabs and shells are visually appealing, but their curves have to be correct from an engineering standpoint. Interestingly, as engineering criteria are perfected, their visual results tend to look like natural forms. Some of the

Elevated highway, Berlin. 1963

opposite above: **Louis I. Kahn. Interior, Kimbell Art Museum, Fort Worth, Texas. 1972**

opposite below: **Fritz Wotruba. Church of the Holy Trinity, Vienna. 1965–76**

most dramatic ferroconcrete structures exhibit curves that resemble the organic forms we see in seashells, honeycombs, mushrooms, and soap bubbles. Like the egg, the strongest and most pleasing containers exhibit a harmonious relationship between external forces and material structure: this relationship is what reinforced concrete seems ideally suited to create.

It is generally agreed that joints are the weakest points in classical structures: that is where loads change direction and complex stresses occur. But curved ferroconcrete members virtually eliminate joints. As with the eggshell, loads are distributed over the entire surface. This is accomplished by placing steel rods at the points of greatest tensile stress—the points where concrete particles would tear or pull apart. At points of greatest compression, the concrete is thickest: that is where the particles might be crushed. The steel rods are covered with enough concrete to prevent rusting, and they are given slight surface irregularities to prevent slippage after the concrete hardens. As a result, ferroconcrete has the virtues of steel and stone without their disadvantages.

Aside from its practical value, ferroconcrete appeals to designers because it offers so many possible structural solutions; also they can express their forming and shaping impulses in a variety of ways. Of course, these "sculptural" impulses are limited by the wooden forms that have to be built to hold concrete during pouring and curing. But as ferroconcrete technology advances, the wooden framework may become a thing of the past. As more is known about aggregates and the usefulness of additives to lower weight, speed up drying, add color, and transmit light, the range of aesthetic effects possible in ferroconcrete will greatly increase.

One of the supposed disadvantages of concrete is its unsuitability as a surface material. As with steel, many architects use it for structural purposes only, covering it with veneers of brick, stone, marble, metal, and so on. Others cover concrete with stucco and paint. But these cosmetics should be unnecessary; Le Corbusier has shown what rich textures can be obtained by exposing concrete and letting the marks of the formwork show. Furthermore, rough concrete surfaces enhance the quality of smooth materials like metal and glass.

Together with the steel-frame skeleton, ferroconcrete has transformed architecture by eliminating the weight-bearing masonry wall. Combined with recessed columns, steel or concrete skeleton construction permits a skin composed almost totally of glass. That is what we see in Dallas: one crystal palace after another. The structural revolution produced by steel and ferroconcrete has changed the overall appearance of our cities. Furthermore, it has changed many of our deep-rooted attitudes about space and shelter, privacy and strength. We are a much more open society than we used to be, largely because we can move so freely in and out of our public spaces. Steel and concrete have done a great deal to make that possible.

THE STRUCTURAL DEVICES

To enclose space, materials must be systematically organized; that means structure. Architectural structure is the art and science of shaping, organizing, and fastening materials to resist the opposition of gravity, the attacks of weather, the wear caused by human use, and the processes that cause fatigue within materials themselves.

To experience architectural forms intelligently, we have to understand structure, which also adds to our enjoyment of architecture. We must be able to. "see" the forces that work to make a building safe and durable. And beautiful. Architecture is more than the interplay of pleasing shapes and surfaces, important though they are. We must be able to see architectural surfaces and shapes in terms of their thickness and strength, in terms of the weight they support, in terms of the space they enclose, and in terms of the forces they resist. This type of seeing and sensing has to be informed by awareness of the way materials are organized to stretch or squeeze, brace or bend, span or cover, lift or hold. Notice that these processes suggest the activities of our bodies: buildings are bodies, too. We enjoy them in the same way—by feeling the exertion, coordination, and relaxation of our bones, muscles, sinews, and skin as we go about the business of living.

The Post-and-Lintel   The post-and-lintel is the most ancient of construction devices, and it is still widely used. It consists of two vertical supports bridged over by a horizontal beam. The prehistoric dolmen was an approximation of the post-and-lintel, with upright stones serving as posts and a horizontal table rock acting as a lintel. The Egyptians used the post-and-lintel exclusively because of its stability and capacity to support great weights. Visually, the system offers a distinct separation between supporting and supported members, a feature that was especially appealing to the Greeks, admirers of clarity and precision in all things.

Stone was the principal material used in ancient post-and-lintel construction. But steel and ferroconcrete are preferred in modern post-and-lintel construction, especially in large buildings. It is a system that resolves all forces into vertical and horizontal components, permitting an exceptionally rational organization of space and considerable efficiency in the use of materials. Since each structural member is very specialized, a high degree of standardization becomes possible: that leads to mass production, prefabrication, and lowered costs.

The post-and-lintel system is also responsible for the strong emphasis on window walls in modern building. The steel cage affords large openings, which permit wide windows, wide vision, and generous display possibilities. With supporting posts set back from exterior walls, these windows need not

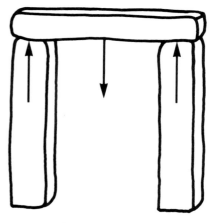

Post-and-lintel

Walter Gropius. Laboratory Workshop, The Bauhaus, Dessau, Germany. 1925–26

be interrupted: window design is limited only by the size of glass panes and the framework needed to hold them in place. In the Bauhaus building, designed by Walter Gropius, we see an early use of continuous bands of glass uninterrupted by walls or posts. This type of design became common for buildings requiring a great deal of daylight—factories especially. Today, designers rely mainly on artificial illumination for factories, office buildings, department stores, and so on. But the glass wall is still popular—especially those constructed of one-way or tinted glass—because its reflections help to harmonize a building with its environment.

In addition to its role in glass-wall design, the post-and-lintel system provides regular spacing of posts and partitions, creating interchangeable cubical spaces. These spaces lend themselves to modern business enterprise: efficient sale and rental of space; standardized design of fixtures and furnishings; orderly circulation of people. From a commercial and technocratic standpoint, the space created by arches, vaults, and domes is wasteful: the lofty spaces in a church, a library, or a museum represent uneconomic expenditures of funds. So the post-and-lintel system makes sense to engineers; and it suits capitalism. But socialists like it, too.

The Cantilever　A cantilever is basically a beam or slab extended horizontally into space. Its free end is unsupported, and the point where it rests on its post acts like the fulcrum of a lever. If the inside end of the beam were not bolted down, the cantilever would rotate around that fulcrum. But since that end is fixed, the free end is rigid. So the cantilever is secure if its material does not break and its internal end is firmly fastened.

The cantilever principle could have been seen in the first overhanging stone ledge. A tree branch also resembles a cantilever; but the earliest human societies saw no reason to build cantilevers. That may explain why we are slightly fearful of them: we think they might break. But today, cantilevers are very popular because strong materials are available at reasonable cost. Wooden cantilever beams are used in many domestic dwellings, even though they cannot be extended as far as steel. Multiple dwellings use them, too, as narrow balconies or sunbreaks. But the dramatic impact of cantilever construction is not felt unless an extension approaches the limits of the material it uses. As with the suspension bridge and the lightweight truss, the beauty and excitement of the cantilever seem to depend on defying gravity.

In buildings with a continuous window band, the portion of the floor projecting beyond the columns is cantilevered. Supporting columns can be concealed inside the wall partitions so that no posts are visible. Thus, instead of being extended freely in space, the edge of the cantilevered floor becomes an attachment for a curtain wall of glass or metal panels. So, although the cantilever is invisible, its operation is essential for curtain-wall treatment.

The most exciting uses of the cantilever, however, are seen in roof structures, canopies, grandstands, aircraft hangars, and theater balconies; usually, they are made of ferroconcrete. Here the imagination of the architect and the ingenuity of the engineer combine to create some of the most striking buildings in contemporary architecture. Nothing excites the imagination like a massive concrete form hovering in space.

The Truss　The truss is an application of the geometric fact that no angle of a triangle can be changed without altering the dimensions of the sides. A truss is a system of triangles arranged to work like a beam, or lintel. Because truss systems can be made very rigid—and thus capable of bridging very wide spans—they are used where great spaces must be spanned with few or no interior supports. Wood and metal are the principal materials used because these materials possess high tensile strength for their weight; most of the members of a truss are in tension. In bridges, theaters, convention halls, gymnasiums, and assembly plants, the truss is indispensable.

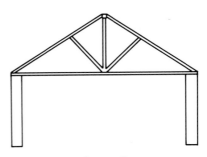

Wooden roof truss

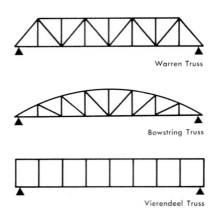

Warren Truss

Bowstring Truss

Vierendeel Truss

Types of trusses

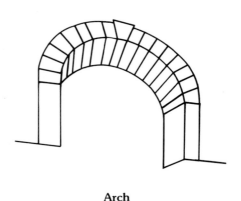

Arch

Roof truss, Old Ship Meetinghouse, Hingham, Massachusetts. 1681

The Greek temple pediment may be the most beautiful application of the truss in the shape of a triangle. It is so firmly established in our consciousness that it is hard to imagine a traditional house, barn, or church without a triangular gable. Even though the short distances between the walls of houses can be spanned in other ways, the triangular-gable roof "feels" safe. We accept a flat roof very reluctantly, if at all, in low structures. In addition, the space *inside* the gable is very useful—in the form of a loft, an attic, or merely as insulation. In the sturdy Cape Cod cottage, Yankee ingenuity used gable space for extra bedrooms, which accounts for the popularity of the New England saltbox today. In more modern houses, flat ceilings can be eliminated, and the gable space can be converted into the prestigious "cathedral ceiling." More practically, the gable roof sheds snow and rain conveniently and offers a profile of low resistance to wind.

Although trusses are systems of triangles, their overall shape need not be triangular: most trusses are long rectangles shaped like a beam. This beam-truss places stiffening struts, braces, or bars where the solid material in a wood, metal, or stone beam would be. Another truss—the so-called bowstring truss—is straight along the lower edge and arched along the top. Structurally, the upper edge of a truss is in compression; the lower edge and the diagonals are in tension.

If we travel over a bridge supported by trusses, or if we stand under a roof made of trusses, we may wonder how so much space can be spanned by such thin members. We feel slightly insecure because we underestimate the strength of materials—especially of steel—in tension. But the parts of a steel truss have been designed so that loads work to *pull apart* rather than *bend* the metal. Because of steel's crystalline structure, it is almost impossible to pull it apart; and its braces are given a cross-sectional shape that stubbornly resists bending. So, those fears based on our prehistoric memories can be set aside. Of course, a little fear produces architectural excitement; too much, and we would rather stay home.

The Arch   The post-and-lintel represents the simplest way of using gravity to enclose space; the arch is much more sophisticated. In both cases, vertical posts or columns are used, but the means of bridging over space—always the central problem of architecture—is very different. The arch relies on the compressive strength of bricks or cut stone. As the separate units of an arch, called *voussoirs,* are squeezed together by the weight above them, they are, in effect, "welded" into a single curved member. The arch does not start to function until the voussoir in its center—the *keystone*—is set in place. But since the

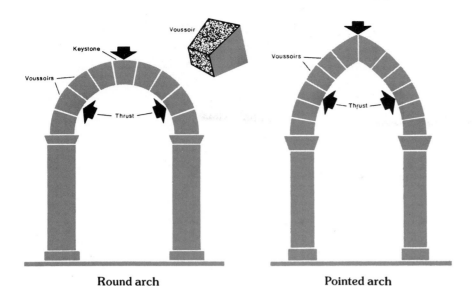

Round arch	Pointed arch

keystone is the last stone to be placed, the arch has to be supported during construction by a structure of wooden forms, called *centering*. Centering is expensive, but it results in a uniquely beautiful curve.

The arch that the Mesopotamians developed—about four thousand years ago—is semicircular. The load it carries to its supporting posts develops almost horizontal reactions, called thrusts, which tend to force the posts outward, leading to collapse. These outward thrusts have to be resisted by some type of buttressing or by a heavy masonry wall, called a *spandrel*. A spandrel prevents bulging of the arch under pressure; it was the principal mode of reinforcement used by ancient builders. A *free* arch, on the other hand, relies on the correctness of its design and the strength of its materials. In medieval architecture, buttresses began to be used in place of solid-masonry spandrels to counteract the outward thrusts of the free arch. Necessary from an engineering standpoint, these buttresses also produced much of the aesthetic effect of Gothic architecture.

In Renaissance construction the arch was employed in combination with the post-and-lintel, but usually as part of a wall and without external buttresses. The triangular pediment shape, based on the roof truss, was commonly alternated with the arch over windows and doors, often as a decorative rather than a structural element. Builders of this period had the engineering capacity of their Gothic predecessors, but their architectural tastes differed: they concealed structural functions while using arches, pilasters, pediments, and blind arcades—the full range of classical building—for largely aesthetic purposes.

The arch tempts builders to become great engineers. It permits large, high openings, and the successive positions of its frames can establish a rhythmic pattern of forward movement. The arch is also a versatile device, lending itself to the rugged honesty of early church architecture in which coarse masonry walls were used for abutment; or to the delicate, soaring effects of Gothic structures in which weight-bearing walls were virtually eliminated. In both cases, tall, vertically shaped space was the objective. The early churches had darkly mysterious interiors, lit mainly from within; they seemed indifferent to their outer garments, like the early Christians themselves. By contrast, Gothic interiors were richly illuminated by outside light passing through their stained-glass windows.

Because the pointed Gothic arch sent its thrusts in a more downward direction, its buttresses could be quite slender, and its stained-glass windows could be relatively free of thick masonry abutments. In addition, the pointed arch raised the ceiling height, increasing the overhead space. Eventually, Gothic ribs, or half arches, created vaults that were in effect segmented domes. The area between the ribs was filled with a masonry fabric that functioned almost like the membrane materials used in today's thin-shell structures.

opposite: Pont du Gard, Nîmes, France. 1st century A.D.

Crypt, Speyer Cathedral, Germany. 1040
The round Romanesque arch, resting on columns that look like massive tree trunks, generates a powerful sense of order and stability.

The modern, free arch is used mainly to support bridges or large domed and vaulted structures. Made of reinforced concrete, steel, or laminated wood, the modern arch is monolithic, and it is much stronger than its brick or stone ancestors. In wide-spanning arches, as in Eero Saarinen's Kresge Auditorium at M.I.T., supporting posts are omitted. The arch springs (begins its curve) at ground level; it resembles the action of a huge bowstring truss. But true arch action is involved: the entire curve is in compression while the ground itself acts as a kind of tie-rod.

Today, the arch combined with stressed-skin shells produces enormous curved openings (see Saarinen's TWA Terminal, page 400) and floating ceiling effects that would have amazed the ancients. Architects have achieved a mastery of structure that permits an almost organic unity of form. There is hardly any separation between skin and bone. Increasingly, we build the way nature builds.

Eugène Freyssinet. Airport hangar, Orly, France. 1921
A modern arch structure so beautiful that it has been converted into a museum.

Eero Saarinen. Kresge Auditorium, Massachusetts Institute of Technology, Cambridge. 1954
This is not a true arch; it is an archlike opening in a spherical, thin-shell structure. Like the Gateway Arch in St. Louis, this arch functions aesthetically and symbolically; the shell does the work.

left: **Nave (vaulted c. 1095–1115), St.-Savin-sur-Gartempe, Poitou, France. Barrel vault**

right: **Nave (vaulted c. 1115–20), St.-Etienne, Caen, France. Groined vault**

opposite: **Nave (vaulted c. 1288–1308), Exeter Cathedral, England. Gothic ribbed vaulting**

The Vault The classical vault was a series of identical arches in file order—one behind the other. A bridge or an aqueduct was an arcade, a series of arches in rank order—side by side. Interior space of any size was spanned by arches in the form of a semicylinder—the so-called barrel vault. Even the dome was based on the arch; we can think of it as an arch rotating around its vertical axis. The groined vault used in Romanesque and Gothic building was a great advance; it was originally produced by the intersection of two barrel vaults, creating four ribs, or half arches.

The disadvantage of the old barrel vault was that it could not be pierced by windows without being greatly weakened. That is why early Romanesque churches were so dark. By replacing barrel vaults with groined vaults, however, church naves could go higher: their vaults were lighter in weight, and they did not require such heavy walls for support. By the twelfth century, the round Romanesque arches and heavy groins began to be replaced by Gothic pointed arches and rib vaulting. These Gothic ribs were lighter than the groins they replaced, so they could be placed wherever they were needed—not just at the points where the old barrels would have intersected. Then, by adding ribs, the stone panels between them could be narrowed and constructed with lighter-weight stone. The ribs then multiplied—for decorative and structural reasons—and their weight-bearing function was spread over the whole vault surface.

Again, we witness a dynamic pattern of distributing loads, as in modern stressed-skin and shell construction. What is the architectural principle here? Structures based on the arch disperse their stresses and tend to seek organic form; structures based on the post-and-lintel concentrate their stresses and tend to seek geometric form. We get the classic confrontation of styles—between natural and abstract, between biological and mechanical, between free and measured.

The Dome The vault evolved as a solution to the problem of bridging great spaces without interior supports while avoiding wooden trusses, which might burn, or stone lintels, which could break. As we have seen, this solution was based on arch combinations. The dome represents another solution. Essentially a hemisphere, the dome can bulge into the bulbous shape of an onion,

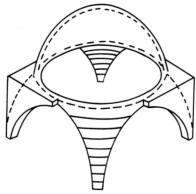

A dome on pendentives

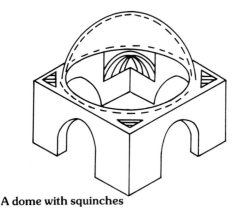

A dome with squinches

The Pantheon, Rome. A.D. **118–125**

as in the multiple domes of the Cathedral of St. Basil in Moscow. Often a circular opening, or skylight—called an *oculus* (or a *lantern* if it has a tower)—is placed at the top. Of course, the tower's weight increases the tendency of a dome to bulge. For that reason, chains or metal rings were embedded in the masonry of classical domes. Or a high, thick mass of masonry surrounded the dome up to its haunch (a point about halfway up to the dome's top). From the outside, that destroys the dramatic exterior form of the dome, as in Rome's Pantheon: it looks like a shallow mound; compare it to St. Peter's.

Placing a dome on a cylindrical drum over a circular foundation is logical from the standpoint of geometry and construction. Yet most domed structures—in the West, at least—rest on rectangular foundations. Why? Because Western churches required a rectangular plan. Eastern churches favored a central plan, a plan that focuses attention on a point directly under the dome. In the Middle East, where the dome probably originated, its ceiling was regarded as an image of the cosmos; frequently it was covered with stars. (Is that why today's planetarium is dome-shaped? Is outer space shaped like a dome?) So the dome has had religious and cosmological meaning from the beginning.

A number of devices have been used to transfer the load from the circular edge of the dome to the rectangular foundation on which it usually rests. The most common are called *pendentives* and *squinches*. The pendentive system places the dome on a drum that rests on four arches springing from four powerful piers located at each corner of a square plan. The arches touch the drum's rim at only four points. Between these points are four curved triangular sections, called pendentives; they connect the curves of the arch to the rim of the drum and carry its weight down to the piers.

Michelangelo. St. Peter's, Rome. 1546–64
(dome completed by Giacomo della Porta, 1590)

Hagia Sophia in Istanbul, built in A.D. 532–37, offers the oldest and perhaps best example of a dome on pendentives. The great outward thrusts developed in its arches and pendentives are carried to the ground by a beautiful system of half domes and powerful exterior abutments. The dome itself has no oculus; it is pierced instead by windows running continuously around its lower edge. This device creates the impression that the dome is floating—a miracle in itself, considering the dome's great weight. It also adds to the "cathedral effect" of being in another world.

DOMES: SOLEMN, TRIUMPHANT, PLAYFUL...

left: **Cathedral of St. Basil, Moscow. 1555–60**

right: **John Nash. The Royal Pavilion, Brighton, England. 1815–18**

...FANTASTIC

Corn Palace, Mitchell, South Dakota. 1921

Domes, turrets, cones, and annually rotated mosaics made of corn. This is folk architecture: all building traditions are fair game; anything goes.

Philip Johnson. Roofless Church, New Harmony, Indiana. 1960

A wood-shingle dome that looks like a magician's trick handkerchief. This dome, without a building underneath, sits in a walled garden; it has overtones of a mosque, a Hindu temple, and a revivalist tent. But where do the people sit?

The squinch system, used mainly by Islamic builders, is not as rationally articulated as the pendentive solution. It too rests the dome on four arches sprung from four corner piers, creating a square support for a circular edge. But instead of pendentives in the corners, smaller arches called squinches are substituted, forming an octagonal support at eight different points. The octagon approximates a circle better than a square; and so, with some adjustments in the masonry, the dome rests on what is, in effect, a polygonal drum.

Squinches have this advantage: they create opportunities for numerous niches in the corners between the main arches. These form semidome shapes

...AND EXUBERANT

Detail of Mosque of Ahmed I (Blue Mosque), Istanbul. 1609–16

View into outer portal, Masjid-i-Shah, Isfahan, Iran. 1616

E. H. Brenner. Women's Clinic, Lafayette, Indiana. 1965

A complex of seven interlocking domes built by spraying concrete over a wire-mesh framework resting on a structure of curved polystyrene planks.

R. Buckminster Fuller. American Pavilion, EXPO 67, Montreal. 1967

Buckminster Fuller's geodesic dome was ideal for a World's Fair exposition building. It could also be used by the military for radar stations in the Arctic. But despite high expectations, it never caught on as "architecture." Most people associate civilized living with square-shaped spaces.

that rhythmically repeat the shape of the major dome. But, as can be seen in the interior of the mosque in Isfahan, squinches are very prolific; they seem to breed more squinches, and we get an effect like a honeycomb. The surfaces between the arches are so richly decorated that the sense of architectural structure is lost. The effect is gorgeous, but we cannot see how the space is created.

Shell Structures   Modern shell structures enjoy the advantages of reinforced concrete and superior mathematical tools for calculating stresses and strength of materials. Compared to classical domes, our shell structures are flatter and wider: they don't need deep masonry drums. Concrete shells are so thin that their dead weight is negligible; the engineering problem lies in maintaining their stability and resistance to buckling because of stresses caused by rain, snow, or uneven heating by the sun. But shells are worth the trouble: they enclose a great deal of space with very little material; they are economical to build and easy to maintain.

Architects persistently seek the tent experience—for religious or secular purposes—because of the sense of protection it fosters while we feel bathed in a wonderful overhead light.

left: **Umbrellas over trade section, Swiss National Exposition, Lausanne. 1964**

below left: **Frank Lloyd Wright. Interior, Wayfarer's Chapel, Palos Verdes Estates, California. 1951**

below right: **Wallace K. Harrison. Interior, First Presbyterian Church, Stamford, Connecticut. 1958**

Shells can be made of metal as well as of concrete. R. Buckminster Fuller's (1895–1983) geodesic domes have been made of aluminum, steel, wood, concrete, plastics, and even paper. Eventually, plastic and Fiberglas sheets stretched over cable systems or metal-mesh supports will compete with concrete in shell construction. These materials produce forms similar to those we see in tents, kites, and umbrellas. Shell structures can also be constructed by spraying cement over inflated rubber balloons. Sprayed plastics and weatherproof fabrics are being seriously investigated, too.

Fair and exposition architecture is temporary, so it is often used to experiment with new materials and structural systems. The Berlin Pavilion at the New York World's Fair of 1964–65 consisted of a tent structure made of vinyl-coated canvas stretched and supported by steel masts and tension cables. The result was visually pleasing as well as inexpensive. In the future, such buildings may be permanent if problems of long-term durability and weather resistance can be overcome. Because our social, industrial, and domestic needs continually change, innovative structures of this type might come into widespread use.

The ability to enclose enormous spaces safely and efficiently may lead to the design of total communities in single structures—in so-called *megastructures*. We already house small cities in our great hotels, ocean-going superliners, shopping centers, industrial parks, and universities. By locating all building units on a single raised platform, architects have suggested the direction of the future: comprehensive design of communities through integration of their major forms, utilities, and systems in a single structure to which additional units can be added—"clipped on"—or removed as necessary. This idea is not as radical as it seems; it confirms in architectural terms what is already a fact—namely, that communities are multicelled organisms increasingly interrelated by common systems of power, transportation, communication, and administration.

THE ARCHITECTURE OF INTERIOR SPACE

Frank Lloyd Wright. Interior, The Solomon R. Guggenheim Museum, New York. 1959
Wright's museum is like a cathedral—much in the tradition of early Christian domed churches. But unlike the mosaics of St. Mark's or Hagia Sophia, the pictures in this "church" keep changing. The building and its art do not explain, they only tolerate, each other.

opposite: **Interior, Hagia Sophia, Istanbul.** A.D. **532–37**

opposite above: Le Corbusier. Interior, Notre-Dame-du-Haut, Ronchamp, France. 1950–55

Rectangular openings in a thick concrete wall visually dramatize the process of light entering an interior at many eye levels. It is as if a sculptor had reinvented the window.

opposite below: Eero Saarinen. Interior, TWA Terminal, Kennedy International Airport, New York. 1962

The sweeping structural shapes and curved edges are clearly meant to suggest the trajectories of flight. The interior spatial expression is of a great womblike cave, with light from a multitude of organic openings penetrating its earthly recesses.

left: Safdie, David, Barott, and Boulva. Detail of Habitat, EXPO 67, Montreal. 1967

Superb opportunities for light modulation and a truly sculptural environment present themselves in the sheltered transitional spaces formed by interlocking units.

below: Schoeler Heaton Harvor Menendez. Interior, Charlebois High School, Ottawa, Canada. 1971–72

A Post-Modernist conception of space in which ducts, plumbing, and trusses are brought out of concealment and used as "sculpture" or as symbols of change and growth. This, after all, is what a high school is all about.

James Stirling and James Gowan. Interior, Engineering Building, Leicester University, England. 1959–63

An inspiring space for engineers. Stirling shows how standard industrial parts can be organized to express a poetical idea; the horizontal, no-nonsense working levels are framed by angular glass-and-steel planes to create a strong sense of upward striving.

I. M. Pei. Interior, Everson Museum of Art, Syracuse, New York. 1965–68

A monumental room achieved in a small museum by attention to fundamentals: honest and uncomplicated enclosure of space, a practical device for bathing the walls with light, and a modest amount of wall punctuation that allows the art objects to breathe.

Paul Rudolph. Project for Graphic Arts Center, New York. 1967

For the center of Manhattan—a mega-structure visually if not functionally—Paul Rudolph has proposed one immense, articulated building complex that would carry out rationally the unwitting logic of the island's architecture since the skyscraper mania began in the early twentieth century.

CONSTRUCTORS AND SCULPTORS

Can we see any pattern in contemporary architecture as a whole? Is there a common idea about building shapes or structural systems that pervades architectural practice now? The answer has to be No. Almost everywhere, buildings are being erected that express divergent philosophies while using similar materials and structural devices. Yet, in all this diversity it may be possible to discern two main tendencies expressed through two types of architect: constructors and sculptors. What are their typical attitudes toward form, engineering, architectural emotion, and the purposes of design?

Constructors are designers who favor the dramatization of engineering devices to create exciting architecture. The word "constructor" is used in Europe to designate a person who practices what Americans call structural engineering. In both Europe and America, however, architecture and structural engineering are independent though cooperating professions. Although the professions are formally distinct, each shares many of the competencies of the other. That is why we can think of some architects as constructors—for them, the engineering solution is fundamental; architecture is, as Nervi has called it, "structural truth."

The label "sculptor" can be applied to designers who are mainly interested in plastic and symbolic form as sources of architectural emotion. Naturally,

they use structural devices to build, but the devices are regarded as means rather than as ends. Sculptural architects are interested in the play of light over forms for the sake of visual excitement; they try to invent space-enclosing shapes that will symbolize the purpose of a building or the attributes of its users. Such designers believe that architecture should express ideas and feelings more than building systems.

In today's Post-Modernist architecture, the form of many buildings goes beyond the strict requirements of structure and utility. Philip Johnson's orchestration of domes for the Dumbarton Oaks Museum shows the "sculptor" at work; it involves the decorative rather than the structural employment of a building device. Here the symbolic—not the engineering—function of the dome is exploited. The idea of the dome as a complete and separate world has been used to create a contemplative and mystical atmosphere for the examination of small, exquisitely displayed art objects.

From the standpoint of the constructor, sculptors have turned away from the basic principles of modernism. Their work seems to be a revival of the old architectural traditions, using modern materials and devices in place of classi-

left: **Reed, Torres, Beauchamp, Marvel. Chase Manhattan Bank, San Juan, Puerto Rico. 1969**

Two branch banks, both in warm climates. One expresses the engineer's mind and method; it works but it lacks the power to stir the imagination. The other strains for the picturesque. (Are the arches supposed to echo palm trees?) The result is kitschy.

right: **Wimberly, Whisenand, Allison & Tong. Model of Waikiki branch, Bank of Hawaii. 1965**

left: **Philip Johnson. Museum of Pre-Columbian Art, Dumbarton Oaks, Washington, D.C. 1963**

right: **Philip Johnson. Plan of Museum of Pre-Columbian Art**

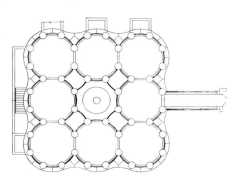

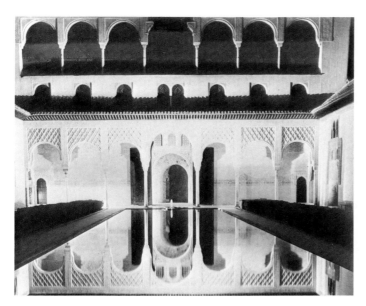

Court of the Myrtles, The Alhambra, Granada, Spain. 1368

above: **Naramore, Bain, Brady & Johanson and Minoru Yamasaki & Associates. IBM Building, Seattle. 1961**

Steel arches at ground level covered with marble: they may be strong and secure, but they look funny at the corners. A cantilever made of half arches is not very reassuring.

left: **Edward Durell Stone. Beckman Auditorium, California Institute of Technology, Pasadena. 1960**

cal orders and decorative systems. For example, in Minoru Yamasaki's work we can see Gothic arches made of metal, and pagoda-like roof canopies made of ferroconcrete. The symbolic associations of old construction systems have been "borrowed" and adapted. Edward Durell Stone (1902–1978) also used modern materials and devices to resurrect architectural memories—particularly of Persian and Moorish structures built during the late Middle Ages. His arcades, columns, and perforated walls remind us of Islamic palaces; at the same time they represent a search for symbols by a designer who was not too proud to learn from the past. In theory, materials and technology change, but symbols never lose their power. So Stone's Beckman Auditorium at the California Institute of Technology goes back seven centuries to a Moorish-Spanish palace, the Alhambra. Does that make sense for nuclear physicists and genetic engineers?

Constructors take pride in an unsentimental approach to design. As a result, the harsh label "new brutalism" was applied to the work of a British group of architects in the 1950s. We can see an example of their tough-minded approach in the Hayward Art Gallery in London. It seems to combine the ideas of sculptors and constructors. The rugged strength of the building is not

opposite: **Michael Graves. Portland Public Services Building, Oregon. 1980–82**

Post-Modern architecture (see the examples by Philip Johnson, page 250, and Charles Moore, page 101) is both a reaction against Bauhaus design and a reassertion of the importance of color, ornament, and symbolism in building. Graves creates a medley of arbitrary shapes, mechanical proportions, and geometric patterns. Form and function seem almost completely divorced; instead we get playful allusions to ancient Egypt, Art Deco, and downtown signage, with Greek temples set on top of everything, like icing on a birthday cake.

left: **Pier Luigi Nervi. Palazzo del Lavoro Exhibition Hall, Turin, Italy. 1959**

below: **Pier Luigi Nervi. Little Sports Palace, Rome. 1957**

merely the result of coarse, poured-concrete surfaces; it also grows out of a no-nonsense solution to the light and space requirements of an art museum and the job of managing circulation through its galleries. There are no signs of axial design, or of traditional ornament and symbolism. Instead, we get a harsh, aggressive statement of what the building does. It looks like sculpture, but its forms are justified as engineering.

CONSTRUCTORS

Skidmore, Owings and Merrill. Alcoa Building, San Francisco. 1968

The crisscross beams designed to brace the structure against earthquakes convert the facade of this building into a single, huge truss.

opposite: **John Warnecke & Associates and Peterson, Clark & Associates. Hennepin County Government Center, Minneapolis. 1968–76**

Here the crisscross braces add visual excitement as well as strength. Notice how light and buoyant they look against the windows.

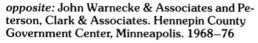

SCULPTORS

The "sculptors" do not invent forms arbitrarily; they just pay close attention to the visual meaning of materials under stress.

Riccardo Morandi. Parco del Valentino Exhibition Hall, Turin, Italy. 1958–60

Eugène Freyssinet. Basilica of Pius X, Lourdes, France. 1958

Eric Mendelsohn. Einstein Tower, Potsdam, Germany. 1920–21. (Destroyed)

Eric Mendelsohn. Drawing for Einstein Tower. 1919

Mendelsohn's powerful ink drawing reveals his approach as a sculptural designer—one who initially *feels* a form and then creates a structure to match his emotion.

left: **Minoru Yamasaki & Associates. North Shore Congregation Israel Synagogue, Glencoe, Illinois. 1964**

Reinforced concrete is versatile enough to convey the slender grace of Yamasaki's synagogue or the formidable power of Bennett's art gallery.

below: **Hubert Bennett & Associates. Hayward Art Gallery, London. 1968**

Pier Luigi Nervi was one of the great constructors, but he probably used more columns than were structurally needed in his Palazzo del Lavoro in Turin, Italy. The same is true of Wright's Administration Building for the Johnson Wax Company (page 82). Nervi designed a modern equivalent of Gothic fan vaulting; like all man-made "trees," these columns provide a sense of scale, a structural reference to which people can relate and thus "feel" the dimensions of a great interior space. We often find bodily references in the work of the constructors: Morandi's Parco del Valentino Exhibition Hall in Turin and Freyssinet's Basilica of Pius X in Lourdes express a sense of powerful supporting legs, arms, and ribs. Both structures are earth-covered and both employ prestressed-concrete arches and braces. These enormous "caverns" are humanized by concrete forms that function structurally and symbolically at the same time.

Architectural emotion, therefore, arises from multiple sources: it may result from the careful adjustment of spaces and solids—from the magic of geometry; or it may rely on deep memories of life under ledges, before caves, or underneath woven boughs and bundles of straw. It may depend on the tent experience—a thin membrane barely separating a private world from the vastness of infinite space. Or it may recall huge stones modeled to resemble bodily parts, the places where procreative power lives. At different stages of human development we have tried to live in the bowels of the earth or on the tops of mountains. Depending on luck or mood, we return to one or the oth-

RHETORIC AND RESTRAINT IN REINFORCED CONCRETE

Paul Rudolph. Interior, Southeastern Massachusetts Technological Institute, North Dartmouth. 1966

Louis I. Kahn. Stairwell in residence hall, Bryn Mawr College, Bryn Mawr, Pennsylvania. 1964–65

er. Some of us are still nomads, psychologically, and that is why architecture is so changeable.

The superiority that constructors feel toward "sculptors" reflects an age-long conflict between abstraction and empathy, between geometric designers and pictorial designers. One camp believes architecture is structure, and structure is measure, and measure is geometry, and geometry is reality. The other camp believes architecture is sculpture, and sculpture is magic, and magic is illusion made real. Of course, both of them are right.

CHAPTER THIRTEEN

PHOTOGRAPHY

J ames Agee, a great friend of photography, once said: "It is doubtful whether most people realize how extraordinarily slippery a liar the camera is." The camera is also sensitive, seductive, and instructive, but photographs have to be closely analyzed if we want to enjoy them without being deceived. And that is what we propose to do in this chapter: examine photography as a remarkable way of seeing, knowing, and remembering. Photographs have tremendous power to please our eyes and persuade our minds; if we could understand that power—the product of an intimate man-machine collaboration—we might gain access to some of the deepest secrets of visual art and human communication.

Today, we are surrounded by photographs and photographic reproductions. Children encounter photographic (or televised) representations of reality before they can speak. For the rest of us, pictures made with light have almost become substitutes—*preferred* substitutes—for the real world. But it is important to emphasize that at the earliest stage of consciousness, the stage where the attitudes and habits of a lifetime are established, we experience photographs as real in the same sense that people, places, and things are real.

It should be remembered, too, that photography is closely connected to graphic reproduction. This book would be impossible without both. Art as it is understood today could not be taught or studied without photography and its supporting technologies of duplication and reproduction. Photographs of artworks and photographs *as* artworks give us access to more places and objects than we could possibly visit in a lifetime. In this sense, photographs are like books that introduce the words and ideas of persons we cannot meet personally because they live too far away, or because they are no longer alive. The photographic reproduction of a building or a sculpture is not identical to the original. Still, it resembles the original more closely than an English translation resembles an ancient text.

Faults can be found with the photograph as a copy. And certainly it is better to visit a museum than to see its holdings in a catalogue of reproductions. Yet, we should not forget the profound changes that photographic copies have wrought in our lives. They have given us the capacity to see the faces of humanity throughout the world, the places where people live, the work they do, the things they make. If these gains have been won at the expense of demystifying original artworks, divesting them of their remoteness, uniqueness, and preciousness, so be it. The fact is, photographs are one of our most enjoyable ways of transcending time and space.

In this chapter photographs are juxtaposed with paintings or sculptures to bring out their principal similarities and differences. The similarities lie in their fundamentally visual character, no matter how the image was made. The differences are mainly due to the superior accuracy of the photograph. This superiority creates an illusion of objectivity and authenticity that has established photography—plus film and television—as exceedingly powerful instruments of information and education. Also, by comparing photographs with other visual media, we become more aware of their distinctive aesthetic effects. Finally, in examining photographs seriously we should gain insight into *all* visual sources of knowing, feeling, and valuing.

PHOTOGRAPHY AND REALITY

A close connection between the photographic print and objective reality was assumed almost from the nineteenth-century beginnings of the art. As the lens, camera, and plate were perfected, the painter's hand and eye came under suspicion as truthful recorders of reality. But if the photograph seemed more reliable from an optical standpoint, it was painting that gained ground as a vehicle of psychological expression. The split between photography and painting—or between science and art—is still with us. Ironically, its basis lies in the fact that the camera resembles the human eye: it captures light rays and records them by a process that excludes the human hand. The painter's hand—more than his eye—raised doubts about the artist's ability to represent reality in complete detail. And his brain—the neural tissue behind his eye—raised doubts about the artist's ability to tell the truth objectively.

The camera seemed to circumvent human imperfection. At least that is the impression created by its capacity to receive and record visual facts automatically. As a result, viewers attributed a special kind of credibility to the photograph, a credibility they would not grant to any painterly style, no matter how realistic. The photograph was seen as truthful in a scientific and historical sense; from that combination of virtues we got the idea of a photographic "document," the man-made image that is more reliable than words, less time-consuming than reading, and free of human bias.

Because it records only what is seen by a neutral "eye," the photograph offers viewers a fundamentally new way of knowing; the photographic print

left: **Diane Arbus. *Mexican Dwarf in His Hotel Room in New York City.* 1970. © 1971 The Estate of Diane Arbus**

The secret of a photograph by Diane Arbus lives in her matter-of-fact approach to individuals who are condemned to be outsiders. Because she refused to be shocked by their abnormality, Arbus forces us to look at them as persons when our instinctive reaction is to look away.

right: **Diego Velázquez. Sebastian de Morra. 1643–44. The Prado, Madrid**

assures us that its imagery is more complete and honest than the data delivered by human sensory equipment. No matter that the photographer chooses his subject, selects "the decisive moment," and manipulates a print in a thousand ways. The photographic record of reality still seems completely true. This has led viewers to believe that in seeing a photograph they come into actual, as opposed to symbolic, contact with the world. Today, that conviction is part of a general consensus. Like perspective in the fifteenth century, photography entered human consciousness as an art that controls a superior cognitive technology.

PHOTOGRAPHY AND PAINTING

Historically, photography emerged from painting. Its earliest practitioners were portrait painters. When the daguerreotype was perfected—about 1839—lifesize painted portraits went into decline and hand-painted miniatures died out; it was a simple case of technological obsolescence. The same process took place as history painting was replaced by still photography and then newsreel photography, which, in turn, gave way to television film and videotape. But, as always, technological change produced unanticipated social and cultural side effects.

Today, almost everyone owns dozens—even hundreds—of photographs. And almost everyone owns one or more cameras—often miniature cameras that can be carried anywhere. So photography is now a folk art as well as a fine art. It is practiced by far more persons than ever practiced the

Sandy Skoglund. *Radioactive Cats*. 1980. Courtesy Castelli Graphics, New York

Skoglund changes the relation of photography to reality: her photos are staged. The tenement room, its people, furnishings, and cats were arranged, or installed, and then photographed. Of course, this is what cinematographers do—and some photojournalists, too. But in straight still photography the effect is surreal.

Evelyn Hofer. *Brownstones on the West Side.*
1974. New York Times Pictures

Edward Hopper. *Sunlight on Brownstones.*
1956. Wichita Art Museum, Kansas. Roland P.
Murdock Collection

Both Hopper and Hofer are poets of urbanism. But Hopper is more strictly wedded to the city's rectangular relationships; notice how his couple look at nature wistfully through a square opening in the canvas. Hofer, on the other hand, finds delight in a format of converging diagonals; she sees a speedier, more dynamic harmony in the repeated masonry forms. The result is a brownstone counterpoint that skips and sings. Hofer discovers melody where Hopper felt a pervasive silence.

arts of drawing and painting. In this connection, we should remember that a few centuries ago most people saw themselves only in a mirror (which gives a limited view as well as a reversed image). The rich might see themselves in painted portraits, but the working classes and the poor had no idea—no visual idea—of themselves. Now that has changed: rich and poor see themselves in dozens of images—large and small, old and young, formally posed or caught off guard. In other words, all of us have seen ourselves, our friends, our relatives, and our ancestors photographically; and these images confirm the fact that we exist. Thus photography has had immense importance for the development of a genuine sense of self. (As the folk saying goes: "You don't know how you look 'til you have your picture took.")

Photography has also taught us how much artists change what they see. Oddly enough, we are less conscious of the fact that the camera also changes reality: we do not realize that the photographer manipulates what the camera sees. Most of us believe that the photograph cannot be false no matter who operates the camera. (We are much more suspicious of statisticians.) So photography has taken over the "truth" franchise in our culture. Only photography represents reality in a manner that commands universal acceptance; today, even painters use photographs.

In the past, painters used photographs in secret. Most of them regarded photographs as a crutch, a device employed by artists who were weak in drawing or too lazy to analyze and reconstruct what they saw. The history of the relationship between painting and photography has been brilliantly written by Van Deren Coke (see Selected Bibliography, page 509), who provides an abundance of evidence about the painter's use of photographic "aids." It runs from pure and simple copying to highly sophisticated references to photographic ways of seeing. Indeed, the camera's one-eyed optic is widely celebrated: Photorealism is now a major painting style.

But photography creates problems for painters who prefer the record of the camera's glass eye to their own human mode of perception. In copying photographic imagery, painters also reproduce its frozen, or "stop-action," quality. Or they reproduce the camera's typical distortions of form and space.

left: **Dong Kingman.** *The "El" and Snow.* **1946. Whitney Museum of American Art, New York**

Both Dong Kingman and Berenice Abbott see the "El" as a kind of carnival or bazaar. However, Mrs. Abbott stresses the grittiness of the city scene whereas Kingman is impressed with its melody. The watercolor medium seems ideally suited to Kingman's lyrical vision of steel girders and cast-iron lightposts because it subtracts from their mass and presents them as a collection of light, dancing surfaces. The photograph, on the other hand, retains the weight of the steel: no danger of turning the city's shadow patterns into tissue paper and lace.

below: **Berenice Abbott.** *"El" at Battery.* **c. 1933–37. Courtesy The Witkin Gallery, New York**

Inevitably, the camera distorts because of its monocular way of seeing; as a result, the painter's copy may have an inauthentic or "dead" look. Some artists can conceal their photographic sources: they can use the camera without being used by it. Others deliberately simulate the photograph's frozen action; they use it to make a statement about the artificiality, the sameness, or the reproducibility of everything we see and do. In any case, photographic imagery can be dangerous because it is so seductive. The painter who sets out to use it can easily become its captive. Instead of an image that has passed through a human consciousness, we may see no more than a painted snapshot.

above: Arman. *Little Hands.* 1960. Collection the artist

Arman and Hartmann converge, not only in their choice of doll or mannequin parts to express the obscenity of Buchenwald, but also in their use of "real" objects to suggest the horror of a real event. Notice that Arman's hands do not touch; they are clearly dismembered and mutilated. Hartmann's hands and arms are intertwined and they reach toward the viewer rather gracefully. We have a more complex idea expressed in the photograph: it is a peculiar grace of writhing bodily parts. As viewers we are caught in a tension that is both moral and aesthetic—the contradictions between what we know and feel. Hartmann forces us to view the concentration-camp murders as a kind of high-fashion ballet. It is a deeply disturbing experience.

right: Erich Hartmann. *Mannequins.* © 1969 Magnum Photos

left: **Ivan Albright. *Self-Portrait.* 1935. Collection Earle Ludgin, Chicago**

Ivan Albright's *Self-Portrait* and Douglas Jeffery's photograph of John Gielgud portraying the aged Shakespeare offer an unusual opportunity to compare a painting and a photograph dealing with the same theme—the irony and disillusionment of old age. An interesting difference emerges: Albright's painting is hyper-realistic, more than photographic in its accumulation of detail. The photograph of Gielgud, on the other hand, is realistic by definition. Albright builds a case against himself; the symbols of life's futility are patiently and lovingly assembled. Jeffery focuses our attention on a different sort of drama—the spectacle of a great Shakespearean actor, late in his career, playing the role of his aged master. The photograph functions simultaneously as a theatrical document and a work of visual art.

below: **Douglas H. Jeffery. *John Gielgud as Shakespeare in Edward Bond's* Bingo. August 25, 1974. Royal Court Theatre, London. © Douglas H. Jeffery, 1974**

above: **George Tooker.** *Government Bureau.* **1956. The Metropolitan Museum of Art, New York. George A. Hearn Fund, 1956**

The contrast between the photograph and the painting enhances our understanding of the distinctive excellence of each, that their common theme is the impersonality of bureaucratic existence. How does each picture make its point? In Tooker's case it is through precise repetition of human and architectural forms within a fast-receding space. Duane Michals uses the same device: the central figure is much reduced in size compared with the foreground figure. His people are also destined to be swallowed up in a prison-like office-tomb. But Tooker dwells on the paranoid atmosphere of the bureau, the sense of being spied upon; Michals emphasizes the alienation of man from man. His theme is Giacometti's theme—isolation. Here a photographic liability becomes an asset: the monocular lens of the camera produces an optical shrinking of the older, bald-headed man in the corridor. Thus we witness his tragic reduction in spiritual size.

right: **Duane Michals.** *Intersecting Corridors.* **1974. Courtesy Duane Michals**

420

THE AMATEUR WITH A CAMERA

The rudiments of taking a photograph are quickly and easily learned, and cameras are inexpensively available to almost everyone. This combination of factors has spawned a multitude of amateurs—persons who make photographs well or badly for their own enjoyment. So photography can be called a folk art without detracting from its status as one of the so-called fine arts. Actually, a good photograph is good regardless of the training or status of the person who made it. A more important question has to do with the consequences of the fact that millions of people now have the means of making pictures.

One result of photography's popularity is the discovery that everything that can be seen can be photographed. The idea that anything can be recorded by a camera is similar to the child's discovery that anything in the world can be named: it is a linguistic and cognitive revelation. As millions made this discovery, the philosophic outlook of our time was fundamentally changed. People realized that the scientific developments beginning in the eighteenth century had yielded immense technological benefits for the twentieth century—benefits going beyond the substitution of machines for human or animal effort. Machines seemed to be adequate, or more than adequate, substitutes for human perceptual and mental work. Who can doubt this today, in an age of electronic computers?

The mechanization of seeing began with the perfection of the camera. And from this initial success a marvelous feeling of cultural confidence emerged: not only seeing but also perceiving and thinking could be mechanized. That is, we began to believe that machines would enable us to think faster and better. Because millions of people could record the environment almost as spontaneously as they could see it, they developed a new sense of mastery over that environment; to "capture" something on film was the psychological equivalent of controlling it. In a very real sense, the invention of photography in the nineteenth century was as revolutionary as the invention of printing in the sixteenth century.

Because the masses could take pictures of themselves and pieces of their world, photography raised the possibility that most people could understand what they were looking at. In addition, the amateur photographer became something of a critic—not only of photographic prints but also of photographic reality. This does not mean that amateur photographers became sophisticated connoisseurs of art. Generally, the amateur is more interested in the realism of a snapshot than its aesthetics. But the fact that cameras are used by millions has produced a fundamental change in the history of art and society.

First, the privilege of owning images has been extended to the masses. Second, the ownership of images has produced a quantum leap in the capacity of ordinary people to see themselves and their environment objectively. Third, the ability to take photographs, and to judge them, seems to confer more capacity to participate in cultural affairs in general. Fourth, greater participation in cultural affairs increases participation in politics. Fifth, collecting paintings seems to have become a more specialized interest, mainly of old elites whose status is secure, or of a new class that aspires to elite status.

Not surprisingly, the invention of photography and the steady improvement of photographic reproduction have led to a general democratization of life in the technologically advanced countries. A "revolution of rising expectations" began when large numbers of people could see pictures of places, products, and life-styles that were normally beyond their experience. Then motion pictures, followed by television, created a second "revolution of rising expectations." But there can be little doubt that photography started the process: this new art-technology changed the modern world.

INSTANTANEOUS SEEING

Because of the realism of the photographic image we may not realize that its "stop-action" image is unnatural: we do not see the way the camera sees. A still

John Pregulman. *The Rebecca Kelly Dance Company.* 1985.

Stop action: the flow of time and motion condensed into a single, instant image.

opposite above: Film still from *The Grapes of Wrath:* the Joad Family. Directed by John Ford. 1940. © 1949. Twentieth Century-Fox Film Corp.

There is a continuous exchange of influence between photojournalists, documentary filmmakers, and film and television directors. The Arthur Grace photograph here is very reminiscent of John Ford's film which, in turn, descended from the motion-picture documentaries of Pare Lorentz and the photographs of Walker Evans, Dorothea Lange, and Margaret Bourke-White. Their common theme is the timeless reality of rural poverty.

opposite below: Arthur Grace. *Nellie Hart and Sons.* 1974. New York Times Pictures

frame taken from a roll of 35-millimeter motion-picture film gives us a better idea of what the human eye sees: it catches a generalized glimpse of things, a glimpse that becomes an image which is somewhat blurred and indistinct. In other words, film reality depends on the illusion of *motion* more than on sharpness and clarity of *contour:* motion pictures prove that "there are no outlines in nature." But the still photograph is different; it produces a "high resolution" image—an image so sharp, clear, and instantaneous that it seems to stop time.

When we say the photograph "stops" time, we mean that it condenses the flow of time into a single instant. That instant is a moment in real time; the camera isolates a split second in the life of the object. This visual isolation of a moment can be understood in terms of the physics of the camera. However, it also has a psychological and aesthetic dimension: because we simulate what we see internally, we try unconsciously to "stop" our personal or biological time as we view a photograph. As a result, photographic forms acquire a quality that we rarely experience when looking at painted forms. That quality might be called "immediacy." The camera reveals what the naked eye cannot catch. Or, we realize that the camera has caught what the eye sees but the brain does not register.

So photography gives us access to a dimension of reality that normally eludes us. That seems to be the reason why photographs cast a spell over the spectator. Clearly, the modern, high-speed camera is a magical instrument even before we consider the outlook and artistry of the person who uses it. Like the microscope or the telescope, the camera "invades" an invisible realm and makes it visible.

PHOTOJOURNALISM

"Art" photography, scientific photography, and portrait photography are older than photojournalism. But it is mainly the association with print journalism and inexpensive print reproduction that accounts for the success of pho-

Barbara Gluck Treaster. *Huyn Thanh and Descendants.* **1972. New York Times Pictures**

Paul Strand. *The Family.* **1953. © 1971 The Estate of Paul Strand**

Paul Strand gives us a family of distinct individuals, mutually supportive but absolutely independent. Barbara Gluck Treaster's people are entirely dependent on each other. Where Strand emphasizes the spatial separation and parallelism of his figures, Treaster gives hers a common root in the old man's feet. All the forms in the photograph seem to converge on a little area where man and earth meet. Form and idea coincide. Each of these photographs is a masterpiece.

tography. By "success" I mean more than popular acceptance or high commercial value; I mean that many of the world's best photographs have been made by newspaper and magazine photographers. The photojournalism tradition of *Life* and *Look* continues to operate vigorously in today's newspapers and newsmagazines; it is also a strong influence on television news coverage and motion-picture photography.

As the documentary photograph became our most trusted medium of information, its cheap reproduction by the printing press made it a prime contender with the printed word in a continuing struggle for the minds of the public. If we reckon the progress of that struggle by the changed ratio of words to pictures in printed or electronic form, it seems clear that photographs have won the battle. When advertisers decided to shift most of their expenditures from magazines to television, they shifted to a medium that was almost wholly visual, with words heard mainly in "voice-over" commentary. Unfortunately, the consequences for verbal literacy have been disastrous. Still, the public is not uninformed about national and international events. It might even be argued that functional illiterates know more about world affairs than literate persons knew two or three generations ago. From the standpoint of disseminating general information, the technology of the cheaply reproduced image seems to be superior to the printed word.

Photography, then, provides the masses with an eyewitness account of contemporary history. To them it seems more truthful than written history or print journalism; becoming informed becomes fun. What accounts for the immense appeal of photojournalism? Aside from low cost and ease of access, the following factors can be cited: (1) Photogravure and photo-offset printing yield very good reproductions of original photographs. (2) The arrested or frozen-action qualities of the photograph—its candid quality—make viewers believe they are looking at authentic, unposed events. (3) The realism of the photographic images gives it an inherent advantage over the abstract language of print when it comes to reconstructing "the sense" of what actually happened. (4) Photojournalism satisfies our voyeuristic impulses better than any other medium of visual or literary art.

424

Photojournalism became the parent of today's flood of books, magazines, and posters devoted to visual gossip, sexual imagery, and hard and soft pornography. This potential was always latent in photography as a medium, and now it has become an actuality. The camera's functioning as a detachable eye—an instrument capable of seeing quickly, secretly, and from odd angles—made photography the ideal medium of voyeurism. Here again, literature could not compete. The candid camera made it possible to see without being seen, to investigate reality without interfering in reality—a kind of triumph over Heisenberg's law.

In the photojournalism of Mathew Brady, people could see the gory side of the Civil War—a dead Confederate sniper—up close. Erich Salomon let us into meetings of international statesmen; we could watch Mussolini's facial acting—up close. Perhaps that is why a great war photographer, Robert Capa, said: "If your pictures aren't good, you're not close enough." Eventually he was killed. So were Werner Bischof and David Seymour ("Chim"): they changed the imagery of war as presented by painting and prints; war became a painful, almost tactile, experience. The ugly facts of battle had always been softened by verbal accounts. Literary journalism and historical painting had built-in conventions for creating psychological distance. But photojournalism changed all that: it transformed the viewer from a spectator into a participant. The hand-held camera (still or video) placed the viewer's eye so close to the action that he felt totally involved. This was the "pornography" of war. In peacetime it became the pornography of civil violence. From there it was a short step to pornography in the erotic sense of the word.

PRINCIPLE OF THE FRAME

The painter's picture frame has architectural roots. This is clear when we realize that mosaics and frescoes were a kind of "fill-in" art: their shapes were defined by a building's structure. It was not until the late Middle Ages that the pictorial image became a window image—the result of seeing *out* of an enclosed space, a room. At this point painting and photography merged in their fundamental outlook: the first *camera obscura* was in fact a darkened room that admitted light through a small opening in one wall, forming an inverted image on the opposite wall.

Photography might not have been invented if Renaissance painters had not begun to think about art in optical and scientific terms. The development of perspective was a reaction against the flat, conceptual approach to imagery that we see in Byzantine art. The Renaissance artist, inspired by classical models of realism and encouraged by a new spirit of openness to sense experience, substituted his eye for the *framed* opening—the window—of a room. And that is essentially what a photographer does.

left: **Erich Salomon.** *Visit of German Statesmen to Rome.* **1931. International Museum of Photography, Eastman House, Rochester, New York**

Erich Salomon pioneered the use of photography to show how statesmen actually operate. Visually, at least, his candid camera broke the barrier between the small circles of powerful men who negotiate the fate of mankind and the large body of humanity that looks on. His pictures are historical documents as much as they are works of art. In Teresa Zabala's picture the political photograph is carried beyond journalism: she gives us a psychological reading of these men that transcends the event itself. Whereas Salomon used the grouping of furniture and figures to generate an ominous conspiratorial quality among his politicians, Zabala probes people's faces, appraising them with a thoroughness we have not seen since the doctors in Rembrandt's *Anatomy Lesson.*

right: **Teresa Zabala.** *Carter with Congressional Leaders.* **1977. New York Times Pictures**

If we look at a landscape through a window or look at an object through a rectangular opening in a piece of paper, we get the idea of framing as it was understood by the Renaissance painter—and the modern photographer. Moving the "window" closer or farther away from the eye enlarges or reduces the size of the visual field. Moving the "window" around in the same plane has the effect of composing reality as if it were made of flat shapes collected—seemingly organized—within the frame. This concept of composition relies on the idea of a portable window that can be moved with almost as much freedom as the human eye itself. The camera, of course, is the photographer's movable window frame.

A further refinement of framing is the device of cropping, a way of *re*-framing the imagery captured in the photographer's print. Cropping represents the photographer's "second chance" to arrange life. The "first chance" was the selection of a piece of reality to be photographed and to live again. That is a seemingly godlike act. Not only does the photographer choose what viewers will see; he also states what is there to be seen. This is creation in an almost primal sense.

The ability to frame and crop reality lies at the heart of the photographer's art. These operations go by names borrowed from painting—"composition" or "design"—but in photography they have different meanings. The photographer isolates and juxtaposes objects already created; painters *make* the forms they arrange, and the process takes time. When viewers see a photograph, they think the photographer has seen the image, recorded it, and framed it all at once. That is why they believe the recorded image does not lie. But it does. The photographer's manipulation of edges and tones, negatives and prints, changes the *gestalt,* or configuration, of the image. And if the gestalt is changed, the whole image is changed.

PHOTOGRAPHY AND ABSTRACTION

Every photograph (like every artificial image) is an abstraction. Its flatness, small size, frozen action, and color (or lack of color) produce simplifications and generalizations of reality. For a variety of reasons we accept these simplifications and generalizations: we agree to see the part for the whole, black-and-white for color, flatness for depth, and stillness for continuous action. *Deliberate* photographic abstraction goes even further: it tries to investigate visual form by surrendering the representational function of photography.

There are essentially two kinds of photographic abstraction. The first might be called "straight abstraction" because it involves no alteration of the camera's optics and very little manipulation of the print during development. Instead, the photographer uses close-ups, unusual angles of vision, or unfamiliar fragments of familiar wholes. Our attention is drawn to patterns and structures that, although they are real, cannot be easily recognized. The purpose of this type of abstraction is to persuade viewers that the real world holds infinite resources of undiscovered beauty. Underlying the work of the straight abstractionist is the well-known formalist aesthetic—the conviction that every part of the universe has been harmoniously designed and assembled.

We have to admit, however, that in modern photography it is ridiculously easy to produce thousands of these formal revelations. They may be aesthetically interesting at first, but the public finds them increasingly boring. Why? Because discovering the world's microscopic realities needs to be done only once. After that viewers lose interest: formal patterns and textures hold our attention only to the extent that we can see their connections to larger patterns of human concern.

A second type of photographic abstraction might be called "synthetic" abstraction. Here the image is more artificially created and is virtually independent of objective or "seen" reality. The connection with the camera itself is somewhat thin: synthetic abstraction relies on the fact that visual forms can be recorded directly on a light-sensitive surface. Man Ray's *rayographs* and Mo-

Paul Caponigro. *Rock Wall No. 2, W. Hartford, Connecticut.* **1959**

Photographic abstraction. The rocks are real; this is a "straight," not a manipulated, photograph. But we are forced to concentrate on form and texture rather than on symbol and context. Indeed, light, shape, and texture have been lifted *out of context* and presented purely as aesthetic phenomena.

László Moholy-Nagy. *Untitled (Abstraction) Photogram.* **1924. Courtesy The Art Institute of Chicago. Gift of George Banford, 1968**

Synthetic abstraction. Real objects are recorded on photographic paper without the intervention of a camera lens. Through multiple exposures, reversals of light and dark, and manipulation of tones we get an essentially nonobjective, photographic image.

Willie Vicov. *Heavy Turnout for Philippine Elections.* **1984. UPI/Bettmann Newsphotos**

Photographic abstraction. Again, this is "straight" photography; but here we have to concentrate on *patterns* of repetition and variation. The overall image is abstract because it is not about nuns or voting. Not really. The real subject is the variation of similar shapes in similar enclosures. Our pleasure is mainly aesthetic: the contrasts between dark and light, the tilting and turning of forms, and slight changes in size relationships.

holy-Nagy's *photograms* tell us through their terminology that they are an essentially new art form—image construction without an eye or a lens.

For the art historian a new classification must reflect a fundamental artistic change, and in synthetic abstraction a new conception of artistic imagery is clearly at work. The idea of the lens as a surrogate eye, or witness, or advocate, is substantially abandoned. The synthetic abstractionist works more like a nonobjective painter or printmaker. So, from the standpoint of art history, this type of imagery represents an antiphotographic step—the continuation of a painterly idea with new materials; it simply redefines photography as painting with light.

THE PHOTOGRAPHIC SLIDE

Today, many photographers make slides instead of prints. In fact, more film is sold for slide transparencies than for any other purpose. Unlike the film negative, which has to be printed to make a positive, the slide carries a positive image as soon as it is processed. To see that image, the photographer merely projects it on a screen. So making slides rather than prints has grown in popularity among serious photographers. The advantage of slides lies in their low cost and ease of storage for easy retrieval. Also, color slides kept in a dark box are less subject to fading than color prints. For this reason alone, slides are very useful in scientific and educational work. We may be reluctant to think of the slide as an art object because we do not usually see it, only its projected image. But we do not see the film in a movie or the tape in a video-cassette, either.

One of the truisms of our time is that weddings and birthday parties are staged for the benefit of the photographer. As for the old-fashioned touristic pilgrimage, many of us do not really see the monuments because we are too busy taking pictures. Mostly, these pictures are processed as slides that will be shown at home. So the ridiculous spectacle of a photographer thrusting himself into the most solemn moment of a wedding, for example, has a serious significance: the authentic witnessing of the event does not take place until a few close friends and relatives meet in a dark room to see the slides. The wedding or Bar Mitzvah was not a charade—not exactly. It was a piece of folk theater meant to be solemnized under the auspices of the slide projector.

Aesthetics comes into play as we consider the image created when the slide is projected on a screen. What the viewer sees is light reflected back from a screen, or, in the case of rear projection, light transmitted through a screen. The image can be quite large—cinema size, if desired—and it can be seen by many persons at once. It can even be projected into the night sky; at Las Vegas any citizen can pay five dollars and have his image spread out across the heavens. More importantly, when the image consists of transmitted light, it is capable of carrying a wider range of color and tonal values than an image printed on paper. Thus the slide projection has all the blown-up realism of cinema imagery, with the exception of motion.

The photographic print produces an image by a process of darkening a surface—usually paper—covered with a photographic emulsion. The forms we see are created by *subtracting* light from a surface that is white, or off-white, but not as bright a source that seems to generate its own light. However, the slide projection glows (special screen coatings enhance that effect) and thus it has more vividness. Perhaps this is why students accustomed to slide lectures are disappointed when they encounter originals: an oil-on-canvas image cannot compete with the silver screen.

The slide image represents only one line of photographic evolution—the line that connects it to film and television. The other line connects photography to graphic art. Here the frame format inherited from painting is important. It would be difficult to conceive of "art" photography apart from pictures matted and framed like drawings, etchings, or easel paintings. However, traditional paintings and prints are limited in size; only a few persons can see them at once; they become mass media only through cheap print reproduction. The slide projection, on the other hand, is ideal for low-cost, high-quality mass viewing. The slide image (or the image created by projecting several slides simultaneously) is unaffected by graphic constraints; its edges are not governed by carved moldings or printed pages. Also, slide projections are not graspable objects; they enter experience in a dematerialized fashion, like light or air. So the future of the projected image may be limited only by the physiological and cognitive capabilities of the human organism.

It seems likely that slide images will evolve into something beyond photography as we know it. At the same time, photographic *prints* will probably consolidate and perfect themselves along traditional, pictorial lines. Thus photography behaves like the older art forms; it spawns new offspring while itself remaining the same.

THE PHOTOGRAPHER AS ARTIST

Oddly enough, amateurism strongly affects the practice of photography as a "fine art." The same factors that account for the spread of amateurism influence serious photography. An inexpensive and easily used technology enables photographers to function more independently than painters, sculptors, or filmmakers. Photographs can be cheaply reproduced and they are not hard to display; indeed they can be passed from hand to hand. Unlike writers, photographers do not depend on the costly technology of the printing industry; they need not contend with editors and publishers; they can function without a literate reading public. Photographers are more like independent craftsmen; they can reach the public without too much trouble, and most people can afford to buy photographs.

Because the same equipment is available to almost everyone, the professional photographer's *attitude* becomes the distinctive instrument of his art. A painter's eyes, fingers, and wrist are unique; they are integral parts of the act of painting. But we cannot make the same claim for the photographer's finger on the shutter-release. It is the photographer's visual and intellectual equipment

left: **Claes Oldenburg.** *The Stove.* **1962. Private collection**

The bitter, derisory statement made by Oldenburg's stove relies, in a sense, on the homely old image of a stove in the Evans photograph. Before he could make it ridiculous, Oldenburg had to festoon the stove with large portions of specially constructed, inedible food. Evans, on the other hand, celebrates the beloved cast-iron monster as the only solid, durable object in a seedy environment. The photographer's manipulation of context—the frontal "pose" of the stove, the decision to "place" the pots and pans at eye-level—is less obvious than Oldenburg's manufacture of a sleazy meal. But it is no less an act of artistic selection and organization.

right: **Walker Evans.** *Frank's Stove, Cape Breton Island.* **Yale University Art Gallery, New Haven. Director's Purchase Fund**

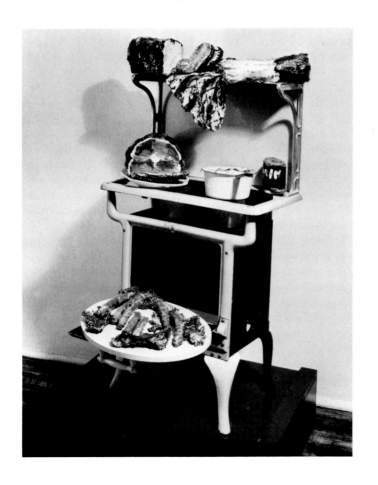

Christo. *Package on Wheelbarrow*. 1963. Collection, The Museum of Modern Art, New York. Blanchette Rockefeller Fund

The bound or wrapped figure has been used as a symbol of confined power from Michelangelo to Rodin (see the *Balzac*, page 314) to Christo. Carolyn Watson's photograph retains the form but changes its meaning: her figures are more nearly related to Henry Moore's sleepers in the London underground during World War II. Why is this a great photograph? Because Watson saw a universal image in these two sleepers. Her print transcends the fact that two Americans had to bed down on a bench in London because of a shortage of hotel rooms. It is the capacity to leap from the recording of a local event to the representation of a general idea that accounts for the extraordinary potency of *Crash Pad*.

Carolyn Watson. *Crash Pad*. June, 1971. Courtesy Monkmeyer Press Photo Service

that are crucial. A camera has no built-in mechanism of selection, so the photographer's decision-making turns out to be the most creatively significant aspect of his art. But choices made instantaneously depend on a lengthy period of incubation. Photography is more than a type of mechanical seeing; it presupposes a capacity to sense what is interesting, to recognize what is humanly *worth* seeing.

In stressing the photographer's mental and cultural preparation we stress the importance of knowing what makes a picture good to see. A photographer who consistently takes good pictures has more than luck on his side: he is obviously *looking for something;* good pictures are proof of *focused knowledge* as well as of darkroom skill. Viewers expect a photograph to be the product of informed seeing: they want to believe their perceptions have been shaped and guided by an exceptional human intelligence; otherwise the values of a photograph become a matter of good or bad optical recording. Ultimately, the great photographers give us the sense of encountering the world through an artist's mind—an artist whose ideas and biases are visible. Whether we share those biases or not, we need to be convinced they are there. In photography, point of view has both philosophical and optical significance.

PHOTOGRAPHIC CRITICISM

The criticism of photography is largely undeveloped for three reasons. First, in its perfected form the medium is less than a century old—not long enough for a solid body of aesthetic theory to develop. Second, most scholarly writing about photography deals either with technical questions or the history of photography, that is, the history of camera equipment, developing processes, and the biographies of famous photographers. Third, in the struggle to free itself from the parent art of painting, photographic criticism often neglects the theories developed in the older visual arts.

It is unfortunate, too, that conventionally trained art historians have paid little attention to the evolution of photography as an art. They may mention the influence of photography on Courbet, or on Degas and the French Impressionists, but they rarely discuss the role of photography in our visual culture as a whole; they ignore the changes photography has wrought on contemporary modes of seeing and thinking. Without addressing these questions, however, photographic criticism cannot rise above shop talk; the central problems of aesthetic value are encountered only if critics deal with photography as it confronts the major questions of society and mankind.

The battle to recognize photography as a full-fledged art form has been fought and largely won—by Alfred Stieglitz, Edward Steichen, Beaumont Newhall, Minor White, Helmut Gernsheim, John Szarkowski, Aaron Scharf, Peter Pollack, Van Deren Coke, and many others. For criticism, winning this battle has important consequences: membership in the fine arts "club" means that photographs can be judged like other works of visual art. The early status of photography as a bastard art form excluded it from serious consideration. That has now changed. But does the emergence of photography as a new art form create a new set of aesthetic expectations? No. The sources of artistic form may vary, but human needs with respect to any visual presentation are remarkably consistent. So the factors that make a good photograph are similar to those that operate in the case of drawings, paintings, and prints.

But if the criteria of greatness in visual art are much the same, there are nevertheless "local" factors that operate uniquely in each of them, including photography. These grow out of the technical features of the camera, the physical character of photographic prints, and the economic factors that govern their reproduction and distribution. The small size of the photograph should be mentioned—its portability and accessibility as a hand-held object. The photograph is a possession that can be carried everywhere because it fits into a wallet or a purse. Like books, photographs can be privately studied and savored. Yet they can also be vastly enlarged. As large-scale images for advertising, information, and display, photographs are perhaps the most public of visual art forms. Small or large, photographs have become as influential as film and television in shaping popular consciousness.

We come, then, to the specifically photographic criteria of excellence. What separates a great photograph from a good one? Naturally, we must judge a photograph according to the way it uses the opportunities and overcomes the limitations presented by the medium. At the same time, we cannot forget that photography is an art of ideas as well as of images. Therefore, our critical method should enable us to see connections between quality of technique and quality of thought or feeling; it should enable us to recognize and evaluate the interactions between medium and meaning.

The qualities that photographs must possess in order to be judged excellent can be identified. They can be designated as positions on six scales, or *continua;* one end of each scale stands for a minimum of quality, and the other end represents a maximum. Since any given photograph is unlikely to fulfill every ideal expectation, we have to estimate its cumulative achievement on all six scales to form an overall judgment of its merit.

Following are the scales, each of which goes from low to high: (1) from surface to depth, (2) from optical to tactile, (3) from pattern to idea, (4) from

Chuck Close. *Susan.* **1971. Courtesy Pace Gallery, New York**

A painting that looks like a photograph; a photograph that looks like a painting. Are we witnessing two kinds of identity crisis? Whatever the answer, we are faced with serious problems of photographic criticism. Siskind didn't *make* this photograph, he *took* it—and created an image with all the Abstract Expressionist power anyone could want. Now what would you do if you were a painter?

Aaron Siskind. *Lima 89 (Homage to Franz Kline).* **1975. Courtesy Light Gallery, New York**

part to whole, (5) from singular to typical, and (6) from record to original. The first three scales emphasize technical qualities. The last three scales stress the conceptual factors affecting the evaluation of a photograph, assuming it has met our technical requirements. A photograph that scores "high" on any one of these six scales would be interesting; a high evaluation on several scales would suggest the possibility of a masterpiece. In Chapter Fifteen of this book, the section "Kinds of Critical Judgment" presents the general criteria on which these photographic scales are based.

From Surface to Depth: Obviously, we are not referring to depth-of-field—the right aperture and focal length of the camera lens. Photographic depth refers to the volumetric quality of form; its lack is felt as thinness, lightness, or flatness. Lightness means an unconvincing representation of the mass or weight of forms. Lightness or thinness may be due to improper exposure and/or poor lighting. But more fundamentally, it results from the photographer's failure to represent the invisible tensions and strains that contribute to the weight and shape of an object. Flatness is the failure of the image to account photographically for the distribution of objects in space.

Andreas Feininger. *Cemetery in New York City.* **1948.** *Life* **magazine. © 1948, Time, Inc.**

Walker Evans. *Graveyard in Easton, Pennsylvania.* **1936. Library of Congress. Farm Security Administration Collection, Washington, D.C.**

FROM SURFACE TO DEPTH

The convincing distribution of objects in deep space calls for skillful technical control of the photographic medium. But technical control, while indispensable, cannot of itself produce depth as we intend it here. The ability to capture surface changes has to be the servant of a poetic sensibility. That is, textural change and spatial differentiation must be subordinate to the cognitive and emotive requirements of the image. Evans does only an adequate job of rendering the textures of the limestone cross, the scrubby grass, the brick-front houses, and the smokestacks. Edward Weston or Ansel Adams could have produced a better print. But Evans's point of view and his choice of a flat light over his shoulder have yielded a type of depth that no amount of textural detail could equal. It is his angle of vision—just next to the large cross—that gives the spacing to the other grave markers. This is what causes the rapid reduction in size relationships, especially between the cross and the brick dwellings. It even helps to compress the layers of rooftops, chimneys, and buildings near the horizon. Thus a squeezing down in the distance produces a pressure that seems to spread out the foreground objects, thrusting the graves toward us. This manipulation of depth, as much as the symbolism of the cross, creates photographic quality. The principal objects receive precisely the amount of space and light needed to define their forms and, more importantly, to reach a significant level of human meaning. Feininger is a more "scientific" photographer; hence his approach to physical, or three-dimensional, depth is a model of technical control. Yet it is a poetic device that creates the aesthetic depth of the work. Feininger has to contend with the fact that his telephoto lens inevitably foreshortens space, pressing distant forms into the frontal plane. To some extent he can cope with this flattening effect by relying on an Oriental pictorial device: movement upward means movement inward. But how can Western viewers be persuaded to accept this way of seeing? Feininger eliminates the horizon as well as any enclosing or framing lines. As a result we are forced to see the photograph very much as if it were a tapestry of gravestones. Our perceptual energies are concentrated on the texture of the fabric, so to speak. Now we can see subtle changes of light and dark seeming to form an S-curve that leads the eye very gradually into the upper fifth of the picture. There the gravestones lose much of their detail; they retain only their rectangular shapes, like the crisp gray notes around the edges of a Cubist composition. This Cubist dissolution of mass, accomplished before our eyes in a gently ascending movement, suggests a lovely analogy. In the bottom of the photograph the dead have begun to exchange their identities; by the time we reach the top their souls are dancing.

FROM OPTICAL TO TACTILE

Here are three strong photographs that rely heavily on the sense of touch. Which is not to say they are merely textural studies. They do, however, demonstrate the power of the medium to create monumental effects without pictorial trickery. What we see is optical rendering carried to a peak of tactile expressiveness. Notice that the subjects are all presented frontally; the problems of composition are quite uncomplicated; and there is little or no appeal to narrative values. To be sure, Strand's *Ranchos de Taos* inevitably touches on regional and historical ideas, but it is mainly the weight and volumetric quality of the architectural forms that account for the impact of his image. The Weston *Cabbage Leaf* is an even purer demonstration of the power of photography to generate plastic, i.e., sculptural, values with very commonplace materials. It is significant, I believe, that Weston achieves a lyricism here that one cannot imagine in any other visual medium. Raymond's photograph is a tactile triumph of another sort. To be sure, the soft chenille fabric receives much of its sculptural quality from the bed and pillow underneath. But Raymond has also been attentive to the active notes struck by the folds at the head and foot of the bed. Finally and most photographically, these are contrasted to the flat, quiet texture barely visible in the wallpaper pattern. We know that black-and-white photography operates within a very narrow visual range. Hence our criterion—from optical to tactile—emphasizes the control of volumes through the visual orchestration of textures. It shows that although still photography is capable of suggesting some of the qualities of the nonvisual senses—sound, taste, kinesthesia, and even smell—it is through rendering tactility that photography's claim to represent reality is most powerfully supported.

Edward Weston. *Cabbage Leaf.* 1931. Courtesy Cole Weston

Paul Strand. *Ranchos de Taos, New Mexico.* 1931. © 1977 The Estate of Paul Strand

Lilo Raymond. *Bed in Attic.* 1972. Courtesy the photographer

434

The formal values of a good print depend very much on the photographer's ability to represent three-dimensional volumes with a monocular instrument. We are binocular creatures and we expect to see depth. In the pictures of Edward Weston or Ansel Adams, we think we see depth—beautifully. It is because we are aware of a masterful control of light gradations. That control gives us the physical substance and spatial location of forms through purely photographic means. Something of this quality must be present in every good print.

From Optical to Tactile: Photography approaches reality from a distance and from a wholly visual standpoint. Yet the reality of matter is best recognized through the feel, or tactility, of forms. Now, photography employs a developing process that subtracts light; but the loss of light can produce a loss of textural detail. Painting has the advantage of being able to construct form by adding light, or adding shadow, or both—achieving texture either way. Thus the photographer is caught between a rock and a hard place: he needs optical detail to suggest the weight and texture of reality; at the same time the chemistry of photography tends to darken prints and to eliminate detail. So the photographer is always engaged in seeking an optimal balance between light and dark to preserve visual facts and textural quality.

Connoisseurs know that the grain of photographic emulsions and papers can supplement or "improve" upon the visual facts. Beyond a certain point, however, this sort of manipulation becomes nonphotographic—the simulation of painting or printmaking. Our rule here is: the tactility of a good photograph must be perceived as the product of an ocular process. In other words, the tactile values of a print must be photographic in origin; that excludes effects achieved through darkroom maneuvers.

From Pattern to Idea: The photograph devoted to pure pattern is a commonplace achievement for the camera; often it represents good technique com-

George Gerster. *Sahara Pollution.* © 1976 Foto George Gerster. Courtesy Photo Researchers, Inc., New York

An exceptionally eloquent example of pattern employed in a cognitive, as opposed to a purely formal, context. It is the juxtaposition of beautifully patterned sand and seemingly casual deposits of trash that makes the forms work expressively. By themselves, the wavelike sand forms would look like a thousand other photographs of desert rhythms. As for the trash piles, they are curiously, almost perversely, satisfying. Perhaps that is because the endless regularity of the sand patterns makes us hunger for signs of visual randomness. Notice, too, how the human figures on the upper left horizon provide a sense of scale for the picture as a whole. At the same time they hint at the essential idea of the picture—the painful connection between human settlement and pollution.

bined with a modest level of insight. But the camera is better employed as a machine that sees in order to know, to admire, to express, and to explain. The mere recording of patterns becomes photographic kitsch—a pretense to aesthetic profundity. Of course, patterns can be truthful as visual reports, but to sustain our interest they have to *signify* something beyond their own existence.

Patterns that require labels to be understood must be judged unsuccessful as photographic art. For a pattern to succeed aesthetically we have to *see* its meaning or significance, not read it. In other words, the formal values of a photograph require a larger context—the context of mind—as an essential support. Discovering patterns in nature or the manufactured environment becomes aesthetically potent when the photographer *shows us* their connections to the unfolding processes of nature or reveals them as products of human powers of invention and transformation. Otherwise we feel we are looking at a kind of vacant ornament, easily seen and easily forgotten.

From Part to Whole: The camera can only record fragments but art has to reveal universals. This is not a question of picturing large subjects or panoramic scenes. It is rather a problem in selecting and organizing what is partial or incomplete so that viewers believe they see what is finished and whole. Bad photographers seek the effect of wholeness by manipulation—usually by simulating the painter's tonalities and subordination of detail. This might be called "forced" unity. Good photographers rely on (a) selecting the significant feature of a subject; and (b) framing and composing a subject so that we sense its belonging to a complete universe. Obviously, choosing the significant de-

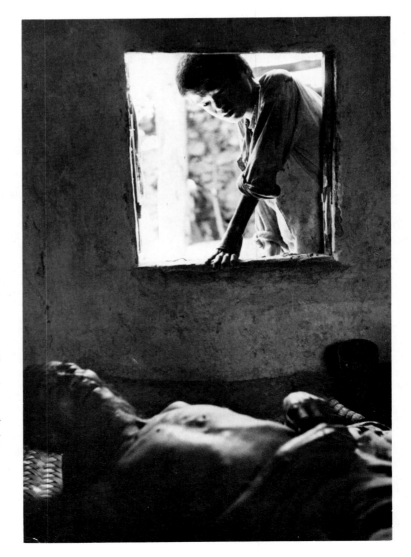

Werner Bischof. *Boy Leaving His Sick Grandfather, Korea.* **Undated. Courtesy Magnum Photos, New York**

The purpose of photographic composition is to make fragments of reality enter into complete relationships. Here portions of two figures have been organized into a whole that augments the expressive power of each part. The square window does more than frame the boy and concentrate our attention on his anguish: its placement initiates all the visual events within the image; it explains the darkness of the room; it dramatizes the somber texture of the wall; it contrasts the glaring outdoor illumination with the soft light barely crossing the grandfather's body. Most important, the diagonal formed by the boy's arm movement connects the pieces of the image with its narrative: it gives the angle and destination of his gaze; it makes us attend to the direction of the old man's stare—over the viewer's right shoulder and into the distance. Finally, it opposes the weight of the boy's arm and shoulder to the weightlessness of the sick man's hands. In purely design terms it relates the window to the room; in symbolic terms it compares the vertical situation with the horizontal situation. Bischof believed, and here demonstrates, that the pictorial dynamics of a great photographic statement are inseparable from its human meaning.

tail is crucial; that choice may be visual, intellectual, or intuitive. The important point is that viewers should be able to sense the totality of a situation through seeing the part.

From Singular to Typical: Compared to the other visual arts, photography can easily capture the exotic, the peculiar, and the freakish. It can readily gratify the human interest in weird people and strange actions. That is what photojournalism often does in carrying out the responsibilities of reportage. But photography as art must go beyond the recording of shocking events or grotesque phenomena. Otherwise it degenerates into a search for perversity, abnormality, and violence.

Henri Cartier-Bresson. *Children Playing in the Ruins, Spain.* 1933. Courtesy Magnum Photos, New York

In the introduction to his book *The Decisive Moment*, Cartier-Bresson says: "Above all, I craved to seize the whole essence, in the confines of one single photograph, of some situation that was in the process of unrolling itself before my eyes." Our criterion—from singular to typical—stresses this same objective. Cartier-Bresson's famous photograph illustrates the concept perfectly; both incident and idea are captured in a single image. Notice how Ben Shahn's *Liberation* (page 180) employs the same notion of a picture; it is essentially a photographic approach: the grotesque incident frozen and transmuted into an idea. To some extent we can explain the expressive force of Cartier-Bresson's photograph in compositional terms: the children in the rubble-strewn street distributed along an S-curve that comes to an abrupt halt with the boy on crutches; the jerky rhythm created by the repeated angles of the children's bodies. But there are psychological factors at work here, too: in the tension caused by our fear that the boy's crutches will be caught in the stones and he will fall down hard; in the cruelty of boys at play; and in the contrast between the laughing faces and the rough frame created by a shell hole. Most important is the rapid divergence of the lines forming the wall against which this drama unfolds; it propels the crippled youngster forward like a shot. These devices, and more, lie beneath the photographic surface of the work. It has taken me some time to see them and a paragraph to describe them even briefly; Cartier-Bresson caught them in an instant. Such mastery must be the product of a long apprenticeship, a quick mind, an intelligent eye. By "intelligent eye" I mean the photographer's ability to make an immediate, almost instinctive connection between what he sees in a scene, what it signifies at the moment, and what it means in depth—what it means as an idea that can occupy the mind permanently.

Robert Walker. *Find Coffee House.* 1971. New York Times Pictures

Here is a work that epitomizes my distinction between a photograph that serves to copy or record an event and a photograph that makes a discovery that is aesthetically and humanly significant. Walker's photograph, in my judgment, bears comparison with the masterpieces of Pieter Brueghel, Adriaen Brouwer, and even of Rembrandt. Consider the Caravaggio-like lighting that bathes the figure in the upper left: it is a little masterpiece in itself. The hand and head of the woman in the lower right could have been taken from an interior by Vermeer. Now these comparisons are not made to establish the greatness of a photograph by demonstrating its genealogy in the history of painting. It is rather to say that the same factors which make a masterwork of a Brouwer or a Vermeer operate in the present instance. Notice how the size and focal properties of the man advancing with his crutches create a superb, tension-filled space between him and the figures in the background. It is a space modeled in the tradition of the great Baroque canvases. At the same time, the scale relationships and perspectival effects are purely photographic. The ground plane moves up and away from us about as fast as the central figure moves toward us. The result is a powerful and dramatic pair of opposed movements, each culminating in an episode that demands our compassion in a different way. An isolated figure, almost lost in shadow (right middleground), provides precisely the right amount of interest and space modulation needed in that quadrant of the composition. The photograph satisfies our surface-to-depth requirements; it nourishes our tactile feelings through optical representation; it transcends the unusual or special character of the place and its people. And it takes up several great themes: helplessness, courage, loneliness, and love.

Some photographers confuse visual or moral shock with aesthetic surprise. Here Velázquez is our best model: he could portray human deformity without losing sight of what is noble in human beings. Diane Arbus skates on much thinner ice: she brings us face-to-face with physical and psychological abnormalities, but it is uncertain whether she is exploiting freaks or asking us to realize that her people are fellow sufferers (see page 414). Now, discovering universal human qualities in people who are outcast, ugly, or afflicted is morally and aesthetically admirable. The photographer's rule should be: Show us the truth about the human condition but do not use human misery as a source of thrills.

From Record to Original: The photograph as record tells us what we would have seen or known if we had been "there." This kind of image is a convenient mechanical substitute for personal witness: it enables us to travel without leaving home, to remember without summoning up mental images. Such pictures are valuable to the extent that they are reliable, that is, accurate. An "original" photograph, on the other hand, represents a fresh discovery. That "discovery" is partially related to the character of the photographic act: "taking" a picture means searching, getting warm, getting hot, and finally finding something new.

So it is not enough for the photographer to be "there" with his or her camera; it is necessary to be humanly "there." Otherwise the photograph will merely record what a mindless machine would record. Great originals result from a combination of alertness to the unusual—an instinctive recognition of images that say something new. Good photographers are allergic to visual clichés and stereotypes. Again, the mental preparation of the photographic artist has to be emphasized. When the preparation is right and when the execution is timely, the photograph represents a live birth—in the creator and the spectator. We may have seen an object or a place a thousand times before, but it has to strike us as a revelation. Great photographs should enable us to see innocently—like children.

CHAPTER FOURTEEN

IMAGES IN MOTION: FILM AND TELEVISION

Until there is a chapter on film in every textbook of art ... we shall not have firmly established in the consciousness of our generation this most important artistic development of our century.
(Bela Balazs, Theory of the Film, *1952.)*

A complex technology stands behind motion pictures and television, yet it is correct to think of both media as extensions of painting and picture-making. The pioneers of still photography operated on the basis of a painterly sensibility, and, even today, a long pictorial tradition supports the work of photographers and cinematographers. This will remain true as long as film and television are seen in a two-dimensional, rectangular format. The great change, of course, was the creation of a credible illusion of motion on a flat surface: it opened up the ancient art of painting and transformed it into a revolutionary force in modern life.

The illusions created by film and TV are so convincing that we are hardly aware of their pictorial connections. We are like Renaissance viewers discovering the optical miracles created by the newly discovered science of perspective. In the fifteenth century, the convincing representation of objects in depth liberated the imagination of artist and viewer alike. A long-standing goal of the pictorial tradition had been the creation of lifelike illusions; each new tri-

Film still from *Modern Times*. Directed by Charles Chaplin. 1936

Chaplin's tramp, a born loser, gets caught up in the wheels and gears of industry. Here we see how the main idea of the film—the crazy conflict between man and mechanization—can be captured in a single image.

umph in pictorial representation encouraged viewers to believe they were watching man's conquest of reality. Now, motion pictures and TV seem to have accomplished the ultimate—the complete simulation of reality. But technology does not stand still: lasers and holography promise to make the three-dimensional simulation of reality even more convincing.

Motion pictures and television depend on two separate but interdependent factors. First is the long artistic tradition that tries to re-present our world and our experience. Second is the continuous stream of new technologies that record reality: the camera, flexible film, film projection, synchronous sound and imagery, color photography, the iconoscope or videocamera, videotape, holography, and so on. From these technical inventions we have created aesthetic devices like montage, close-up, slow motion, split screen, wide screen, freeze-frame, and instant replay. It can be argued that artistic necessity motivated these technical developments. Or, perhaps, technology changes according to its own internal laws. In either case, we have to consider the interaction of technical and aesthetic factors—media-meaning relationships—to understand film as an art form.

THE MANIPULATION OF SPACE-TIME

Artists have always tried to represent movement: they blurred the edges of forms, added "speed" lines to contours, and visualized the imagined positions of bodies in motion. Without the capacity to use real motion, they relied on suggestion—something close to magic. Well, some forms of magic are more convincing than others: motion pictures rely on magic, too. If you look at some film footage you will see that it consists of thousands of fixed images.

Why are we willing to believe in the filmmaker's magic—the illusion of reality created by little pictures on film passing across a beam of light at the rate of twenty-four frames per second? Apparently, more than magic is involved; there is a physiological effect, too. Each picture lingers as an after-image; that image is not instantly extinguished in the viewer's eye; our eyes fail to see the empty intervals (lasting 1/48 of a second) between the separate still images. Neither can we see the swift motion of the electronic beam that scans the TV tube to create pictures with little points of light. The optical persistence of the still image (or the "running together" of points of light on the TV tube) combined with our delayed perception of the changes from image to image makes us believe we are witnessing real movement. Movement, in turn, is one of the most reliable indicators of life. So a chain of physical, physiological, and psychological events identifies the viewing of motion pictures with the viewing of reality.

Marcel Duchamp. *Nude Descending a Staircase, No. 2.* **1912. Philadelphia Museum of Art. The Louise and Walter Arensberg Collection**

When exhibited at the Armory Show in 1913, some smart critic called this picture "an explosion in a shingle factory." The germ of truth here is more important than its attempt at humor: Duchamp did in fact paint movement as an explosion; his painting resembles a strip of motion-picture film seen very quickly. It looks like an explosion until the projector runs it past our eyes at a speed of twenty-four frames per second.

As technology succeeded in representing motion believably, a new artistic exploitation of space and time became possible. Film artists were able to manipulate space and time for two reasons: (1) because they controlled a technology that converts time into lengths of film; and (2) because viewers identified cinematic space-time with real space-time. The cinematographer was no different from the Renaissance draftsman who could draw lines converging on a horizon and thus convince viewers that they were seeing reality in depth. The Renaissance perspectivist could speed up or slow down a viewer's optical journey by shortening or lengthening the lines moving toward the horizon. (The horizon line was also an illusion.) Similarly, cinematographers can represent the crossing of great distances or the passage of long time periods by their control of film lengths. Short distances can be extended, and brief events made to last seemingly forever. Using slow motion, reverse motion, or speeded-up motion, cinematographers have a "time machine" that lets them control pieces of reality captured on film. Through editing, or montage, they compose with film footage and, in effect, play with the viewer's perception of the "real" world. Actually, the viewer lives in *his* (the cinematographer's) world. Oddly enough, the technology that makes these things possible is primitive compared to much of modern applied science—the computer, for example. Still, it is revolutionary as far as human imaginative life is concerned. The wheel was a simple machine, too.

Film Devices   The artistic devices available to the filmmaker can be divided into two categories: (1) those that simulate the natural activity of the eye as it examines objects in space and (2) those that simulate our mental activity in experiencing the duration and quality of time.

The basic tool of cinematic space and object scanning is the *visual continuity sequence*. This consists, very simply, of the long shot, the medium or transitional shot, and the close-up. The camera imitates the eye as it scans a scene: it establishes the overall situation, selects a subject within the situation, moves closer to it, and concentrates on significant details of the subject by inspecting its details and enlarging their size on the screen—the close-up.

David W. Griffith is generally credited with the earliest use of the close-up, a device he employed sparingly but eloquently. As an aesthetic device, the

Film still from *The Sea*. Directed by Patroni Griffi. 1962

Even though cinema is a public medium, it gives us access, through the motion-picture camera, to scenes of the utmost intimacy and tenderness. The film close-up breaks the conventional distance between ourselves and other people; this nearness, plus over-lifesize imagery, creates over-lifesize emotions.

Film still from *The Loves of a Blonde*. Directed by Miloš Forman. 1967. Courtesy CCM Films, Inc.

close-up is tremendously powerful; it exaggerates the most subtle and transient visual effects, and it generates a unique sense of intimacy. The close-up, in turn, created a distinctive type of screen style—facial acting. On the cinema screen, limited facial movements acquire immense expressive meaning. In addition, the enormous enlargement of persons and objects emphasizes the tactile qualities of film imagery. Thus a director can draw attention to significant details while generating an intense awareness of their texture and slightest movement. In addition, film close-ups destroy cultural conventions about the "right" distance between a viewer and another person. As these conventions of distance are broken down, visual images generate tactile feelings that produce strong emotional reactions.

When visual continuity is established, objects and persons are located in space. However, the visual continuity sequence is only a primitive unit of the motion-picture art; it corresponds to words, phrases, and sentences in writing. By themselves, their meaning is limited; they have to be assembled and orchestrated in paragraphs and chapters to support the sort of meaning encountered in a story or a novel. We need visual narrative or plot—the combination of images in sequences that express developments *in time*.

The assembling and orchestration of images would be only decorative if it did not attempt to shape the viewer's experience of time. In films, time is *abstracted from* things and felt increasingly for its own qualities. The other visual arts—painting, sculpture, and architecture—also try to manipulate time, but they do not enjoy the technical advantages of the motion-picture or TV camera, which converts time into linear-feet of film or tape. By cutting, inserting, and splicing film, the filmmaker manipulates time more directly than the painter or sculptor. Thus the filmmaker governs the amount of time you and I spend on objects and events. The result is an extraordinary degree of control over the viewer's imaginative life for a real-time period of two hours or more.

MOTION PICTURE TERMS, DEVICES, AND TECHNIQUES

Frame Shot	A single picture on a strip of film.
Shot	The fundamental compositional unit in a film sequence; a visual unit consisting of many frames. One element in a film scene, sometimes called a "take."
Sequence	A single filmic idea consisting of one or more shots or takes. It corresponds to a paragraph in prose.
Montage	The editing of film through various sorts of cutting and dissolves.
Cut-in	Insertion of a detail, usually a close-up, taken from the main action of a film sequence.
Overlap	Repetition of action from an immediately preceding sequence at the beginning of a new sequence.
Fade-in	The gradual emergence of the film image from darkness.
Fade-out	The gradual disappearance of the film image into darkness.
Dissolve	The fade-out of one image as another image, which has been superimposed, takes its place.
Wipe	The displacement of a film image by another image or shape; it takes any direction across the screen as it erases its predecessor.
Dollying	Continuous motion of a platform-mounted camera toward or away from a subject, causing its image to grow larger or smaller on the screen.
Panning	Following the action of a subject with the camera, or moving the camera across relatively stationary objects.
Zooming	Rapid movement toward the subject by dollying or by using a zoom lens, which achieves the same effect with a stationary camera.

FILM AND TV TYPES

Like all new media, movies and television began as new ways of presenting established art, information, and entertainment forms. Film and television continue to use the older forms: the novel, the stage play, the lecture, the sermon, the magazine, the short story, the outdoor poster, the carnival sideshow, party games, and combinations of all of them. Because of this mixed and varied ancestry, the film critic Pauline Kael may have been right when she described film as "a bastard, cross-fertilized super-art."

Translated into the new media, the older art forms become documentaries, commercials, daytime serials, sitcoms, sermonettes, celebrity interviews, and game shows. To the extent that they adapt themselves to the new media, the traditional art forms acquire new aesthetic identities. This is especially true of the film documentary, the soap opera, and the TV commercial. But when the older art forms are reproduced unchanged, their aesthetic power is usually weakened. A televised lecture—the well-known talking head—can be very dull. But sometimes, skillful camera work manages to create new and exciting visual content, as in thirty-second TV "spots" for boring politicians. Thus film and TV do more than enlarge the audience for traditional forms of information and entertainment; they fundamentally change what is said and how it is seen and understood: today's media managers also manage content.

"I didn't read the book but I saw the movie." Does that mean I "know" the novel? Of course not; even the plot was probably changed in the movie. But a more fundamental change occurs when a novel becomes a film, or a magazine ad becomes a TV commercial. The basic difference lies in the organization of space—unilinear and unidirectional in the case of print; multilinear and multidirectional in the case of film. The rules for reading print are quite strict, whereas the rules for reading film are more lenient, if only because there is so much more to see. So we get more information with less effort in the film or TV presentation. Because the visual media tell several stories at once, they accomplish more than print in a given amount of space.

No wonder, then, that advertisers favor visual images over words; they get "more bang for the buck." It is a matter of selecting a superior technology for the delivery of their message. Does this mean that aesthetic values are sacrificed in the transition from old to new media? Not at all. The new media simply exercise a different set of aesthetic capacities. The film- and TV-viewing public seems to know this very well: people watch TV commercials for detergents, deodorants, and "lite" beer with a great deal of pleasure. Why? Because of the simultaneous imagery; the multidirectional organization of space on TV is very good. As for the words, no one pays any serious attention to them.

Scene from the television show *All in the Family*. Courtesy Columbia Broadcasting System

The Archie Bunker family eating, talking, and complaining all at once. Small as it is, the TV tube manages to carry a great deal of simultaneous action, dialogue, and detail. How? By using old-fashioned pictorial composition; the same grouping of figures can be found in nineteenth-century genre painting. Of course, Archie has a great nineteenth-century mind.

FILMED VERSUS TELEVISED IMAGERY

The technical differences between filmed and televised imagery can be exaggerated. Both media use basically similar tools: the creation of images with light and the realistic reproduction of motion. Of course, there are differences in accuracy of color, the size of their pictures, and the quality of their images. Also, we view each medium under different circumstances. Still, these differences will probably be minimized by technical improvements in television, which, in any case, relies heavily on the broadcasting of film. In all likelihood, the media will converge because both are responsive to one central drive: the convincing representation of reality on a flat surface.

A fundamental difference between filmed and televised imagery lies in their social effects, which, in turn, grow out of differences in their modes of production, distribution, and presentation. These differences account for the special qualities of television: representation and transmission are simultaneous; only TV permits us to witness events immediately—as they occur. When viewing a "live" telecast, we know we are "there," and this knowledge becomes a factor in our aesthetic experience. However, motion-picture film must be processed; there is a time lapse between an event and its presentation to the public. This provides opportunities to heighten or isolate events through editing. Accordingly, film is the more "artistic" of the two media, whereas television seems to be more "historical." TV news can be edited to

left: **Film still from *Potemkin*: woman holding wounded child. Directed by Sergei Eisenstein. 1926. Courtesy Rosa Madell Film Library. Artkino Pictures, Inc.**

Eisenstein's films are designed visually. Their emotional and ideological impacts rely on more than the accumulation of realistic detail. They are composed like the pictorial masterpieces of Goya and Picasso.

right: **Pablo Picasso. Detail of *Guernica*. 1937. The Prado, Madrid**

Photograph from a *Dick Cavett Show*. From left: Noel Coward, Cavett, Lynn Fontanne, and Alfred Lunt. 1970. Courtesy Daphne Productions, Inc., New York

The collective TV interview has become an electronic version of an old, perhaps obsolete social form—conversation. Emphasis is on the glamour, opinions, and wit of famous guests. The popularity of the genre demonstrates the effectiveness of the medium in exploiting more-or-less spontaneous human interactions.

445

shape the record, but there is less time for subtle manipulation of events and contexts.

Motion pictures are normally seen by a large audience, although it is possible to attend private screenings. Accordingly, films are planned with the expectation of group responses. Television shows are also intended for groups—millions of viewers—but often they are seen by individuals alone or by the family alone. So, television cannot depend on a large audience to influence viewer response. Unfortunately, television often tries to *simulate* large audience response with recorded noise and laughter or by televising performances before live audiences recruited to be heard and seen. Here, TV tries to reproduce the experience of theater, but the result feels false.

The closeness of television to living events is best exploited in sports coverage and news reporting in general. Here TV demonstrates its superiority over the old filmed newsreel, which reached an audience only after it had learned about events through radio and the newspapers. However, our awareness of the simultaneous TV coverage and transmission can give us a false idea about the accuracy of the medium. (The same is true of photography.) We tend to believe in the truth of what we see—compared to spoken or written accounts—and may not realize that events can be staged, abbreviated, or isolated from context while appearing photographically accurate.

The public has not yet built adequate defenses against partial or biased TV presentations. Ironically, our political life is endangered by the same source that deepens and extends our historical experience. Although we know more about what is happening, too much of what we know is wrong, slanted, or out of context. Perhaps it is only in televised sports events that we can suspend historical judgment and surrender to the purely aesthetic pleasures of a magnificent visual medium. As for the news—especially political reporting on TV—it needs to be supplemented by outside reading.

FILMS AND DREAMS

The darkened theater; a soft, comfortable seat; controlled temperature and humidity; and thousands of shadowy images moving across the screen—these strongly suggest the dream world. Cinema can be thought of as the manufacture of synthetic dreams. Psychological experiments reveal that individuals deprived of dreams—allowed to sleep but awakened when they begin to dream—move into a psychotic state. Clearly, dreaming is a biological and cultural necessity; in some mysterious way our human psychobiological equipment is purged and regenerated while we sleep. Our sanity is maintained, it seems, by a curious, illogical flow of images called dreams. But why do we need dreams during the waking state?

It might be argued that art has always served mankind as an alternative source of dreams. That is, we have always manufactured visions to supplement our real dreams. Science may not be able to demonstrate that dream-deprived individuals are satisfied by artificial dreams such as those evoked by pictures and films. Or perhaps such experiments have not been attempted. But speculation does not have to be carried that far: from the evidence of art history, daydreaming, and our obsession with film and television viewing, it is plain that people have a strong need for a waking fantasy life.

Here, it is the technical resemblance of films to dreams that arouses our interest. One of the first uses of motion-picture photography was in the study of animal movement. Today, films have great value as tools of scientific investigation. But that is not the use which has stimulated their highest development. Films have moved steadily in the direction of imitating the kind of perception associated with our imaginative life. Indeed, it is possible that film and TV images are technically superior to the images—the dreams—we build inside our heads.

Apparently, our civilization, which has created the most complex technology in history, needs to create dream-generating devices for the people

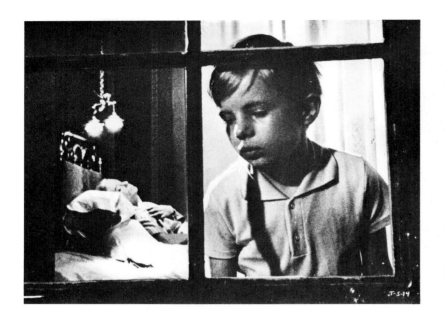

who use that technology. In other words, the need for synthetic dreams grows in direct proportion to the growth of complex technical systems in our work, play, and interpersonal relations. The dreams we create biologically have to be supplemented by dream machines so we can maintain some sort of human balance, or sanity, in our culture. Perhaps this explains the invention in the twentieth century of two major art forms—cinema and television—both of which simulate our dream-life. The timing of these inventions does not seem to be an accident.

THE DEMOCRACY OF FILM

Film and television tend to eliminate distinctions based on money or class, because access to them is relatively inexpensive. But they are democratic in a more fundamental sense; every seat in a motion-picture theater is equal. That is, each viewer sees the same imagery; film actors cannot play to the boxes; seats in the balcony are as good as seats in the orchestra; sound is audible throughout the house. As for TV, despite a certain amount of family scrambling, each viewer has a prime location. Film or TV imagery tends to devour the space between the screen or tube and the viewer; each member of the audience feels that the performance is being played for him or her alone. Furthermore, the moving camera has a compelling power to lead the viewer's eye into its represented spaces and places. We forget our physical location as we enter cinema space. Happily, there is room in it for everyone.

Close-ups, especially, eliminate the distance between actors and audience—a distance that is social as well as spatial. Early in the film industry, this produced the star system and the phenomenon of the fan who takes a deep personal interest in the lives of actors. More important, cinema encourages very active processes of psychological identification; film and television audiences experience life-styles that are not necessarily available to them in reality. But film fantasies can become economic and cultural facts. As people "enjoy" products and services normally reserved for the rich and successful, they acquire tastes for products and services that they want to satisfy in their real lives.

Obviously, the democracy of film can lead to commercial exploitation, but it can also play more constructive roles. The first lies in its educational influence on the lives of illiterate or impoverished people. Cinema gives them access to types of personal and social behavior normally associated with educated persons. Film and TV viewing may not solve basic problems of igno-

left: **Film still from** *The Silence:* **boy in room of dying aunt. Directed by Ingmar Bergman. 1962. Courtesy Janus Films, Inc.**

Two Scandinavian masters using the same device to express the pain of dying and living. The tension between old and young is rendered in the stark contrast between horizontality and verticality.

right: **Edvard Munch.** *The Dead Mother.* **1899–1900. Kunsthalle, Bremen**

Film still from *The Grapes of Wrath:* **the Joad Family. Directed by John Ford. 1940. © 1949. Twentieth Century-Fox Film Corp.**

Every generation and every group need their own image—the mythic or historical account of their founding. For the displaced Southern and Midwestern farmers of the 1930s, that account was provided by John Ford's version of Steinbeck's novel. Using a realistic style based on the documentaries of Pare Lorentz, Ford fashioned a classic epic of migration and resettlement on a continental scale.

left: **Film still from *The African Queen*: Katharine Hepburn and Humphrey Bogart. Directed by John Huston. 1951. Horizon, United Artists**

The test of a very good film image: it tells us a great deal about her, about him, and about them—without words.

right: **Film still from *Kramer vs. Kramer*: Dustin Hoffman and Justin Henry. Directed by Robert Benton. 1979. Stanley Jaffe Productions, Columbia**

Again, the silent image speaks volumes: mother isn't there; daddy is new to shopping; the little boy's thoughts are far away. Notice how ironically this plays against the screaming soapbox graphics: BOLD (Hoffman is cautious); DASH (both of them seem to be dream-walking); JOY (no one is happy).

rance and poverty, but it is probably the chief contributor to a desire for change—personal as well as social and political change.

A second democratizing result of films and television applies mainly to advanced industrial societies—the capacity to generate a large-scale sense of community and social cohesion. Television, especially, unites the alienated citizens of a depersonalized mass society. As spectators of the same media events, millions share a common set of actual and imaginative experiences. It is especially through televised events that the masses have an opportunity to recognize and validate powerful symbols of communal anxiety, hope, and achievement. Without these events, it would be difficult to satisfy our need for identification with a community larger than the family or the neighborhood—social units that appear to be increasingly fragmented and temporary. So, apart from their merits as art, the moving-picture media perform a vital civic function: they help create a national community out of millions of separate, more or less isolated, viewers.

THE CRITICAL APPRECIATION OF CINEMA

Despite a vast literature devoted to the film—historical, technical, and sociological—very little material tells viewers how to look at films for increased pleasure and understanding. Critics give us plot summaries; they praise or condemn actors and directors; and they publish anthologies of their best writing. Most of all, they discourse learnedly on the theory of filmmaking. But interesting though it is, this literature does not tell viewers how to look at films, how to enjoy them as art.

Our approach is based on one theoretical assumption: whatever else it is, film is fundamentally a visual medium. Such great film directors as Eisenstein, Bergman, and Fellini are supreme visual artists. This means that our critical approach to the other visual arts applies to film as well. After all, movies are like other pictures in many ways; they are still seen on flat surfaces within a rectangular frame.

But what about the elements of time and motion? Are they not genuinely new factors that have led to the creation of a genuinely new art form? Yes, provided we recognize that time and motion in the film are illusions created by still images. Again, look at a strip of motion-picture film. From our standpoint, a film is as good (or bad) as the sum of impressions made on us by those thousands of little images that constitute its shots and sequences.

We may remember a film's dialogue and sound effects, its actors' voices and diction, the physical interaction of the characters, the development of its

Film still from *La Dolce Vita*: party scene. Directed by Federico Fellini. 1960

The combined man-and-woman forms are skillfully used here to suggest animality—the loss of human dignity in Fellini's image and a crude parody of physical love in the Antonioni image.

Film still from *Blow-Up*: photographer and model. Directed by Michelangelo Antonioni. 1966. © Metro-Goldwyn-Mayer, Inc., 1966

below: **Nam June Paik. Charlotte Moorman wearing *TV Bra for Living Sculpture*. 1969. Photo © 1969 by Peter Moore, New York**

The bra consists of two small television sets fastened to Ms. Moorman's body. As she plays the cello, the TV images change in response to the musical vibrations. This is video art—high-tech and old-tech joined to create a new kind of visual imagery. The arrangement is ingenious, to be sure, but as for the pictures themselves . . .

plot. Obviously, these are important aesthetic components of a film experience—auditory, literary, and dramatic. Still, it is visual imagery that converts sounds, words, and movements into the phenomenon we call *a film*. We may not remember what Bogey said to Lauren Bacall (people often get it wrong), but we cannot forget how they looked.

One final point: study of films, talk about films, and writing about films takes place *after we have seen* a film. This means that film criticism is something we do with *remembered* images. Here a book is useful: it can reproduce certain images—still images, of course—to help us recollect and concentrate on our film experience. That is what we have done here, modestly, in a context provided by the other arts. I hope the lesson is not lost: the criticism of film art, like the criticism of painting or photography, begins with the examination of visual images.

CONCLUSION

Writing in *The New Yorker* about film, television, and literature, the critic Michael Arlen recently said: "The audience for the serious music of language seems to be drifting away, as if mesmerized by paintings, photographs, moving pictures, videotape—by the new power of visual imagery." He spoke also of a "childish battle . . . between the print and visual interests . . . in which the visual team now appears to have the upper hand." Then he concluded that "the real issue remains in doubt: respect for man and his art." Arlen sounds unhappy about the closing of a cultural gap, the equalization of the visual and verbal arts in our media of communication and expression. He fears that fine literature is taking a beating from the visual media, and, as a result, the prospects for art and humanity don't look very good.

A major premise of this book is that the visual arts—including the newer media of photography, film, and television—have been engaged in restoring balance to a cultural situation that has grown badly out of kilter. Over the centuries the dominance of printed words in our arts of communication and expression has produced an underdevelopment of our visual sense and, perhaps, a distortion of consciousness itself. The rise of today's visual media does not mean that civilization will revert to barbarism. It is just that new and almost forgotten forms of power are being developed. When these forms are fully developed and understood, it is unlikely that our visual sense will ever be so powerfully repressed again.

Film still from *La Dolce Vita*: Christ figure suspended from a helicopter. Directed by Federico Fellini. 1960

In one of the great symbolic sequences of film art, Fellini defines modern decadence. Cynical promoters exploit popular religious feeling by staging a fake miracle. Fellini includes himself among the promoters: he, too, creates spectacles and encourages people to believe in them. That is what a filmmaker does.

PART FIVE

THE PROBLEMS OF ART CRITICISM

Most of us think we are art critics. At least, we deliver critical opinions regardless of what we know about art or art theory. Perhaps this is because in a democracy citizens are encouraged to believe their views on any subject have equal weight, just as their votes count equally in politics. As a result, there is a great deal of heat generated in critical discussions of art—especially contemporary art. Here we would like to add some light to that heat. Unfortunately, in our educational system, very little time is devoted to developing a foundation for practicing criticism. Well-informed persons—even artists—find themselves delivering opinions that have been foisted on them, or offering their views without knowing how they came to hold them. When it comes to art criticism, most people seem to rely on instinct.

In an effort to approach the subject rationally, the next two chapters are devoted to critical theory and method. My main goal is to give viewers a commonsense approach to the business of forming interpretations and making judgments about works of art. Although there are no permanently correct interpretations and evaluations of particular artworks, there are systematic procedures for going about the work of criticism. We should know what those procedures are and be able to use them. At least we should be able to defend the way we arrive at our opinions.

Whatever else it is, criticism is something we *do*. It is a practical activity (with theoretical underpinnings) in which it is possible to gain proficiency. But first we need to know what criticism is for, what different kinds of critics do, and how critics justify their judgments. Finally, we need critical procedures that work—procedures that advance our understanding of art without spoiling the fun of looking at it.

Vernon L. Smith. *Looking at John Chamberlain's* **Essex** *(1960) at the Guggenheim Museum.* **1972. New York Times Pictures**

Everyone does criticism but not everyone does it well. Is this because some of us have a "good ear" for art while the rest of us are tone deaf? No. Can we get better with study and practice? Yes. Do artists make the best critics? Not necessarily. What about art historians? Same answer. Then who can be trusted? You must judge that for yourself.

CHAPTER FIFTEEN

THE THEORY OF ART CRITICISM

T he chief goal of art criticism is understanding. We need a way of looking at art objects that will yield a maximum of insight into their meanings and merits. Although a work of art yields information to the trained viewer, we are primarily interested in how that information is related to its excellence. For this reason, archaeological, historical, and biographical data *about* art and artists may be interesting but not necessarily useful in art criticism. Our main goal is to understand the causes *in* the work of the effect it has upon us.

A second goal of art criticism—perhaps as important as the first—is pleasure or delight. To be sure, we get pleasure from understanding, from knowing what it is in art that causes our gratification. The trained viewer should also be able to experience more of the satisfactions a work is capable of yielding; criticism enables us to carry on the search systematically. The satisfactions we get from art depend on two things: the quality of the object itself and our capacity to use our own experience in seeing it. So art criticism should increase pleasure while teaching us to focus our knowledge and experience in an aesthetic situation.

Some people think that serious study of art kills the pleasures it can yield. Perhaps they think that too much knowledge—about art or love—is deadening. Some kinds of art scholarship seem to confirm those fears. But the information sought by critics is mainly about the sources of their satisfaction, about the bearing of a work on their world, and the meaning of their existence in it. As we look at art we may discover that we are stimulated or depressed, frightened or excited, angered or soothed. Then, being human and curious, we want to know why.

But the search for meaning and pleasure is not the only function of art criticism: we have a real desire to share what we have found. It is very difficult to know or enjoy something without thinking about the reactions of someone else. That is probably why we talk about art, music, films, and books: we want to find out whether others have the same responses. Or we may want to persuade them to accept our interpretations and opinions. So there is always a social motive in criticism—assuming that, whatever else it may be, *art criticism is talk about art*.

Why do we enjoy talking about art? Because it is one of the best ways to

Jack Levine. *The Art Lover.* **1962. National Collection of Fine Arts, Smithsonian Institution, Washington, D.C.**

A caricature of the aesthete: his standards are so high that he doesn't like anything. Actually, liking and disliking are only minor features of criticism; the important task is to *understand* a work, and that requires interest, sympathy, and imagination. If we can't understand the work, we can't judge it.

communicate our feelings without embarrassment. That may be why few people can resist the impulse to deliver critical judgments: we want others to *know* us in a special way. But the great critics have more than a desire to talk; they have an unusually rich and varied capacity for aesthetic pleasure. By disclosing their discoveries they enlarge our capacities for understanding and delight. In this sense, art criticism is like teaching; it is the communication of ideas about art—and often about life, the soil in which art is nourished.

One commonly accepted purpose of criticism is to make a statement of the worth or rank of an art object. Indeed, the purposes mentioned above may be considered preliminary to judging "how good" a work is. Here we face a persistent human tendency—the need to say that something is "better than" or "worth more than" something else. This probably derives from our wish to possess what is valuable, a very human motive that may account for the development of art criticism as a serious discipline.

So we need a sound foundation for judging what is good, better, and best. Why? Because we want to feel secure about what we like. Furthermore, fame, wealth, and prestige are rooted in our critical judgments. To some extent, art history began as an effort to sort out artists and artworks. Then, as the "greatness" of artists was established, the discipline developed ingenious ways of determining the authenticity of artworks, especially when dealers wanted to sell them. If a work could be attributed to an important master, it would be *worth* a great deal in money. (Money values and aesthetic values are not complete strangers.) But scholars found that in answering questions of origin and authenticity, they learned much that is *humanistically* valuable. The history and criticism of art became disciplines that enabled us to see connections between art and the major patterns of human thought and behavior.

Collectors are involved in criticism, too, since their purchases confirm their own or someone else's critical judgment; all the activities surrounding the buying, selling, and display of art have critical significance. Criticism carried on by reviewers and journalists in newspapers and magazines and—by implication—in galleries and museums influences what artists create. This leads to an interesting result: criticism affects the production of what it criticizes. Artists need the support of the public, whose expectations have been shaped and defined by critics. In their pursuit of recognition, they try to discover the critical standards by which they will be judged in the places where they wish to be admired.

Criticism may begin with the need to understand and enjoy art, but it ends with the formulation of ideas and opinions that act as standards for artistic creation. We may not have set out to influence what artists create, but in teaching art, talking about art, and buying art, we bring critical standards into being. These standards shift, of course, and they are difficult to formulate with precision. Nevertheless, a process of critical communication seems to be constantly at work. In one way or another, all of us participate in an activity that affects the politics, the economics, and the aesthetics of art. So we need to do the job of criticism with as much integrity as we can muster.

THE TOOLS OF ART CRITICISM

What kind of equipment does a critic need in order to function adequately? What must we know, what skills must we have, what experience is needed to be a critic?

Obviously, wide acquaintance with art—especially the kind we expect to judge—is fundamental. Usually, this is acquired through study, especially of art history. It is important that this knowledge be gained through seeing original works of art as well as reproductions. Also, it helps to see student work, unfinished work, even "bad" work. Artists have a considerable advantage here: they can recognize errors of technique that theoreticians often miss. Acquaintance with masterpieces seen in color slides is fine, but not enough by itself. We have to go to galleries and museums and studios. All over the world, if possible. Seeing the world's art is the best excuse for leaving home.

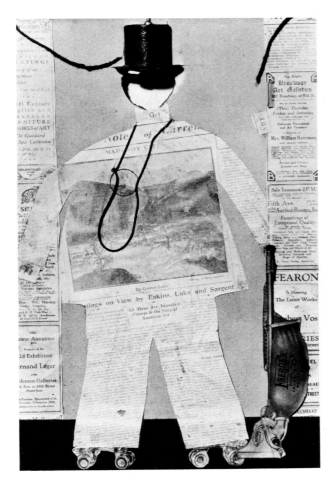

Arthur G. Dove. *The Critic.* 1925. Terry Dintenfass Gallery, New York. Arthur G. Dove Estate

The artist's mischievous image of the critic—a ridiculous, top-hatted figure who rides around the galleries on roller skates wielding a vacuum cleaner.

Knowing about art implies more than visual recognition of the monuments of art history. It also calls for understanding the styles and functions of art, the social and cultural contexts in which artists have worked, the technical factors that affect artistic execution in various media. The chief benefit of a broad acquaintance with art is breadth of taste. A critic should appreciate a wide range of artistic creativity as a defense against critical narrowness—the tendency to employ standards based on a meager knowledge of styles and limited experience with technical methods. Fortunately, we have access—through reproductions and travel—to art created throughout the world. This was not possible for most people only a few generations ago. As a result, our standards of art criticism are richer and more complex (or they *should* be) than those of our grandparents.

Artists would probably have more respect for critics if their judgments were based on artistic experience. Of course, some critics have had this experience, and some are artists themselves. But most criticism is done by persons with mainly literary and theoretical preparation. Still, scholars have an advantage: they are presumably free of the rivalry, partisanship, or jealousy that can color artists' opinions of other artists' work. Some have argued that artists are constitutionally incapable of judging their peers objectively—a harsh judgment in itself. The question will probably be argued as long as there are artists and critics. For a long time, colleges and universities employed only theoreticians to teach art. Today, happily, they employ theoreticians *and* practitioners—persons who often have both kinds of training.

Critics with only theoretical preparation are poorly equipped to assess quality of execution in works of art. Some have a tendency to denigrate technical facility; they think of it as superficial, and often they do not recognize faulty craftsmanship. The art world is regularly embarrassed when the work of amateurs, practical jokers, and animals is given serious attention (or prizes!) in art exhibitions. These stunts—probably intended to ridicule modern art—have little to do with the achievement of serious artists. Nevertheless, they constitute a scandal in the practice of art criticism; certainly they raise questions about the competence of some critics. In an effort to be fair and open to all forms of artistic expression, some critics simply abdicate their role. To be more than art publicists or promoters, critics must be reasonably good judges of artistic technique; technique plays a major role in determining form; and form is inseparable from content. Without *some* technical expertise, our critical judgments may be entertaining but hardly defensible, except as literature.

Another requirement of the critic might be called "breadth of sensibility." This designates the capacity to respond to a wide range of artistic expression. We know that individuals vary in the kind and quality of emotion they feel in connection with real-life events. Likewise, they vary in capacity for feelings encountered in art. Critics, however, must have access to a generous range of aesthetic emotion; they must be supple in the realm of feelings and ideas; otherwise, their usefulness is limited. It is possible that many of our differences of opinion about art are due to restricted sensibility or limited capacity for aesthetic perception. Enlarging and deepening our responses to art—extending our aesthetic range—is a humanly enriching enterprise. That is why the development of critical capacity should be one of the main goals of a liberal education.

Of course, a critic is more than an empty slate. He or she carries a host of biases and unconscious preferences. So another item of critical equipment might be called *judicious temperament*. This means the ability to withhold judgment until all the aesthetic evidence is in. Many of us make judgments too quickly: we state conclusions and then look for reasons to justify them. A judicious temperament, however, allows time for sensations, impressions, associations, and half-formed valuations to interact; it permits our intelligence to carry out the work of sifting, sorting, and organizing. When we examine a work of art, our feelings are being skillfully assaulted; so we need time to exercise logic and rationality. In art, or in a court of law, there should be no "rush to judgment."

TYPES OF ART CRITICISM

Although we speak of a person called an art critic, there are in fact several kinds of critic, differing according to the social or professional role each performs. The most familiar type is probably the *journalistic* critic—someone who writes reviews of exhibitions, plays, books, and concerts. There are several varieties within this category; sometimes a newspaper employs only one reporter to "do" art, music, and drama criticism. Those journalists might better be called "art writers." On the other hand, an art magazine may employ a number of critics with specialized art backgrounds. Another kind of criticism takes place in schools, colleges, and universities—wherever art is taught. This criticism, conducted by teachers, might be called *pedagogical* criticism; spoken rather than written, it has tremendous influence. In addition, there is *scholarly* criticism, which appears mainly in learned journals; it can affect artistic production and art collecting, though somewhat indirectly. There is also the *popular* criticism conducted by lay people. They clearly constitute the majority of critics, and although they vary in expertise, their opinions cannot be ignored.

Finally, the artist, too, is a critic. Every decision he or she makes has a critical dimension. The creative act is one of continuous revision, that is, acceptance or rejection of forms and meanings in the light of the artist's expressive goals and critical standards. This subject—the artist's use of mental images and ideals during the process of creation—would be worth a book in itself.

Following is a more detailed examination of the critical types outlined above.

Journalistic Criticism   The main point about journalistic criticism is that it is a category of news. It is meant to inform readers about events in the art world and to retain their loyalty to a particular newspaper or journal. Usually, we read a "review"—a brief summary of an exhibition; it is rarely long enough to constitute a systematic analysis of the works in a show. Indeed, there is a style of review writing that endeavors to create verbal equivalents of the artworks in an exhibition. Obviously, criticism that reports the news and tries to substitute words for visual and aesthetic experience—while also giving critical judgments—labors under an impossible burden. Usually, the brevity of journalistic criticism forces the writer to eliminate analysis and to rely on critical conclusions to create exciting copy. Unfortunately, this kind of writing also appears in longer magazine articles where there is less excuse for pages and pages of long-winded opinion and speculation passing as critical analysis.

Still, considering that journalists have to satisfy the curiosity of many readers and have to describe works their readers have not seen, some fine critical writing can be found in newspapers and newsmagazines. Specialized monthly journals have the space to go further: they engage in aesthetic debates, promulgate a "party line," or scold museums and foundations for failing to support their favorite artists. But they serve a good purpose. They stoke the fires of critical controversy, and by expressing their biases forcefully, they help create the atmosphere of striving and rivalry that artists, collectors, and the general public seem to require.

Journalistic critics write under pressure of deadlines, so their output can suffer from the perils of much newswriting: inaccuracy, hasty conclusions, the substitution of opinion for analysis, and a tendency to be witty at the artist's expense. But discriminating readers learn to discount the errors and biases in advance. Or they compensate by reading several critics, comparing them for accuracy. Best of all, they try to see art shows personally. Without these safeguards, our critical understanding would consist of trendy opinions about the principal current reputations. Coteries and intrigues are not unknown in the art world; art journalism is certainly part of the endless jockeying for position that characterizes a realm where talented people struggle for recognition. So we can use journalism for news while reserving critical judgment for ourselves.

Pedagogical Criticism   The purpose of pedagogical criticism is to advance the artistic and aesthetic maturity of students. Beyond rendering judgments of their work it should enable students to make judgments themselves. To do this well, the teacher of art must be familiar with the art of beginners and amateurs as well as "museum art." The art of young and old; naive and sophisticated art; the art of the technically adept and the technically inept; the art of trailblazers and plodders, innovators and imitators: art teachers must know them all. Pedagogical criticism calls for tremendous range.

An important task of the teacher of art, one that demands great sensitivity and critical skill, is the analysis and interpretation of a student's work *to the student*. This is how students learn to analyze and interpret their own work; this is how advanced students learn to see the direction their work is taking. For beginning students, an instructor functions as a critic *during* the process of execution. Student work, therefore, represents a delicate kind of critical collaboration, a collaboration that should not become a form of artistic dependency.

In the past students sought out teachers whose art they admired and wished to imitate. Most of them wanted criticism to inculcate the standards visible in an artist-teacher's work. As a result, a teacher would often reproduce his artistic personality endlessly among his students. Robert Henri (1865–1929) was an exception; he had strong artistic views, but his instruction did not constrict the growth of students. Thomas Hart Benton (1889–1975), on the other hand, produced "little Bentons," as if on an assembly line. Either from the force of his personality or the narrowness of his vision, he dominated his students technically and aesthetically. Jackson Pollock was one of them; his early work was touchingly Bentonesque. But as history shows, he changed. The lesson here is that strong teachers can nurture a student, strangle a student, or create the foundation for a lifelong rebellion.

Today's philosophy of pedagogical criticism seems to call for a certain amount of restraint on the part of the artist-teacher. Its main goal is to assist in the development of critical standards *within* the student—standards that are compatible with the student's emerging artistic personality. Yet the art teacher worth his or her salt has strong convictions, too. So achieving the right blend of qualities in a teacher is not easy; we need a combined father, mother, and midwife who possesses well-developed artistic skills, great powers of aesthetic discrimination, plus the ability to recognize genius in others.

Scholarly Criticism   Scholarly art criticism is the fully developed product of long study, specialization, and refined critical sensibility. Its function is to provide the kind of analysis, interpretation, and evaluation that academic detachment makes possible. In other words, it takes time. For the living artist, scholarly criticism represents an approximation of "the judgment of history." Settled in the safety of academic tenure and undergirded by traditions of scrupulous research and disinterested truth-seeking, scholarly critics are in a position to render the informed and sensitive judgment that serious art deserves. Unfortunately, not all artists live to see that judgment, but it is reassuring to know that it will eventually come to light.

Academic critics often reexamine styles and reputations that have been categorized and set aside. Since each era has its characteristic way of seeing, artists who were scorned in their own day may be shown to have fresh meaning now. Museums perform this function when they resurrect the reputation

above: Thomas Hart Benton. *Arts of the West.* 1932. The New Britain Museum of American Art, New Britain, Connecticut. Harriet Russell Stanley Fund

Early in his career Pollock fell under the Benton spell. We can see what he got from his teacher: the extreme contrasts of light and dark; the torn, jagged contours; the explosive composition; the taste for violent action.

right: Jackson Pollock. *Untitled.* c. 1936. Collection Mrs. Lee Krasner Pollock, New York

of an artist, a school, or a style that has fallen into disesteem. Think of the current vogue for Art Deco—a style that was considered of only minor decorative value; today, it is having a lively revival. We should remember, however, that the history of art does not repeat itself identically. Originally (during the 1930s), Art Deco was part of a very progressive thrust in the arts of design; today, it is bathed in nostalgia, a nostalgia colored mauve, dusty rose, off-white, and teal blue. Why have we rediscovered these colors? Because a few scholars and critics decided they had meaning for our time.

Popular Criticism Any discussion of art takes place against a background of criticism by the public at large. Average citizens continue to judge art whether we think they are qualified or not. Therefore, the existence of a large body of popular critical opinion has to be considered in its effect on the total art situation. We should also remember that the general public does not consist entirely of fools. As Mark Twain said: "The public is the only critic whose opinion is worth anything at all."

If critical opinion influences what artists create, we have to consider popular as well as elite criticism. The concept of an avant-garde, of a body of artists working in advance of popular taste, assumes the existence of masses of people who are too sluggish and dull to keep up with the latest thing. But if it were not for these dull people and their backward tastes, there would be nothing for the avant-garde to rebel against! Actually, the idea of progress in art—of advanced and retarded taste—is a myth: it confuses progress in history with progress in aesthetics. Nevertheless, that myth has considerable influence, especially among those who think of art as a branch of the fashion industry.

Popular criticism changes very little; it judges art in terms of its representational power. Most people believe normal vision is adequate equipment for the conduct of art criticism. The critical consensus of these people is consistent through history, so their standards cannot be easily ignored: they want art to be faithful to the visual facts. We have discussed this type of art in connection with the style of objective accuracy (Chapter Four). Today, photography and film satisfy the popular desire for visual truth; indirectly, this gives artists a good reason for departing from purely optical realism. But abandoning reality entirely seems to be something that popular criticism will never forgive.

Perhaps aesthetic education will enable people to discriminate among the various types of realism. It should not be impossible to see the difference between styles of unselective, mechanical realism and styles that portray the character, the inner existence, of persons and places, objects and events, while remaining faithful to their surfaces. Within its own standards of fidelity to human vision, popular criticism can become wise and discriminating; it is a matter of having access to a full range of visual options.

KINDS OF CRITICAL JUDGMENT

How do critics justify their evaluations? Or do they judge art intuitively? Do they measure each work against a master they happen to admire? Or do they have general standards, formulated in advance, for judging each new work of art?

From our standpoint, it would be well if critics withheld judgment until they had carried out the preliminary tasks of description, analysis, and interpretation. After that, judging would be more responsive to the character of the art object. But when they "rush to judgment," certain ideas of excellence seem to underlie what they say is good. Following are the main ones.

Formalism   Once we have abandoned the notion that great art is the skillful imitation of appearances, we can turn to what is called formalist criticism. Here excellence is located in visual organization—in the relationships among the visual elements of an artwork regardless of labels, associations, or symbolic meanings.

For a formalist, successful relationships are *designed;* they result from an artist's calculation and planning rather than a viewer's subjective tendencies. Artists such as Poussin, Cézanne, or Mondrian appeal to the formalist because they minimize accidental effects; they aim deliberately at a harmony of forms. We have no uncertainty about the artist's purpose or method: it is to create a work that does not depend on "extraneous," that is, nonartistic, considerations to be effective.

Formalist excellence does not require a geometric, a hard-edge, or an abstract style. For example, Poussin gives us softly rounded representational forms moving in naturalistic space. But his compositions, considered as a whole, are organized so that the main shapes, masses, and directions are related to each other with remarkable precision: every tree, hill, and figure has been measured, weighed, and balanced. So we witness a perfect reconciliation of visual forces; we experience a pleasure that must be like that of an accountant auditing a perfect set of books.

Formalist critics can find interest in subject matter; they can learn about religion, history, or politics from the persons and objects represented in artworks. However, they consider an artwork excellent only insofar as its *form*, its underlying organization, is responsible for their enjoyment. For example, they must admire the bronze-metal skin of Mies van der Rohe's Seagram Building, not just because bronze is inherently beautiful, but because the bronze parts have the right dimensions and are located at the right intervals in relation to the window size, the color of the tinted glass, the overall shape of the building, and the size of the space around it.

Formalist criticism takes an interest in craftsmanship, since putting things together carefully and working them to the "right" degree of finish suggests a search for pleasing relationships. But craftsmanship is based on the logical and economic use of tools and materials—essentially utilitarian concerns. The formalist responds to this logic only if it produces results that seem to harmonize great forces in the universe. In other words, the formalist wants works of art to depend solely on the principle of *unity in variety*. The unity or harmony or *beauty* of the artwork should be a kind of grand reconciliation—like the unified field theory that Einstein never quite discovered.

Formalism has had a healthy influence on art mainly in its negative teaching, that is, when it has insisted on the unimportance of literary or historical association as vehicles of aesthetic meaning. But on the positive side, formalism has trouble in establishing what its idea of excellence is. That is, how do we know which formal relationships are pleasing or significant? The formalist critics Roger Fry and Clive Bell never really specified the criteria of formal excellence. Mainly, they told us what it is not. Their expression, "significant form," sounds good but it doesn't help much in doing criticism.

If pressed, the formalist might say that an organization is good when it embodies the ideal structural possibilities of the forms we see in it. ("Structural" is an acceptable word for formalists to use since it has no literary or historical associations.) But how do we *know* when a visual organization embodies the *ideal* possibilities of its components? Here, formalists must fall back on the quality of their perceptions—that is, they must feel that their perceptions in the presence of the work are inherently satisfying. Bernard Berenson relied on formalist ideas of aesthetic value when he employed the term "life-enhancing" to describe the most important characteristic of art. This term (which is really an elegant way of saying "good") represents a viewer's conviction that great art makes us feel stronger, more confident, or more vigorous. It does this *regardless* of subject matter.

The qualities we call "beautiful" or "life-enhancing" are presumably the qualities any sensitive and intelligent person would consider pleasing. In other words, there are *norms* or *ideal standards* in art which connect with something in us that seeks such norms. Thus we come to a theory of communication that underlies the formalist's idea of excellence. He believes there is an ideal or perfect embodiment of all things, and that excellent art reveals or *communicates* that ideal—to certain people. Who are they? They are persons who, because of their biological, psychological, and cultural makeup, can recognize and enjoy ideal form. This sounds like a circular argument, and it is. Formalism is ultimately a philosophy of art that enables certain people to realize that they like the same things or the same combinations of qualities.

Many artists and critics are formalists without knowing it. Their ideas of excellence are based on intuitive feelings of sympathy with the organization of an art object. Perhaps those feelings come from affirmative signals received from their glandular, nervous, and muscular systems. But, as mentioned above, formalism provides us with a guide to the values it rejects as aesthetically irrelevant: social and historical information, literary and emotional association, mechanical imitation of objects and surfaces. Beyond that, it offers us the form preferences of the normal person—the sensitive and cultured normal person. Artists and critics have to hope they fall into that category.

Expressivism Expressivist criticism sees excellence as the ability of art to communicate ideas and feelings vividly, intensely, and truly. It is not especially interested in formal organization for its own sake. Children's art offers a

opposite above: Nicolas Poussin. *Landscape with the Burial of Phocion.* 1648. Hôtel Matignon, Paris

opposite below: Fernand Léger. *Nudes in the Forest.* 1909–10. Kröller-Müller Museum, Otterlo, The Netherlands

above: Paul Cézanne. *Lac d'Annecy.* 1896. Courtauld Institute Galleries, London

THE FORMALIST AS PAINTER

First, the formalist tries to capture nature within a measured, orderly framework (Poussin); next he tries to represent nature's vitality without losing control of its underlying structure (Cézanne); finally, he fits nature into his vision of the universe as a perfect machine (Léger).

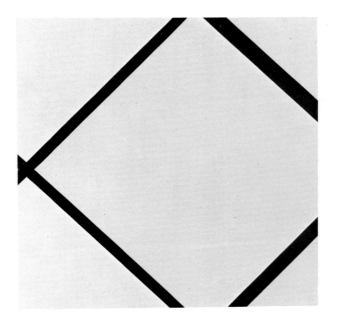

Piet Mondrian. *Painting, I.* **1926. Collection, The Museum of Modern Art, New York. Katherine S. Dreier Bequest**

The formalist sensibility. To understand this work, we measure and compare forms: lengths, thicknesses, angles, convergences, and divergences. We do this with the negative spaces, too. When all the measuring and comparing are done, we can examine our feelings of balance and imbalance, tension and harmony, action and repose. Some bodily responses are involved, but they are based almost wholly on our optical activity. The experience has nothing to do with history, religion, philosophy, sociology, or politics.

Drawing by a four-year-old child

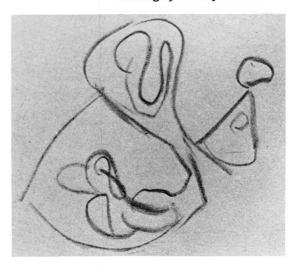

Paul Klee. *Shame.* **1933. Paul Klee Foundation, Kunstmuseum, Bern**

The expressivist sensibility. Klee uses a childlike way of seeing to represent an adult way of feeling. The goal here is emotional resonance, psychological reality, primal truth.

good example of what expressivist critics admire. Children usually lack the patience or skill to produce art that exhibits a finished and calculated organization of form. For them, the impulse to communicate—to describe an event or express an emotion—is stronger than the desire to adjust forms so they will be "perfect" or "beautiful" as adults understand these words. The art of children pleases us because of its uninhibited color, design, and imagery—its naiveté. In describing their world, children "tell it like it is."

Now, all art, regardless of style, communicates ideas or feelings. Consequently, expressivist criticism must give us a way of deciding whether a work goes beyond "mere" communication. To deal with this problem, we have the idea of *intensity* of experience. Art is best when it arouses intense feelings—feelings stronger than those we experience in everyday life. We must be simultaneously aware of the real-life and the artistic sources of our feelings. Consider the photograph of an air attack. We know what it represents, but the image looks mechanical and ordinary: it does not communicate the violence of the event *even though* it is obviously accurate. But when Grosz or Dix deals with the same theme, we realize that our emotional responses have been heightened by the artist without destroying the underlying truth of the event.

Clearly, expressivist critics believe art should "have something to say," which implies that *artists* should have something to say. Expressivists, like many lay people, want art to be a source of insight about life: the great artist should be wise in a way that others are not. That is, the artist discovers certain truths about life, and, through skill and imagination, finds a way to express them forcefully. Therefore, *originality, relevance,* and *cognitive validity* become expressivist criteria of aesthetic excellence. Technique and formal organization are important only insofar as they help communicate significant ideas.

The expressivist standard of relevance amounts to a demand that art contribute to the meaning of existence *now*. The emphasis on "now" suggests that a work of art succeeds when it conveys feelings and ideas that have immediate meaning in our lives. "Immediate meaning" for the expressivist is tied to originality and truth—ideas that have almost scientific force. The reasonably perceptive individual knows when these standards have been met. Again, we have the concept of the normal person, but now that mythical individual has been recruited for a new task—the establishment of a standard of relevance that includes all of us.

Instrumentalism   Instrumentalism conceives of art as a tool for advancing some moral, religious, political, or economic purpose. Therefore, excellence does not depend on the artist's ability to solve problems inherent in the use of materials or the creation of form—problems *internal* to the artistic enterprise. Neither is excellence based on the expressivist criteria of vividness, credibility, and relevance. Instrumentalists are concerned with the *consequences* of the ideas and feelings expressed in art; they want art to serve ends more important than art itself.

The instrumentalist idea of art might be illustrated by the background music for a film. The music should support the dramatic action, heightening its meaning and anticipating climactic moments but never calling attention to itself. The relation of art to social, political, or moral goals should be the same.

Pablo Picasso. *Woman Weeping.* 1937. Penrose Collection, London

This is not a pretty picture: expressivist art is not meant to please us. Picasso's achievement is to employ form in a fresh way (originality), to make an honest statement (truth) about the human condition as it really affects us (relevance).

above left: Otto Dix. *Lens Bombed.* **1924. Philadelphia Museum of Art. Gift of anonymous donor**

above right: George Grosz. *Punishment.* **1934. Collection, The Museum of Modern Art, New York. Gift of Mr. and Mrs. Erich Cohn**

right: **Photograph of an air attack on a tank during World War I**

Another example of this idea of art might be seen in the illustration for an ad. It should visualize the words or the message as a whole; in presenting that message it can be funny or beautiful, but not so funny or beautiful that we forget the name of the product.

In a sense, the history of art is the history of its service to society's principal institutions and ruling elites. It is only in the modern era that art has functioned as a free-floating activity, unattached to a particular church, state, or ruling family. Today, museums, universities, and foundations have emerged as the main sponsors of art and artists, but usually they do not try to change the unattached character of artistic creativity. Artistic support does not seem to require aesthetic loyalty. However, when it comes to the kind of art that is not aimed at museums, galleries, and foundations—commercial art, graphic communication, or product design—then it is clear that instrumentalism is very much alive. The people who sponsor this art have very clear ideas about what it is for, and they employ artists and designers who can do the job they want done. The results—like the instrumentalist art of the past—are very impressive.

Instrumentalist criticism seems to be in difficulty when we consider art that is admired for reasons other than those for which it was created. Medieval art was meant to communicate the doctrines of the Church to people who could not read. But *we* can read—most of us; our religious indoctrination comes from other sources. Still, we admire Romanesque sculpture for its vigor, its emotional honesty, and its unity of form and expression. Does this mean that with the passage of time instrumentalism loses its validity as an explanation of artistic greatness?

Not exactly. Instrumentalist theory is really based on a shrewd analysis of artistic creativity. Instrumentalists realize that art which once served purposes outside itself may eventually be prized for formal or expressive qualities. However, these qualities were originally "built into" the art object so that it would function effectively; the service of king or church or state requires excellence in all respects. The instrumentalist maintains that the highest motivation is indispensable for the creation of great art.

Is the instrumentalist critic really a formalist or expressivist who requires that art have extra-artistic motivation? No, because the instrumentalist maintains that motivation and purpose cannot be separated. For instrumentalists, aesthetic values do not exist independently; the meanings and pleasures of art are fully experienced only when we recognize their involvement in the larger goals of life. Michelangelo's *Pietà* is a masterpiece not only because it illustrates a central religious event but also because it supports crucially important ideas about maternal love and grief. Form, purpose, and idea are identical. Thus, instrumentalists experience the visual organization of forms and their expressive function at the same time. They need not speculate about whether an organization has realized its ideal possibilities; they know the purpose of the work when they see its forms. If they cannot "see" or feel or understand the purpose of the work, they *know* it has failed. Criticism becomes much easier that way.

Michelangelo. *Pietà*. 1498–99. St. Peter's, Rome

Instrumentalism: its masterpieces are formalist masterpieces, too. But the forms are organized to serve purposes above and beyond form.

Diego Rivera. *Night of the Rich*. 1923–28. Ministry of Education, Mexico City

Diego Rivera. *Two Women*. 1941. The Arkansas Arts Center, Little Rock. Gift of Abby Rockefeller Mause, 1955

These works employ approximately the same form-language, using it to express bourgeois complacency or revolutionary disgust, which shows that Cubism supports formalism or instrumentalism, depending on how the artist feels at the time.

Jean Metzinger. *Tea Time.* 1911. Philadelphia Museum of Art. The Louise and Walter Arensberg Collection

David Alfaro Siqueiros. Detail of *New Democracy.* 1945. Whereabouts unknown

The fusion of voluptuous form with the idea of revolutionary violence.

There is a vulgar kind of instrumentalism that expects art to deal with stereotyped political ideas. Marxist critics, for example, want artists to illustrate class struggle, capitalist oppression of the masses, imperialist exploitation, the heroism of workers, and so on. At its best, Marxist criticism offers an interesting explanation of the economic relations between creators and users of art, but it tends to be unsatisfactory in the formulation of criteria of artistic

Pieter Brueghel the Elder. *The Painter and the Connoisseur.* c. 1565. The Albertina, Vienna

In the sixteenth century the critic might be literally *there*, observing the birth of a masterpiece and probably offering advice. Today's critic is rarely present in the flesh, but the artist is well aware of his spirit: it hovers over everything, occasionally holding back the brush or making the paint hard to spread.

excellence. In the mural art of Diego Rivera, for example, we see numerous scenes depicting the oppression of the Mexican masses. The purpose of these murals was to create the motivation for revolutionary change. But their form language is indistinguishable from nonrevolutionary works painted by Rivera and other Cubists early in this century. In other words, Rivera's enduring reputation rests on formalist grounds; apparently, Communist content was added to bourgeois formalism.

The Soviets are notorious for their sponsorship of art that illustrates the official views of the state; most of it has been consistently mediocre. But this may not be due to instrumentalism; more likely the culprit is bureaucratic rigidity and clumsiness. In the Western democracies, too, citizens and politicians often adhere to theories of vulgar instrumentalism: art is good when it celebrates officially proclaimed goals; art is bad when it makes us uncomfortable. Art is especially bad when it is ugly; the problem here may be that vulgar instrumentalists are really closet formalists.

Despite its abuses—especially in official censorship—instrumentalism provides useful grounds for criticizing art. First, it encourages critics to seek out the social, moral, or economic purposes that art serves. Second, it emphasizes the worthiness of art that is related to society's dominant concerns. Third, it acts as a corrective to the tendency of artists to become excessively involved with purely technical problems. In other words, instrumentalism is not a bad critical philosophy; certainly, it is a durable philosophy, but it can become a crude weapon when bureaucrats take hold of it.

CONCLUSION

There are so many kinds of art that no single critical theory is adequate for evaluating all of them. When it comes to the criticism of architecture, the crafts, and industrial art, for example, we must find ways to consider the aesthetic value of utility, workmanship, and the expressiveness of forming and fabrication processes. What we must *not* do is decide that certain classes of objects are aesthetically irrelevant; we have to guard against the tendency to consider only the kinds of art that fit our favorite critical principles. When we say that something is not art, we are probably avoiding the task of criticizing what we do not like. If we want to understand art, theories that exclude objects before we have examined them are not very useful. We should employ a definition of art that includes potentially everything that human beings make. Then, equipped with suitable critical procedures, we can examine the merits of any work that "asks" to be judged.

David Seymour. Photograph of Bernard Berenson at the Borghese Gallery in Rome, 1955

The critic as connoisseur. Is it an original? By whom? When did he make it? Who has owned it since then? Has it been altered or retouched? How much was done by the master and how much by assistants? How much was "created" by restorers? What do the other experts think? Why are they wrong? Why am I right? Incidentally, is it any good?

CHAPTER SIXTEEN

THE CRITICAL PERFORMANCE

Having discussed the qualifications of critics, the purposes of their work, and the kinds of arguments they use to support judgments, we can turn to the critical performance itself. Much of the commentary in this book consists of criticism. That would be true of most statements about art, since it is difficult to discuss the subject without carrying out some critical operations. But now it is time to describe the critical performance in detail; we want to stress that it is an orderly and sequential process.

Our guiding assumption is that there is a systematic way of acting like a critic, just as there is a systematic way of behaving like a lawyer. For lawyers there is a form for presenting evidence, refuting adversaries, citing precedents, appealing to jurors, and so on. Although art criticism does not have the form of legal debate, it *does* have form. To do criticism well, consistently, we need a form or system that makes the best possible use of our knowledge and intelligence and powers of observation.

Art-critical *performance* can be divided into four stages: Description, Formal Analysis, Interpretation, and Evaluation, or Judgment. To some extent these stages overlap, but they are fundamentally different operations; their sequence proceeds from easy to difficult, from the specific to the general. That is, we focus on particular visual facts before making inferences about their overall meaning and value.

DESCRIPTION

Description is a process of taking inventory, of noting what is immediately visible in an artwork. At this stage we are interested in *avoiding* inferences, judgments, or discussion of personal feelings. We want to arrive at a simple account of "what is there." In description, the language of the critic should be as "unloaded" as possible; it should not contain hints about the meaning or value of what is being described.

The reason for deferring inferences and value judgments is to make certain that our description is as complete as possible. Making value statements at this stage might tempt us to justify them, and that would prevent us from completing the description, finding what is "there" to be discovered. Interpreting or judging a work on the basis of partial evidence can be very embarrassing.

Gerald Gooch. *Hmmm.* 1968. Hansen-Fuller Gallery, San Francisco

What do we try to describe in a work of art? First, the most obvious things. In dealing with a realistic work, we mention the *names* of the things we can see, and we try to use terms that will minimize disagreement. For example, we might say that Picasso's *Les Demoiselles d'Avignon* shows the figures of five women. But, despite the title, it may seem that one of the figures is not a woman. Then we should say the painting has five *figures*, four of which appear to be women. It would be better for the critic to *prove* that the fifth figure is a woman. Perhaps the uncertainty about that figure will be useful in forming an interpretation.

As artistic imagery grows abstract, it becomes difficult to name persons, objects, places, and so on. The things we normally recognize disappear or become something else. Then we should describe the main shapes, colors, and directions we see. A shape may be ovoid or rectangular, large or small, hard-edged or soft-edged. But we should not say it is beautiful or ugly, crude or harmonious. The same applies to the other visual elements: they can be described without being judged. The point of this operation is to give us *time*—time to see, time to build up a body of perceptions, time to let the visual facts "soak in."

We can also call attention to characteristics of execution—ideally the *visible* characteristics. We can see whether paint has been brushed out or mixed on the canvas. We can tell if a surface consists of several transparent layers or has been applied in one coat. In architecture, we can recognize cast iron or steel or concrete or brick. Often, but not always, we can see how these materials have been shaped and assembled. In the case of handcraft or manufactured objects, we should describe processes of fabrication: is a container turned, built up by hammering, stamped out, cast, welded, or soldered? Can we see the marks of the tools that formed and finished it? Answers to these questions affect our perceptions of an object, our understanding of its form, our feelings about its use.

For discussions of technique, viewers depend on the critic's knowledge. Again, the critic should deal with technique in terms of its visible effects. In other words, we do not want a lecture on lost-wax casting while we are looking at a Rodin bronze. Professor Vincent Scully gives us just enough technical information in architectural criticism: "Moreover, the Beinecke Library wall is actually a Vierendeel truss; it thus need be supported only at the four corners of the building. But the truss does not look structural to the eye, which therefore sees the building as small, since the span looks to be a little one. Yet the building is huge and therefore disorienting to the viewer." Scully seems to be saying that the engineering qualities of the span have been visually violated. The little squares that make up the wall deceive us about the way the building is actually constructed. According to Scully, structure and appearance should correspond. And since they don't, the building is "disorienting to the viewer." In this brief excerpt, we see how technical analysis can lead to an aesthetic judgment—visual disorientation—hardly a virtue in a great library. Scully concludes: "It all ends, I think, by creating an atmosphere of no place, nowhere, nobody, matched only by some of De Chirico's images of human estrangement and by a few similarly motivated Italian buildings of the Thirties and early Forties."

Devastating as it is, Scully's critique is based on more than subjective opinion; he lays a technical foundation for his view. He also tries to *persuade*

Skidmore, Owings and Merrill. Beinecke Rare Book and Manuscript Library, Yale University, New Haven, Connecticut. 1963

Scully's comparison of the Beinecke Library to one of De Chirico's "images of human estrangement" shows how the aesthetic sense operates in the work of criticism. The library and the painting do not look alike, but they convey a similar feeling.

Giorgio de Chirico. *Delights of the Poet*. c. 1913. Collection Helen and Leonard Yaseen, New York

473

us by sharing aesthetic impressions of the library—using an analogy to the forlorn imagery of Giorgio de Chirico (1888–1978) and comparing the building to the architecture of Italy during the Fascist era. Whether we agree with Professor Scully or not, it is clear that he has earned the right to pronounce judgment.

FORMAL ANALYSIS

In formal analysis, we try to go beyond a descriptive inventory to discover *the relations* among the things we have named. We may have identified five female figures in *Les Demoiselles*, but now we want to examine their organization as shapes, colors, and textures—as forms with particular locations in space.

Some of the figures in *Les Demoiselles* are made of flat, angular planes of color, whereas the two central figures are more curved; they have gentler transitions of color and seem less distorted. Also, in one of them white lines were employed to show its main shapes. Strangely, the outer figures have heads that are very different from their bodies. And the central figures, while frontally posed, present the nose in profile. Finally, one of them looks insecure, like a statue that might fall off its pedestal; her torso is erect, but her feet are too far to the left to support her body.

This observation about the figure that seems to be falling illustrates an important source of inference in art criticism: the erectness of human posture and the influence of gravity on form. No matter what style of art we examine, certain physical and biological assumptions about people are shared by artist *and* viewer. We cannot look at a tilted representation of the human figure without feeling that it may fall. Thus the expectation of collapse creeps into our perception of the work.

Continuing our formal analysis: the color in *Les Demoiselles* seems to model the forms, but we have very little impression of depth. The figures exist in a shallow space implied by the overlapping shapes. There are no perspective devices, no changes in size, focus, color intensity, or sharpness of edge to suggest a representation of space much deeper than the picture plane. (Does this mean that Renaissance picture-making is finally dead? Is single-point perspective finished, along with the unity of pictorial space?)

Notice that the drawing of the hand in the central figure involves some skill in foreshortening; so it is more or less believable. But the other two hands in the picture are crudely drawn; one is childlike, while the other is stiff and schematic—part of an arm that resembles wood or stone more than flesh. Yet that arm—on the left side of the canvas—is painted in the typical pink tones of European figurative art. There seems to be a conflict between the drawing of the arm and its color and paint quality. Is this the type of unintentional conflict that Scully noted in his architectural critique, or is it an *intended* conflict—part of the meaning of the work?

We can also recognize three kinds of distortion in the heads of the three outer figures. In the head at the left, color shifts from pink to brown, the eye is much enlarged, and the planes of the nose are simplified, as in African wood sculpture. The *shape* of the head remains naturalistic, however, and it is naturally illuminated. Moving to the upper-right head, we depart completely from logical representation. Harsh green lines are used to indicate the nose plane in shadow; a rough, unfinished kind of execution is employed in the head and the area around it. Finally, the breast has a squarish shape.

Still, the upper-right head has a normal connection to the body. But the head on the seated figure (lower right) is very uncertain in its attachment. Its nose has been flattened out, the convention of a shadow plane has been used decoratively—as an element of pure form in what might be called a synthetic composition based on a head. The alignment of the eyes is illogical and the mouth is too small. It seems that a collection of shapes based on a head has

been arbitrarily assembled and placed on the figure's shoulders. From this "head" alone, we cannot deduce the sex, race, age, or any other distinguishing characteristic of a person. Only the hips and thighs—plus the title—confirm that it is a woman.

Finally, at the extreme left of the canvas, we see a brown area that looks like a close-up of a female figure, employing forms typical of African art. Is it one of the *demoiselles*? It seems to be an echo of a woman's back, painted brown to look like carved wood sculpture. Perhaps it announces the *leitmotif*, the subtopic, of the painting. Perhaps it is an enlarged rear view of the figure at the left.

Pablo Picasso. *Les Demoiselles d'Avignon.* 1907. Collection, The Museum of Modern Art, New York. Acquired through the Lillie P. Bliss Bequest

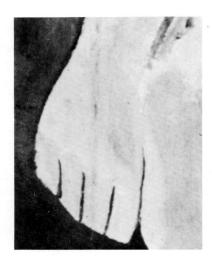

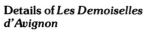

Details of *Les Demoiselles d'Avignon*

The viewer's expectations are very important in formal analysis: on the basis of what we see, what do we *expect* to see? The artist is usually aware of our visual and cultural conditioning. Certainly Picasso knows how to use fixed-point perspective, and he knows that viewers in the Western world expect illusions of depth to create the space for his *demoiselles*. Nevertheless, he deliberately breaks up any possibility of deep space. The still life at the bottom of the painting provides the merest hint of a plane leading *into* the picture space. But Picasso does not follow through: he locates the foot of the figure on the left in the same plane and at the same height as the still life. This foot has to be on the floor, yet the floor cannot be on the same level as the tabletop and the still life. Obviously, the expected logic of spatial representation has been deliberately destroyed.

It is plain that in making a formal analysis, we have been accumulating evidence for interpreting and judging the work. At first, the breakdown of spatial logic suggests that something is seriously wrong. But perhaps a different logic has been created. Or would *any* logic of space be irrelevant here? It seems reasonable to say that the activity of each figure takes place in its own space in a shallow area parallel to the picture plane.

The linear and coloristic clues in *Les Demoiselles* keep us close to the surface. When our eyes try to travel inward, they are turned to one side. Picasso makes us feel we must move to make sense of the profile view of the nose. From a fixed position we cannot deal with a front view of the face and a profile of the nose in the same head. So we must move imaginatively from left to right as we view the two central figures: we move in the *same direction* as the "falling" central figure. That movement reinforces our tendency as Westerners to "read" everything in a clockwise direction. But there are numerous violations of our *other* expectations. Western ideas of form and proportion have been repeatedly disobeyed. By the time we reach the seated figure at the right, we are ready for anything; we may even be willing to accept the joining of the shoulder, arm, forearm, and hip in a single continuous form: emphasis has shifted from the shape of the limbs to the *shape of the openings* they form.

Our analysis has begun to move from an objective description of forms to a statement about the way we perceive them. We seem to be groping for a principle of organization, an idea that can account for the way the work is structured. As observations increase, as information accumulates, it becomes increasingly difficult to postpone the work of interpretation. But now we can undertake that job with modest feelings of security: we have *tried* to be objective in our description; we have identified the subject matter; we have examined the main form relationships; we have tried to build a consensus about the visual facts and their "behavior." Now how do they add up?

INTERPRETATION

Interpretation in art criticism is a process of finding the overall meaning of a work that the critic has described and analyzed. This does not mean that critics find verbal equivalents for art forms. Neither does it mean judging the work. Obviously, we are not in a position to judge a work until we have decided what its themes are, what it means, what problems it tries to solve.

Interpretation or explanation is the most important part of the critical enterprise, and it is tremendously challenging. Indeed, if we have thoroughly interpreted a work, the business of evaluation often seems superfluous: we feel satisfied with what we have found out. Perhaps that is because interpretation involves discovering the meanings of a work of art and stating their relevance to our lives and the human situation in general.

Certain assumptions underlie critical interpretation. We assume that an art object, being a human product, cannot escape the value system of the artist. Values and ideas are almost like germs; we pick them up everywhere. Just as human beings "pick up" values, art objects pick up ideas. As critics, we are not primarily interested in whether these ideas are faithful to the artist's beliefs. That is, we do not use art to find out what an artist thinks. We *are* interested in the fact that art objects become charged with ideas—ideas that may enter a work without the artist's conscious knowledge. It is our function as critics to discover those ideas and communicate them to others.

An important principle of criticism is that the artist is not necessarily the best authority on the meaning of his or her work. As critics, we are interested in what artists think about their work; in fact, we are interested in *anything* they can tell us. But their views cannot be swallowed whole: whatever they say needs to be confirmed by our own methods of analysis and interpretation.

Does interpretation violate or distort the qualities of art that are not readily verbalized? How can we talk about shapes, colors, and textures except in very imprecise terms? My reply is that art criticism is not meant to be a substi-

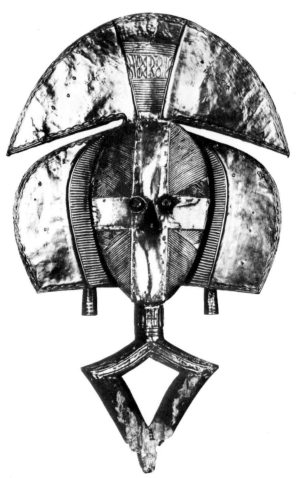

left: **Guardian figure, from the Bokota area, Gabon. 19th–20th century. Ethnographic Collection of the University, Zurich**

Picasso's *Dancer*, painted about the same time as *Les Demoiselles*, gives us a good idea of the way he used African art, and how his powers of visual transformation work. The Gabon figure was a grave marker: symmetrical, armless, and austere. Picasso converts it into a female dancer displaying her charms.

right: **Pablo Picasso. *Dancer*. 1907. Collection Walter P. Chrysler, Jr., New York**

tute for aesthetic experience. If the visual content could be verbally expressed, it would not be necessary to make the artwork in the first place. The function of language in critical interpretation is to deal with the formal and sensuous qualities of the art object in terms of their impact upon our feelings and intelligence. As we examine an artwork, its qualities seem to organize themselves into a perceptual unity, and it is this unity that we try, however badly, to verbalize.

During description and analysis we used words to *direct the attention* of viewers to *actual* colors and shapes in the art object, not to our language about them. Our verbal formulations will vary somewhat, and that suggests perceptual variation, or different emphases in what we see. Now we need a device that can combine our various perceptions in a single statement. In the discussion that follows, we try to reconcile these variations in the form of a *hypothesis*—a tentative interpretation of the facts. Our aim is to arrive at an explanation that will make sense to many viewers of the same work.

Forming a Hypothesis   How do we begin the work of interpretation? Well, during description and analysis, several possible explanations presented themselves almost spontaneously. Now we have to formulate an explanation deliberately: we want it to fit the evidence we have been assembling. The explanations that came up as we analyzed the art object were based on incomplete evidence; technically, they were *explications*—partial explanations of the work as it unfolds. But partial explanations contain useful hints: we can use one or more of them as *hypotheses* to see if they will work as explanations of the whole.

In science, more than one hypothesis can account for a given phenomenon. And the same is true of art: more than one hypothesis can explain an artwork. Since changing social, personal, and cultural conditions affect our perceptions, it is not surprising that the same work can be interpreted differently at different times or by different persons. What is important is that the interpretation be responsive to a particular set of visual facts. Still, in practical criticism, we find that the various interpretations tend to have a "family resemblance." If more than one hypothesis can explain a work, should the critic abandon the effort to develop a single explanation? To some extent the answer depends on the public a critic serves. For example, a teacher of children might explain Seurat's *A Sunday Afternoon on the Island of La Grande Jatte* as a picture of people enjoying a day off: they stroll, rest in the shade, watch fishermen, and meet friends. In other words, an adequate interpretation might consist of little more than an account of the visible subject matter. For others, the picture might be explained in terms of the representation of light, the flattening of forms, the control of contours, and the pointillist application of paint. The critic might contrast the dignity, order, and *silence* of the painting with the sounds (boat whistles, dogs barking, kids shouting) we hear. Or do we hear them? Is this a picture of silent sound?

Finally, we might offer the hypothesis that this is "really" an abstract painting that uses familiar objects to sustain our attention until we become aware of complex formal relationships of light and dark, flat and deep space, and imitations of sunlight with paint. Another hypothesis, not incompatible with the others, is that the picture is a *game* the artist plays with viewers—a game employing the pictorial conventions of linear perspective, dark silhouettes, cast shadows, and a new way of coloring flat surfaces. Seurat persuades us to recognize familiar things in forms that are mainly his own inventions. The viewer is taken in by a few contours and perspective devices; we have been "fooled" into believing these patterns are people.

The Mimetic Theory   How are hypotheses formed? We get a hint from the remarks people make about "modernistic" art—works that seem "wild," "crazy," or "childish," as in Seymour Lipton's *Cerberus*. We know what people say when they are frustrated; they become angry, or they try to be funny. Here is a free-form sculpture that might remind us of a "dog waiting to take a bite out of a mailman's leg." The remark is questionable as humor, but that's what we often hear; it expresses annoyance and embarrassment as much as anything else. It also reveals the normal impulse to use what might be called the "looks-like," "feels-like," and "reminds-me-of" reaction. The mind, confronted with material it cannot organize, struggles to find some correspondence between present, confusing perceptions and past experiences that have been organized. The "humor" is only a symptom of the struggle.

At a certain level, Lipton's (born 1903) sculpture *does* look like a watchdog waiting to bite someone. But the comic strip saga of dog biting mailman explains few of the visual facts. So we must employ the "looks-like" reaction at a more sophisticated level. What is there about a dog-bites-man episode that corresponds with the art object? This fierce little beast, with his sharply pointed equipment, has only one aim in life: to bite strangers. Which makes him a marvelous guardian. Yet somehow, man—a noble creature—becomes entangled in the low concerns of this single-minded creature. So the Cerberus episode may be an "excuse" for the artist to deal with the opposite themes of animality and dignity. No humans are present but we respond to those forms like humans: we're ashamed to be afraid of *Cerberus*.

A simple "looks-like" or "reminds-me-of" reaction can lead to a fairly complex hypothesis *if* the visual evidence will support us. If not, we must modify our statement until it fits the facts.

Interpreting *Les Demoiselles* To illustrate interpretation, let us return to Picasso's *Les Demoiselles*. We can discard some hypotheses first; the work is not a celebration of female beauty (although it does evoke works of that type: Rubens's *The Judgment of Paris* or Raphael's *The Three Graces*). But notice that it displays very little artistic virtuosity—skill in drawing and brushwork, painterly modeling of forms, or sensitive representation of light. Color and shape are not employed as a source of sensuous delight. In other words, the value of the painting lies in something other than optical enjoyment of its surface. The forms we have analyzed serve mainly to designate or symbolize ideas. Indeed, it is possible that *Les Demoiselles* expresses ideas that are original in a historical or philosophical sense.

We can build our interpretation on the basis of the clue offered by Picasso's left-central figure; it *looks like* a statue on an insecure base. The figure seems to be falling, but, being a statue, it maintains a serene expression. The statue does not *know* it is collapsing. This work of art tells us that someone or something is in a state of collapse—without being aware of it.

We noticed earlier that Picasso used white lines to delineate forms in the central figure. It is a use of line we may have seen in classical art. (The probable source is Greek vase painting of the sixth century B.C.) The faces of the two central figures also have the expressionless stare that is characteristic of archaic Greek female images. A more recent ancestor of the central figure might be found in a highly sentimental work, *Venus Anadyomene* by Ingres. But even without this information, we can sense the origins of the central figures: they embody the classical ideal of female beauty developed in the cultures of the ancient Mediterranean world; they belong to Picasso's own tradition (indeed, they look like Picasso!). By contrast, the other standing figures are derived from non-Western sources—African or Pre-Columbian. And, as observed earlier, they employ angular as opposed to curvilinear shapes. These figures disappoint the expectations of Mediterranean pulchritude aroused by the central figures: the upper-right figure is aggressively ugly; and the left figure has the sort of leg we do not see in the cities of the West.

So we witness a change of race along with a change of artistic treatment. Picasso has intentionally juxtaposed Western and non-Western racial types to

express the *fall* of Western ethnocentrism. First, the classical beauty symbolized by the central figures is contrasted with the angular forms of the other standing figures; then they are synthesized in the hybrid figure at the lower right. Its head is based on non-Western plastic forms subjected to a type of Western cerebral play. In the *fall* of the classical figures we see the fall of a culture in which beauty is the object of serene contemplation. The ideal of female passivity is displaced by ideals of female activity and magical aliveness.

Historians tell us that Picasso originally intended to paint a brothel scene showing a sailor surrounded by nude women, fruit, flowers, and a symbolic intimation of death. The final version of the canvas does not carry out this

Georges Seurat. *A Sunday Afternoon on the Island of La Grande Jatte.* 1884–86. The Art Institute of Chicago. Helen Birch Bartlett Memorial Collection

Photograph of staff assistant and children before the *Grande Jatte* at the Art Institute of Chicago, 1970

Jim Dine. *Five Feet of Colorful Tools.* **1962. The Sidney and Harriet Janis Collection. Gift to The Museum of Modern Art, New York**

After attending to the objects, their colors, their negative shadows, their placement, the space below them, the paint spatters, the board on top, the hooks, and the frame—we are about ready to interpret. Some suggestive hypotheses might help, and we get them by raising the following questions: Is this work about carpentry? About neatness? About craft in relation to painting? About dancing tools? About the souls of useful objects? About what happens between the real objects and their airbrushed echoes? Has the glossy paint changed the identity of the tools? What caused the vertically shaped paint spatters? Are the hammers and saws bleeding? Are they perspiring in color? Are they happy to be what they are, where they are? Are we looking at musical notes? Should we sing?

Seymour Lipton. *Cerberus.* **1948. Collection Mr. and Mrs. Alvin S. Lane, New York**

482

Pablo Picasso. *Les Demoiselles d'Avignon*. 1907. Collection, The Museum of Modern Art, New York. Acquired through the Lillie P. Bliss Bequest

Can this work be explained wholly on the basis of what we see? Or must it be approached via the history of art? Must we know the Western conventions for dealing with the pose and composition of female nudes before we can adequately appreciate Picasso's departure from those conventions? The answer depends on whether we regard the work as one document in a continuing story or whether we see it as an independent, organic thing. It is possible, however, with agility in shifting one's perceptual gears, to understand the work through visual sensibility *and* scholarly intelligence. But that obliges us to discipline our seeing and knowing.

Raphael. *The Three Graces*. 1500. Musée Condé, Chantilly, France

Raphael uses these women for a superb demonstration of classical equipoise: they are balanced on their feet, within the pictorial space and on the picture plane. Is it essential to remember this painting as we look at Picasso's?

Peter Paul Rubens. *The Judgment of Paris*. 1638–39. The National Gallery, London

In Rubens's picture, as in Picasso's, the display of female flesh is an important part of the story. The women compete with one another—one even addresses herself to the viewer. Again, must we keep her in mind as we look at the central figures in *Les Demoiselles*?

Jean-Auguste-Dominique Ingres. *Venus Anadyomene.* **1848.**
Musée Condé, Chantilly, France

This insipid painting embodies the ideals of nineteenth-century French academic art. Surely Picasso reacted against everything it represents: *Les Demoiselles* is, among other things, a picture of that reaction.

Pablo Picasso. *Head of a Woman.* **c. 1909. The Art Institute of Chicago. The Charles L. Hutchinson Memorial Collection**

Further support for our interpretation of *Les Demoiselles.* In 1909—two years after *Les Demoiselles*—Picasso was still trying to fit African sculptural forms into a European pictorial format.

plan. But it should be stressed that a defensible interpretation of the work need not follow Picasso's intent; indeed, we can be misled by the artist's plan (assuming it is possible to know what it was). Our critical procedure is designed to get at meanings that can be *visually* confirmed in the work—meanings the artist may not have consciously intended.

In 1907, well before World War I and the dissolution of European colonialism in Africa and Asia, Picasso's painting represented, at the very least, a remarkable anticipation of the political and cultural changes that would take place some forty years later. So, if my interpretation is right, Picasso's painting has meaning for general history as well as for the development of artistic style. Generally regarded as the first Cubist picture, this work also represents a great advance in the capacity of painting to deal with important ideas.

Our interpretation of *Les Demoiselles* has led to an appraisal, or judgment, of its importance. Clearly it has enormous artistic and intellectual significance. In the following section we take up the subject of making value judgments about works of art.

JUDGMENT

Judging a work of art means giving it a rank in relation to other works of its type. This aspect of art criticism is much abused and may be unnecessary if a satisfying interpretation has been carried out. Nevertheless, for a variety of motives, human beings often want to rank art objects. Also, there are practical situations where ranking and appraisal are unavoidable. Museums are anxious to acquire works that are "important"; there are "good" collections of French

Impressionists and there are "great" collections of French Impressionists. As for individuals, they tend to buy what pleases them, but they like to feel that what pleases them is good, that is, *comparatively* good—better than something else.

Certain kinds of critics are called connoisseurs—persons who "know" a great deal about matters of artistic reputation and excellence. When dealing with older artworks, connoisseurs concentrate mainly on authenticity. For example, the importance of Giorgione has already been established; therefore connoisseurship involves deciding whether he did, in fact, execute a certain work; when in his career the work was done; whether other versions exist; and whether it is a *good* example of his style. (If the "Giorgione" is really a Titian, then it is probably worth less; paintings by Giorgione are rare, but Titian lived a long time and painted many pictures—not all of the same quality.) In general, connoisseurs seem to be best at judging artworks in comparison with other works *by the same artist.*

In the case of contemporary art, different problems arise. Authenticity is not usually a problem; most of the facts about the work are known. But many collectors and gallery owners want to acquire works of art *before* their creators have become famous—and expensive. They exercise critical judgment almost like an investor in low-price mining stock: gold or uranium might be discovered. Such persons want to identify artistic excellence before it is widely discovered. Hence, the criticism of contemporary art is closely related to the *prediction* of aesthetic values. Somehow, the critic must know what people are going to like. Hopefully, they will like good art. Well, what makes it good? The judgment of history.

Comparisons with Historical Models   In making a critical judgment, we should relate a work of art to the widest possible range of comparable works. A common error of young artists and critics is to form judgments with reference to a very recent or narrow context of artistic creativity. But to take a critical judgment seriously, we must feel assured that it is based on the consideration of a wide range of comparable objects in time and space. Since we know examples of artistic creativity beginning over twenty thousand years ago and continuing to the present day, the range of relevant objects is enormous. Knowing the history of art (as much of it as possible) is the best defense

John Sloan. *Connoisseurs of Prints.* **1905. International Business Machines Corporation, New York**

Connoisseurs are critics of a special type; they often specialize in a particular kind of art or in the style of a particular artist. Their expertise is gained by close scrutiny of the minutest details of material and technique. That is what Sloan satirizes here—connoisseurs concentrating on every stain, blemish, or scratch in a print. Does this mean they miss the big picture?

we have against pure subjectivity in critical judgment. Fortunately, modern education, the wide dissemination of reproductions, and the frequent display of original works greatly extends the known history of art. So there is little excuse for the critic who judges according to standards based only on the work of a certain "school," geographic location, or historical period.

It may seem paradoxical to say that judging art calls for relating it to historical examples while we expect it to express current needs and values. But a comparison with the best work of the past does not imply *imitation* of the past. Historical examples are not supposed to be copy models; we employ them intelligently when they serve as benchmarks or touchstones of excellence. When judging excellence in sculpture, for example, the masters from Michelangelo to Henry Moore shape our ideas about the capacity of genius operating within specific historical and cultural contexts.

Accordingly, we can admire Max Beckmann's *Self-Portrait in a Tuxedo* as well as the *Portrait of a Young Man* by Agnolo Bronzino. Both works use form to describe the outer man and his inner ideals. Bronzino, in addition to establishing the grace and self-confidence of a young man, concentrates on creating a credible illusion of skin, clothing, and architectural surroundings. The hand at the waist is magnificently drawn and modeled. Beckmann, facing himself, portrays an older person—a man with an experienced and cynical expression. The pose has a certain elegance, but the portrait is hardly a celebration of manly beauty. Despite the formal clothes and the nonchalance of the hands, we get an ominous and troubled impression. In the Bronzino portrait, psychological analysis is minimal; in the Beckmann portrait, psychological analysis predominates, especially in the grim set of the mouth, the lighting of the face from two sides, and the exaggerated sharpness of the facial planes. Bronzino's young man symbolizes an age of reverence for learning: he holds a book to suggest the intellectual interests of the Renaissance. Beckmann's man

left: Agnolo Bronzino. *Portrait of a Young Man.* c. 1535–40. The Metropolitan Museum of Art, New York. The H. O. Havemeyer Collection. Bequest of Mrs. H. O. Havemeyer, 1929

right: Max Beckmann. *Self-Portrait in a Tuxedo.* 1927. Busch-Reisinger Museum, Harvard University, Cambridge, Massachusetts

holds a cigarette, also symbolizing an age—an age of neurosis. Both men desire poise and serenity, but they go about it very differently.

The more we examine Beckmann's portrait, the more it is clear that we are in the presence of an important work of art. Obviously its values are different from those of the Bronzino. Yet both pictures belong to the same type or genre. It is this similarity that enables us to compare them, to seek a range of meaning and a power of expression in the modern work that is comparable to the range we find in the sixteenth-century work. We do not seek the same values, but the same *capacity to support values*. The harshly manipulated planes in the Beckmann become a vehicle of aesthetic expressiveness much like the flawless surface of the Bronzino. Which means that the Beckmann is as good as the Bronzino.

The Relevance of Technique   For the purposes of art criticism, what is the role of craftsmanship, mastery of technique, skill and facility in the use of materials? To answer, we can begin with the proposition that *art is making;* it is what the Greeks called *techné*. Art is not an idea *followed* by technical expression; art is idea and materials simultaneously united by technique. The notion of technique as subordinate to idea is a philosophic error that has bedeviled aesthetics and art criticism for a long time. In criticism we cannot afford to ignore craft or technique because making and forming processes are expressive or satisfying in themselves.

Technical analysis has already been mentioned in connection with critical description. Now we want to study craftsmanship as a vehicle of aesthetic value. Technique is not only a means toward an end, it is an end in itself. There is a special sort of aesthetic pleasure we derive from technique; it probably comes from our strong identification with our hands and hand tools. The logical and effective use of tools is one of the most fundamental demonstrations of our mastery over the environment. We are, after all, tool-using animals.

How do we judge whether a work is technically good? Is it good if it works, or is it good because it looks good—because it is well crafted? In the past, good technique was chiefly concerned with the durability, expressiveness, or magical effectiveness of an object. Craftsmanship was also a visible sign of labor and materials expended; it signified the power to command skilled labor. Durability remains important but it is less prominent in today's art because modern materials permit even badly crafted works to survive. As for the evidence of human labor, it is less significant as a mark of status since many of our most costly possessions are made by machines. For us, then, craftsmanship or technical excellence means (1) logic in the use of tools and materials; and (2) close correspondence between appearance, meaning, and function. Technical excellence is difficult to judge, but we can be alert to certain qualities: utility (in practical objects), logic and economy (in the use of materials), and closeness of form, function, and meaning.

Since the physical properties of materials govern what can be done with them, craftsmanship consists of extracting the maximum of performance and meaning from materials without violating their nature. Perhaps craftsmanship can be defined as the *morality* of materials and technique: certain things that can be done with materials *ought not to be done*. Plastics can be treated to look like anything from marble to wood, but we usually feel cheated when we discover the deception. Still, our notions about the appropriate use of tools and materials cannot be fixed forever; a new "logic" of materials can be invented. Engineers continually extend our ideas about the use of old materials in new contexts. Artists and designers do this, too. And sometimes they employ a *perverse* logic of materials: they deliberately violate our sense of rightness in craft or technique; *anticraftsmanship* can become one of the meanings of a work.

This is often the case with Pop art. In *Two Cheeseburgers, with Everything*

Aristocles. *Stele of Aristion*, from Attica. 510–500 B.C. National Archaeological Museum, Athens

Pablo Picasso. Detail of *Les Demoiselles d'Avignon*. 1907. Collection, The Museum of Modern Art, New York. Acquired through the Lillie P. Bliss Bequest

The resemblance between these two figures may be entirely accidental. Or maybe Picasso was using the archaic Greek figure in the same way he used African wood sculpture: to contrast the early, vigorous stage of culture with the late, overripe stage of civilization.

Claes Oldenburg. *Two Cheeseburgers, with Everything (Dual Hamburgers)*. 1962. Collection, The Museum of Modern Art, New York. Philip Johnson Fund

(Dual Hamburgers) by Claes Oldenburg we have an intentionally "ugly" sculpture of an everyday object. These oversized hamburgers are made of plaster painted in vivid, garish colors. Because of the crudely painted plaster, the distorted scale, and the general lack of "finish," the artist achieves a strong sense of cheapness and vulgarity. Technique has been used to violate our feelings about size, color, finish, and logic in the use of materials. Oldenburg tells us that we are looking at something meant to be eaten, but his craft makes it look exceedingly unappetizing. Imagine sinking your teeth into painted plaster; the "aesthetic" reaction becomes physical revulsion. Has this ruined us for fast-food burgers forever?

Correspondence between appearance and function calls for the use of craftsmanship to express the meaning or use of an object. Our rule is that objects should *look like* what they do. From this rule we get what amounts to an *ethical* position in the crafts and industrial art: inferior materials and poor craftsmanship should not be "covered up" with skins that deceive us about what is going on inside. Honesty in materials also implies honesty in appearance. Here ethics and aesthetics meet; they require that surfaces satisfy our

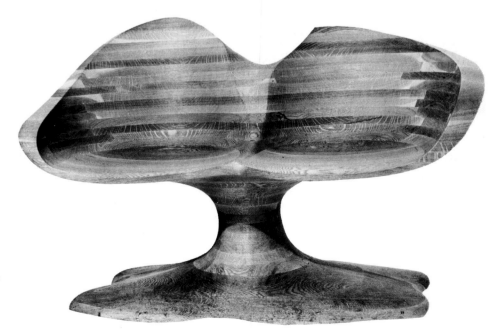

Wendell Castle. Double chair. 1968

The criticism of craft objects raises special problems: the work asks to be judged as sculpture and as seating equipment simultaneously. Thus Wendell Castle puts himself in double (or triple) jeopardy—and wins his case! The chair succeeds as skilled performance, utilitarian form, and expressive image.

visual needs for reliable information about weight, dimension, surface quality, and structural purpose. But in speaking of "inferior materials" we do not mean that some materials are intrinsically superior to others. Materials become "inferior" only when they are used inappropriately from the standpoint of durability, honesty, and logic of forming and fabrication.

Craftsmanship becomes especially elusive in the criticism of painting, drawing, and graphic arts. This is because technique in the pictorial arts is closely associated with the capacity to create illusions, whereas the crafts stress utilitarian results. In modern painting and design, however, technique is almost independent of illusionism (although Photorealism is an important exception). Accordingly, the critic examines technique in terms of artistic *performance*. We study execution—the application of paint, the control of surface quality, the handling of color—to see whether the artist's performance is satisfying in itself. Does it display inventiveness, dexterity, and eloquence in the use of the medium? Is the technique consistent with the design of the work as a whole? Does it heighten our awareness of material, form, and idea *at the same time*? This is the great challenge of technique: to display skill or virtuosity while keeping in touch with the idea or purpose of the work.

Isabel Bishop. *Nude.* 1934. Whitney Museum of American Art, New York

Technique. The mood and idea of this work are inseparable from the paint application. Through half-covering glazes alone, Bishop carries us a long way—from the surface of a woman's skin to the center of her dreams.

493

Stuart Davis. *Visa*. 1951. Collection, The Museum of Modern Art, New York. Gift of Mrs. Gertrud A. Mellon

Words constitute an integral part of the imagery of this work; the critic has to consider them from the standpoint of color, shape, size, and meaning—and even of sound.

CONCLUSION

This discussion of technique and its connection to the main idea of an artwork has broad implications. For one thing, it suggests that there is such a thing as too much craft—overdoing or over-finishing a work. That would apply to a book as well as a painting. The process of creation is alternately frustrating and satisfying. I think the pleasures outweigh the frustrations, and for that reason we are reluctant to stop working. But the author of a book dealing with criticism should recognize the perils of over-finishing or over-writing. If nothing else, that author should know when the danger point has been reached. I think the time has come: this book is done.

GLOSSARY

Cross references are indicated by words in SMALL CAPITALS.

ABSTRACT EXPRESSIONISM. A style of painting (mainly American, 1950s and 1960s) emphasizing spontaneous execution, large brushing gestures, bursts of muscular energy, and non-representational imagery. See "ACTION" PAINTING.

ABSTRACTION. The essential form after superficial or changeable features have been taken away; sometimes used (incorrectly) to mean any image that does not resemble its model in reality.

ACADEMIC. The artistic approach taught in the eighteenth- and nineteenth-century art academies of Europe; a philosophy of art based on bland imitations of ancient CLASSICAL art; by extension, any systematic, traditional, anti-experimental type of art.

"ACTION" PAINTING. A style in which the meaning or content of a picture relies strongly on the implied activity of the painted surface, especially the signs of brushing, spattering, and dripping paint; related to ABSTRACT EXPRESSIONISM.

AERIAL PERSPECTIVE. Creation of depth illusions in painting through the use of diminishing intensity of colors, the use of cooler colors for distant objects, softening of edges, and blurring of focus.

AESTHETIC. Pertaining to art theory or matters of taste and appreciation in art; the beautiful as opposed to the good, true, or useful; any vivid or intense experience. Also *an* aesthetic: an artistic or stylistic point of view; a philosophy of art.

ALLA PRIMA. Italian for "all at once"; DIRECT PAINTING; immediate achievement of final effects; the painting has one "skin" rather than many layers; the opposite of indirect painting.

ARABESQUE. Imagery that resembles the flowing interlaces of Islamic art; stylized ornamental motifs based on plants and flowers; intricate and fantastic decorative pattern of ORGANIC or geometric origin.

ARCHAIC. Primitive, antiquated, or obsolete; Greek art before the seventh century B.C. Also, archaic smile: the expression, almost a smile, of Greek sculptured heads before the seventh century.

ARCHITECTONIC. Architectural. Paintings, sculptures, or craft objects that exhibit the structural or textural traits of buildings.

ARMATURE. The skeleton or framework inside a wax or clay (usually) sculpture; it supports the work while it is being modeled.

ART NOUVEAU. French for "new art" (JUGENDSTIL in German); highly decorative style of the 1890s; emphasis on the whiplash curve, rich color, flat patterns, floral ornamentation, vertical attenuation.

ASSEMBLAGE. Creation of imagery by the aggregation of different materials, often fragments of recognizable images and objects.

AUTEUR THEORY. The view that the artistic quality of a motion picture is mainly the responsibility of the film director, who is the real cinema "artist."

AVANT-GARDE. French word for those who are advanced, "ahead of the times"; artists who point out the direction others will follow.

AXIS. The center line, real or imaginary, around which the parts of a work of art are composed and balanced.

BAROQUE. Art of the seventeenth century in Europe; characterized by irregularity of form, illusions of infinite space, theatricality of color and lighting, grandiose gestures, over-life-size figuration.

BASILICA. Originally a Roman building used as a court of law or for public meetings; evolved under Christianity into the church, a building with a long, narrow NAVE, side aisles, and an apse at the end, formerly occupied by the judge or emperor's representative.

BAUHAUS. The school of art and industrial design founded in 1919 by Walter Gropius to promote the unity of all the arts; closed by the Hitler regime in 1933.

BIOMORPHIC. Having the qualities of living form. See ORGANIC.

BROKEN COLOR. Painting technique typical of IMPRESSIONISM; short touches of bright color, often complementaries, placed side-by-side to create a vibrating effect.

BRUTALISM. An architectural style of the 1950s featuring exposed steel and large areas of coarse, undecorated concrete; the building treated almost like an Expressionistic sculpture.

BYZANTINE/BYZANTINE ICONS. The art and architecture, mainly religious, of the Byzantine Empire; icon paintings of sacred persons venerated in the Eastern Orthodox Church; style of strict frontality, little or no naturalistic modeling, rich decoration, otherworldly outlook. See MOSAICS.

CALLIGRAPHIC. Pertaining to the art of beautiful writing as in the scripts of Persia, China, and Japan; an artistic style characterized by graceful flowing curves.

CANTILEVER. The free part of a horizontal member that projects into space, seemingly without support, while its internal end is anchored in the main structure.

CAPITAL. The head or topmost part of a column or pier; depending on its characteristic shape and decoration, it may be called Doric, Ionic, Etruscan, or Corinthian.

CARTOON. A full-scale preparatory drawing for a painting, MURAL, or tapestry; a humorous sketch or caricature; a series (as in a comic strip), usually made for a newspaper or magazine.

CHIAROSCURO. In painting, the MODELING of form with light and dark; any artistic treatment that stresses the contrast between light areas and shadows.

CHROMATIC. Pertaining to color, especially HUE. See also POLYCHROMATIC, MONOCHROMATIC.

CLASSICAL. The art of ancient Greece and Rome; any work exhibiting the traits of ancient Greek art; an art of formal order stressing simplicity, dignity, clearly defined intervals, mathematical proportion. A "classic" is, by extension, a work generally accepted as a masterpiece.

CLOSED FORM. The sense of unbroken space characteristic of CLASSICAL composition in painting, sculpture, and architecture.

COLLAGE. From the French *coller*, to paste; any artistic composition made by gluing assorted materials (cloth, newsprint, wallpaper, wood veneers) to a flat surface, usually a canvas or a panel.

CONCEPTUALISM. An art movement (after 1960) emphasizing the transient character of the creative act rather than its outcome; art objects become the report, written or spoken, of an event; deemphasis of visual imagery. Related to Process Art.

CONNOISSEUR. Literally, one "who knows" and is therefore competent to offer critical judgments of art; an expert in a particular branch of art who can recognize certain techniques, establish dates, verify authenticity, estimate prices; a person of discriminating taste in art, cooking, etc.

CONSTRUCTIVISM. Twentieth-century nonrepresentational sculptural style, associated with the Russians Naum Gabo and Antoine Pevsner; theoretical foundations in modern physics, engineering, and technology; an endeavor to treat volume with a minimum of mass.

CONTRAPPOSTO. A twisting of the human figure in such a manner that the head, chest, abdomen, hips, and thighs may face in different directions. The various directions create an opposition of forces within the figure, which is felt as emotional tension by the viewer.

CRITICISM. The act of describing, analyzing, interpreting, and judging works of art; informed talk about art; incorrectly used to mean censure or fault-finding.

CUBISM. A style of art originated by Picasso and Braque in Paris about 1907; emphasis on the geometrical foundations of form, the two-dimensionality of the picture surface, multiple views of the same objects, superimposition and interpenetration of forms. Intellectual phase is *Analytic Cubism* (1909–12); decorative, playful phase is *Synthetic Cubism* (1912–14).

DADAISM. Post-World War I style stressing accidental images and events, the "logic" of absurdity, irrationality in art, literature, and morality. Related to SURREALISM.

DAGUERREOTYPE. An early photographic process (1839) named after L. Daguerre, employing silver salts, iodine, and mercury vapor in developing a picture.

DIRECT PAINTING. See ALLA PRIMA. A technique that stresses spontaneity or the appearance of spontaneity in execution; a minimum of reworking; avoids transparent effects and "building up" a surface with several layers of paint.

DOCUMENTARY. A photographic, motion-picture, or television presentation of unposed or uncontrived events; a style of art that *seems* to report actual events.

EARTH SCULPTURE. A form of art in which the sculptor excavates earth, relocates boulders, digs water channels, etc., to create

pleasing or expressive aesthetic effects. Also Earthworks and ENVIRONMENTAL ART.

ECLECTICISM. A style based on many borrowings; the combination of recognizable elements from several styles to fashion something new.

ENCAUSTIC. A painting medium using hot wax to bind colors to a wood panel or a wall.

ENTABLATURE. The portion of a CLASSICAL building facade between its column capitals and its roof; it contains the architrave, frieze, and cornice.

ENTASIS. A slight convexity or swelling in the shaft of a CLASSICAL column; it counteracts the optical effect whereby perfectly straight columns seem to be narrower in the center.

ENVIRONMENTAL ART. Any ordered arrangement or reconstruction of the natural or built environment; a garden, for example. See EARTH SCULPTURE and HAPPENINGS.

EXPRESSIONISM. A style of modern painting, originally Central European, emphasizing intense color, agitated brushwork, and violent imagery to express painful emotions, anxiety, and hallucinatory states.

EXPRESSIVISM. A term used here to describe the critical position that greatness in art results from the vivid, intense, and convincing expression of emotion.

FAUVISM. From the French *fauve* (wild beast). An early twentieth-century painting style emphasizing the juxtaposition of extremely bright areas of color, arbitrary drawing unrelated to the color, and distorted linear perspective. Main aim is breakdown and reform of traditional pictorial structure; not as anguished as German EXPRESSIONISM, which it resembles.

FETISH. A charmed or magical object; often a sculpture regarded as the home or embodiment of a spiritual substance, much as the *ka*, or other self, of an Egyptian pharaoh is believed to reside in the many statues of him; a psychological obsession with an object or part of the body which results in an erotic response.

FORESHORTENING. The representation through drawing of three-dimensional forms on a flat surface to create the illusion of their depth, as of an arm and hand extended toward the viewer. See Mantegna, *The Lamentation* (page 138).

FORMALISM. A term used here to describe the critical position that greatness in art results from the ideal juxtaposition and treatment of the basic elements of visual form.

FRESCO. A type of MURAL, or wall painting, in which dry colors are mixed with water and applied to a wet plaster surface; *fresco* means "fresh" in Italian.

FRONTALITY. The full-face or head-on presentation of the human figure; planarity in the organization of forms, that is, emphasis on forms parallel to the frontal plane.

FUNCTIONALISM. The doctrine prominent in the early twentieth century that architecture, furniture, and other useful objects should be designed to reveal their materials and process of making, to work well and to endure, and to express their practical purpose; the view that aesthetic excellence results from successful utilitarian design and performance.

FUTURISM. An Italian painting style (about 1910) derived from CUBISM; devoted to the celebration of speed, the representation of motion, and the dynamization of civilized life.

GEODESIC. Word invented by R. Buckminster Fuller to describe his basically hemispherical domes, which rely for strength on a geometric grid of thin, straight members in tension and compression.

GESSO. The mixture of chalk or plaster and glue applied to wooden panels and (rarely) to canvas to serve as a ground for tempera painting.

GLAZE. A semitransparent film of pigment and oil or varnish used to color or model an underlying painting that is usually MONOCHROMATIC or limited in color range; imparts a lustrous effect.

GOTHIC. Originally applied to the art and architecture of France, then Europe, from the twelfth to the mid-sixteenth century; emphasis on vertical space, basilican plan, long, narrow NAVE, slender masonry construction, progressive enlargement of window area, ribbed groin VAULTS, flying buttresses, stained glass.

GRAPHICS. Also the graphic arts; from the Greek word for drawing or writing. Applied to engraving, etching, woodcut, lithography; any method of printmaking or communication through line, especially when reproduced in books, magazines, posters, and by electronic transmission.

GUILDS. Free professional and social associations of medieval artisans, merchants, and tradesmen, organized to protect their interests, to maintain standards of craft, to govern the training of apprentices and journeymen, the admission of members, the preservation of trade secrets, and the control of business and work.

HAPPENING. A quasi-theatrical event staged or contrived in nonrepeatable form, employing people, places, and objects to make a visual-sculptural-satirical statement. See ENVIRONMENTAL ART.

HATCHING. A drawing and printmaking technique; a kind of shading in which fine lines placed close together create a tone that models form; in painting, a series of parallel strokes (as in Cézanne) that create the appearance of planes or facets of form.

HEDONIC. Pertaining to pleasure; art created to generate agreeable sensations.

HUE. The name of a color, such as red, blue, or yellow; the quality of light (wavelength) that separates one color from another.

ICONOGRAPHY. The conventional meanings of the images used to convey or symbolize ideas in works of art; an artist's distinctive use of visual SYMBOLS.

ICONOLOGY. The historical study and interpretation of visual SYMBOLS in art, with particular attention to their literary origins; the study of religious symbolism.

IDEALIZATION. Visual representations that omit defects or imperfect variations in a form; a type of ABSTRACTION; a type of STYLIZATION; representations that follow perfect models.

IMPASTO. From the Italian word for paste; paint applied in thick slathers or lumps.

IMPRESSIONISM. A late nineteenth-century (mainly French) style of painting; the extension of REALISM to the scientific analysis of color and light; stress on capture of transient atmospheric effects; use of BROKEN COLOR and color complementaries to render form; outdoor painting and direct observation of subjects emphasized.

INSTRUMENTALISM. A term used here to describe the critical position that greatness in art results from effectiveness in advancing the objectives of humanity, usually as defined by one of a number of major social or economic institutions: family, church, state, GUILD, firm, political party, corporation.

INTENSITY. In color, a high degree of brightness; the fullest manifestation of a color's chroma, its freedom from black, white, or gray. In AESTHETICS, high emotional excitation.

INTERNATIONAL STYLE. First applied to Gothic art; the style of architecture and utilitarian design developed in the 1920s by Walter Gropius, Mies van der Rohe, and Le Corbusier; an outgrowth of the Bauhaus philosophy.

JUGENDSTIL. See ART NOUVEAU.

JUNK ART. The use of rubbish and trivial objects (by Schwitters, Duchamp, Dubuffet, and others) to create images and objects; an extension of the COLLAGE idea.

KEYSTONE. The wedge-shaped stone in the center of a masonry arch.

KINETIC ART. Mainly three-dimensional or sculptural art that seems to move spontaneously in space (as in a Calder mobile) by the aid of a mechanism or through some naturally recurring force, such as tide, wind, or water.

KITSCH. Mediocrity in the highest degree. In aesthetics, pretentiously bad art; bad taste in art; cheap, mass-produced objects and images designed to arouse easy emotions.

LANTERN. An open cylindrical construction that lets light in through the top of a dome. See OCULUS.

LINEAR. Pertaining to line. One of Wölfflin's categories stressing the creation of form by outlines or contour lines. Also a main trait of the graphic arts.

LINTEL. The horizontal member of the POST-AND-LINTEL structural device that supports the weight above an opening in a wall.

LOCAL COLOR. The natural or daylight color of an object, seen closely, as opposed to its OPTICAL COLOR, as seen from a distance or as influenced by reflections, weather, or surrounding objects.

MANNERISM. A post-Renaissance, mainly sixteenth-century aristocratic style, characterized by elongation of the figure, artificial poses and gestures, strange distortions of the figure, forced perspective, and strident color; affectedness in art as well as behavior.

MATTE. Having a dull, almost nonreflective surface; the opposite of glossy. Matte varnishes protect a painting without adding gloss.

MEGALITHS. Immense stones such as were used in the construction of Stonehenge. Menhir: a single, uncut, prehistoric megalith.

MIMESIS. The Greek word for imitation or reproduction; the theory, generally attributed to Aristotle, that art is the imitation of human beings in action.

MINARET. The tall, slender tower attached to a mosque; it has one or more balconies from which the muezzin calls Muslims to prayer.

MINIMALISM. A style of nonrepresentational art restricted to very few visual elements, organized as simply as possible.

MODELING. In sculpture, the direct forming of materials such as wax, clay, wood, stone. In painting, the creation of more-or-less sculptural illusions.

MODULE. A standard or unit for measuring and designing; in architecture a device for standardizing the sizes and proportions of building parts and furnishings.

MONOCHROMATIC. Pertaining to a single color or HUE; a composition organized around tonal variations of one color.

MONTAGE. A method of composition in photography, cinema, and television; the technique of combining imagery from various sources to create a unified visual presentation; film editing: superimposition, intercutting, overlapping, etc.

MONUMENTALITY. The combined quality of dignity, grandeur, and impressiveness, especially in architecture and sculpture, regardless of actual size.

MOSAICS. A surface decoration or picture made with pieces of colored glass, stone, or ceramic (called TESSERAE) set into cement or mastic; typical of wall, apse, and dome decoration of BYZANTINE churches.

MURAL. Any large wall painting. See FRESCO.

NAIVE ART. The art of untrained or self-taught artists; the art of preliterate peoples. See PRIMITIVE ART.

NATURALISM. The doctrine that art should consist of the exact transcription of visual appearances. See Chapter Four, "The Style of Objective Accuracy."

NAVE. The central part of a church, used by the congregants, running from the main entrance to the altar; usually flanked by side aisles and bordered by piers and columns.

NEOLITHIC. Also New Stone Age; starting about 10,000 or 8,000 B.C.; beginnings of settled living: farming, animal husbandry, spinning and weaving, fired pottery.

NEO-PLASTICISM. A twentieth-century style of painting, mainly associated with Piet Mondrian and the De Stijl group in Holland; characterized by limited palette (black, white, and the primaries) and restriction to absolutely vertical and horizontal forms.

NONOBJECTIVE ART. Literally, art without objects, wholly nonrepresentational art; an art whose images have no obvious models in physical reality. Should not be confused with abstract art.

OCULUS. The "eye," or circular opening, at the top of a dome. See LANTERN.

OP ART. A style of painting in which disorienting effects are created by juxtaposing vibrating colors, after-images, perspectival illusions, and subtle, progressive changes of repeated shapes.

OPTICAL COLOR. The perceived color of an object; color modified by intervening conditions. See LOCAL COLOR.

ORGANIC. Pertaining to forms that resemble the structure of living things; shaped like the parts of plants and animals rather than machines; natural.

ORPHISTS. A school of abstract painters in Paris about 1912—grouped around Robert and Sonia Delaunay—who combined Cubist form with bright, vivid color.

PALEOLITHIC. Also Old Stone Age; from 32,000 B.C. to about 8,000 B.C.; the period of the cave dwellers who employed tools of stone and bone and lived mainly by hunting and gathering.

PALETTE. The thin panel (often with a thumb hole) on which a painter mixes pigments; also the colors usually employed by an artist.

PAPIER-MÂCHÉ. A sculptural material made of pulped paper or strips of paper mixed with paste; can be pressed, molded, or modeled when moist; dries hard.

PATINA. The mellow, greenish-brown film created on a copper or bronze sculpture either through natural oxidation or by applying chemicals and heat.

PEDIMENT. The triangular space formed by the gable end of a CLASSICAL building; the shape created by the sloping roof and the horizontal cornice; usually holds sculptured figures.

PENDENTIVES. The curved, triangular areas of masonry that support a dome resting on a square base.

PERSPECTIVE. A system for creating illusions of depth on a flat surface; usually a linear system is meant. See also, AERIAL, or atmospheric, PERSPECTIVE.

POLYCHROMATIC. Made of many colors, as in painted statuary or the multicolored ceramic sculpture of the Della Robbia family. See MONOCHROMATIC.

POP ART. A style of painting (and sculpture) originating in the 1960s, employing enlarged images and motifs from commercial art, road signs, comic strips, and outdoor advertising.

POST-AND-LINTEL. The principal structural device of CLASSICAL Greek architecture employing two vertical members, or posts, and a horizontal beam, or lintel.

PRIMITIVE ART. The art of preliterate peoples; a slightly opprobrious term for untrained or unsophisticated art; mistakenly applied to European paintings before the Italian Renaissance. See NAIVE ART.

PROVENANCE. Also prevenience; origin or source, especially of a work of art.

REALISM. A nineteenth-century style of painting associated with Gustave Courbet and related to the novels of Zola; emphasis on a truthful account of human existence; opposed to idealized and academic art. See SOCIAL REALISM.

RENAISSANCE. Also Renascence. The fifteenth-century "rebirth" of art and letters, that is, the revival of CLASSICAL art in Italy and afterward throughout Europe. The Renaissance style displaced medieval GOTHIC and BYZANTINE art.

ROCOCO ART. A late form of BAROQUE architecture and decoration, but more intimate and secular; playful, witty, and often erotic; ornate decor; light colors; irregular form; reflects the effeteness of the French court in the late eighteenth century.

ROMANESQUE. The art and architecture of Europe from the ninth to the twelfth century; characterized by heavy masonry construction, dark church interiors, and mystical, restless sculptural forms.

ROMANTICISM. In art, an eighteenth- and nineteenth-century style emphasizing subjective feeling and the emotions associated with exotic life-styles, escape from the present, extreme danger, suffering, nostalgia, myth, and historical evocation.

SERIAL ART. Also series painting, systems sculpture, and "ABC art." A style of the 1960s and 1970s in which simple geometric configurations are repeated with little or no variation; sequence becomes important as in mathematics and linguistic theory.

SFUMATO. The soft, "smoky" treatment of contours, notably by Leonardo, to avoid edginess and to create an impression of rounded volume.

SHAMAN. Sorcerer, magician, medicine man, priest of the Old Stone Age hunting cultures; he was probably responsible for the pictures of animals painted on the cave walls and ceilings.

SOCIAL REALISM. The style of art, allegedly Marxist, which is based on the doctrine that painting and sculpture should accurately represent the workers' experiences, especially their oppression by class enemies and their triumphs of production.

STYLING. As used in industrial or product design: superficial change. The stylist alters the appearance of the product for marketing, rather than functional, reasons.

STYLIZATION. The process of making visual representations conform to a conventional model. See IDEALIZATION.

SURREALISM. A literary and artistic style stressing the subconscious and nonrational sources of imagery; influenced by Freudian psychology. See also DADAISM and Chapter Seven, "The Style of Fantasy."

SYMBOL. In art, an image employed to designate something else. Symbolism: the systematic use of visual symbols according to mythical, religious, literary, etc., traditions; see ICONOGRAPHY. Symbolists: a late nineteenth-century school of painters (including Gauguin) who used color especially to suggest ideas and emotions; also Synthetists.

TACTILE. Pertaining to the sense of touch; in painting, the use of textured materials or the treatment of surfaces to induce sensations of touch. "Tactile values": an expression of the connoisseur Berenson to designate the convincing or authentic qualities of a painting.

TECTONIC. Pertaining to architecture and construction; one of Wölfflin's categories meaning "closed-form," where it applies to painting and sculpture, too. Also, ARCHITECTONIC.

TEMPERA. A type of paint whose medium or binder is egg yolk, glue, or casein; water soluble until it dries.

TERRA-COTTA. A reddish-brown baked clay used for earthenware, sculpture, and building construction, as in terra-cotta tiles, pipes, and fire insulation.

TESSERAE. Pieces of colored glass, stone, or ceramic used in making MOSAICS.

TONAL BLENDING. In painting, modeling a form by changes in tones of a single color instead of changes in HUE.

TOTEM. The protecting creature, usually an animal or bird, to which a clan believes itself related; the emblem that represents a clan or family. Totem pole: a carved and painted wooden post showing figures of totemic protectors or ancestors.

TRANSEPT. The crossarm in a basilican church; it meets the NAVE at right angles, separating the NAVE from the apse; the main altar is usually under the crossing of NAVE and transept.

TROMPE-L'OEIL. "Fool the eye" in French; a highly illusionistic method of painting, as in the works of Harnett and Peto; see also NATURALISM.

UNDERPAINTING. The first stage of the indirect painting method; the establishment of the chief shapes, lights, darks, and masses, usually with a limited palette or in monochrome.

UNITY. A coherent relationship among the parts or elements of a work of art.

VALUE. The lightness or darkness of a color. In aesthetics: any perceived quality; any source of appeal in a work of art; the artistic satisfaction of a human interest.

VAULT. A masonry, brick, or concrete arched structure forming a ceiling or roof over a hall; *barrel* vault, *groin* vault, *ribbed* vault.

VEHICLE. The binder or glue that holds the coloring matter in pigment and makes it adhere to a surface.

VOUSSOIR. A wedge-shaped block used in the construction of a masonry arch. See KEYSTONE.

WASH. A thin, semitransparent film of paint, highly diluted with turpentine or water (as in watercolor painting), and applied with a broad, continuous sweep of the brush.

ZIGGURAT. The almost pyramid-shaped monument of the ancient Babylonians and Assyrians, consisting of four or five stages or stories stepped back to form terraces; outside stairways lead to temples and a shrine at the top.

ZONING. Partitioning a city or town by ordinance into specific areas or zones for manufacturing, recreation, and residence.

ZOOMORPHIC. Pertaining to animal art; ascribing animal forms or attributes to humans, especially to gods and goddesses.

TIME-LINES PRIMAL, PREHISTORIC, AND ANCIENT ART

TYPICAL OBJECT, IMAGE, MONUMENT	MAKER, ARTIST	MATERIAL, MEDIUM, PROCESS	TIME	PLACE	PERIOD OF CULTURE	USER, SPONSOR, PATRON
Child's Drawing (page 464)	Four-year-old child	Crayon and paper (any pointed instrument; any surface), 4″ high	No Date	Universal	All cultures	Autonomous creation; art sponsored by the artist
Venus of Willendorf (page 15)	Unknown shaman-artist	Limestone carving, 4⅜″ high	c. 30,000–25,000 B.C.	Austria	Upper Paleolithic (Old Stone Age, Aurignacian culture)	Child-bearing woman; mother cult (?); fecundity rites
Ancestor figures of the Dogon tribe (page 315)	Tribal carver; village smith/medicine man (?)	Wood carved with iron adze and knife; rubbed, charred, and oiled, 26¼″ high	No Date (probably 19th century)	Mali (Sudan), West Africa	Neolithic Metal Age (Dogon culture)	Probably commissioned by secret society of male elders and priests
Portrait jar (of ruler?) with stirrup-spout handle (page 313)	Unknown potter-portraitist	Painted sun-baked clay, 4¾″ high	A.D. 400–600	Chicama Valley, Peru	Late Neolithic (Mochica; pre-Inca); (comparable to pre-Dynastic Egypt)	All classes used effigy jars decorated according to social status
Pharaoh Khafre (Chephren) with hawk-god, Horus (page 323)	Unknown temple sculptors	Green diorite; carved, abraded, and polished	c. 2600 B.C.	Giza, Egypt	Old Kingdom, Fourth Dynasty	The pharaoh is sponsor and only beneficiary
Stonehenge (page 365)	Bands of farmers and herdsmen supervised by priests and skilled stoneworkers	Upright stones with lintels (about 13′ high, up to 50 tons) arranged in ritual circle, or *cromlech*	c. 1800–1400 B.C.	Salisbury Plain, England (Also Carnac, Brittany; Maltese Islands)	Late Neolithic (Bronze Age), megalithic, pre-Celtic	Bronze Age farming, herding-hunting community
Snake Goddess (or priestess) (page 362)	Unknown sculptor/priestess (?)	Faience (glazed, multicolored pottery), 13½″ high	c. 1600 B.C.	Knossos, Crete	Aegean (Late Minoan Bronze Age)	Cult of mother goddess (?)
Tutankhamen's throne (page 117)	Unknown palace craftsmen under direction of priests of Amon	Gold-sheathed wood, carved and inlaid with precious stones	c. 1350 B.C.	Thebes, Egypt	New Kingdom, Eighteenth Dynasty	Commissioned by king for his tomb

FUNCTION, PURPOSE	SOCIAL ORGANIZATION AND CHARACTERISTICS	KEY EVENTS: POLITICAL, ECONOMIC, RELIGIOUS, TECHNOLOGICAL
To overcome fear of outside world; to control environment through magic; to "name" things; to assert own existence	Any kind of human family	Discovery of fingers and thumbs as tools of expression; discovery of relationship between visual form and real world; ability to control reality through representation; beginning of separation of world from the self: people, places, and things organized *around* the self. This art, or something very much like it, preceded the specimens of prehistoric art known to us
To promote fertility, induce pregnancy; good-luck charm, amulet; sympathetic magic	Nomadic hunting band, about 60 people; some division of labor between sexes; everyone forages; males hunt	Homo sapiens emerges; Cro-Magnon man supersedes Neanderthal man; incest taboo defines family relationships; improved tools for hunting and fishing: better spears, harpoons; bow and arrow invented; animal trapping; burial of dead; red ocher a symbol of blood and life
To preserve the spirits of ancestors; to guard and advise the family; to accompany genealogical accounts of clan's founding at annual feast; to express dualism of male and female principles	Tribal, extended family; polygamous, exogamous (girls marry outside the group); men hunt, women cultivate small plots; men's and women's societies act as check on power of chief, govern initiation of boys and girls	Settled agriculture, hoe cultivation, some hunting; ruling class descended from stock raisers, mounted warriors; local wars produced captives who become slaves; monopolies of metalwork (especially in gold) exercised by king's family and courtiers
Placed in boxlike grave; held liquid believed to sustain life of deceased	Warrior-hunter caste enslaved farmers; served by priests, artisans, dancers; close village life, some leisure; human sacrifice practiced	Copper, silver, and gold work; textile manufacture; frequent wars; irrigation systems; maize farming, ocean fishing; pyramids of adobe brick; worship of sun, moon, jaguars, serpents; no potter's wheel, no wheeled vehicles, no draft animals; no written language
To provide a permanent home for the *ba*, or soul, of the king in case his mummy is damaged or stolen; hawk symbolizes the sun-god, Re, and the royal descent of Khafre	Matriarchal; brother and sister marriages in royal house; pharaoh (who could be a woman) is god-king and absolute ruler	Unification of Upper and Lower Egypt, c. 3100 B.C.; royal household governs through small group of priests and officials; hieroglyphic writing, 3000 B.C.; great pyramid construction (2680–2500 B.C.); Hyksos invasions (1730–1580 B.C.) end isolation of Egypt
Shrine for worship of Great Mother deity; possible observatory to sight solstices, plot solar and lunar movements, predict eclipses; mother goddess causes sunrise, return of spring, renewal of earth's fertility; for rites connecting earth and sky gods	Egalitarian farming communes; tribal chieftains; some matriarchal survivals; fear of witches among herdsmen	Gold trade with Ireland; amber trade with Baltic countries; copper trade with Near East; flint mining; stone imitations of bronze weapons; wood, mud, reed houses; underground burial in gallery graves; cattle, sheep, and swine raised to supplement low-yield agriculture
To worship woman as embodiment of fertility principle; snakes symbolize earthly insemination (the male principle), controlled by the goddess	Mercantile aristocracy; luxury-loving leisure class; matriarchal customs survive in freedom; flirtatiousness of upper-class women	Palace civilization based on Mediterranean sea trade; Linear A writing; Hyksos invasions, earthquakes destroy palaces, 1720 and 1450 B.C.; high style of fresco painting, no monumental art; elaborate dresses for women: full skirts, bared breasts
To show King "Tut" as upholder of *maat* (truth/justice) as evidenced by sun's rays bathing him and his queen	Powerful priesthood and priestly bureaucracy control throne; drive out "subversives," including rebellious army officers	Ikhnaton's monotheism challenges priesthood (1372–1358 B.C.); his successor, 18-year-old Tutankhamen, restores priests and ancient cult; stonecutters obliterate sun-disk, the name of the one god, Aton; priests interpret Amon's oracle, thus control politics; restoration of gigantic architecture and statuary

CLASSICAL AND MEDIEVAL ART

TYPICAL OBJECT, IMAGE, MONUMENT	MAKER, ARTIST	MATERIAL, MEDIUM, PROCESS	TIME	PLACE	PERIOD OF CULTURE	USER, SPONSOR, PATRON
Stele of Aristion (page 491)	Aristocles	Carved and chiseled Pentelic marble; color added	510–500 B.C.	Attica, Greece	Archaic Greek (transitional)	Family of Aristion or his fellow *hoplites*
Doryphorus (Spear Bearer) (page 144)	Polyclitus	Carved marble (Roman copy of bronze original, which was decorated with colored stones, pastes, gold, and silver)	c. 450–440 B.C.	Argos, Greece	Classical Greek	Citizens of Athens
Dying Gaul (page 35)	Epigonus	Carved marble (Roman copy of bronze original)	c. 225 B.C.	Pergamum, Asia Minor	Early Hellenistic (Greek)	General Attalus I
The Pantheon (page 392)	Unknown architects	Coffered dome on cylindrical base; brick, stone rubble, marble, granite, concrete, and gilded bronze	A.D. 118–125	Rome	Late Hellenistic (Roman)	Emperor Hadrian
Cathedral of Hagia Sophia (page 399)	Anthemius of Tralles and Isidorus of Miletus, architects	Dome-on-pendentive construction; brick, stone rubble, marble, mosaics, and fresco	A.D. 532–37	Constantinople (Istanbul)	Byzantine (First "Golden Age")	Emperor Justinian
Animal head, from the Oseberg ship-burial (page 321)	Unknown carver/ shipwright	Carved and drilled wood	c. A.D. 825	Oslo, Norway	Early Medieval (Northern Carolingian)	Crew of Viking longship
Nave, St.-Savin-sur-Gartempe (page 390)	Unknown masons, craftsmen, and painters	Hall church; barrel- or tunnel-vault construction; painted ceiling of nave, cut-stone arcade; pillars painted to imitate marble	c. 1095–1115	Poitou, France	Western Romanesque	Religious community and people
The Last Judgment (page 187)	Master Gislebertus	Stone relief carving	c. 1130	Cathedral of Autun, France	Romanesque	The Cluniac Order

FUNCTION, PURPOSE	SOCIAL ORGANIZATION AND CHARACTERISTICS	KEY EVENTS: POLITICAL, ECONOMIC, RELIGIOUS, TECHNOLOGICAL
Gravestone marker; memorial to aristocratic "warrior-gentleman"	Tribal, aristocratic: gods, heroes, heroic dead, kings, noble families, free workers, peasant farmers, slaves; "barbarians" the lowest caste	Rule of *polis* (Greek city and surrounding pasture) by old Dorian clans; armored infantrymen (*hoplites*) replace horsemen; the phalanx (*hoplites* fighting in unison); military comradeship weakens tribal ties; egalitarianism of warriors extended to civic life; poor farmers enfranchised; more money spent on public building
To symbolize the union of reason, action, and correct proportion in the ideal Greek man or god; to establish a perfect, i.e., geometrical, standard of physical beauty	Old aristocracy weakened by insurgence of mercantile class and prosperous laborers; *polis* becomes democratic city-state	Greek cities defeat Persians, 448 B.C.; Athenian fleet and merchants dominate Eastern Mediterranean and Black Sea; spread of Hellenism—Greek art, language, and literature; emergence of Athens as model of an open society: free speculation unfettered by priests and tyrants, but for citizens only; Athens defeated by Sparta in Peloponnesian War (431–404 B.C.)
To celebrate victory over Celtic or Galatian invaders; to memorialize bravery of barbarians, their worthiness as men and foes	Oligarchic control of Hellenistic cities; large estates; independent farmers disappear; emergence of small, rich leisure class living off land rents and slave labor	Alexandrian conquests (336–323 B.C.); Oriental colonization; spread of Greek culture (330 B.C.–A.D. 100) to Rome, Egypt, Syria, Asia Minor, Persia, India; imperial bureaucracy, standardized city planning; great library in Alexandria; much prestige in philosophy; Roman conquest of Corinth (146 B.C.), Greece controlled by Rome
Officially dedicated to the gods of the seven planets; to create a vast interior space symbolizing the cosmos; to glorify Hadrian	Imperial state; cosmopolitan capital city; large-scale importation of European slaves; laborers and artisans live in tenements	Growth of mystery religions, Zoroastrianism, Manichaeism, astrological cults; Roman economic exploitation of the provinces; death of Jesus (c. A.D. 30); Jewish rebellion (A.D. 60); death of Paul (c. A.D. 65); Christian underground; slave revolts; growth of large proletariat in Rome; free "bread and circuses" for urban masses
To express the Eastern Christian idea of the unity of God and light in a great vertical space; announces emperor is God's deputy on earth, empress is God's wife	Absolute monarchy supported by urban aristocracy of merchants, monopolists, priesthood, civil service, and army of spies; the commercial model for Venice	Roman legalization of Christianity in A.D. 313; Constantine establishes new imperial capital at Byzantium, 330; Rome sacked by Goths, 410; Justinian and Theodora rule in Constantinople, 527–65; Gregory the Great becomes Roman pope, 590; birth of Muhammad, c. 570; Muslim conquests begin, 632; Jerusalem taken, 638; Arabs defeated at Poitiers by Charles Martel, 732; Charlemagne becomes Holy Roman Emperor of the West, 800
Figurehead (dragon?) for sailing vessel/war galley protects raiders, terrifies farmers and villagers; ship buried with chieftain	Tiny kingdoms subsisting on farming, fishing, trapping, and piracy; polygamy and primogeniture produce younger sons without property, looking for loot	Viking sea raiders invade Ireland, England, France, Italy, and Sicily, penetrating inland on shallow-draft ships (830–900); Central Asian nomads invade Europe, 890; feudal system in Europe; monastery at Cluny, France, founded, 910
To express the Latin Christian idea of salvation in a long, horizontal space culminating in the chancel, altar, reliquary, and choir	Manorial feudalism and monasticism well established; conversion of Roman estate slaves into serfs by victorious raiders who set themselves up as new nobility; employment of foreign artisans as builders	Norsemen and Huns become Christians, c. 1000; England conquered by William of Normandy, 1066; international pilgrimages to holy sites, veneration of saints' relics; schism between Roman Catholic and Eastern Orthodox Churches, 1054; Capetian dynasty in France under Louis VI guided by Abbot Suger (1081–1151); reconquest of Spain from Arabs begins, 1085
To remind the faithful, as they enter the church, that they must answer for everything they do in life	Restless and pugnacious nobility addicted to feuds, killings, destruction; higher clergy (abbots, bishops) chosen from their peaceful sons	St. Bernard preaches Second Crusade, 1146; sends knights to fight Islam for possession of Jerusalem; European barbarians exposed to Middle Eastern wealth, learning, and civilization; deep-cutting plow opens northern European plains to agriculture, rotation of crops; more protein in diet; peasants more vigorous

503

RENAISSANCE AND BAROQUE

TYPICAL OBJECT, IMAGE, MONUMENT	MAKER, ARTIST	MATERIAL, MEDIUM, PROCESS	TIME	PLACE	PERIOD OF CULTURE	USER, SPONSOR, PATRON
The Last Supper (page 256)	Leonardo da Vinci	Egg tempera plus oil glaze on stone wall covered with plaster and sealed with varnish	c. 1495–98	Refectory of Sta. Maria delle Grazie, Milan	Italian Renaissance (Florentine School)	Commissioned by Duke Ludovico Sforza for the monastery of Sta. Maria delle Grazie
The Three Graces (page 484)	Raphael	Oil on wood panel, 6¾ × 6¾"	1500	Perugia (?), Italy	Italian Renaissance (Roman School)	Made for the artist himself (?)
Study for Adam (page 248)	Albrecht Dürer	Pen and sepia wash on paper	c. 1507	Nuremberg, Germany	Northern Renaissance	Study for the artist
St. Peter's (page 393)	Michelangelo (dome completed by Giacomo della Porta, 1590)	Stone, marble, mosaics; metal chains in dome fabric; fusion of central plan and basilican plan; 452' high	1546–64	Rome	Early Baroque	Pope Paul III
The Agony in the Garden of Gethsemane (page 221)	El Greco	Oil on canvas	c. 1580	Toledo, Spain	Mannerism	Church in Toledo (?)
The Judgment of Paris (page 485)	Peter Paul Rubens, his pupils and assistants	Oil on canvas	1638–39	Antwerp, Flanders (Belgium)	Northern (Flemish) Baroque	Private patron
Pope Innocent X (page 266)	Velázquez	Oil on canvas	1650	Rome	Spanish Baroque	Painted for the pope during Velázquez's trip to Italy (1649–51)
Christ Healing the Sick (page 238)	Rembrandt	Etching, 11 × 15"	c. 1648–50	Amsterdam	Northern (Dutch) Baroque	For sale by the artist through his dealer, Pieter de la Tombe; price: one hundred guilders

FUNCTION, PURPOSE	SOCIAL ORGANIZATION AND CHARACTERISTICS	KEY EVENTS: POLITICAL, ECONOMIC, RELIGIOUS, TECHNOLOGICAL
To enable the prior and monks, while eating, to contemplate Jesus' last meal with his disciples; to create psychological studies of Jesus and each of his disciples	Italy's city-states ruled by feudal princes (dukes), bankers, landed aristocrats, and mercenaries (condottieri); brief republic in Florence (1494–1512)	World exploration: Columbus (1492), Vasco da Gama (1497–99), Balboa (1513), Magellan (1519–22); Byzantine and Gothic styles repudiated; classical Greek and Latin texts published in Italy; intellectual life flourishes in ducal courts; artists emerge from artisan class
To express ideas drawn from ancient humanistic texts; to revive the classical ideal of beauty in the nude; to visualize perfection embodied in human form	Roman popes and curia dominate regional dukedoms (except Venice)	Alexander VI (Borgia) and Julius II consolidate power of papacy; best artists go to Rome, now the world's financial center; Michelangelo paints Sistine Chapel ceiling (1508–12) while Raphael works on frescoes for papal apartments in the Vatican; nominally religious art with strong pagan-classical flavor
To master "the science of proportion" in preparation for his figure paintings and engravings; to represent nature truly, i.e., in the "new" Italian manner	Mercantile aristocrats in Nuremberg and Augsburg (the Fuggers) imitate Italian princes, patronize artists and scholars, resent flow of funds to Rome	Martin Luther posts his theses, 1517; Luther excommunicated, 1521; Luther publishes German Bible in 1522 with woodcuts by Lucas Cranach the Elder; Peasant Revolt in Germany (1524–25); iconoclasm, confiscation of ecclesiastical art and property (1520–40)
Rebuilding initiated by Julius II in 1505 to contain his tomb; to restore prestige of city of Rome after sack in 1527; to combine dome-of-heaven symbolism of the early Church with the longitudinal orientation of Latin Christianity	Papal household dominates Rome; cardinals and bankers compete in self-glorification	German army sacks Rome, 1527, artists scatter; Henry VIII breaks with Rome, 1534; Council of Trent (1545–63) fails to reconcile Protestants; Spain rules much of Italy through local surrogates; Michelangelo paints Last Judgment (1534–41)
To combine the qualities of Spanish religiosity with the aims of the Counter-Reformation; to render the Passion of Christ in terms of noble suffering and mystical transcendence	Feudal Spain is bankrupt; imperial Spain milks American colonies; nobility impoverished; intense otherworldly religious feeling	Reconquest of Spain completed; Jews expelled by Ferdinand and Isabella, 1492; Ignatius Loyola founds Jesuit Order, 1540; large infusions of American gold and silver destabilize Spanish economy; Spanish naval power destroyed by English pirates; Armada defeated (1588) by Drake
To express the compatibility of Catholic courtly culture, Renaissance humanism, and the grandiose lifestyle of the aristocratic merchants of Flanders	Jesuits control art, education, and architecture; sponsor devotional art for the masses, classical studies for sons of the rich	The Netherlands gains freedom from Spain, 1609; Antwerp, Amsterdam, Augsburg, and Ulm become major banking centers; French, English, and Dutch settlements established in North America; Hudson's Bay Company organized, 1670; Spanish Hapsburg influence lingers in Flemish art, education, and upper-class behavior
To emphasize the power and sagacity reposed in the head of the Roman Catholic faith	Spaniards dominate Italian politics and religion; Roman Baroque dominates art of Europe	Galileo tried for heresy by the Inquisition, 1633; end of Thirty Years' War, 1648; Catholicism triumphs except in northern Europe; skepticism of Descartes (d. 1650) undermines intellectual authority of Rome; France becomes most powerful nation in Europe; French Academy established, 1635
To render the miracles of Jesus according to the egalitarian ideals of Protestant Christianity and the realistic outlook of the prosperous Dutch burgher class	Dutch towns ruled by wealthy, conservative bourgeoisie supported by Calvinist clergy	Dutch East India Company (chartered 1602) monopolizes Southeast Asian trade; Harvey discovers circulation of blood, 1628; Rembrandt paints Anatomy Lesson, 1632; Dutch ruling class sponsors secular art, realistic style, everyday subject matter

FROM ROCOCO TO MODERN

TYPICAL OBJECT, IMAGE, MONUMENT	MAKER, ARTIST	MATERIAL, MEDIUM, PROCESS	TIME	PLACE	PERIOD, STYLE, CULTURE	USER, SPONSOR, PATRON
Miss O'Murphy (Nude on a Sofa) (page 224)	François Boucher	Oil on canvas, 23⅝ × 25⅜″	1752	Versailles (?) (now in Alte Pinakothek, Munich)	Rococo	Louis XV
Man with a Hat (page 266)	Jacques-Louis David	Oil on canvas	c. 1816	Brussels	Neoclassicism	Portrait commission
Liberty Leading the People (page 44)	Eugène Delacroix	Oil on canvas	1830	Paris	Romanticism	Painted for first Salon, sponsored by Louis Philippe
The Burghers of Calais (page 309)	Auguste Rodin	Bronze, 85 × 98 × 78″	1886	Calais, France	Romanticism-Impressionism-Symbolism	The people and town fathers of Calais
The Card Players (page 215)	Paul Cézanne	Oil on canvas, 25½ × 32″	1890–92	Aix-en-Provence	Post-Impressionism	Painted for himself; later (1895) exhibited by the dealer Ambroise Vollard
Robie House (page 77)	Frank Lloyd Wright	Steel beams, wood, brick, glass, stucco; cantilever and masonry pier construction	1909	Chicago	International Modern Prairie style	Frederick D. Robie
Guernica (page 51)	Pablo Picasso	Black, white, and gray oil paint on canvas, 11′6″ × 25′8″	1937	Paris (now in The Prado, Madrid)	Late Cubist-Expressionist	For Spanish Pavilion, Paris World's Fair
Homage to New York (page 357)	Jean Tinguely	Piano, drums, wheels, gears, typewriter, electric motor, Coke bottles	1960	Museum of Modern Art, New York (self-destroyed)	Abstract Expressionism, kinetic "metamatic" art	For audience in the garden of the Museum of Modern Art, New York

FUNCTION, PURPOSE	SOCIAL ORGANIZATION AND CHARACTERISTICS	KEY EVENTS: POLITICAL, ECONOMIC, RELIGIOUS, TECHNOLOGICAL
To portray the king's mistress as his plaything; to express a lighthearted, spontaneous approach to love; to join the idea of childlike innocence with eroticism	French aristocracy concentrated in royal court, loses governing function; people impoverished by royal wars and extravagance	Louis XIV rules France as absolute king (1643–1715); "Glorious Revolution" and English Bill of Rights, 1689; Hobbes (d. 1679) questions absolute monarchy; Locke (d. 1704) urges representative government; J. J. Rousseau (d. 1778) justifies revolution; Watt perfects steam engine, 1765; Adam Smith writes *Wealth of Nations*, 1776; American Revolution, 1775–83; French Revolution, 1789–94
A tribute to the elegance and fastidiousness of Europe's newly rich class of businessmen and industrialists; David integrates the noble form language of Neoclassicism with the naturalistic detail desired by his wealthy clientele	Powerful entrepreneurial class struggles to control European society after revolutionary radicals are overthrown in France	Napoleon dominates French and European history (1799–1814); David is artistic dictator during French Revolution *and* under Napoleon; Goya portrays Spanish resistance to Napoleonic invasions, 1814; Napoleon defeated at Waterloo, 1815; David exiled; French Academy reinstated, 1816
To idealize fighting on the barricades; satisfies bourgeois appetite for a life of action and danger; substitutes exciting color and brushwork for controlled feeling of classical drawing and modeling	Bitter alienation of artists from society; bohemianism; growing split between art and science; doctrine of art for art's sake	Revolution of 1830 in France and throughout Europe in 1848; Daguerre perfects photography, 1839; Marx's *Communist Manifesto*, 1848; Courbet paints *The Stone Breakers*, 1849; Baudelaire publishes *Fleurs du Mal*, 1857; Darwin publishes *Origin of Species*, 1859; serfs nominally freed in Russia, 1861; American Civil War, 1861–65
To dramatize the heroism of a group of ordinary citizens; to demonstrate the possibility of a democratic public monument; to analyze the emotions of men facing death by execution	Factory system establishes new managerial class; terrible exploitation of industrial workers; middle class firmly controls art, politics, and education	Tolstoy writes *War and Peace* (1863–69); Marx writes *Das Kapital* (1867–94) in England; Edison invents light bulb, 1879; germ theory of disease demonstrated by Pasteur, 1881; Roebling builds Brooklyn Bridge (1869–83); Manet paints Emile Zola (1868)
To create a harmony of colors, shapes, and their interrelations; to demonstrate the geometrical roots of form; to fix and record the artist's perceptions of objects in space	Industrial societies dominate the world; Western imperialism; strong belief in progress through education, science, technology, business enterprise	Monet paints haystack series, 1891; Spanish-American War (1898); U.S. emerges as world power; skyscraper invented in Chicago (1885–1900); revolutions in China and Mexico begin, 1911; World War I (1914–18); Russian Revolution, 1917; League of Nations, 1919
To express the unity of the house with the land by emphasizing horizontality; to make the dwelling seem to belong "organically" to its site; to create decorative and textural effects by exposing natural building materials	Boom atmosphere in U.S.; massive immigration, powerful corporations; blacks and women still disenfranchised; culture essentially WASP	Freud publishes *Interpretation of Dreams*, 1900; Planck's quantum theory, 1900; Wright brothers' flight, 1903; Einstein's relativity theory, 1905; Ford assembly line, 1909; Futurist Manifesto, 1909; U.S. opens Panama Canal, 1914; Griffith directs *Birth of a Nation,* 1915; Americans in World War I, 1917
To protest Franco's bombing of civilians and to denounce Fascism; to create a form language that can simultaneously describe the bombing and its emotional impact; to relate modern war to ancient, subconscious memories of violence	Worldwide depression, unemployment, wild speculation destabilize capitalist societies; mass communication plus charismatic leaders results in mass-movement dictatorships	Mussolini's Fascists take over Italy, 1922; Surrealist Manifesto, 1924; Wall Street "Crash" and Great Depression, 1929; Hitler's Nazis take over Germany, 1933; Gropius and the Bauhaus (1919–33); F. Roosevelt and the New Deal, 1933; Spanish Civil War, won by Franco's Nationalists (1936–39); Hitler-Stalin nonaggression pact, 1939; World War II (1939–45)
To entertain; to ridicule mechanization; to dramatize the "suicide" of a machine; to condemn industrial civilization and the "machine aesthetic"	Growing independence of "Third World" peoples; "loss of nerve" in Europe and America; "backward" Russia emerges as "superpower"	Atomic bombs dropped on Hiroshima and Nagasaki, 1945; United Nations formed, 1945; British leave India, 1947; State of Israel founded, 1948; Marshall Plan for Europe, 1947; Soviets explode atomic bomb, 1949; U.S. explodes hydrogen bomb, 1954; Soviets launch Sputnik, 1957; Cuban missile crisis, 1962; John F. Kennedy assassinated, 1963; Solzhenitsyn describes Gulag (1962), wins Nobel Prize (1970), moves to U.S.

SELECTED BIBLIOGRAPHY

Following is a list of books related to the major subjects discussed in this volume. It is by no means complete; it is intended to suggest the range of published material that can be consulted in connection with questions raised in the text. Specialized monographs and publications about individual artists have been omitted. The listing of periodicals, too, has been kept to a minimum. World histories of art are not included, on the assumption that the reader is already familiar with them or has access to a bibliography of the outstanding works of comprehensive art history.

THE FUNCTIONS OF ART

Antal, Frederick. *Florentine Painting and Its Social Background*. London: Routledge and Kegan Paul, 1948.

Dorner, Alexander. *The Way Beyond "Art."* New York: New York University Press, 1958.

Feldman, Edmund B. *The Artist*. Englewood Cliffs, NJ: Prentice-Hall, 1982.

Hauser, Arnold. *The Philosophy of Art History*. New York: Knopf, 1959.

Huyghe, René. *Art and the Spirit of Man*. New York: Abrams, 1962.

Kostof, Spiro. *A History of Architecture: Settings and Rituals*. New York: Oxford University Press, 1985.

Mayor, A. Hyatt. *Prints and People: A Social History of Printed Pictures*. New York: The Metropolitan Museum of Art, 1971.

Morris, William. *On Art and Socialism*. London: Lehmann, 1947.

Pelles, Geraldine. *Art, Artists and Society: Origins of a Modern Dilemma*. Englewood Cliffs, NJ: Prentice-Hall, 1963.

Read, Herbert. *The Grass Roots of Art*. New York: Wittenborn, Schultz, 1947.

Selz, Peter. *Art in Our Times: A Pictorial History*. New York: Harcourt Brace Jovanovich and Abrams, 1981.

THE STYLES OF ART

Ackerman, James. "Style," in Ackerman and Rhys Carpenter, *Art and Archaeology*. Englewood Cliffs, NJ: Prentice-Hall, 1963.

Hauser, Arnold. *Mannerism: The Crisis of the Renaissance and the Origin of Modern Art*. 2 vols. New York: Knopf, 1965.

Nochlin, Linda. *Realism*. New York and Baltimore: Penguin Books, 1971.

Ortega y Gassett, José. *The Dehumanization of the Arts*. Garden City, NY: Anchor Books, 1956.

Panofsky, Erwin. *Meaning in the Visual Arts*. Garden City, NY: Anchor Books, 1955.

Rosenblum, Robert. *Cubism and Twentieth-Century Art*. New York: Abrams, 1966.

Rubin, William S. *Dada, Surrealism and Their Heritage*. New York: The Museum of Modern Art, 1968.

Schapiro, Meyer. "Style," in *Anthropology Today*. Edited by A. L. Kroeber. Chicago: University of Chicago Press, 1953.

Wölfflin, Heinrich. *Principles of Art History*. Translated by Mary D. Hottinger. New York: Dover, 1950.

Worringer, Wilhelm. *Abstraction and Empathy: A Contribution to the Psychology of Style*. Translated by Michael Bullock. New York: International Universities Press, 1953.

THE STRUCTURE OF ART

Anderson, Donald M. *Elements of Design*. New York: Holt, Rinehart and Winston, 1961.

Arnheim, Rudolph. *Art and Visual Perception*. Berkeley and Los Angeles: University of California Press, 1954.

Chermayeff, Ivan, *et al. The Design Necessity*. Cambridge: Massachusetts Institute of Technology Press, 1973.

Gombrich, E. H. *The Sense of Order*. Ithaca, NY: Cornell University Press, 1979.

Hill, Edward. *The Language of Drawing*. Englewood Cliffs, NJ: Prentice-Hall, 1966.

Itten, Johannes. *Design and Form: The Basic Course at the Bauhaus*. New York: Reinhold, 1964.

Klee, Paul. *Pedagogical Sketchbook*. New York: Praeger, 1953.

Moholy-Nagy, László. *The New Vision*. 4th rev. ed. New York: Wittenborn, Schultz, 1949.

Richardson, John Adkins; Floyd W. Coleman; and Michael J. Smith. *Basic Design: Systems, Elements, Applications*. Englewood Cliffs, NJ: Prentice-Hall, 1984.

Sommer, Robert. *The Behavioral Basis of Design*. Englewood Cliffs, NJ: Prentice-Hall, 1969.

Wölfflin, Heinrich. *The Sense of Form in Art: A Comparative Psychological Study*. New York: Chelsea, 1958.

PAINTING

Arnason, Harvard H. *History of Modern Art*. New York: Abrams, 1968.

Doerner, Max. *The Materials of the Artist*. Translated by Eugen Neuhaus. New York: Harcourt, Brace, 1949.

Goldstein, Nathan. *Painting: Visual and Technical Fundamentals*. Englewood Cliffs, NJ: Prentice-Hall, 1979.

Haftmann, Werner. *Painting in the Twentieth Century*. 2 vols. New York: Praeger, 1960.

Henri, Robert. *The Art Spirit*. Philadelphia: Lippincott, 1923.

Janis, Harriet, and Rudi Blesh. *Collage: Personalities, Concepts, Techniques*. Philadelphia: Chilton Books, 1962.

Read, Herbert. *A Concise History of Modern Painting*. New York: Praeger, 1959.

Seitz, William C. *Abstract Expressionist Painting in America*. Cambridge, MA: Harvard University Press, 1983.

———. *The Art of Assemblage*. New York: The Museum of Modern Art, 1961.

Selz, Peter. *New Images of Man*. Prefatory note by Paul Tillich. New York: The Museum of Modern Art, 1959.

Williams, Hiram. *Notes for a Young Painter*. Englewood Cliffs, NJ: Prentice-Hall, 1963.

SCULPTURE

Elsen, Albert E. *Origins of Modern Sculpture: Pioneers and Premises*. New York: Braziller, 1974.

Giedion-Welcker, Carola. *Contemporary Sculpture: An Evolution in Volume and Space*. New York: Wittenborn, Schultz, 1955.

Hammacher, A. M. *The Evolution of Modern Sculpture*. New York: Abrams, 1969.

Moore, Henry. *Henry Moore at the British Museum*. New York: Abrams, 1981.

Read, Herbert. *A Concise History of Modern Sculpture*. New York: Praeger, 1964.

Rickey, George. *Constructivism: Origins and Evolution*. New York: Braziller, 1967.

Schmalenbach, Werner. *African Art*. New York: Macmillan, 1954.

Tucker, William. *Early Modern Sculpture*. New York: Oxford University Press, 1974.

———. *The Language of Sculpture*. London: Thames and Hudson, 1974.

Wittkower, Rudolf. *Sculpture: Processes and Principles*. London: Allen Lane/Penguin Books, 1977.

ARCHITECTURE

Arnheim, Rudolf. *The Dynamics of Architectural Form*. Berkeley and Los Angeles: University of California Press, 1977.

Burchard, John, and Albert Bush-Brown. *The Architecture of America*. Boston: Little, Brown, 1961.

Conrads, Ulrich, and Hans Sperlich. *The Architecture of Fantasy: Utopian Building and Planning in Modern Times*. New York: Praeger, 1962.

Drexler, Arthur. *Transformations in Modern Architecture*. New York: The Museum of Modern Art, 1979.

Giedion, Sigfried. *Space, Time and Architecture: The Growth of a New Tradition*. 3rd rev. ed. Cambridge, MA: Harvard University Press, 1954.

Jeanneret-Gris, Charles E. [Le Corbusier]. *New World of Space*. New York: Reynal and Hitchcock, 1948.

Jencks, Charles A. *The Language of Post-Modern Architecture*. New York: Rizzoli, 1977.

Norberg-Schulz, Christian. *Meaning in Western Architecture*. New York: Praeger, 1975.

Rasmussen, Steen Eiler. *Experiencing Architecture*. Cambridge: Massachusetts Institute of Technology Press, 1959.

Rudofsky, Bernard. *Architecture Without Architects: An Introduction to Non-Pedigreed Architecture*. New York: The Museum of Modern Art, 1964.

Salvadori, Mario, and Robert Heller. *Structure in Architecture*. Englewood Cliffs, NJ: Prentice-Hall, 1963.

Scully, Vincent J. *American Architecture and Urbanism*. New York: Praeger, 1969.

Torroja, Eduardo. *Philosophy of Structures*. Translated by Milos and J. J. Polivka. Berkeley and Los Angeles: University of California Press, 1958.

CITY PLANNING

Bacon, Edmund N. *Design of Cities*. New York: The Viking Press, 1967.

Blake, Peter. *God's Own Junkyard: The Planned Deterioration of America's Landscape*. New York: Holt, Rinehart and Winston, 1964.

Goodman, Paul, and Percival Goodman. *Communitas: Means of Livelihood and Ways of Life*. New York: Vintage Books, 1960.

Halprin, Lawrence. *Cities*. Cambridge: Massachusetts Institute of Technology Press, 1972.

Jacobs, Jane. *The Death and Life of Great American Cities*. New York: Random House, 1961.

Lynch, Kevin. *The Image of the City*. Cambridge, MA: Technology Press and Harvard University Press, 1960.

Mumford, Lewis. *The City in History*. New York: Harcourt Brace Jovanovich, 1961.

Rosenau, Helen. *The Ideal City: Its Architectural Evolution*. New York: Harper & Row, 1972.

Rudofsky, Bernard. *Streets for People: A Primer for Americans*. New York: Doubleday, 1969.

Sitte, Camillo. *The Art of Building Cities*. New York: Reinhold, 1945.

Zucker, Paul. *Town and Square*. New York: Columbia University Press, 1959.

THE CRAFTS AND INDUSTRIAL DESIGN

Banham, Reyner. *Theory and Design in the First Machine Age*. New York: Praeger, 1960.

Giedion, Sigfried. *Mechanization Takes Command*. New York: Oxford University Press, 1948.

Gropius, Walter, and Ise Gropius. *Bauhaus, 1919–1928*. Edited by Herbert Bayer. New York: The Museum of Modern Art, 1938.

Klingender, Francis D. *Art and the Industrial Revolution*. London: Royle Publications, 1947.

Lucie-Smith, Edward. *The Story of Craft: The Craftsman's Role in Society*. Ithaca, NY: Cornell University Press, 1981.

Mumford, Lewis. *Technics and Civilization*. New York: Harcourt, Brace, 1934.

Papanek, Victor. *Design for Human Scale*. New York: Van Nostrand Reinhold, 1983.

Paz, Octavio. *In Praise of Hands*. Greenwich, CT: New York Graphic Society, 1973.

Pevsner, Nikolaus. *Pioneers of Modern Design from William Morris to Walter Gropius*. New York: The Museum of Modern Art, 1949.

Pye, David. *The Nature and Aesthetics of Design*. London: Barrie and Jenkins, 1978.

Read, Herbert. *Art and Industry*. London: Faber & Faber, 1934.

PHOTOGRAPHY

Boorstin, Daniel. *The Image*. New York: Harper Colophon Books, 1964.

Coke, Van Deren. *The Painter and the Photograph*. Albuquerque: The University of New Mexico Press, 1972.

Coleman, A. D. *The Grotesque in Photography*. New York: Summit Books, 1977.

Ivins, William M., Jr. *Prints and Visual Communication*. Cambridge: Massachusetts Institute of Technology Press, 1969.

510

Kahmen, Volker. *Art History of Photography*. New York: The Viking Press, 1973.

Lucie-Smith, Edward. *The Invented Eye*. New York: Paddington Press Limited, 1975.

Newhall, Beaumont. *The History of Photography*. New York: The Museum of Modern Art, 1964.

Pollack, Peter. *The Picture History of Photography*. New York: Abrams, 1969.

Scharf, Aaron. *Art and Photography*. London: Allen Lane/The Penguin Press, 1968.

Schuneman, R. Smith (ed.). *Photographic Communication*. New York: Hastings House Publishers, 1972.

Sontag, Susan. *On Photography*. New York: Farrar, Straus and Giroux, 1977.

Szarkowski, John. *The Photographer's Eye*. New York: The Museum of Modern Art, 1966.

FILM AND TELEVISION

Eisenstein, Sergei M. *The Film Sense*. Translated and edited by Jay Leyda. New York: Harcourt, Brace, 1942.

Kael, Pauline. *Deeper into Movies*. New York: Bantam Books, 1971.

Kracauer, Siegfried. *Theory of Film: The Redemption of Physical Reality*. New York: Oxford University Press, 1960.

MacGowen, Kenneth. *Behind the Screen: The History and Techniques of the Motion Picture*. New York: Delacorte Press, 1965.

Monaco, James. *How to Read a Film*. New York: Oxford University Press, 1977.

Newcombe, Horace (ed.). *The Critical View: Television*. New York: Oxford University Press, 1976.

Nilsen, Vladimir. *The Cinema as a Graphic Art*. New York: Hill and Wang, 1959.

Sarris, Andrew. *The Primal Screen*. New York: Simon & Schuster, 1973.

Spottiswoode, Raymond. *Film and Its Techniques*. Berkeley and Los Angeles: University of California Press, 1966.

Tyler, Parker. *The Three Faces of the Film*. Cranbury, NJ: Barnes, 1967.

Whitaker, Rod. *The Language of Film*. Englewood Cliffs, NJ: Prentice-Hall, 1970.

Williams, Raymond. *Television: Technology and Cultural Form*. New York: Schocken Books, 1975.

ART CRITICISM

Armstrong, Robert P. *The Affecting Presence: An Essay in Humanistic Anthropology*. Urbana: University of Illinois Press, 1971.

Berger, John. *Ways of Seeing*. New York: Penguin Books, 1977.

Boas, George. *A Primer for Critics*. Baltimore: Johns Hopkins University Press, 1937.

Cahn, Walter. *Masterpieces: Chapters on the History of an Idea*. Princeton, NJ: Princeton University Press, 1979.

Chipp, Herschel B. *Theories of Modern Art: A Source Book by Artists and Critics*. Berkeley and Los Angeles: University of California Press, 1968.

Clark, Kenneth. *What Is a Masterpiece?* London: Thames and Hudson, 1979.

Feldman, Edmund B. "The Critical Act," *The Journal of Aesthetic Education*, Vol. I, No. 2, Autumn, 1966.

————. *Thinking About Art*. Englewood Cliffs, NJ: Prentice-Hall, 1985.

Greene, Theodore M. *The Arts and the Art of Criticism*. Princeton, NJ: Princeton University Press, 1947.

Hughes, Robert. *The Shock of the New*. New York: Knopf, 1981.

Hunter, Sam, and John Jacobus. *Modern Art: Painting, Sculpture, and Architecture*. New York: Abrams, 1985.

Jacobs, Jay. "What Should a Critic Be?" *Art in America*, No. I, 1965.

Krauss, Rosalind E. *The Originality of the Avant-Garde and Other Modernist Myths*. Cambridge: Massachusetts Institute of Technology Press, 1985.

Margolis, Joseph. *The Language of Art and Art Criticism*. Detroit: Wayne State University Press, 1965.

Panofsky, Erwin. *Studies in Iconology*. New York: Oxford University Press, 1939.

Pepper, Stephen C. *The Basis of Criticism in the Arts*. Cambridge, MA: Harvard University Press, 1949.

Russell, John. *The Meanings of Modern Art*. New York: The Museum of Modern Art, 1981.

Stolnitz, Jerome. *Aesthetics and Philosophy of Art Criticism: A Critical Introduction*. Boston: Houghton Mifflin, 1960.

Venturi, Lionello. *History of Art Criticism*. New York: E. P. Dutton, 1936.

INDEX

PHOTO CREDITS

The author and publisher wish to thank the libraries, museums, galleries, and private collectors named in the picture captions for permitting the reproduction of works of art in their collections, and for supplying the necessary photographs. Photographs from other sources are gratefully acknowledged below.

Copyright A.C.L., Brussels: 266 above right; Courtesy Air India, New York: 316; Alinari (including Anderson and Brogi), Florence: 73 above, 73 below, 238 above, 254, 256, 258, 264 above left, 264 above right, 344 right; Alinari-Art Reference Bureau, Ancram, NY: 392; American Crafts Council, New York: 111 above; Amigos de Gaudí, Barcelona: 212 below left; Architect of the Capitol: 368 below; Art Institute of Chicago: 481 below; © Craig Aurness, West Light, Los Angeles: 297; Australian News and Information Bureau: 245 above; Courtesy Austrian Press and Information Service, New York: 381 below; © Morley Baer, Carmel, CA: 385 below, 408 below; Ronald Baldwin, New York: 445 below; Bank of Hawaii, Honolulu: 405 above right; H. Baranger, Paris: 410 above right; Ken Bell Photography Ltd., courtesy University of Toronto Public Relations Department: 105 above; Henry Belville: 182 below; Oscar Bladh, Stockholm: 93; Hans-Ludwig Blohm/Public Archives Canada/PA-145886: 401 below; Blue Ridge Aerial Surveys, Leesburg, VA, courtesy of Gulf Reston, Inc.: 88 below; Lee Boltin, Croton-on-Hudson, NY: 117 above; Grace Borgenicht Gallery, New York: 338; Office of E. H. Brenner, Lafayette, IN: 396 above; The Bridgeman Art Library, London: 194 below; Photographie Bulloz, Paris: 187 below; Hillel Burger, Cambridge, MA, 69-30-10/1609, T700-B1., © President and Fellows of Harvard College 1981: 308; Rudolph Burckhardt, New York: 107 above, courtesy of Leo Castelli Gallery, 120 below left, 304 below, courtesy of Sidney Janis Gallery; R. D. Burmeister, Clovis, NM: 284 below; Robert Burroughs/NYT Pictures: 373; California Division of Highways, Sacramento: 95 below; California Institute of Technology, Pasadena: 407 below; Canadian Consulate General, New York: 396; Ludovico Canali, Rome: 100 below, 370, 490; CBS Television Network, New York: 30 below right; Ron Chamberlain, Warwick, NY: 342 right; Victor Chambi, Cuzco, Peru: 368 above left; Chase Manhattan Bank, New York: 280 below, 405 above left; Chicago Architectural Photo Company: 375 below; Geoffrey Clements, New York: 69 below, 130 above left, 130 above right, 305 below, 341 left; Colorado Highway Commission: 96 above; Commonwealth United Entertainment, Inc., Beverly Hills, CA: 449 above, 450; Community Service Society, New York: 54 below right; Craft Horizons, New York: 114 above left, 355 right; Craftsmen Photo Company, New York: 447 above left; Thomas Y. Crowell, Inc., New York: 119 above, from *Primitive Art* by Erwin O. Christensen; George Cserna, New York: 151 below left, 397 below right, courtesy of Harrison & Abramovitz; © 1985, Mark C. Darley, New York: 104 top; Design M—Ingo Maurer, Munich: 235 below left; Dwan Gallery, New York: 360 above left, 360 above right; John Ebstel, New York: 412 below; Edholm & Blomgren Photographers, Lincoln, NE: 250 left; Susan Einstein, Santa Monica, CA: 56 above; Richard Einzig © Arcaid, England: 402; Michael Fedison, courtesy of Western Pennsylvania Conservancy: 77 below; Fischbach Gallery, New York: 350, 351 bottom right; Courtesy Fischer Fine Art, Ltd., London: 242 below; Ford Motor Company, Dearborn, MI: 108, 356 top right; Copyright David Gahr, New York: 357 above left; Roger Gain, Paris: 115 bottom; Lynton Gardiner, New York, 155 above; General Instrument Corporation, Microelectronic Division, New York: 217 below; Alexandre Georges, Ponoma, NY: 372 left; German Information Center, New York: 410 below right; John Gibson, New York: 360 center; Giraudon, Paris: 484; Goodman, New York: 357 below; Greater London Council: 411 below; Gulick, St. Louis: 33 below; Juan Guzman, Mexico City: 298; Hassia, Paris: 360 below; Office of Zvi Hecker, Montreal: 94 left; Hedrich-Blessing, Chicago: 78, 80 center, 80 below right, 104 center, from Bill Hedrich; Lucien Hervé, Paris: 82 above, 83 above, 84 below, 91, 213 above, 400 above; Hans Hinz, Allschwil: 19 below, 237; Hirmer Verlag, Munich: 323, 366 below; Michael Holford, London: 321 left, 321 right; Martin Hürlimann, Zurich: 393 below left; Illinois Institute of Technology, Chicago: 80 below right; Alexander Iolas Gallery, New York: 275 left, 275 right; Office of Philip Johnson, New York: 81 above, 81 below, 250 right, 394 below; S. C. Johnson & Son, Inc., Racine, WI: 82 below, 102 left, 102 right; © A. F. Kersting, London: 391; Kitchens of Sara Lee, Deerfield, IL: 103 below; Ray Kutos, New Orleans: 113; Alicia B. Legg, New York: 343 below right; Courtesy Light Gallery, New York: 427 above; Terry S. Lindquist, Miami: 292 below; Studio Lourmel 77, Paris: 462 above; Roger Lucas: 358 below right; Norman McGrath: New York, 101, 406; Magnum Photos, Inc., New York: 74, 178, 470 below; Manhattanville College, Purchase, NY: 368 above right; Michael Maor, Jerusalem: 374 left; Foto Marburg, Marburg/Lahn: 389 top; Marlborough Fine Art, Ltd., London: 40 below, 179 left; Foto MAS, Barcelona: 134 above, 213 below left, 345 below left; Pierre Matisse Gallery, New York: 70 above; Meyer, Vienna: 335; Marshall D. Meyers, TX: 318 above; Ministerio de Información y Turismo, Madrid: 407 above left; Ministry of Information, Baghdad: 369 right; Monkmeyer Press Photo Service, New York: 89 right, from Hugh Roberts; Peter Moore, New York: 246 right; Riccardo Morandi, Rome: 410 above left; © Copyright Museo del Prado, Madrid: 255 right; Museum of Modern Art, New York: 80 above, 345 above left, 378 left, 383, 385 above; Museum of Modern Art/Film Stills Archive, New York: 432 above right, 439, 448 above left; Museum of New Mexico, Santa Fe: 94 right; Museum of Pre-Columbian Art, Dumbarton Oaks, Washington, D.C.: 408 below right; National Aeronautics and Space Administration, Washington, D.C.: 531 above left; National Film Archives, London: 442 above, 443 below; National Gypsum Company, Buffalo, NY: 374 right; © 1978 W. R. Nelson Trust: 340 above left; Studio Nervi, Rome: 376 below, 408 above right; Sidney W. Newbery, London: 208 below right; Irving J. Newman, Greenwich, CT: 185 below; New York Times: 75, 95 above, 233, from Gene Maggio, 292 above; New York Zoological Society: 212 below right; Niedersächsische Landesgalerie, Hanover, West Germany: 290 above; Nordness Gallery, New York: 179 right; North Carolina Department of Conservation & Development, Raleigh: 104 above right; Courtesy the Pace Gallery, New York: 197 below; T. Harmon Parkhurst, NM: 94 right; Perls Galleries, New York: 169; Robert Perron, CT: 88 above, 98 below; Phaidon Press, London: 310 left; Philadelphia Museum of Art: 154 below; Studio Piaget, St. Louis: 33 below, 184; Pictorial Parade, Inc., New York: 45 above right, 57; John Pitkin, New York: 108; Planair Photography, Edinburgh, 92; Eric Pollitzer, New York: 15 left, 124, 293, 343, 346 left; Portland Cement Association, New York: 411 above; Dorothy Prather, Mitchell, SD, courtesy of Mitchell Chamber of Commerce: 394 above; Progressive Architecture, New York: 408 above left, from Jan C. Rowan; Nathan Rabin, Chicago: 348 below; Rapho-Guillumette, New York: 43, from Marc and Evelyn Bernheim; George Rickey, East Chatham, NY: 534 below right; Rijksmuseum, Amsterdam: 238 below; Courtesy Rizzoli International Publications, Inc., New York: 216; Robert Associates, Minneapolis: 409; Rockefeller Center, Inc., New York: 371; Morris Rosenfeld & Sons, New York: 214 below left; Bruce Rosensheet, Toronto: 361 above left; Routhier, Paris: 129 above left; Office of Paul Rudolph, New York: 412 above; Sandak, Inc., New York: 30 left, 66 right, 192 left, 386 above right, 389, courtesy of Lamar Dodd; Oscar Savio, Rome: 35 below; George H. Schenck, Jr., Charlotte, NC: 145 below right; Hans Schiller, Mill Valley, CA: 410 below left; Schipporeit-Heinrich, Inc., Chicago: 379 right; Julius Schulman, Los Angeles: 397 below left; Der Senator für Bau- und Wohnungswesen, Berlin: 380; Walter Seng, North Versailles, PA: 359; Shunk-Kender, New York: 543 above; © Sandy Skoglund 1980: 415; Steven Sloman © Copyright, 1981: 39; Edwin Smith, London: 393 below right; Office of Smith & Williams, Pasadena, CA: 367 left; Jerry Spearman, New York: 401 above; Lee Stalsworth, Washington, D.C.: 174 below, 286 above; Artur Starewicz: 363 above; Stilnovo, Milan: 363 below right; Dr. Franz Stödtner, Düsseldorf: 79, 389 center; © Ezra Stoller/ESTO, New York, 103 above, 104 below, 376 above, © 1964, 400 below, 403, 404; Eric Sutherland, Minneapolis: 322; Taylor & Dull, Inc., New York: 191 below right; Thames & Hudson, Ltd., London: 255 left; Frank J. Thomas, Los Angeles: 298; Thomas Airviews, New York: 99; Enrique Franco Torrijos, Mexico City: 96 below left; Marvin Trachtenberg, New York: 365, 388, 399; Tseng Kwong-chi, New York: cover, 349; Turner Ltd., New York: 82 below; TWA, New York: 400 below; © Copyright 1984 by The Type Director's Club. Reprinted by permission of Watson-Guptill Publications: 68 below; Charles Uht, New York: 203 right, 354 above right; UNESCO Photographic Service, Paris: 35 above; United Press International, New York: 466 below; University of California Press, Berkeley: 377 right, from Eduardo Torroja, *Philosophy of Structures*; University Properties, Inc., Seattle, WA: 407 above right; Upjohn Pharmaceutical Company, Kalamazoo, MI: 175 above; Malcolm Varron, New York: 289 below; Victoria & Albert Museum, London: 378; John Waggaman, La Jolla, CA, courtesy of Lamar Dodd: 375 above; Morris Warman, New York, courtesy of Lincoln Center for the Performing Arts: 100 above; John Weber Gallery, New York: 361 below; Etienne Bertrand Weill, Paris: 212 above; Cole Weston, Carmel, CA: 151 above left; Myron Wood, Colorado Springs: 345 above left; Yale University News Bureau, New Haven: 84 above; Yan, Toulouse: 344 left; Zehr Photography, IL: 300.